Czech Writers and Politics
1945-1969

A. French

EAST EUROPEAN MONOGRAPHS, BOULDER

DISTRIBUTED BY COLUMBIA UNIVERSITY PRESS
NEW YORK

1982

EAST EUROPEAN MONOGRAPHS, NO. XCIV

CONTENTS

AUTHOR'S NOTE

I wish to put on record my appreciation of the help which I have received from Czech authors and critics both in Czechoslovakia and abroad whilst I was writing this book. Realising that my subject was likely to be found controversial, I did my best to document as carefully as I could what I had to say, and I apologise in advance for any inaccuracy which may have escaped my notice.

I must also express my appreciation to the Australian Research Grants Commission for its help; to Wolfson College, Cambridge, which provided a congenial atmosphere for studying and writing whilst I was in England, and to Adelaide University which generously assisted with a grant towards publication.

A. French

'It is a matter of general knowledge', wrote Palacký, 'that it was the Czech writers who, instead of letting the nation perish, brought it back to life, and gave it noble aims to accomplish.' It is the Czech writers who were responsible for the very existence of the nation, and remain so today. For it is upon the standard of Czech literature, its greatness or meanness, its courage or cowardice, its provincialism or its universality, that the answer to the nation's existential question largely depends, namely: Is its survival worthwhile? Is the survival of its language worthwhile?

These, the most fundamental questions at the roots of our latterday nationhood, are still awaiting a definitive answer.

Milan Kundera 1967

I

Legends and History

Future historians may note how closely the cultural scene of today has come to resemble our physical habitat. The mounting output of printed matter, which is a measure of our enlightenment, now clogs the transmission of its message to the receivers. The freeways of the mind are jammed with speeding traffic, heading relentlessly towards who-knows-what targets. The toxic fumes create an immense miasma, confusing the signs and concealing the known ways.

The goals of our hurtling automobiles are multifarious and apparently self-cancelling: their general impact upon the society they serve seems highly destructive. What is the impact of our equally uncomputed cultural vehicles? To what extent, and in what ways does literature affect human behaviour? What are the writers trying to do, anyway? How important or negligible, planned or unforeseen are their effects? It would be unrealistic to imagine that in this age the main function of literature is mere entertainment: a glance at the contents of any large bookshop should dispose of that idea. No novel can compete in sales with the text book or the bible. Literature has a wide range of functions – doctrinal, cathartic, scientific, imaginative, denotative, educative, persuasive. There are some who believe that the book has little effect on the organisation of man's world: this is quite evidently not the view of those who have long preached the message of the *Good Book*; or, at a different level of aim, those who practise or approve of the censorship of literature. In their eyes it can improve, and does deprave – morally and politically. The gospeller with his bible, the censor with his blue pencil, manifest the belief that the printed word can bend man's judgement, appoint his goal, and direct his steps.

The barbarians who fell upon Europe in the Dark Ages acquired the habit of burning books. This was on their part a philistine, but in the setting, a reasonable pattern of behaviour. Books were burned for fuel; and in preference to more obviously useful commodities. The barbarians burned books because they were of little interest and no use to them. In our own time we have witnessed a similar pattern of behaviour, but from dissimilar motives. It was indifference and ignorance that induced the vandals of old to destroy literature: today it is destroyed by men who have rather a high opinion of its social impact, and fear it. Paradoxically the present-day suppression of books and silencing of writers can be regarded as an acknowledgment of their social importance. None should doubt that, as a social force, literature has arrived.

The significance of the written word has implicitly been long acknowledged by society at large – sometimes with embarrassing emphasis. The conversion of an oral tradition to a written text has at times equalled the conversion of tentative belief into dogma - from hypothesis to holy writ. Consulted by priests, expounded by seers and teachers, the book in antique times retained an authority surpassing that of its forgotten authors. The written word can, it appears, change the mind, hence the actions, of men. Writers are therefore, at least potentially an important element in society. But it does not follow that they have ever been a powerful force. The poet, like the oracular priestess, was regarded as a mouthpiece rather than a creator. Those who *interpret* scriptures have long been recognised as their masters, and the scriptures adopted and adapted to suit varied ends. Never so much as today has it been seen how doctrine can be used to indoctrinate. The writer is powerless without his audience; and he who controls the channels of communication, eventually can control the message. The poet whose revelations can move men (if not mountains), is at the mercy of those who govern his audience. In a free society he must await the pleasure of publishers, critics, book societies, libraries. In a totalitarian state he can be promoted or crushed directly through administrative action, indirectly by the guided influence of public opinion. At one moment he appears as society's standard bearer; leading, because he first expresses the ideas which others put into effect. At another moment he appears as the prisoner – the mouthpiece, the court philosopher, who is hardly distinguishable from the court fool. Upon this paradox is piled another, no less strange. The writer with an insignificant, or no, appeal, is free to write what he wishes. He whose work touches the lives or aspirations of thousands, is to a varying extent the prisoner of his public. The higher is the public estimation of literature's importance, the greater the threat to the freedom of the writer. The more detached and ineffectual he is, the more ignorant and philistine the society in which he serves, the safer he is intellectually, if not economically.

How exactly does art and literature change society? At the most obvious level their social function seems primarily persuasive – almost, one might say, pseudo-commercial. The twentieth century has perfected the techniques of selling: (its efforts have been especially heroic on behalf of goods which do not sell themselves, because they are unwanted, or actively harmful.) Literature has not kept pace with the spectacular advance of television advertising technique; it seems that it is harder to sell unwanted ideas than to sell plastic gadgets or lung cancer. What then are the commodities retailed by serious, creative literature? Ethical standards? New living styles? Blue-prints for a changed society?

Any change, even for the better, is subversive of the old. Artists of all types have long been under suspicion of being by their very nature inclined to subversion. The writer's non-conformism is taken for granted. A creature of subtle intuitions, a visionary of strange dreams from which ordinary folk are excluded, an irredeemable, unteachable champion of lost causes – always he seems to be looking for trouble. A profession dominated by freaks, neurotics, and social misfits?

If writers were really like this, one would properly expect imaginative literature to be a seed-bed of rebellion and a seismograph of social change. One might see in the literature of the years preceding revolution, the great wave swelling to its climax: by studying current literary trends, one might even predict social changes. Such an idea is as unrealistic as is the picture of the artist suggested above. A few writers, at certain times, see themselves as heralds of social reform or even of violent revolution. But as a matter of fact, when such cataclysmic events occur, the literary sector of society seems to be as surprised and bewildered as others. Socially orientated histories of literature earnestly seek the signs of things that were to come, in the output of the years preceding them: they are careful to stress the forward-looking character of books published on the eve of great changes. Such a selection consigns to oblivion the enormous mass of work which shows no sign of awareness that changes were afoot. Looking back at Russian literature in the years preceding the revolution, who can say, without hopeless distortion, that Russian writers were in the vanguard of rebellion? It is at least as plausible to argue that literary radicalism actually diminished in Russia after the reforms of 1907. During the war years 1914-17 Russian literature was more under the inspiration of patriotism and Messianism than revolutionary fervour. One thinks of the few works of Blok and Majakovsky as symptomatic of a literary trend: but how many talented Russian writers fled abroad, or later struggled to come to terms with the new system, often with little success! The literary output of an era rarely gives ground for generalisation of social trends. Its lines of approach, aims, methods, outlooks and presuppositions are bewilderingly diversified. That part which could by any standards be regarded as socially avant-garde is quant-itatively insignificant: its social significance is acquired only in retro-spect. The mass of imaginative literature seems in fact incorrigibly conservative. Rarely does it see as its task the submission of social blueprints: it is rather the transmitter of cultural tradition: and this is the function which it carries out with varied fidelity and grace. At its best, creative literature, by its re-interpretation of inherited values, preserves the momentum of cultural development. It is this role which, though in no sense revolutionary, gives it the characteristics of an avant-garde movement.

The literature of social ferment can therefore be conceived as operating in a hostile literary, as well as social, environment. Out-numbered, ignored, rejected, divided, and self-consciously ineffectual, the heralds of revolution have themselves little expectation of actual-ly changing society. Their very feeling of impotence at times increases their irresponsibility and helps to give them immunity from reprisals. Society can afford an indulgent smile at the fierce predictions and colourful threats of what is manifestly a literary circus. Politicians collect with secret pride the caricatures which vilify them: rich men promote the sale of books which preach the overthrow of their system. The literary rebel may even combine a proud contempt for society's rewards with a modest private affluence. Attaining the distinction he affects to despise, he may accept from crown or commissar the reward of his lovable mischief. There is a danger of overestimating the leader-ship qualities of writers: it is easy to oversimplify their social role. So far from dictating the pace of change, it is they who frequently suffer dictation. At times they make the bullets to be fired by others: at other times they fire bullets made for them: sometimes they are the target.

Modern studies of East European literature tend to stress its ideo-logical and overtly political aspect: in this, western critics have much in common with the communists. But the social functions of literature are more than merely political. Those who advocate the censorship of literature in our own society rarely mention politics. They are concern-ed that books affect life by setting patterns of moral behaviour which are imitated by readers. Such a notion is not demonstrable to the satisfaction of a sceptic; but it is probably accepted by a majority of those who think about it at all. The more superficial aspects of human behaviour, such as talk, dress, hair styles etc. seem to be influenced by the public media, as they are so susceptible to imitation. The influence of books on individual behaviour has been documented by some curious illustrations. When Goethe published his novel *Werther*, even he could hardly have anticipated that men would not only adopt the dress of his hero, but would actually shoot themselves in his fashion. Although Kipling spent so little time in India, his work seems to have left an indelible impact upon Anglo-Indian society. (As one of the oddest ripples from that literary venture one may quote the extraordinary career of Kim Philby, so mesmerised by the literary associations of his upbringing and name that he actually lived the part of a Kiplingesque spy). One wonders how many adventurous souls have illegally crossed frontiers in the self-conscious imitation of the Scarlet Pimpernel. During the Second World War German security officers are said to have combed the work of a certain English writer of thrillers to discover the secrets of the British Intelligence Service; while members of the latter organisation were doing the same to gain inspiration for their own efforts. Young Nazi Germans participating in the romantic, medieval rallies around Rhine castles in the 'thirties were living the legends written for them by writers of the Weimar Republic: the superman of blood and iron was conceived by Nietzsche before he was made flesh by the SS. Hitler himself modelled his career on Napoleon: Napoleon thought of himself as another Caesar: Caesar trod in the steps of Alexander the Great: and Alexander enacted the role of Achilles; who never existed outside poetry.

It appears that styles of behaviour, made famous in literature, are so convincing that they become true. Once a national or group portrait is established, people live up to the legend. The national image which the Czechs had of themselves before 1920 can be well documented from literature. The legendary Czech was a peasant, serious, longsuffering, protestant, with a passionate longing for freedom and social justice. Then, after Hašek published his novel *The Good Soldier Schweik*[1], the image changed. Czechs began to see in themselves unsuspected resources of broad humour. The national hero (or anti-hero) became a stumpy figure whose imbecillic expression concealed unplumbable depths of low cunning. Hašek's character has so stamped himself upon Czech consciousness that without reading the book one can scarcely understand why his fellow countrymen still regard with such amusement and pride the ruinous tactics of the industrial go-slow, the inextricable muddling of directives, and the cultivated, obstinate incomprehension of even the simplest bureaucratic procedures.

It is possible to argue that Czech history has been profoundly influenced by national legends created by modern writers. During the nineteenth century a small group of Czech writers made the theme of a national revival the central motif of their work. The smallness of the group is illustrated by the anecdote that, at one of their regular meetings it was said: 'If the ceiling fell in upon us, it would be the end of the Czech national movement'. By the end of the century the movement dominated both art and political thinking in Bohemia. In 1918 the legend became a political reality. Needless to say, the Czech national revival was not entirely the work of writers: had economic, social, and political conditions been different, their work would have taken its place with other romantic visions. But the poetry of Kollár and Svatopluk Čech, the novels of Rais and Jirásek, the journalistic sketches of Havlíček and Neruda, built up so consistent, so insistent, a picture of a Czech nation struggling to revive past glories, that they lent an aura of inevitability to a movement towards independence. A great Moravian kingdom of pre-history; a centre of medieval culture in the fourteenth century; a bearer of protestant freedom, and a torch of humane enlightenment to Europe, crushed by Austria and plunged into a dark age by German oppression and Jesuit witch-hunting – such was the past of the nation, as portrayed by nineteenth century romantic writers. It was a past that clamoured for a resurrection of national pride and freedom. The whole sequence reached a definitive form in the masterly and exhaustive *History* of Palacký, which stood for decades as the classic reconstruction of the Czech past.

The history of a nation is open to varied interpretations, and in the last fifty years Palacký's version has often been challenged. His picture of the early Hussite community was rather idealised: the idea that the humanist literature of the fifteenth century marked a peak is hard to substantiate: the representation of the Counter-reformation as a dark age for Czech art is hard to reconcile with the surviving masterpieces of baroque literature, including the sublime lyrics of Kadlický, Michna, and Bridel. The Romantics seem to have exaggerated the effects of the decay in order to make more dramatic the revival; the early Czech peasant art which they idealised did not always possess the antiquity which they attributed to it. But the gap between history and legend is small; it is the nature of all who recreate the past to select and elaborate. So the Czech national legend was savoured, improved, refined, and took its place of honour in the consciousness of the community. Those who preach of the second coming of Christ prepare public opinion one day to receive a new mystic, if his gospel is convincing. The literary apostles of nihilism who proclaim the coming collapse of civilisation induce in their readers not only an agreeable thrill of horror, but also a state of mind that is ready (in theory) to accept such a cataclysmic end. For a century Czech literature prepared public opinion in the homeland for a new era of political independence: the legend became itself a fact of history and an inspiration for men of action. Masaryk, Beneš, and Štefánik were all under its spell. In 1918, when the independent Czechoslovak republic was established from the collapsing fabric of Austro-Hungary, it seemed that the legend had come true. Art had dictated a pattern to life.

But even as those who give intellectual assent to prophesies of doom would be astounded by their literal fulfilment, so the fulfilment of the Czech legend was received by writers with a more qualified enthusiasm than might have been predicted. Fanfares of nationalistic triumph, hymns of noble gratitude, the deep consciousness of national fulfilment - such are the motifs which might have been expected to dominate the early post-war literature of Czechoslovakia. Work of this kind was written; but for the most part it has been ignored and long forgotten. The literature of the time reflected prevailing attitudes - or rather, the attitudes which the writers *thought* were prevailing - but triumph seems to have played little part in them. If one must single out one dominant mood amid the bewildering tangle of Czech literary trends after 1918, it would perhaps be the mood of *expectation* - a belief that tremendous social changes were afoot, and a new world was coming to replace one which was bled white by the war, and so manifestly discredited. War as a tremendous crime against humanity (a crime to which, regrettably, Czechoslovakia owed its political renaissance) demanded some great expiation. While nothing could justify the unparalleled suffering which war had created, it could at least be understood, if it were a prelude to some great change for the better in the human condition. The first President, the writer and philosopher T. G. Masaryk, regarded the war as merely an episode in a larger sequence, which he termed the 'era of world revolution'.

In the Czech lands the struggle for independence had been led by the so-called Young Czechs, with Dr Kramář at their head. After presiding over the first provisional government after independence, he and his party found themselves rejected by the electorate at the first elections arranged under the new constitution. The rejection of old leaders in favour of more radical ideas was symptomatic of public feeling in Czechoslovakia once war was over. Those who had thought themselves to be in the vanguard of a movement suddenly found that their leadership was not required: the ideas which had been regarded as so progressive were already outdated. The actual achievement of national independence ended its interest as a moral cause and a theme of art. At a time when progressive thinkers all over Europe were raising the cry of internationalism, the assertion of Czech nationalism seemed an anachronism. The mood expressed by the mushrooming periodicals of radical student groups was closer in sympathy to pacifism than to patriotism: the call of anarchy was sweeter than that of the discipline so necessary for the tasks of reconstruction. Those who had fought for freedom in the Czech legions abroad came home almost as strangers to the sons who had grown up in their absence. Fighting and the resistance are themes which soon become boring to those who have not participated in them: the young found it easy to ridicule Czech jingoism, cruelly identifying the liberationists with the imperial era from which they had emerged.

Only the legionaries had first-hand knowledge of the revolution which had overturned the social order in Russia; but here, if anywhere, seemed the shape of things to come. A deep note of Messianism sounded in the most modern Czech post-war poetry: in holy Russia, motherland of the Slavs, a new lamp of hope seemed to have been kindled. Together with these touching hopes went an almost mystical belief that the coming era belonged to the common man. The new hero of war was not the general on his white horse, but the Unknown Soldier in his tomb. The sympathies of men went out not to the triumphal cavalcades, but to the legions of the dispossessed and displaced, the poor and the oppressed: for virtue was in them. In the youngest Czech literature a new school appeared, that of the so-called Proletarian poets, of whom the most gifted were Hora and Wolker. Reviving the folk ballad in modern form, Wolker portrayed social issues in an industrial setting: Hora pictured the Madonna as a woman of the slums, and the new Christ-child as the appointed leader of the workers in the hour of their liberation. The young poets wrote almost with reverence of the power and solidarity of the proletarian class, identifying themselves with it in the pictured panoramas of revolt. The writers who saluted the spirit and the coming triumph of the workers, were themselves almost without exception of middle-class origin and upbringing. Inspired by the slogans of Marxism they appointed themselves as spokesmen of the soon-to-be victorious proletariat, and claimed for the poet his historic role as a teacher and prophet. In retrospect such poems seem romantic and naive, imaginative without a touch of scepticism. They are dated by their adherence to a passing phase; yet at their best they reached a high level of art; and their effect on later work was to be great.

An advantage of Proletarian poetry was that it had the appeal of literature addressed to immediate, contemporary issues; lacking the thoughtful scepticism of much prose work of the time, it aimed straight for the heart rather than the intellect. Whatever else the Proletarians lacked, they had plenty of faith, an endearing quality in poetry. The prophetic writer can claim for his visions an authority which rests on revelation rather than argument; and his views can assume a startling, apocalyptic air. Yet his themes, though on the grand scale, are built not on personal experience but on hearsay, reading, and the doctrines of others. As he calls for assent to a doctrine, his presentation tends to be simplistic, sweeping away his readers on a wave of emotion. The exploitation of mass emotion opens the way to theatrical and embarrassing posing: the limitation of doubt and intellectual reservation can lead to shallow vulgarisation. Such are the pitfalls of prophetic literature. They were avoided by the leaders of the Czech Proletarian movement, but their later followers were not so circumspect. They set an example which was to have a delayed, but appalling harvest some thirty years later. In their theoretical work, as well as in their imaginative creations, the early Proletarians took a rash step. Proclaiming that the prime duty of literature was to change life by the liberation of industrial man, they placed their art unreservedly at the service of the radical cause, rejecting all claims for the autonomy of art. While the poems of Wolker himself reflect more the spirit of the evangelist than the agitator, he supplied a doctrine and an example for those who later were to declare that literature is properly the servant of politics, and that the criteria of literary value are social and political, rather than aesthetic. The Proletarian movement, as a trend of serious literature, lasted only a few years; its demise was aided no doubt by the tragic death of Wolker at the age of 24.

The strength of the movement lay in poetry; but a number of serious, attractive novels were also written in this style, notably by Olbracht, Vančura, and Marie Majerová. But in their popularity and influence they were dwarfed by Hašek's realist satire *The Good Soldier Schweik*. Critics denounced it for its crude vulgarity and technical defects of composition: its disorganisation and corrosive humour seemed typical of its author, who had once actually been expelled from the anarchist party for indiscipline. Hašek portrayed in his hero the underdog of modern industrial society, as Wolker had done, but with much greater skill and insight. Compared to the schematic, heroic worker of the Proletarians, Schweik really comes to life; and this unflattering portrayal of the Czech 'little man' won acceptance for its endearing realism.

Set next to Schweik, the hero of Proletarian literature seems romantic – a nineteenth century 'noble peasant' dressed in the garb of a modern industrial workman.

Far more subtle and intellectual was the exploration of social themes in the work of Karel Čapek. In his play R.U.R.[2], first produced in 1921, he portrayed the collapse of man's society through the revolt of the robots against their creators. While the Futurists, with their Czech apostles, were glorifying the theme of technical progress – the 'miracles of the electric century' as they termed it – Čapek explored the theme of man's capacity to destroy himself; combining it with the contemporary theme of revolution. In his play the humans lose their capacity to reproduce themselves: but after the fall of man the robots take upon themselves human characteristics, and a new Adam and Eve commence a fresh cycle of life. The humans become as robots, the robots humans: so the current of life flows on, too powerful for human folly to destroy. *In spite of* science, *in spite of* revolution, the spirit of man survives.

From his plays, novels, essays, and criticism Karel Čapek, together with his brother Josef, became identified with a definite social philosophy, that of American pragmatism. The best-known of the Czech pragmatists, who carried his philosophy directly into politics, was the President, T. G. Masaryk himself. The trend of thought in the Čapek's writing, the personal association between Karel and Masaryk, and the fact that the former published several books of intimate *Conversations with T. G. M.*[3], all contributed to give to Karel Čapek the air of a spokesman for the existing regime, and consequently a defender of the political status quo. Perhaps it would be truer to say that Čapek reflected attitudes widespread among the intelligentsia of post-war Czechoslovakia. These attitudes were: – an attachment to the values of western democracy; a dislike of crude nationalism and militarism; a feeling for rational compromise and the organisation of affairs according to enlightened, but businesslike, principles; above all a deep distrust of all forms of fanaticism, either in politics or religion. Karel Čapek's early novels, *Factory for the absolute* and *Krakatit*[4], were both science-fiction essays on the theme of the deadly danger to humanity of man's release of energy, either spiritual or physical, which would be beyond his control. Čapek thus displayed, in both fiction and drama, a warning distrust of the miracles of experimental science: no less intense was his scepticism towards the current revolutionary faiths which promised to solve man's social problems by reorganising his economic and institutional arrangements. Though Čapek thought highly of Wolker as a poet, he deflated the wild pretensions of Proletarian art, regarding the literary revolutionaries as neo-Romantics.

Čapek's reservations toward religion made him unpopular with Catholic writers, who found in his liberal humanism a form of moral neutrality; the humanists were accused of putting man, not God, at the centre of their world. On the other hand strong nationalists, like the poet Viktor Dyk, found Čapek's work insipid, excessively cosmopolitan, and lacking in idealism. Of the Pragmatists it was said that they loved the whole world, and believed in nothing. They were identified with the prevailing system and with the political philosophy of the ruling group: as such they were the target for attack by dissenters of all types.

Distrust of the government, and dissent from official views, has been a commonly observed attitude of the Czech intelligentsia. No doubt the attitude had good historical reasons, stemming from the fact that for centuries their culture represented a minority struggling for recognition against alien rule. After the Czechs became masters in their own land, attitudes were slow to change. Czech politicians merely replaced Austrian officials as targets of abuse. People were so accustomed to seeing public policy managed from abroad that they regarded with suspicion and incredulity Czechoslovakia's independent role, and claimed that the Republic was a virtual puppet of the Western powers. Every political compromise, every rumour of corruption, added to the suspicions of the dissenters. It was claimed that the ideals of the pre-war struggle had somewhere been lost: the legend of Czech revival had been a noble one; the reality somewhat disappointing. Public life seemed more commercialised, materialistic, more smug and inequitable than was appropriate to an ideal republic.

For writers of principle political independence brought fresh problems. Before the war pacifism had been a patriotic ideal, combining humanism with a practical determination not to fight Austria's wars for it: ideals and national interests thus happily coincided. But when the first Czechoslovak army was formed, the issue changed. The poet Šrámek had made the hatred of militarism a theme of his art: after 1918 he altered his stance and abandoned pacifism. The ex-legionaries Medek and Kopta wrote a vigorous prose literature based on their wartime experiences. The Czechoslovak state had benefitted by the war, which had brought its independence; and militarism seemed to have been rehabilitated now that it was in Czech national interests. Such an attitude seemed to the young radicals quite unprincipled. The dilemma of Šrámek was that of his generation. Those who, in their youth had been the dissenters, had become in their middle years a new Establishment. The political leaders of the new Czechoslovakia were accused of selling their ideals for a mess of Western pottage - in particular of abandoning their anti-imperialist views in consideration of loans, credits, and military assistance from imperial France. In the old legend the historic model for a revived Czech state had been Tábor, the fifteenth century Hussite brotherhood. Then the Czech protestants had faced the scorn and enmity of Europe for the sake of their principles. Now the one state which seemed to be following in the steps of Tábor was not Czechoslovakia, but Russia. Even through the later years of disillusion with the realities of Soviet life, this image of an idealistic, struggling, persecuted community prevailed, while Czechoslovak political leaders, not excluding the President-Liberator T. G. Masaryk himself, were a target for criticism from all sides. Radical and Catholic writers alike used the freedom of the liberal democratic system to denounce its humbug, hypocrisy, and spiritual impotence.

Critics were fond of referring to the 'official' literature of Prague, and by this they meant especially that of the Pragmatists. Just as the left-wing writers were in close personal touch with Communist political organisers, so the Pragmatist writers tended to associate with politicians of the liberal persuasion. While the radicals openly advocated social revolution in their writings, the Čapeks and their friend F. Peroutka, threw their weight behind the 'state-building' programme common to the democratic parties. A conscious effort to bring together men of literature and politics was made by Karel Čapek, when he organised a literary salon at his house in Prague. The salon, composed of artists, intellectuals, and public figures, met regularly. Dr E. Beneš and T. G. Masaryk were among its members. Inevitably this association caused Čapek to be regarded as something of a spokesman for official cultural policy; and this unfortunate impression was increased when he became president of the Czech branch of the International P.E.N. Club.

But those critics who vigilantly espied political influence in the literary salon, or the corridors of powers in the Čapeks' suburban villa, seem to have been deceiving themselves. There is no reason to suspect that the co-operation of Čapek and other Pragmatists with politicians had any direct influence on public policy. How far their literary efforts aided policies made by others is doubtful. Čapek and his friends did more to propagate the liberal viewpoint in general than the platform of any political party, and their appeal was always more to intellectuals than to the common voter. At the other end of the political spectrum the fiery communist writers who plunged so eagerly into political affairs in the early twenties found their efforts crowned with futility. The avant-gardists soon abandoned the cause of politically committed literature, and proclaimed the total autonomy of art. Poetism was the name they gave to their new love – art devoid of all ideological content. They ridiculed all didactic art as a relic of medieval scholasticism, and gaily swept into oblivion the literary-political tenets they had themselves defended a short time before. Beginning like the French Dadaists they produced a stunning impression with their verbal pyrotechnics, dazzling surprises, and the literary exploitation of techniques derived from vaudeville and films. The Poetists, whose most splendid example was V. Nezval, had emerged from a revolutionary tradition, and the chaotic or barbaric element so natural to revolutionary art, became their guiding principle. They contributed some astonishing and brilliant work to the repertoire of Czech modern literature, but in its final stages their work descended into macabre surrealism, which unkind critics likened to infantile exhibitionism.

Although wedded to the idea of 'pure' art, the radical modernists in literature consistently proclaimed their adherence in politics to the communist cause: but radical principles were one thing, Party organisation another. Left wing artists and communist functionaries became increasingly exasperated with each other. To the latter the writers seemed irresponsible, undisciplined, uninterested in day-to-day problems of assisting the revolution. To the writers party officials seemed dreary, unimaginative, often officious and ruthless. Above all, the leaders who professed the cause of political revolution showed themselves in matters of art hopelessly conservative, not to say reactionary. The uneasy marriage between party revolutionaries and avantgarde art broke down in 1929, when a group of writers was expelled from the Party for gross violation of discipline. The attitude of the artists was that they had not abandoned their principles, as they were accused of doing; communist principles were more important than the Communist Party. They declared that the present Party leadership was hopelessly out of touch with reality – mouthing trite slogans, publishing unreadable journals, and lacking all understanding of, or influence over, the working people.

The crisis brought to light some of the problems faced by writers who attempt to engage their talents directly in politics. Where Čapek and the Pragmatists found frustration, the communist writers ran into even more exasperating conflicts, which brought them to the depths of

disillusion. Between the revolutionary artists and the political revolutionaries the intellectual gulf was immense. The political leaders
found it impossible to fit the artists into their plans; the artists found
that the behests of the Party, the needs of vigilance in the 'class struggle',
were empty phrases of little relevance to their literary work. By hard
experience they discovered that the connection between literature and
society is much more complex than they had imagined. Literary critics
had committed the crude error of supposing that a writer was a mere
reflection of his society. It was left for communist journalists to proclaim that the writer's true function was to propagate the social blue-
prints of the theoreticians. It thus appeared that the writers had seriously overestimated the political importance of their own efforts. Instead
of leading the cause, they were being led; and at times manipulated.
The dedication of the young poets to the communist cause was basically on ethical and aesthetic grounds: they rarely attempted to demonstrate to others, or even to themselves, the economic advantages of a
socialised system, and it is unlikely that they ever bothered to study
the complex economic and sociological arguments in favour of it.
Their adherence to the cause was an act of faith, based on revulsion
from social injustice, and on a desire to help build a better world. To
them therefore principles were everything, expediency nothing. When
they thought that the party leadership was itself acting in an unprincipled way, they appealed over its head to the members; and this
was the unforgivable crime for which the writers were driven from the
fold in 1929: their fault was disloyalty to party leadership. The point
was well taken by one of the victims, who declared that for a writer,
loyalty to principle must come before loyalty to a committee. When
conflict arose, an artist must adhere to his own vision of truth, which
no party boss could dictate to him.

Yet in spite of conflict and disillusion the cause of communism retained its appeal for many young Czech artists in the period between
the wars. By their talents they graced the movement and lent it intellectual respectability. The Party was glad of their support and proud
of the progressive and intellectual air which they gave to it. The sensitive social consciences of the writers were applauded by communist
theoreticians, who even extended a mild tolerance to artistic deviations
which would not have been permitted in Russia itself. But when the
artists put their intuitions above political directives, and refused to
toe the party line, they were reproved and disciplined. When the
writers defiantly asserted their right to dissent from the Party, as well
as from the government, then they were denounced as social-fascists,

their work was described as unhealthy and reactionary, and the faithful were instructed not to read their books. The shape of things to come already cast its long shadow over Czech literary life.

During the twenties the cause of world revolution through the Third International seemed to have been quietly abandoned by Moscow, and news from Russia gave no reason to suppose that a millennium of human happiness had been achieved. It might reasonably have been expected that the cause of social revolution, embraced by humanists all over Europe with such enthusiasm in the early post-war years, would also wither away. In fact despite tremendous disillusion this did not happen. Partly the credit for the active survival of the communist faith abroad must be given to its resolute opponents. The abuse directed at the Bolsheviks attained such hysterical proportions, and the anti-communist cause was espoused by such manifestly reactionary elements that an air of injury and persecution lay like a halo on the Reds. It seemed that some good must lie on a cause which attracted the hostility of such an anachronistic troupe of dispossessed aristocrats, political primitives, Nazis, Jew baiters, and Fascists. A tremendous incentive to the radical cause was provided by the great financial depression which hit Europe about 1930. The situation was construed as the imminent breakdown of the whole capitalist system, and the darkest hour before a new dawn. Once more the banners of socialism appeared in full array on the streets of Western Europe. Socialism, as an idea, became a magic word, conjuring up hopes for a better world washed clean of the greed and folly of the old. It was in 1931 that an eminent English journalist returned from Moscow with the slogan: 'I have seen the future – and it works'. An international movement developed whereby brain-workers of all kinds sought to link up with the working class in the hope of ousting the bourgeoisie from power. French, British, and American artists themselves proclaimed the need to put their talents at the service of the cause, and give their work a social content. It was the era of international writers' congresses, when Europe grew accustomed to slogans such as 'Artists for Peace', 'Writers for Progress'. Seeking for support from the Socialist world, the writers turned hopefully to Moscow: but the Russians, already insulated for a decade from the intellectual ferment abroad, were slow to respond.

In 1930 a Writers' Congress had been held at Kharkov which effectively ended official support for a pluralist conception of literature in the USSR. The past rivalry between the Proletarian and the non-Proletarian schools concluded with the total rout of the latter. The

liberal doctrine that no literary current could speak in the name of the
Party, or monopolise literary production, was finally and completely
abandoned. The Revolutionary Association of Proletarian Writers
(R.A.P.P.) was founded on an international basis, proclaiming the
doctrine that literature was merely a superstructure of economic
relations, and the class struggle was the key to artistic criteria. The
crude doctrine of the Rappists found little sympathy outside the USSR,
even among the dedicated admirers of communism; and the Rappist
branch set up in Prague was joined by hardly any serious writers. But
by 1932 R.A.P.P. was abolished in Russia, and a single Union of Soviet
Writers was formed, with Gorky at its head. This appeared to be a
dramatic liberalisation of policy, and there was a keen response from
abroad.

Hoping for closer co-operation with their Russian colleagues a
group of Czech artists attended the Moscow Writers' Congress in
1934. By this time the book burnings in Germany had begun: there was
street fighting in Paris between Communists and Fascists: a liberal
left-wing movement in Vienna had been ruthlessly suppressed: and the
danger of a new European war had drawn closer. The conference
assumed the nature of an international anti-Fascist demonstration.
The French had sent a powerful delegation, and the presence of artists
of the calibre of Aragon, Malraux, and Bloch, and the participation of
Russian non-conformists like Pasternak and Ehrenburg made a great
impression on the Czechs. The Russian Futurists had apparently been
rehabilitated, and when the name of Majakovsky was mentioned, the
audience broke into a storm of applause.

Bukharin, who had been for some time under the shadow of official
disfavour, made a long, well argued speech which included fearless
criticism of certain trends in Soviet literature. He had recently become
the editor of the influential newspaper *Izvestia*, and to the Czechs his
liberal views seemed to represent a new Soviet cultural policy, one
with which they would be happy to co-operate. (Evidence of such co-
operation was the formation of an Anti-Fascist group of Czechoslovak writers.)

But the optimism was premature. Although the Russians had a-
bandoned the sterile policy of the Proletkult period, it soon became
depressingly clear that the change was one of doctrine, not of outlook.
What had divided the communists from their liberal allies was the
question of whether artists should choose their own way of aiding the
cause, or whether they should operate according to directives laid
down by the Party. Only the former alternative was acceptable to the

Western writers, who included the Czechs. The policy of the Russian literary establishment was unequivocally in favour of a Party line to be followed by the artists. The new guidelines had been enunciated by Zhdanov at the Congress: the doctrine of the Proletkult had been dropped, and that of Socialist-Realism had been put in its place.

Among the radical Czech writers an issue of the time was the adherence of certain artists to the international literary movement of Surrealism[5]. In Prague, as elsewhere, the Surrealist movement was espoused by artists who were in fact among the strongest supporters of the Communist Party; the leading figures were the poets Nezval and Biebl, and the theoretician Karel Teige, who had been the leading spirit of the Poetist movement. From the outset the Czech Surrealist group aroused the hostility of orthodox Marxist critics, who denounced it as an example of bourgeois decadence and a betrayal of the methods of dialectical materialism. When the Surrealists spiritedly defended their methods, arguing in strictly Marxist terms, they were declared to be Trotskyists, and ordered peremptorily to follow the line dictated from Moscow. Meanwhile the atmosphere in Prague grew more tense as news came in of the Russian political trials: the Meierhold theatre closed; attacks on Shostakovich and Eisenstein; Bukharin, the hero of the thaw, arrested and shot. The more depressing was the news, the more unquestioning was the loyalty demanded by the Party and its cultural spokesmen. Finally they had their way with the Surrealist group, which was liquidated by Nezval after a violent quarrel with Teige. For twenty years Nezval had been the typical avant-gardist, a rebel on principle, gaily rejecting restraints imposed by convention or doctrine. In 1938 he stifled all doubts and insisted on the need for loyalty to party policy, even in face of the Russian political trials and the suppression of cultural freedom in the USSR.

But despite their intolerance of so-called decadents, Trotskyists, and deviationists within their own camp, the Czech Communists were, in the late thirties, eager to co-operate with elements of other political persuasions. During the period 1929-35 the Party, under a new young leadership, and under instructions from Moscow, had isolated itself from other parties, and openly worked for the destruction of the Czechoslovak political system. But as the German threat increased, with the signing of the Czech-Soviet military pact in 1935 and following the VIIth Congress of the Comintern the Party line again changed. Now the Czech communists were eager to co-operate in a wide anti-Fascist front, and welcomed the adhesion even of right-wing elements. The switch of support to the very nationalism which had been previously denounced, was welcomed by liberal elements. The new policy was symbolised by the slogan proclaimed by a Soviet literary delegation, 'Not Schweik but Žižka', as a model of behaviour for the Czech people. (Žižka was the high-born, nationalist champion of the medieval Hussites.) It was a strange paradox that Soviet intellectuals in their choice of a literary stereotype for Czech social behaviour, gave their preference to a nationalistic feudal knight rather than to the proletarian anti-hero of the anarchist Hašek.

The threat of war in 1938 brought together Czech writers of the most diverse views into a common national front: amid the crisis old quarrels were temporarily laid aside. In a joint appeal to the outside world the Czech writers implored intellectuals everywhere to save their country. They won sympathy, but no help; and Czechoslovakia, abandoned by its allies, was mercilessly struck down by the Germans. The hopes of Russian intervention had proved as abortive as the earlier dreams of world revolution. But the greatest disillusion was with the policies of the democratic leaders, for it was the reigning government which took upon itself the responsibility of capitulation. Its careful plans and dearly bought alliances had collapsed like a house of cards. The cautious pragmatism and liberal faith which had for twenty years sustained official state policies and formed its political outlook, had been exposed as powerless before the elemental violence of the Nazis. To men like Čapek, whose whole work had been impregnated with faith in the power of human reason, the catastrophe was stunning. Karel died on Christmas Day 1938; his brother perished in wartime in a German concentration camp. The ending of this talented and humane pair of writers seemed tragically and curiously appropriate. Their democratic ideals of reason and tolerance were made to appear futile and utopian in a world dominated by organised fanaticism. The German occupation not only put an end to the First Czechoslovak Republic, it dimmed Czech faith in democratic institutions and in the civilised values which they represented. The occupation of the land symbolised the triumph of unreason, the practical vindication of the barbaric principles represented by the Nazi New Order. For many Czechs in those bitter days faith in liberal ideas wilted and died, together with their long and frustrating love affair with France. Those who sought to understand the Czech tragedy in a wider context saw in the Nazi movement the end of an era in Europe, the final collapse of the hopes of the Enlightenment and Humanism. The revival of the pogrom, the everyday use of torture, the book burnings and public executions, seemed to indicate that barbarism had won a perhaps final triumph over the civilised values of Europe.

Under German occupation all the media of instruction and propaganda were naturally employed in the Nazi cause; censorship was ruthless and efficient. One result of this state of affairs, which continued for six years, was to interpose between writer and reader a division which later became known as the credibility gap. Scepticism was sharpened to the extent that men acquired the habit of believing the opposite of the official pronouncement: together with incredulity there developed the custom of reading the written word as a code, to detect hidden allusions and cryptic messages. 'A withdrawal to prepared positions' meant a rout; a 'temporary setback' meant a catastrophe: 'Bolshevik terrorists' meant Czech resistance workers; 'traitors' meant patriots: 'official information' meant misinformation; 'justice' meant injustice; 'truth' meant lies. War brings in its trail a reversal of criteria; and once readers have lost faith in the public media, it is difficult to restore it. One legacy of the German occupation has been a lasting feeling of scepticism on the part of Czech readers, a disinclination to take anything at its face value, and the acceptance of the idea that any published work is likely to conceal political allusions and messages which only the eyes of the initiated can perceive.

There were other literary legacies of wartime occupation. Their language, literature, and traditions were the one unifying element of the Czech people, the kernel of their resistance, the only light to sustain the nation through the new Dark Age. Literature became the more precious because it was almost all that the Czechs had left in common; it provided a symbolic refuge from Germanisation. The social function of literature increased, and the role of the writer became over-valued by ordinary standards; in the post-war period men credited artists with real power to change the world. Writers could rejoice in their new-found importance: but the notion that imaginative writers could do immense good or harm to political causes was fatal to their independence, and later was to make them a prime target for political bosses.

A favourite theme of the Nazis was the doctrine of historical inevitability. The New Order was a logical, and inevitable consequence of long historical development. In 1941 the German empire stretched from the Pyrenees to the Near East; and even those who hated the Nazis with all their hearts feared the truth of the prediction that the German Reich was on the crest of a wave that nothing on earth could stop. Even intellectuals fell into a kind of fatalism, acknowledging the existence of irresistible historical forces to which nations must accommodate themselves. Then as the tide of success turned, faith in ultimate German victory ebbed, but the fatalistic attitude remained. Those who had seen the Nazis as carried on an irresistible wave of history, now saw the communists in a similar position. As so often with wartime propaganda, readers dismissed the details presented to them, but accepted the logic behind them. One of the sad intellectual legacies of the war was the belief that certain groups were 'on the side of history', and that common prudence indicated the folly of opposing them. Previously, to win support for a movement it had been necessary to indicate that it was wise, beneficial, or well-motivated: since 1939 it has been sufficient to argue that it is on the side of history, hence inevitable, and its opponents accordingly blind or corrupt reactionaries.

The years of enemy occupation subtly changed the mental climate of the Czechs, and the resulting attitudes were to show themselves in later literature. During the occupation new Czech poems, novels and plays were still published, provided they gave no offence to the occupiers, but the real issues of the time could not be the subject of controversial writing. Czech wartime literature has its own neutral style, and is like an intermezzo between the ferment of pre-war and post-war. A number of young and talented poets made their debut in this period, and among their most endearing legacy is the picture they have left of wartime Prague. Its aspect, like the lives of its dwellers, is humdrum, shabby, austere. The children of hard times and material shortages are strangers to the romantic world of grand gestures and flamboyant heroism. The young poets' obsession with mundane details and down-at-heel reality, their disinclination for romantic escapism, is a mark of their anxiety to convey the bare truth. They wrote of empty streets, stairs that lead nowhere, endless walks through faded suburbs, the sight of buildings which have long since been demolished: a lost world of childhood is conjured up by the sight of a battered textbook, or a childish treasure. Their work avoids pathos as much as it shuns politics: heroism, rhetoric, and sentimentality are rigidly excluded from their narrow world, which is not without a sense of its own absurdity. Kamil Bednář, Ivan Blatný, Jiřina Hauková, Jiří Orten are the stars of this brief period. Their work had common features which mark them off as a group – the so-called lost wartime generation. Orten was killed in 1941; the others survived but never gained the place in Czech literature which they had the right to expect. Their later work, which should have been their triumph, was to be a melancholy post-script to that of the war.

There was a curious gap between the deliberately humdrum world of new writing and the cataclysmic changes going on outside. The incongruity was carried into the lives of the writers themselves. While the critic Václav Černý was editing the austerely intellectual, literary journal *Critical Monthly*[6] he was, until his arrest, active in the resistance, together with the novelist Vančura. Normal life was like a facade covering a network of deadly peril which touched the lives of all. No man was safe from arrest, not even the highest officials of the Protectorate government. No one could be sure that he would not be challenged at any moment to make a terrible decision – to assist the Nazis, or to resist them. In either case refusal could have fatal consequences. Emotions which in normal times are exceptional – intense anguish, searing fear and hatred – became commonplace. The normal had become bizarre, and the bizarre normal. Neutrality was impossible: there was no way to avoid involvement. What took away all security was the necessity to make hazardous choices; the freedom to choose was like a millstone round men's necks. How many people in wartime positively envied prisoners of war, because they alone were absolved from all choice! Exempted from the struggle, they were blessed with non-involvement. Under enemy occupation even the dead at times became objects of envy, and the grave a kind of refuge. The living were inexorably *condemned to be free*. The hero was driven into heroism, the coward into cowardice. The deadly burden of involvement paradoxically reversed the values of freedom and captivity: lacking choice the prisoner attained a desperate kind of security; the free man, able to collaborate or resist, to invite future reprisals or immediate execution, was in the trap. Freedom, like truth and justice, had suffered a curious inversion of meaning. The human experience of wartime was to be the future material of literature: it was a topsy-turvy world, in which many things were the opposite of what they seemed, and words meant the reverse of what they said. In this world was reality to be found in the apparent normalcy of everyday life, or in the anguished conflicts which lay behind it? In the thousand imaginary dangers that beset each day, or in the deadening routine which filled it? And when the day of liberation came, what would be *its* reality?

By May 1945 the fighting was virtually over in Western Europe: Prague, almost undamaged by warfare, awaited her deliverers. The pent-up hatred of the Czechs was about to be released upon the occupiers, but warned by experience, the resistance movement waited until the last minute. The rising began on the morning of May 5 when American help was within an hour's distance from the city. The radio station was seized, and the Germans were ordered to surrender. The American troops, apparently at the orders of the high command and in accordance with a secret agreement with the Russians, made no move towards Prague. Efforts by Czech moderates to effect a peaceful handover of power failed, and all compromise was rejected by the armed resistance movement, which now came into the open. So the heavy fighting began, as German tanks rolled into the city centre, and shelled public buildings. The lovely Spring sunshine witnessed a scene so often foreshadowed in revolutionary Czech poems, the sight of men desperately fighting at the barricades. It was four days before the first units of the Red Army fought their way into the Prague suburbs: meanwhile the city had experienced unprecedented scenes of savagery and carnage, in which prisoners were hanged in the streets and doused in burning petrol. So the German occupation, begun in March 1939 amid heavy omens, ended six years later in a crescendo of violence and horror.

II

The Battle of the Books

'Mankind will return through ruins to the wreckage of the past. Through cities smouldering with burned-out anger. Through alleys of gallows trees. Though pillaged lands. It will stand by the meagre fireplaces of hearths without warmth, in houses without walls. It has not yet lost enough. It will lose even the past'.

A. Hoffmeister

In the Europe of 1945 only a naive person could imagine that the silenced guns symbolised the happy ending to a bad dream. A return to normalcy was ruled out not only by the material conditions, but because people had only dim memories of what constituted normal life: chaos had become normal; and normalcy the dream. Much of the continent lay in ruins: the physical devastation seemed the outward sign of a ruin beyond the powers of rebuilding. Amid the burning cities a traditional and complex fabric of social relationships had been obliterated. The buildings could one day be restored; but the people were gone, or changed; and the system of values which had upheld the structure had lost its validity. Principles of conduct which had once been accepted without question, had become almost curiosities. Where it had been a patriotic duty, as well as a means of survival, to deceive, to steal, or to kill, it was hardly reasonable to expect that criteria could be reversed or restored by parliamentary decree. Where ideas like truth, duty, loyalty, treason, had become simplified into black/white options, the mental climate was scarcely amenable to democratic habits of thought, to the weighing of legal distinctions, and to moral scruples over the rights of dissenting minorities.

Symbols of survival from the holocaust were the pyjama-clad figures whom liberating armies discovered in the abandoned concentration camps. Toothless, sick, starving and broken, they inspired in their liberators horror, anger and revulsion: man had reached life on its lowest terms. The pitiable and grotesque figures, when they became vocal, told of horrors inflicted not only upon them, but by them upon each other in the cruel battle for survival in the camps. For a century or more, men had written of civilisation's breakdown: now the incredible reality was before their eyes as the raw material of journalism and future television programmes. What had happened to the subject peoples of Europe had a parallel in the awesome sufferings of the Germans themselves in their bombed cities: a modern apocalypse revealed itself in the man-made firestorms which destroyed Dresden. Anyone could see that devastation on this scale went beyond the scope of mere rehabilitation. If Europe was to live again, it would evidently be a new land, with perhaps only sentimental attachments to the old.

Many historians have attributed the spread of communism in post-war Europe primarily to the presence of the Red Army. Obviously this is a gross simplification; for the lines of military occupation did not coincide with those of ideological influence. In Greece and Albania, where there were no Russian forces, the communists asserted themselves much more vigorously than in Austria or Finland, which suffered Russian occupation. In ideological fanaticism none surpassed the new communist bosses of unoccupied Jugoslavia: on the other hand Russian-occupied Hungary had a middle-of-the-road government, and was lumped together with Germany as a Western, enemy, country by the nations of the socialist camp. Amid this complex pattern, Czechoslovakia was unique. It was physically by far the least damaged of all the warring countries east of the Rhine. Although liberated mainly by the Russians, its President, the framework of its post-war government, and its ministerial bureaucracy, came from London. To the surprise of many external observers, the Red Army withdrew entirely from Czechoslovak territory within a few months of the war's end; and the political situation developed without overt Soviet interference. The Czech and Slovak communists were very successful in forcing their ideas upon the government, in establishing their position within it, and in winning a majority at the election of 1946. Their success owed much to their position as the favoured sons of Moscow, an advantage ruthlessly and astutely exploited by the Czechoslovak Communist Party: but they were assisted by a mental and political climate favourable to their cause. The Czechs had not forgotten the Nazis' teaching about the inexorable forces of history; only now it seemed that history had been misinterpreted. In the battle of the giants, between Fascism and Communism, history had apparently been all the time on the side of the Communists, and nothing now could stop their triumph. Men of intellect and democratic convictions gave assent to such views: others were prepared to be swept along on a tide of success.

The idea that the future belonged to socialism was widespread in Europe: even in that citadel of conservatism, England, which had retained its living patterns virtually intact through the war years,

Churchill's government was, in the hour of its triumph, paradoxically swept out of office by a landslide socialist vote. In Prague, unlike London, the victory of Marxist-orientated parties was taken as a matter of course. One might well ask how was it that before any elections had been held, people *knew* that Czechoslovakia would be governed by socialists. The idea was common knowledge; it was in the air, so to speak. Actually it came from propaganda, newspapers and radio. The romantic idea that history was on the side of the Communists appeared as an assumption underlying serious political argument, literary discussion, or even theological exposition. A sign of the times was a book published in the USA, entitled *Doom and Resurrection.* [1]

Its author was a talented Czech theologian, J. L. Hromádka. In his book he interpreted the war as the culmination of a great spiritual upheaval. The symptoms of Europe's decay were shallow humanism, sceptical indifference, a growing lack of self-commitment: the cool tolerance on which liberals so prided themselves, he saw as a lack of compassion and a refusal to identify evil. Europe had witnessed a new *treason of the intellectuals*: first they had lost faith in God, then later in reason itself: they had watched the new savagery of Nazism with a paralysis of will – almost with a sense of excitement, almost with envy of its fanaticism. So a continent had died. And the resurrection? As a churchman Hromádka saw the ultimate hope in a return to the evangelical spirit of Christ. As a historian he saw that spirit presently at work in the socialist revolution begun in 1917 and still continuing.

It may seem strange to bracket the spirit of Christ, the peace giver, with that of the armed prophets of Stalinism. Hromádka recognised and accepted the contradiction: how could the resurrection be accomplished by men whose beliefs were atheistic, and whose practices were of a violence verging on the barbaric? And yet there was more hope in them than in liberalism without conviction, freedom without faith, tolerance without commitment. Communism posed a threat to the sanctity of human personality; in its theoretical crudity it tried to reduce man to a mere by-product of a historical process. But by a strange paradox it was atheists who, by their involvement and sense of belief, represented the social impetus of the living church. To insist on their follies and crimes was to refuse to see the wider context: perhaps once to the early Romans, steeped in the culture of the classical world, the Christians too had seemed primitive and fanatical. But their faith had conquered the world.

To Western observers, anxiously following the spread of communism across Europe, it seemed that the struggle for power in Prague was between forces of the Right and the Left; this is in fact the way the struggle was described by the communists themselves. Actually the right wing in Czech politics had been entirely discredited, and had no hope of gaining power. The Czechoslovak government in London, later to be portrayed as a reactionary group, was committed to drastic social reforms; the idea of restoring to private ownership the industrial enterprises annexed, enlarged and capitalised by the Germans, was out of the question. The issues which divided the country went much deeper than questions of nationalisation, social services, or a restructuring of the economy. The basic issue was between democrats and revolutionaries; between those who hoped to revive the liberal-humanist tradition of Masaryk; and those who proclaimed a fresh start, and radical solutions in the spirit of the USSR. Those who believed in the old Europe, and hoped to reform it, faced fatalists and fanatics, who believed that Europe was dead, and a new world had to be made; if necessary, by the destruction of what remained of the old.

In this contest the democrats held many good cards. The values they asserted were traditional, and had been implicitly accepted by the vast majority of thinking people before the war. These values were: belief in the rights and dignity of the individual; the subordination of political expediency to moral principle; the rights of free speech, thought, and belief; the protection of minority and dissenting views; an open door to influences from both East and West. Those of the democratic persuasion (they were not a political group) could look to Beneš himself as an embodiment, and unofficially as a spokesman, of their views. The Czechoslovak government in London had been committed to these principles. They were shared by many in the socialist camp itself.

On the face of it, the future of Czech democracy seemed bright, and prophesies of doom rather romantic. The Czech lands were an oasis of comparative calm in a ruined continent; and the cause of extremism would seem to have suffered a deadly blow with the crushing of Nazism. Nor had Czech Communism a particularly impressive pre-war record. From 1929 to 1935 the communists had campaigned for the disintegration of the Czechoslovak state and the overthrow of its political system: even the accession to power of Hitler in Germany had not persuaded the Party to support the cause of Czech national defence. This was the period when communist fortunes fell to their lowest level, and their cause was abandoned by many of the intellectuals who had supported it. Then in the summer of 1935, following the lead of the Moscow International, the Party had switched to support of the

Popular Front and national defence against Nazism. At the time of Munich the communists had won much sympathy for their patriotic stand: but the signing of the Soviet-Nazi pact in the following year caused a fresh, and agonising, switch. Now the Czech communists affirmed their solidarity with the German proletariat, and denounced Western imperialism as the aggressor in the war.[2] Two years later, the German invasion of Russia simplified issues for the communists, restoring a patriotic Czechoslovak front against fascism. Now Stalin welcomed the co-operation of Beneš, who had useful contacts with the West; and the USSR recognised the exile Czechoslovak government in London.

In view of the Party's erratic record it was, in 1945, by no means certain that the Russians would sacrifice a friendly and co-operative ally in Prague, in order to install a communist group whose primary loyalty had been to the now dissolved Comintern. Decisions taken by the wartime allies at Yalta seemed to have placed Czechoslovakia within the Soviet orbit; but it was a time of change and manoeuvre, and the political – cultural orientation of the country was still an open question; from the beginning a struggle was joined between the opposing factions. The democratic regime set up in Prague assured conditions for the free play of ideas and policies. In cabinet, parliament, trade unions, and National Committees, communists and democrats clashed openly, even while they co-operated in the political field. In less obvious terms the struggle for the minds and allegiance of the people was carried on relentlessly in journalism, radio, and in creative literature. Of course, not all art and writing was politically orientated; but a high proportion of it was committed: and even in the case of apparently neutral work, the wartime experience of reading between the lines, and treating literature as a code for secret messages, caused readers and critics to see political trends even where perhaps none had been intended.

In June 1945 a public meeting was held in Prague to honour the memory of writers who had lost their lives during the war. The meeting was addressed by Václav Černý, critic, professor, and editor of the journal, *The Critical Monthly*, which had been closed down by the Nazis. He had worked in the underground; had been arrested; and had been physically ill-treated by the German occupiers. A man of liberal, left-wing views, he was a scathing critic of everything he considered sham and superficial in Czech literature; and he had no time for what he recognised as the dogmatic attitudes and sectarian methods of many communists. He was above all devoted to the cause

of free expression in literature, and in his speech at the meeting he
quoted from the programme of the underground national-revolutionary
council of writers of which he had been a prominent member:

'For the future development of literature, art, and cultural life as
a whole, it is vital that all writers, artists, and scientists... should
enjoy complete freedom in their thinking, their work, and in their
artistic and scientific expression; that no line, no artistic or scientific school or group should be favoured by the state apparatus at
the expense of others: that there should be free competition of
ideas, and work: its quality should be the decisive factor'.[3]

Speaking from the point of view of a dedicated liberal, Václav Černý
appealed for an effort to reconcile the claims of freedom and authority, the rights of the individual and the community, conscience and the
law, personality and the state. Writers and artists should now, as ever,
be in the forefront of change: and art should, as always, pioneer the
new ways of life.

The most fundamental issue which on the theoretical level divided
the communists from their opponents was the question of the rights
of the individual towards the community, above all, the right of free
expression and dissent. Discussion with the communists overtly on
this issue was fruitless, since they refused to admit that there was any
conflict between freedom and socialism, or that there was any serious
restriction on personal freedom in their model, the USSR. A more
fruitful issue of debate was the future cultural orientation of Czechoslovakia, West or East. In the political field it was the policy of the
democrats to avoid the question by seeking a middle position; and in
the immediate post-war period Czechoslovakia was often hopefully
termed a bridge between Russia and the West. This was the attitude
taken by Černý in the cultural field. He acknowledged readily the
bonds between the Czechs and Russian culture generally; the fact that
the Czechs and their Slav neighbours had recently come closer politically put a historical seal on a cultural sympathy which was very old.
But he rejected the idea that this should mean any weakening of Czech
ties with the West. Indeed the Western character of Czech art, thought,
and literature was attested by five hundred years of development.
Gothic art, Romance culture, French modernism, and American
pragmatism were an inseparable part of the Czech tradition. In any
case Marxism was itself a Western philosophy which had been trans-
planted to eastern Europe, and institutionalised by Slavs. (This latter
was a tactless reminder). In fact Černý could also have pointed out
that until 1945 the main inspiration for Marxist thought in Czecho-

slovakia had come not so much from Moscow as from Paris. The pre-war threads of Czech Communist literature led back to the French avant-garde, to surrealism, futurism, and Dada, rather than to the deadening academism of Soviet art.

For their part the communists consistently denied that they were seeking an exclusively Eastern orientation for Czech culture: on the other hand they claimed that culture did not need the influence of 'decadent, reactionary, exclusive, politically tainted' Western art, based on 'out-dated' ideas. The reckless use of such labels, slapped on whole categories of literature, and the flourishing of crude politico-cultural slogans, was a feature of communist argumentation. They pressed their advantage on the widest possible front; neglecting no opportunity to attack Černý, who became a symbol of resistance to their views. When he published in *The Critical Monthly* two articles by K. Brušák on contemporary English literature, even this apparently innocuous subject provoked angry comments. Brušák, in a comment on J. B. Priestley, had given a brief sketch of wartime England, noting trends towards increased social and economic justice there. Such a view was in sharp contrast with that presented by the communists, who regarded England as a centre of capitalist reaction, exploitation, and imperialism, moving inevitably towards revolution. Even more disturbing was Brušák's account of English writers' disillusion with left-wing politics. He retailed their gradual abandonment of utopian hopes that society could be saved by economic reorganisation from above; their realisation that centralisation of control would bring a dangerous accumulation of power into the hands of a small group; and their regretful conviction that such an accumulation would be the worst threat to society's happiness and freedom. A final result could be a state in which a clique could control the distribution of everything from bread to poetry, and regulate a nation by education, propaganda, rewards and terror.[4]

In retrospect one marvels at the accuracy of Brušák's sketch as a prophesy of Czechoslovakia's own forthcoming society. At first sight English literature might seem an improbable field in which to stage a debate about Czech political orientation, but communist publicists were quick to see the political implications of the article, and they blamed Černý for it, identifying him with the views expressed.

The death of Paul Valéry presented another opportunity for con-temporary Czech issues to be fought on apparently neutral ground. In his journal Černý paid a glowing tribute to Valéry, as a fine example of Western art. His reward was a blast of criticism for praise of a poet of aristocratic decadence, and isolation from popular movements. In the communist daily newspaper *Rudé právo*, Gustav Bareš violently attacked Černý for his choice of literary models. By an unsubtle switch of argument he accused him of trying to cut Czechoslovakia off from the USSR, whose protection was the only guarantee of Czechoslovak existence. 'Increased political and cultural co-operation with the Russians was the only progressive path for the Czechs: but certain re-actionary elements were deliberately trying to put a brake on their co-operations; to hold fast to old, discredited ideas; and to prevent the Czechs from drawing upon the life-giving strength of the powerful, admired, and triumphant USSR'. In such crude polemics the shift from literary criticism to political propaganda was obvious, and the literary question was merely a springboard for the propaganda. Writers like Bareš scarcely bothered to veil the menace which lay behind the ostensibly cultural debate.

Writers in Western countries are accustomed to personal feuds or literary controversies involving politics: but almost never do such controversies have any decisive effect in the world of public affairs. However threatening, grandiloquent, or seductive are the voices of poets or novelists no one expects politicians to take much notice of them: and the polemics take on a reassuringly harmless image. This was certainly not so in Prague. In June 1946 literature's relationship to politics became the main theme of an official congress of the Czecho-slovak Writers' Syndicate, and a speaker was none other than the President of the Republic, Dr E. Beneš himself. In the great debate between democrats and communists there was no doubt on which side his sympathies lay; though in the field of public affairs his position set him outside political debate, and above all contestants.

In his speech to the Congress Beneš drew attention to the close relationship between politics and literature in the past, when Czech writers had spoken as the conscience of their nation. Now their country had become a symbol of international co-operation; and the writers for the first time had the opportunity of propagating their national ideals and tradition on the world stage. But they could be transmitted and represented worthily only by a literature that was free and autono-mous. Czech literature must stand above conflicts of political parties, groups, or classes; and must not become a tool in such conflicts. Above all, freedom of utterance must be vigilantly protected from interfer-ence by party, class, political or other non-literary influences; *and of course from interference by the state itself.*[5]

It was rather a bizarre situation – typical of the topsy-turvy atmosphere of post-war Europe – that a head of state should appeal to a group of writers to safeguard freedom of expression from the state apparatus. The fact that Beneš was willing to make such an appeal suggests that he doubted the ability, or even the will, of many Czech writers to preserve the autonomy of literature: at least one group, the communists, was already openly attempting to harness it to their cause.

In the literary debate both liberals and communists agreed that literature must avoid hypocrisy and deceit: both praised realism, and demanded truth from writers; but their interpretation was different. Truth to liberal critics and writers was a vague conception, a matter of observation, faith, and conscience. For their part the communists embraced a pre-fabricated theory of art, proclaimed at the Moscow Writers' Congress of 1934 by Zhdanov.[6] The style inculcated, the theory, and the method, was known as socialist-realism: basic to the theory is its 'dialectical' view of reality. A flower patch may seem a static tableau of colour; and a photographic, or naturalistic art may so render it. Actually it is a complex of competing elements; the young struggles for life against the old; the flower which will bloom to-morrow rises next to that whose bloom is all but over, and the decaying matter which once bloomed, but supplies the humus for new growth. Abjuring a passive, naturalistic view of the empirical world the Marxist separates the growing from the decaying, the promise of the tomorrow from the dying remnants of yesterday. In his view of the world he selects for emphasis those elements which are young, vital, positive, in contrast to the decadent artist who wallows in the decay of the passing and past. In the panorama of history the Marxist recognises the struggle of the oppressed and exploited to liberate themselves: history is on their side, and they are its future heirs. The artist thus embraces their cause; and engages his art on their side. Needless to say, all that is 'young, positive, vital' etc. is identified with socialism, the order of tomorrow; what is 'decaying and reactionary' is identified with capitalism. The artist who has 'understood the trend of history', or 'thrown in his lot with the working class', contributes by his art to their final triumph. Inevitably therefore his work will be socially engaged, positive, and optimistic. To entertain doubts, to be pessimistic, negative, sympathetic to decay, or even to show 'bourgeois objectivism', is not permitted to those who seek socialist realism. To emphasise the dark side of life, and thus perhaps cast doubt on the final issue, is a mark of a bourgeois mentality, and because of its deceit is, from a dialectical standpoint, untruthful; for it denies the truth of socialist vision. Truth therefore becomes dependent primarily upon political interpretation.

The test of such a theory is its value as a tool of criticism, and the quality of work which it inspires in its followers. In the period 1945-8 actually very little Czech literature was published which fitted the socialist-realist model at all closely, but a great deal was published which was actively sympathetic to the socialist cause. Much of Czech contemporary writing was of a realistic nature: by its treatment of contemporary issues, and by its views expressed or implied, it could be said to be socially engaged. Without attempting to survey the whole field of literature we may take some examples which will illustrate the trend, and the truth or bias of its content.

In Western Europe a literary development of the war years was the increased stature and influence of war correspondents. Their despatches, comments, and analyses served to document the course of operations and also to alert public opinion to the issues at stake. The heightened interest in reportage seems to have been world-wide: nowhere was it greater than in former enemy-occupied countries, which only from 1945 had the opportunity of reading wartime issues described from a non-German point of view. In Czechoslovakia, reportage literature satisfied a need for information, and also for an art which was contemporary, realistic, and directly connected with immediate problems.

A common theme of literary reportage was that of the wartime resistance movement in Czechoslovakia. Its most spectacular achievement was the assassination of Nazi Governor Heydrich. The planning, performance, and results of the deed were documented in a dramatic account *Shadow behind Heydrich*, which straddles the line between journalism and fiction. Other prose works, *That the Nation might live* by R. Rédr, and *Men walk in Darkness*, by J. Marek[7], tell the story of the resistance from the communist point of view. In the latter a group of parachutists is dropped over Czech territory from Russia; their task is to contact and organise partisan resistance by the local underground. A Czech officer guides them to their appointed goal through the night over unknown paths, where the safety of all is dependent on the courage and faith of each. The darkness of the night matches the uncertainty within them; and it is this which threatens the success of the enterprise more than any external peril. The ideological slant of the two works is obvious. It appears not only in the assumption that credit for the resistance belongs almost entirely to the communists; but even more so in the scale of values adopted by the heroes. Emphasis is put not upon the terrors of the occupation, but on the heroism and high faith of the participants. The sacrifice of human life inspires in them not tragic feelings of loss and futility, but pride in duty performed, and a conviction that the example will help others to strive towards the victory of communism.

In similar spirit, but set in a lower key and written in more accomplished style is the collection of stories by Jan Drda entitled *The Silent Barricade*.[8] Drda is an interesting figure, a talented writer whose involvement in cultural politics brought him little good. He had won a name in wartime for his novel *Town on the Palm of a Hand*,[9] which was in fact an adaptation to the Czech environment of the French *Clochmerle*. He was active in the film industry and in popular journalism; after the war he was prominent in the Writers' Syndicate, and became editor of the daily *Lidové noviny* (*Popular News*). In 1945 his comparative youth, talent, and eagerness to co-operate with the communists seemed to promise him a bright future. We shall hear of him again.

In 1945 it was natural that the central theme of interest should be the ordeal from which the nation had just emerged. The terror and suffering produced by Nazi occupation was symbolised in the concentration camps, and one of the strangest literary genres to emerge from the war were the poems composed in the camps, and first published after their liquidation. Poetry is often considered as a luxury product and it may seem bizarre that men and women who were humiliated, starved, and beaten, should have found the will and the energy for verse. Perhaps it was the unbelievable character of the new experiences that drove men even without literary training to try to preserve their impressions: the drama of life, surpassing that hitherto met in the course of their reading, seemed to require only a passive instrument to record reality, and bear witness that the unbelievable had become fact. It was difficult to write in prose, for lack of materials; but short verses could be memorised, and passed on through the camps.

In this way a new, and short-lived, folk literature was created; much of it was of more historical than literary interest; and most of it perished with its unknown composers. Among the prisoners at the Buchenwald camp was Josef Čapek, brother of the novelist Karel: he did not survive the ordeal, but he left a number of poems, and these were subsequently published under the title *Poems from the Concentration Camp*.[10] In 1946 appeared an anthology of camp verse, *Poetry behind Bars*[11]: many of the poets were naturally anonymous or dead. The poems varied in literary sophistication: some were touching in their naivete; in general they kept the impact of direct reportage, often preserving the slang of camp life. Among the motifs of the poems are nostalgic dreams of happier days; hope for survival; prayers for vengeance upon the Germans; and faith in the Soviet Union, which will punish the Nazis for their crimes.

In the prose book of Jiří Beneš, *In German Custody,*[12] is expressed the fear that one day men may forget what the Germans have done, and allow their enormities to be repeated:

> In time many things are bound to be forgotten, and it may happen that our children will see the children of today's Germany with other eyes... they will see only the punishment, and will try to forget the guilt of their parents. Therefore it is essential to register the testimony of those who witnessed German guilt.

Amid the cold recital of horrors comes a touch of poetry:

> One day the prisoners had to stand in line quite naked: it was a cold day, sometime in February... I saw a group of eight or ten naked bodies, with bowed heads leaning against the wall or against each other for the warmth... Some Rodin should have moulded those strange postures of the prisoners of Buchenwald.

The still-life conjured up by Beneš seems more touching because of its conscious association with formal art, recalling familiar associations of tranquillity and beauty. Scenes or details observed in the camp often strike up a memory of a person's lost world of freedom and normalcy. Even more striking is the effect on survivors of later experiences which bring back memories of the camps:

> I saw young people there, young women and children, even babies... Many of them must have choked, for I saw some corpses with the fingers bitten off... There were men on one side, women and children on the other, innocent children... As they had been rounded up from the train, so they lay, one on top of the other, heads on others' feet, hands beneath the skulls of others, legs like sticks...
>
> Later on, when already free, I passed through towns behind the front... I always had a shock when I saw bare mannequin figures lying in the shop windows... those figures lying in the shop windows... those figures looked like that - scattered wax mannequins of the dressmakers' salons, *dernier cri de la civilisation* – the latest fashion of modern time.

After being condemned to death prisoners were kept for ninety days awaiting execution: they were commonly kept fettered in irons night and day. The misery and terror of those days was preserved in a collection of *Last Letters*, written by condemned prisoners, and subsequently published in Prague.[13] An authentic note of careful reportage was struck by Ota Kraus and Erich Schön in the book *Factory for Death*.[14] From Mauthausen camp came a striking collection of short stories by Milan Jariš entitled *They are coming*.[15]

Amid this literary chamber of horrors there is one book which has become a classic of communist literature, *Reportage from the Gallows*, by Julius Fučík[16] it was to become compulsory reading for every Czech schoolchild, and its author was to be held up as a model of heroism. Before the war J. Fučík had been a writer for the popular press and active communist worker. During the war he went into hiding; worked in the resistance movement; was arrested by the Gestapo; and after prolonged interrogation was condemned and executed. His book is a collection of writings said to have been smuggled out of his cell by a sympathetic warder. That a prisoner of such importance should have been allowed to write a book in his cell without detection is certainly surprising, and doubts have been cast on its authenticity.[17] The book consists of a loosely written commentary upon Fučík's prison experiences, feelings, and impressions of his fellow internees. Its most striking feature is its pervading attitude of cheerful optimism: there is nothing really tragic about Fučík – no doubts, remorse, or fear – certainly no classic atmosphere of greatness and doom. In the face of threats, blows, setbacks, and the shadow of death, Fučík maintains the bluff good humour of an energetic scoutmaster: one expects a rescue and a happy ending. There is no rescue; but, for Fučík, the ending is happy; for he reckons his life as a cheerfully offered sacrifice for the communist cause. An intense feeling of solidarity with the comrades is conveyed in a much-translated passage from his diary:

> It is nine o'clock. In the Kremlin tower the clock is striking ten, and the procession is beginning in the Red Square... now they are singing the Internationale; now it is ringing all over the world. Let it sound in our cell... We are not alone: we belong to those who sing in freedom. *Yes, we are with you.*

The recent ordeal of the Czech nation was interpreted by the poet Vladimír Holan in apocalyptic terms of doom and salvation, of physical catastrophe and spiritual regeneration, in two books of post-war verse, *Thanks to the Soviet Union* and *Vigil*.[18] In his visions of the old doomed world Holan, who once described himself as 'drunk with words', combined lurid details of war horrors and refined cruelty with metaphysical overtones of 'Satanocracy' and 'Titanomania'. War had become a sentence of death passed on a world abandoned by God and surrendered to chaos: the liberation of Prague was a symbol of hope for a fresh start. A new world was needed; for there was no way back to the old.

The view that 1945 was a turning point of history appears repeatedly in the work of visionary poets like Holan, Hrubín, and Závada,[19] who now resumed the poet's traditional role as a prophet. Their visions of the future were rather vague; but of the past there were memories which would not be forgotten:

> From the ruins of smouldering towns
> From towns laid low in ashes
> Life long since evacuated...
> Only shattered houses
> Only the shattered souls...
> Only the ferro-concrete skeletons
> The girders of the nerves laid bare
> Vibrating still
> After the earthquake...
> Everything consumed by the fire of the bombs
> Ourselves shrivelled
> To living mummies...

Among the reprisals inflicted by the Germans for the assassination of Heydrich was the total destruction of the Czech village of Lidice in 1942. All adult males were shot; women and children were removed to the camps; the village was dynamited; men who were absent (some on enforced labour in Germany) were hunted down and shot in their turn. Lidice became a symbol of Nazi ruthlessness and Czech suffering:

> It is no more, it is no more,
> the tongueless bells no longer ring,
> only the smoking walls remain
> and one stray dog who walks alone
> searching in vain from stone to stone...
>
> Black beams hang broken from the skies
> and blood and smoke falls on the square:
> a mongrel howls her lost despair
> and scratches vainly with her claws.
> Only the old lime trees remain
> and birds, whose slender carols now
> evoke the old and mourn the new.
> Black beams hang broken from the skies...[20]

An emphasis on the horrors of war was not altogether to the taste of communist critics, as it savoured too much of the negative side of things. War was, after all, a necessary means whereby what was evil or historically outdated was swept away to make room for healthier growth. The literature of terror, anxiety, and inner tension came to be identified by Marxists with Existentialism: it quickly became a term of abuse in Marxist journals, and young writers suspected of the taint were urged to adopt a more positive attitude.

At the Writer's Congress of 1946 in Prague the novelist Drda, among others, emphasised the artist's duty to inspire community effort, to open men's eyes to a new social ethic, to show the way ahead, and to make familiar the process of social change. As he assumed as a matter of course that the present changes were for the better, he added to literature the required functions of strengthening *faith* in the victory of the right cause, and spreading optimism. For writers actively to engage their work in the process of social change meant that they were forced to take up a political position. Neutralism was regarded with disfavour, if not hostility, and many of the poets who had entered literature in the war years were regarded as insufficiently involved in the life of their society, almost as deserters from the social cause.

It would be a great mistake to assume that writers who actively engaged their art in the social process did so necessarily from unworthy motives; or that their efforts were primarily of a propagandist nature. It was regarded as an important function of literature to pay its debt to heroes and victims of war by giving a just picture of events. For novelists especially it was the *interpretative* function of their work which was stressed, that is, to express the spirit of their time, and to put the present situation into its historical context. According to Marxist thought this meant revealing as the culmination of history the liberation of the Czech people into socialism. Several novelists took up the challenge; among them a distinguished pre-war writer Václav Řezáč. Although his reputation was established, it was rather as an exponent of the psychological novel, with more than a glint of decadence. In his book *The Black Light*[21] the central figure had been a man eaten by his sense of inferiority and cowardice; to compensate for his personal inadequacy he cultivates his worst side, so that his only companion becomes the *lie*; reaching the depths of deceit and moral decay, he cuts himself off entirely from the fellowship of men. Řezáč's wartime novel *Turning Point*[22] has as its subject the birth of a novel. A writer, oppressed with his sense of inferiority, creates as his other self a fantasy character; and the action of the book moves on the twin planes of reality and imagination, confusing the levels of consciousness. Such a literary background did not make Řezáč a promising convert to Marxist literature; but in 1945 he was writing for the popular press 'healthy', uncomplicated stories about simple heroes of the resistance. He was accepted into the Party, and set out deliberately to serve its cause by writing a monumental trilogy upon the transformation of society by socialism. The action was to be set in the former German-speaking areas: it was the period when, in one of those acts of massive inhumanity characteristic of the time, more or less the entire population of the area was deported to Germany, and the land was recolonised by Czechs. This was to be the context of the trilogy, and Řezáč went to live in the area to collect material over a long period, while, incidentally, working for a government department. It was six years before the first volume appeared.[23]

Another writer who essayed the difficult task of historical interpretation through fiction was Marie Pujmanová, one of the most talented and attractive of the pre-war novelists. In 1937 she had published *People at the Crossroads,*[24] a novel set in the twenties. Madame Pujmanová did not commit the error of romanticising the life of the proletariat; her novel centres upon a middle class family in an industrial complex (the Bata works), and some of the detail seems to be autobiographical: its meaningful thread is the struggle for the communist cause, to which Pujmanová herself subscribed. After the war she prepared a second volume in the expected trilogy, *Playing with Fire,*[25] which was eventually published in 1948. The novel is set in the period from the Dimitrov trial in Leipzig to the Munich crisis of 1938: significantly the final scene is laid within the walls of the Soviet embassy in Prague. The final volume of the trilogy was not to appear until 1952.[26]

Reading through Czech literature of the period 1945-8 one is impressed by its stress on social, often identified with moral, causes. The individual is dwarfed by tremendous movements which control his fate or hold his salvation. Like a new mystical faith flowering amid the ruins was the idea of a social-ideological redemption for the nation, and its name, for many, was socialism. Even conservative critics like V. Černý, whom communists denounced as a reactionary, left no doubt about his left-wing views, and bolstered his arguments with quotations from the Marxists classics. Nevertheless there was a considerable group of writers who failed to join in the chorus of cheery optimism, and it is significant that many of them were of the younger generation. Those who had made their debut in literature in wartime were often lumped together by critics as if joined by a common programme or outlook, but in fact they had little but their age in common, unless it was an aversion to false heroics and to self-deception. They had graduated in the academy of wartime propaganda, and had learned to weigh the lies of public speakers, and to ignore the beating of drums. There had been in their work a fair amount of experimentation in the avant-garde styles of the thirties; of playing with ideology; and of what was later called Existentialism, in their case little more than an exploration of the feelings of alienation and anxiety.

After the war was over and their work could freely appear, common characteristics of a new wave in poetry became evident. The poems seem at times like an undifferentiated complex of daily trivia – snatches of conversation, imprints of inconsequential detail. Their work has been summed up as 'a search for the metaphysics of the everyday'. Important collections in this style were *Limb and other poems*, and *Odes and Variations*, by Jiří Kolář; *Fates* by Josef Kainar; *That evening* by Ivan Blatný; *The Strange Room* by Jiřina Hauková; and *Along the Fence* by Oldřich Mikulášek.[27] Kainar explored man's tendency to transform reality into the abnormality of dreams, which he termed 'the new myths'. Wartime Prague appeared in cheerless visions of grey, empty streets; its alienated inhabitants were the creators, and simultaneously the victims, of the city life. There was a montage of random detail, like the shots of a movie camera set into a film clip. Wary of slogans and signposts, the young poets avoided a fixed hierarchy of significance, and portrayed reality in its diverse and unpoetic detail:

Places we left behind, live on.

Horse trots. Child cries. Mother opens door.

'Not here. Not here. Don't know

where has it gone'. They search.

They search for something: run round the flat.

They search for places left behind,

places we used to be...

They think: the house.

The house stayed...

The clock is striking in the empty room.[28]

Truth lies in what we see and do, not in the interpretations of others. In the Foreword to one of Jiří Kolář's books appeared a quotation from Henry Miller's novel *The Black Spring*: 'What is not in the open street is false, derived, that is to say, *literature*.'

Such writers were not easily thrown off balance by events, and had equipped themselves with a scepticism that protected them from the deafening blare of post-war political slogans. The young poetess, Jiři-

na Hauková, had by 1946 already gained recognition by her anti-
romantic love lyrics, and her wartime verses that catch a spirit of the
lost, and endearing, 'normalcy' of life. Her work written between
1946-9 is collected in the cycle significantly entitled *The so-called
Spring*[29], which is without a trace of the socialist exaltation then in
mode. Her poems continue in the cold, fearful manner of wartime – the
long, hard Winter: and the delayed Spring:

> At winter's close we thought of winters past,
> that froze; like men of whom we were afraid...

A poem in simple style tells the journey of people who have lost their
way, through a bottle's neck into an unknown barren land, without
flowers of life: as mist falls, the lovers lose one another and are quite
alone, as if they had no more need of each other, and had never met:

> And tree was not tree, and stream was not stream,
> and we were no longer ourselves.
> How did we come to this place, where we met
> not a single trace of man!

Critics who were already judging the worth of literature by its
measure of social engagement and its attitude to politics, were un-
impressed with the poetry of Blatný and Hauková, who did not 'feel
the pulse of the time'. Their vast uncertainty made them seem vulnerable before the self-assurance of those who claimed to have found the
path of progress assigned by History. The young writers also were
concerned with the path along which the nation was travelling; but
they were more sceptical about its end. Jiřina Hauková had translated
into Czech T. S. Eliot's *Waste Land*, and her own poems evoke the
image of an arid landscape of menace and alienation.

Similar in tone was the work of a young novelist Jiří Mucha. The son
of the Art Nouveau painter Alphons Mucha, he had spent much of his
life, and gained much of his education, abroad in Western Europe. He
spent the war years as a war correspondent with the Western Forces,
and while in England he became one of the New Writing group around
J. Lehman. Apart from his intimate knowledge of England, France,
and Switzerland, Mucha travelled extensively in North America and in
the Near and Far East. A graduate of medicine, he had also studied
the History of Art and Oriental literature at the University of Prague.
It would be hard to think of any Czech writer of such cosmopolitan
culture, or one so much at home with Western intellectuals. His book
of wartime short stories *The Problems of Lieutenant Knap*,[30] was in
fact published in English before it appeared in Czech. After the sophisticated and politically sceptical atmosphere of literary London,

Mucha was hardly likely to be carried off his feet by glib slogans in Prague, or to be convinced by talk about the inevitable world revolutionary process by men who had never left Czechoslovakia.

In 1947 Mucha published the novel *Scorched Crop*.[31] The story begins before the war, when a young Czech leaves his native village and unspoiled sweetheart to travel abroad. He reaches Malaya, and in that exotic setting his experience is enriched by a love affair with a beautiful Eurasian girl. War converts him into an allied officer, and gives him travel and adventure. The coming of peace takes him almost by surprise: the victory celebrations around him only emphasise his feeling of isolation, and the knowledge that he is no longer required. His instinct is to head for home; but there too he finds himself a stranger. The rolling plains which he remembered seem curiously shrunken: the gloomy skies and shabby streets are a desolation of the spirit. Meeting again the girl he left behind, he marries her, and tries to settle in a tiny flat: but he cannot bridge the gap between himself and his environment. His disappointment in the post-war world is shared by his former colleagues:

> Once a month I went to collect my pay, and usually met friends from the army. They looked shabby and apathetic. When I asked them how they were, some shrugged their shoulders. Everyone was disillusioned in his own way, and was shy of talking intimately with anyone else and of disclosing his feelings. We had ceased to be interesting figures, and the mere fact that we had come home from the wars did not seem sufficient reason for anyone to give us special consideration... We were above all disappointed with ourselves...

In his dingy suburban existence memories of his life in the Orient wash over him, alienating him still further from his uncomprehending wife, and corrupting their relationship:

> You see nothing but yellow sand and the purple sunset. The deeper the purple of the twilight, the brighter the orange colour of the sand, until suddenly the light goes out. It is night... in other places you see nothing but white surf dashing upon you, out of the deep darkness roaring with a lashing gale. Before it reaches you there are more white crests riding towards you, then more still. Can you come back now with one bound into a cage of four walls, a ceiling, a floor, and a lamp, illuminating nothing but a table. A strange feeling. As if I were a prisoner, and yet enjoying boundless freedom.

To the ex-soldier it seems that the release from exile, the relief from service discipline, have curiously misfired: in his native environment he is an intruder, and his knowledge of the past makes the freedom of home into a prison. There is a violent quarrel, in which his wife receives an accidental injury which paralyses her: he is now fettered to her for life. Filled with remorse and compassion, he accepts his lot, and re-nounces all hope of escape from the trap which he has contrived for himself. His restless search for freedom has ended: he is back at his beginning; and can find peace only by devotion to the woman who symbolises his confinement.

Jiří Mucha's novel was quite unpolitical, in that it hardly touched on public policy. But the atmosphere of post-war Czechoslovakia which it showed was very different from the resolute cheerfulness of socialist literature. Like the poems of Hauková, Mucha's prose struck a sour note: evidently it lacked optimism; and communist critics styled him a 'man of yesterday', wedded to the dying past instead of the un-born future. To expect socialist-realist writing from Mucha would have been as absurd as to expect it from Iris Murdoch or Lawrence Durrell. On the other hand Mucha's work in no sense represented an attack on the system at that time. Those writers who chose to challenge the socialists directly were very few. In the field of serious journalism one figure stands out, that of F. Peroutka, author of several books on public affairs before the war, a middle-of-the road liberal with a powerful contempt for extremists, and currently the editor of the newspaper *Svobodné noviny* (Freedom Press). The struggle which Václav Černý carried on with the communists in the literary field was equalled by that carried on by Peroutka in the field of political journal-ism. But in the area of belles lettres the communists were able to plug their cause the more consistently because their opponents did not care to engage with them directly in the literary field. It was the commu-nists who proclaimed the need to point art towards ideological goals; and generally they got their way by default. In a few cases, however, the game was played against them by writers who engaged their work in the social issue, but not on the socialist side. One such man was the poet Jan Zahradníček.

Born in 1905 he had been recognised before the war as a master of Czech verse, and had influenced the work of younger writers like Hru-bín. Zahradníček had been a personal friend of the left-wing avant-gardists, but in the character of his work he belonged to the Catholic, ruralist school of Czech literature, which had deep roots in the nation-al tradition. During the thirties, when the dangerous times awakened national consciousness, the themes of the native soil and the past of the nation became popular, and Zahradníček won a great following by his books *The Thirsting Summer* and *Greetings to the Sun.* [32] His poems expressed current feelings of anxiety, reverence, and trust in the home land, as the focus of Czech hopes of survival. Such hopes were shattered by the catastrophe of the Munich surrender in 1938, and in the bitter aftermath there were many scapegoats. Left-wingers and liberals were the target of attacks, including attacks from the Catholic right wing. The writer Durych made harsh criticisms of Masaryk in politics, Karel Čapek in literature: this was a sad piece of mistiming, for which Durych was never forgiven. His associates in what was regarded as a Catholic writers' group, Deml, Čep, and Zahradníček, were put in an equivocal position, not pro-German, but hostile to what was left of the democratic Czech leadership. Their stance was regarded as misguided and reactionary, and was interpreted by their opponents as an act of desertion from the common front of resistance. It was a short period in Zahradníček's life, and ended with the German occupation of Prague in March 1939; but his equivocal attitude was not forgotten. He emerged from the war guiltless of collaboration with the Nazis; and in 1946 he published new work *The Old Land*, and *St Wenceslas.* [33] In his poems, many of which were written but unpublished in wartime, Zahradníček portrays the sufferings of occupation as the time of testing for the Czech nation, whose hope of salvation lies only in fidelity to national tradition, and in return to the spirit of St Wenceslas, oldest and most endearing of the Czech saints. When the land is in deepest peril, its people need most the return of his spirit, sweeping like a flood through the land, and bearing away its debris of doubts, cowardice, treason, and compliance with evil.

In 1947 Zahradníček published a long poem, *La Saletta*, which was interpreted as an expression of his feelings towards the trend of events in post-war Czechoslovakia, in particular, as a condemnation of the new course towards socialism. La Saletta is the name of a French mountain village where, a century before, a vision of the Virgin is said to have appeared to two simple children, who reported her message of dire warning to their unbelieving elders. Zahradníček briefly cited the account of the miracle in the chronicle, then told the story in his own way, applying the warning of doom to his own time. The perils and trials of war should have taught men to distrust false prophets, and to put their faith in truth and holiness: instead the poet sees a vista of distrust, hatred, and chaos. Instead of humility and penitence for the terrible crimes of the past, there is blindness and arrogance, as new tyrants demand obedience to their oracular wisdom:

Eyes blinded by seeing the unwitnessed
ears deafened by hearing the unheard-of
at their desks
torn quill from fallen angel's wing
they dip in wells
that blood has filled
from novel battlefields
from novel execution sheds
writing a grievous witness of their times...

The words of the vision warn of the triumph of evil over a world without faith or hope, split by hatred, destroyed by moral blindness and corruption. As socialist writers used literature to express their social and moral attitudes, so now did Zahradníček, but from the opposite point of view. His poem, of high formal quality and written with the authority of a master, totally negated the easy optimism of contemporary writing; and the communists rightly saw it as an oblique attack on their whole moral position.

La Saletta was published in an illustrated, luxury edition of only 1,500 copies: by reason of its subject, format, and limited distribution it clearly was not intended for the popular market. One might therefore wonder why a poem of such mystical overtones should have seriously disturbed the communists and gained dangerous notoriety for its author. By regarding the work as a challenge to their position they tacitly acknowledged their belief in the political importance of literature, even of an esoteric type. One is bound to ask how far such a belief was justified; whether they were not deceiving themselves and others; how important in fact was the social impact of literature at the time.

The reading public had been schooled by wartime experience to a formidable degree of scepticism towards the written word. In dealing with reportage depicting recent events people were able to check its accuracy by personal memory or direct observation. As the exchange of views was relatively free, one might expect that falsification or hypocrisy would be readily exposed. To make any real impact, literature had to carry conviction; a measure of its effect would be the impression it created of sincerity and truth. There is no way of measuring its political effect; but it is possible to estimate what impression of truth it conveyed, and how vulnerable it was to the test of observation.

Of the literary genres mentioned above perhaps the most striking was that of camp reportage. Its impact was due to the sensational nature of its content, and the fact that so many potential readers had

either personal or indirect experience of the subject. The autobiographical style, even the artlessness or crudity of much of the work
helped to give it conviction. In effect it prolonged into the post-war
years the emotions of wartime – fear and hatred of the Nazis, the longing for revenge, and the determination to prevent any German revival:
at the same time it kept alive the image of Soviet Russia as the shield
and avenger of the Slavs, and of Munich as the dramatic symbol of
Western betrayal. This unhappy reminder could not but harm the
cause of those who argued for a Western orientation to post-war
Czechoslovakia. At the same time the theme of revenge, and fear of a
revived Germany, played into the communists' hands. From 1946,
when the Western powers found themselves in increasingly bitter
dispute with the USSR and were attempting to rebuild Western
Germany in general, and Berlin in particular, they were put in a false
position. The image sedulously fostered by communist journalists was
one of England and America attempting to salvage capitalism by re-
arming a new Nazidom to fight against Russia. To this image the
literature of the camps and the resistance contributed in a way perhaps
never intended by its authors; and the impact was increased by its
authoritative realism.

There was obvious ideological value in books like Fučík's *Reportage from the Gallows* or Marek's *Men Walk in Darkness*, which used
the theme of the resistance to exalt the role played by the Communist
Party, and practically showed the fighting spirit of dedicated Party
men as an example for the whole nation to follow. Generally speaking
the communists claimed for themselves the whole credit for the resistance, and attributed to the Russians credit for the allied victory. In
the reportage of war the Western role was not entirely forgotten, and
J. Mucha himself published an attractive book on the African campaign
entitled *Fire against Fire*.[34] But such works, written from a Western
angle, were swallowed up in the spate of publications dedicated to a
different point of view which saw the war as basically a struggle between Fascism and Communism, with Russia in the role of the hero
and the Czechs as their honoured helpers. An appropriate ending was
the liberation of Prague by the Red Army, theme of so many speeches,
stories, poems, and pictures.

Literature of this kind, which had an historical basis and claimed
authenticity, was open to criticism on the grounds of inaccuracy or
bias. In the case of the liberation theme, there were some embarrassing
features which were kept in the background. The heroic image of the
Red Army had been impaired by the behaviour of its members; among

the military assistance rendered to the Czech rising had been that given by the army of General Vlasov, the Russian renegade later executed by the Russians; and in any case Prague could have been liberated days earlier by the Americans but for the Russians, who insisted on their rights in accordance with a previously negotiated understanding among the allies. The liberation was in fact a staged feat, arranged by agreement among the big powers without the prior knowledge of the Czechs.

Literature which attributed to communists an unblemished record of resistance to Nazism, and more or less the entire credit for the resistance, encountered similar doubts. People remembered, but rarely mentioned now, the Nazi-Russian pact of 1939 and the vacillations of communist policy. Those who had personal knowledge of the wartime resistance were aware of its very heterogeneous nature, and the prominent role of patriotic groups like that of the *Sokol* or the ex-legionaries. In any case the most spectacular exploit, the assassination of Heydrich, was planned and executed from London, which was the headquarters of the wartime intelligence network.

The legend of the recent past, and the image of the Party which literature projected, did not square with recollection or even with common knowledge. Such a divergency was not at all fatal to the prestige of the communists, for people were disposed to be indulgent: they had long been schooled to scepticism, and popular reservations were merely a prolongation of a wartime attitude towards the written word. More serious was the effect on literature itself. After the deception and lies of wartime propaganda Czech literature needed nothing more desperately than to break down the credibility gap. In the work of the younger writers one notes an intense search for the truth, however unpalatable: but the desire went unsatisfied. There were certain topics which, even without the intervention of censorship, were practically unmentionable: the Vlasov incident, and Nazi-Russian collaboration were instances. The fact that the writers almost universally accepted the taboos, and that the public knew they had accepted them, undermined the social authority of literature from the outset. Even in 1945, when the way to truth seemed to lie open, there was a known gap between the pretence and the reality. Gradually the gap was to widen until it became a gulf; and the existence of the gulf became the most taboo of all subjects. By an ultimate irony it was the writers who claimed to engage their art in public causes and to write with socialist realism, who shied further and further from reality, plunging ever more deeply into self-deception. Just as war had reversed the meaning of many words, so it was with the terminology of literature, as *engaged* writing came to mean that *disengaged* from reality, and the spokesmen for the nation's conscience were to become the conscienceless mouthpieces of political bosses.

The writers of documentary literature could, when they erred, be convicted of falsehood by contemporary witnesses: the prophetic writers were more fortunate in that the verdict of history upon them was necessarily late in coming. Writing from opposite points of view both Hromádka and Zahradníček saw the aftermath of war as a profound human crisis from which man could rescue himself only by a supreme spiritual effort. Whereas Hromádka trusted that the secular gospel of socialism could set mankind on a fresh life-giving course, Zahradníček accepted the possibility that evil could prevail; and in this he drew closer to the Existentialists. Many of the younger writers shared the view that they were living through a spiritual crisis, and if they saw hope anywhere, it was in socialism. But an unexpected development, which in retrospect made such views seem romantic, was the astonishing speed of the return to an apparent normalcy in Europe. Cities which in 1945 were a desolation of ruins, had within two years been tidied up to a semblance of their prewar condition. Human beings emerged like ghosts from the debris; families were, beyond all hope, reunited; libraries and art collections reappeared from hiding places as by magic. The human urge to recreate the past was so intense that, with the aid of modern technology, it conquered amazing obstacles. A city like Warsaw, totally wrecked by fire, bombs, shelling, and street fighting, began to rebuild its ruins according to the medieval style of the lost structures. In their fears for European civilisation the prophets of doom had underestimated the resilience of its inhabitants and the power of the new technology. Thus, in the face of all probability, normalcy seemed to be returning, and the visions of apocalyptic ruin became themselves unreal. No religious revival took place; and socialism itself soon lost its messianic appeal.

Those writers who interpreted the course of history in less sensational ways were on safer ground. In forecasting the victory of socialism over capitalism in Czechoslovakia they were in the enviable position of prophets who assist in the fulfilment of their own prophesies. For socialism as a model of economic development and a rational use of resources, there was very wide support. Writers like Řezáč and Pujmanová who portrayed in their work the coming of a socialist order, were speaking to the converted: they were also, by creating belief in the new order, helping to hasten its appearance. But the day would come when the public would be able to compare the reality of the order with the visions of it already projected in literature. When that day came, the visions of socialist writers would be subject to stern examination by their public: and the greater the deception, the deeper would be the disillusion with both prophets and their creed.

III

The Hammer and the Sickle

(In 1948) began a new life, a life truly quite different: and the face of that new life was deadly serious. But the odd thing about that seriousness was that it wore not a frown, but the appearance of a smile. Yes, those years claimed to be the happiest ever, and anyone found failing in gaiety fell under instant suspicion of being displeased with the victory of the working class; or else (an accusation no less serious) that he was *individualistically* submerged in his own inner concerns.

M. Kundera (The Joke)

There will be an end to all manoeuvres by friends of reaction sheltering under the umbrella of 'cultural immunity' or 'creative freedom'... Our slogan is above all: A healthy people's culture, a culture of progress, of life, and not a decadent 'culture' of death. That is why we say: Down with all sorts of marasmus and decay. Down with existentialism, pessimism, nihilism; away with the deadly poison of bourgeois reactionary culture and ideology.

V. Kopecký, April 1948

From the national elections of 1946, which were entirely free, the Communists emerged as the largest single party; in alliance with the marxist Social Democrats they held a narrow absolute majority: nevertheless the government formed was a coalition of national unity. Although the communists claimed key ministries, in particular those of Information and the Interior, there was a genuine sharing of power between marxist and democratic (now dubbed 'bourgeois') parties. All parties co-operated in a more or less businesslike way in the task of getting the country back on its feet. The keystone of foreign policy was by general consent the military alliance with the USSR, and there was a close working relationship between Prague and Moscow on government, and also on Party level. The Russians were always careful to distinguish between government-to-government and party-to-party relationships, and in this separation there lay the seeds of future conflict.

Since the 'thirties Czechoslovak communist policy had oscillated between two distinct policies, set at different times by Moscow, between participation in parliamentary government within the legal system, and active subversion to overthrow it. In the immediate post-war period it seemed that Stalin intended to prolong the wartime co-operation with the West, at least until the USSR had made substantial recovery from the shattering blows it had received. During this period Gottwald and the Party leadership understood that they were playing the Kremlin game by a policy of moderation and legal reform. The policy suited Czechoslovakia very well: and its effect was to enlist the co-operation of both masses and intelligentsia under the freely accepted leadership, of the Party. At the same time the latter kept alive, through its own apparatus and press, the alternative policy, of 'heightening the class war', should Moscow policy change. The ultimate intentions of Stalin were almost certainly as obscure to the Czech communists as they were to the rest of Europe: for the time being it was necessary for them to keep both options open. It was deeply in the interests of Czechoslovakia as a whole that the policy of East-West co-operation should continue, and that international tension should not grow. It was also in the interests of the Czech communists in government office: their co-operation with the 'bourgeois' parties and with their 'class enemies' was both genuine and comprehensible. But the whole precarious situation depended on the progress of relations between the USSR and the Western governments, and the continuation of co-operation on the international level.

Unfortunately for the Czechs the deterioration in international relations was rapid. The mentality of war, once created, did not fade with the armistice: a sad aftermath of the fighting was the war hysteria which lingered on, not only in Moscow but also in Washington. The eclipse and impoverishment of the medium powers had left the USSR and the USA as the two remaining super-powers (as they were now styled) confronting each other across Europe. Having gained victory at such a cost, neither intended to give away lightly its advantages, and an understandable international rivalry was heightened by the ideological gap. When civil war broke out in Greece between the communists and their opponents, although neither of the super-powers was directly involved, it seemed that the ugly rift was already developing into a new armed conflict. From 1946 to 1953 the possibility of atomic war in Europe was always near, poisoning the international atmosphere and leading the great powers into a new policy of 'defence in depth' abroad. The tension was accompanied by a wave of anti-reformism in home policies. While anti-communist feeling spread in the USA, Russia's policies grew harsher towards any signs of liberalism among her own intellectuals and dissidence among her satellites. In March 1946 Winston Churchill delivered his now famous speech in Missouri, in which he declared that an *iron curtain* had descended across Europe from Stettin to Trieste, leaving all Eastern Europe under the control of Moscow.

Mutual suspicion and fear, active subversion by Russia, crude dollar diplomacy by the USA, dramatic statements and rhetorical gestures, all helped to kill the hope of international co-operation. With its breakdown, the partnership of democrats with communists, which was once seen as the hope of the post-war world, became increasingly difficult and improbable, above all in Czechoslovakia, where the areas of big-power diplomacy met. In 1946 US Secretary of State Byrnes, infuriated by the pro-Soviet stance of Czechoslovak delegates to the Paris conference, cabled home to stop further credits to Czechoslovakia: at the same time Czech negotiations with the Export-Import bank for a loan broke down. The view that the Czechs could already be written off as a prisoner of the Soviets was premature; but the assumption helped to make it come true. In June 1947 the Czechoslovak government accepted an invitation to join in preliminary talks for the Marshall Aid Plan. After the acceptance had been published, the Czechs were ordered by Stalin to withdraw, on the grounds that the treaty of friendship with the USSR prevented Czechoslovakia from joining a hostile coalition. By this public and deliberate humiliation of a supposedly equal ally, Stalin advertised Czechoslovakia's new status as a client state. Preparing for the possibility of war, Russia tightened her hold on all the buffer lands. In each case the pattern was similar. The discovery of an alleged conspiracy led to political arrests implicating the democrat leaders: the collapse of the coalition brought the communists into a position of complete control. After the arrest of Petkov in Bulgaria and Kovacs in Hungary, the democratic politicians of Prague could only look forward with impotent foreboding to their own turn. It came in February 1948 when the democrats themselves forced a crisis by resigning in protest at the packing of the Prague police force with communists. In the crisis the Party showed its power. The radio buildings were occupied by police; all the mass communications media, controlled by the communist Minister of Information, kept up a steady drumfire of party propaganda. Mass demonstrations occupied the streets, and the Party's private army, the armed *Workers' Militia*, moved into factories and public places. Democratic politicians were unable to enter their own offices; the editor of the newspaper *Svobodné noviny*, Ferdinand Peroutka, was thrown out by the Action Committee of his own office. It was an impressive demonstration of direct action, well organised, and armed. The crisis ended when President Beneš authorised Prime Minister

Gottwald to form a new government excluding the democrat leaders. The danger of civil war and the threat of Soviet intervention were enough to break the resistance of the President. By constitutional means Czechoslovakia was delivered into the hands of the communists; and she now took her place among the other dominions of Moscow.

The effects of the political change were soon felt in the cultural sphere. In the USSR the renewed curb of the intellectuals had begun in 1946 with the founding of the journal *Culture and Life*, whose province was the guidance of literary, artistic, and educational work. History textbooks were condemned for lack of ideological force: there were ominous charges of 'bourgeois nationalism' in Ukrainian cultural life. To Russian writers it was made clear that their prime function was not to express themselves, but to interpret to the masses their 'historic destiny' as revealed by the Party; and to assist in its fulfillment. Writers, books, and journals on which fell the displeasure of the party bosses were censured and suppressed. Zoschenko and Akhmatova were among the first victims. Their work was condemned by the Party arbiter of taste, Zhdanov, in a speech of tasteless vulgarity, reprinted in a mass edition in Prague.[1] As the purge spread, it involved some of the best-known figures of Soviet cultural life, including Pasternak in literature, Eisenstein in films, and Shostakovich in music.

It was clear that the era of co-existence between modernistic art and Soviet culture was over. While most Czech writers preserved an apprehensive silence towards the Russian purge, the communists recognised that a new guideline for cultural policy had been set. When Zhdanov wrote: *In Soviet literature there is no place for rotten, empty, vulgar work without ideology*, the party faithful could see that the same applied to Czech literature. Party spokesmen, and critics like Štoll and Taufer, Bareš and Hájek, grew increasingly authoritarian in their pronouncements. The mentality of the cultural purge was already alive in Prague before the February takeover: all the communists needed was administrative authority, and that they now were in a position to assert.

Between 1945 and 1948 there had been a great deal of genuine and spontaneous co-operation on the part of the Czech writers towards the political leadership. Even those who privately were sceptical about the 'building of socialism' and Czechoslovakia's contribution to it, felt a civic responsibility towards the country, and often towards the Party. Where there was dissent, it concerned the means of national rehabilitation, not the general aim, which writers were eager to assist. But from 1948 the relationship between the political leadership and the writers changed: spontaneous co-operation was replaced by required obedience. Just as socialism involved a command structure in economics, so too in literature and art. From February 1948 all political power and initiative passed to the Party: as a matter of course it also took over responsibility for the direction of cultural life. It would be wrong to attribute this to entirely base motives on the part of the communist leaders. Traditionally, Marxists had always assigned a high importance to popular culture, not only as a means of mass persuasion but also for the purposes of general uplift: the aim was to raise men's non-material, together with their material, standards of living. Logically it followed that the Party, as the vanguard of the masses, should direct cultural life and draw art and literature into its master plan for the new socialist age. Socialist artists had long written of the communist millenium; now they would have the opportunity – indeed the duty – of bringing it about.

The Czech writers, who had by now learned a lot about the Soviet model, were aware of the dangers in this blyth picture. In particular the cultural purge in Russia revealed the frightening effects of letting a party boss like Zhdanov dominate the whole field of culture. The Czech intellectuals could calm their apprehensions to some extent by remembering that Russia was not Czechoslovakia. Each state would choose its own way to socialism, which would accord with the traditions and national aspirations of the Czechs and Slovaks. In any case the Czechoslovak Communist Party was not a cadre of desperate men or successful conspirators; it had something of a democratic parliamentary tradition, and a mass popular base at the grassroots of Czech society. When Dr Beneš resigned in June 1948, Gottwald succeeded him in the Presidency with traditional pomp, and attended a *Te Deum* at the cathedral in honour of his enthronement. Politicians who had worked with Gottwald for years dismissed the idea that he was the stuff dictators are made of. Like Gottwald, Zápotocký, now Prime Minister, was a man with a human side and possessed the common touch. Their popular image was of bluff, easygoing men, always ready for a joke with their political opponents. It seemed sensible to suppose that Moscow would value the friendship of their Czech ally, and would do nothing to spoil that friendship. It would be foolish to interfere in Czech affairs and try to impose a system which had its roots in the entirely different traditions of the USSR.

February 1948 has gone down into history as a turning-point in Czech affairs; but at the time not all observers recognised it as a dramatic break with Western traditions and freedom in cultural life.

For several months after the communist take-over there was a lull, in which journals like *The Critical Monthly* continued to appear: books which had gone to press before February were duly published. In retrospect the delay in the imposition of the Soviet cultural model seems without significance. But in fact the imposition may have been dramatically hastened by events over which the Czechs had no control.

Only a month after the Communist Party had gained full power in Prague came the news that Soviet specialists had been withdrawn from Jugoslavia. Even as the Czech communists were establishing themselves, and still wooing sections of the opposition, the international communist movement was rocked by the revelation of the violent quarrel between Stalin and Tito. Publication of the correspondence between the two Parties uncovered to an amazed world the unbelievable arrogance with which the Soviet leadership had treated a supposedly equal ally. Those who had doubted Russia's will to interfere in the affairs of her satellites must have quailed to read these documents. Czech moderates and pro-communist democrats who had underrated the ferocious single-mindedness of Russian policy, had clearly been deceiving themselves. But their confusion was no less than that of the Czechoslovak communist leadership, who had believed that their country would be allowed, even encouraged, to follow its own way towards socialism: in the light of Czech history, it had been thought that this would be a democratic way, free from external threats and interference. But after the breach with Tito it became obvious that nothing would satisfy Stalin but unquestioning obedience to the Russian model. Now that renegades had been discovered within the international communist front, among allies of Moscow, and within the Slavic enclave of Europe, any deviation from the Moscow path was a signal for suspicion. If there were traitors within the leadership of the Jugoslav Party, treachery might well lurk in the top echelons of other fraternal parties – especially among Tito's old friends and collaborators in the Comintern. Overnight, Tito and all Titoists (of any nationality) were turned from heroes to potential traitors and saboteurs. At the same time the slogan of 'national roads to socialism' was dropped like a hot brick.

Only a short period of time separated the assumption of full power by the communists in Czechoslovakia from the full impact of the crisis in the international communist movement. During that brief period there were signs that the Party had intended to pursue a conciliatory policy towards the writers; and the new constitution, promulgated in May 1948, seemed designed to ally fears of cultural repression. Personal freedom, freedom of expression and of the press were all guaranteed: in principle there was to be no advance censorship of publication. The freedom of creative writing was explicitly affirmed. It is in fact one of the oddities of history that advance censorship of the press was not *legally* practised in Czechoslovakia until 1967, although total control of the printed word had long been exercised by Party and government.

From the beginning of the communist era in Czechoslovakia the Party assumed, as its natural right, responsibility for all branches of production; consequently its public image was affected by success or failure in any branch. But in the literary and artistic sphere responsibility was felt more intensely, because results there reflected the image directly, and so were very much a political matter. The communists have often been accused of degrading literature to the level of advertisement and propaganda, and it is an accusation which can easily be substantiated. But in most cases this seems to be the unwished result, not the conscious aim, of communists. In the case of the Czechs, it is hard to believe that the degradation of art was the wish of the Minister and cultural boss, Zdeněk Nejedlý, whose devotion to the Party was equalled by his intellect and breadth of scholarship. Nejedlý understood the need for freedom in cultural matters; unfortunately cultural activity had to be subjugated to a social goal, namely the construction of a socialist order. To this end all efforts were harnessed: the cultural field, like the field of business, manufacturing, and distribution, was mapped out, and its tasks were set like a military operation. Freedom of composition was, it appears, doomed almost from the start; but international crisis, the fear of war, and the shock wave from the Jugoslav heresy helped dramatically to hasten its doom.

Unlike writers in western Europe the Czech writers were already in a state of organisation, which could readily be turned into mobilisation. Recognised writers were almost all members of the Union of Czechoslovak Writers, an organisation whose aims and constitution were similar to that of any other Trades Union. The Writers Union did in fact bring material benefits to its members, including the right to use Dobříš castle, which had been made over to them. But at the same time the organisation exposed the writers more easily to coercion. In this way they accepted, and grew accustomed to, a hierarchy of authority – the rank and file deferring to the central committee, and the latter accepting advice from its elected officials. But the highest authority, as was clear to all, rested outside the ranks of the writers altogether: the leadership of the Union was openly responsive to the directives of the Party.

In March 1949 the Union held its first conference under the new dispensation: the venue was Parliament House – a significant choice. Leading speakers were not writers, but political leaders – Premier Zápotocký, Minister of Education Z. Nejedlý, Minister of Information V. Kopecký. A letter was read out from President Gottwald, in which he quoted Stalin's now famous quotation: 'Be engineers of the souls of our people. Be the harbingers of their desires, their love and hatred! Be their socialist revivalists!' Subsequent speeches left no doubt that literature was being mobilised, and its obedience demanded. Only two camps were said to exist - socialism and reaction: there was no middle way. Writers were reminded of the social responsibility of their art, and the damage they could cause by 'incorrect, unhealthy' views. The first task of literary criticism was 'to drive out of concealment those who tolerated reaction, and favoured compromise': it must be made clear who was for, and who against, socialism. In the evaluation of literary work the class struggle should be the central criterion:

> The main task is to distinguish allies from enemies; to recognise reactionary and progressive forces... We ask: is this work for us or against us? Does it harm or help us? Is the writer on this side of the front or that? This is the principal question: everything else must give way to that... We ask: On which side of the barricade does he stand?

The speaker was Zdeněk Nejedlý. Control of literature had evidently been taken completely out of the hands of the writers. They were already being lectured and threatened like children: socialist realism was prescribed as the only acceptable method of composition; they listened in silence to suggestions that they study the principles of Leninism-Marxism for inspiration, and heed the authoritative pronouncements of Zhdanov in Moscow. At the IXth Congress of the Communist Party in Prague in 1949 ideologists and literary hacks coolly laid down the principles prescribed for artists and writers, to assist them in their work. The watchword of the Party was now '*Strengthen the class war*': at a time when patience was being labelled as faint-heartedness, and tolerance as collaboration with traitors, the idea of a peaceful transition to socialism had been abandoned. The idea of a Czech independent road to socialism was seen as Titoism, the new and dreaded heresy. From September 1948 a commission had been functioning whose aim was the purging of undesirable elements from public life. Even while the writers were supposed to be deliberating about the goals of literature, police terror was doing its work. In the Spring of 1949 Záviš Kalandra,[2] former Party member, popular writer and historian, was arrested, and subsequently hanged. His crime was apparently to have maintained contact with the writers who, unable or unwilling to co-operate with the regime, had departed into exile. They included some of the best living Czech writers, Egon Hostovský, Jan Čep, and the young poet Ivan Blatný. Their exile was physical and permanent. Others, who remained in Czechoslovakia, were to withdraw to an inner exile, less permanent, but no less tragic.

In retrospect the results of the new course in Czech literature give a sad impression of misguided zeal, authoritarian bungling, and desolation of the spirit. They are recorded in publications suspended, new journals founded in hope, soon discredited and abandoned; in novels which have become historical curiosities; and in courtly versi-fication to the greater glory of Stalin. Ideological loyalty and social commitment were now mandatory; and of all forms of literature none seemed to offer more promise to the new course than the novel. By its form it was attuned to mass consumption; in its content it approached most nearly to that of the press, the public lecture, or the secular sermon. It could act as a mirror and an inspirer of social progress; and by cultivating rapport with the masses, it could best fulfill the education-al role now regarded as literature's prime function. From the novels published after 1948 we should be able to estimate the success of the new course in the arts.

Of course the production of creative literature differs radically from the production of steel or toothbrushes: even the heavy-handed bureaucrats could understand that – though they notably omitted to make adequate allowance for the difference. Writers, even if they are genuinely eager to co-operate, are not the most amenable people to discipline, whether imposed from within or without. Their efforts seem to carry them along channels of thought not originally intended; and by the time they have worked out their ideas and pushed their books through all the chores of publication, the tastes and attitudes around them may well have changed. Thus the literary harvest of a given political situation is always hard to define. Diversified in method, orientation, and content, its representation in later literary hand-books as a simple, one-string model, is often illusory: the simplicity is usually the result of the editor's strict selectivity, when it is not due to his own simplicity. The Czech literary harvest of the new course was not entirely without surprises or diversity; nevertheless there was a quite unusual stereotyping of literary production; and this can be explained by the firm organisation of writers by officials, and the strict control of organs of publication by Party nominees. Recurring themes can be seen in novels and short stories, among them are: the appraisal of the past in the light of recent events; the presentation of the theme of socialist construction as the focus of contemporary life; the new morality as the living style of socialist man; and the general superiority of the socialist system, with the USSR as its model, over the capitalist, bourgeois, imperialist world. Under the last-mentioned heading fell not only literature denigrating America, e.g. F. Kubka's *Short Stories for Mr Truman* (1951),[3] but the flood of stories and poems in praise of the Soviet leaders, people, and land.

The building of the new socialist society, as the epic theme of the present, seemed to demand treatment on correspondingly monumental lines. The late 1940's saw the beginning of some vast prose structures, including a number of trilogies, and at least one work (F. Kubka's *The Great Century*[4]) planned to fill seven volumes: the construction of dams, and the transformation of the villages by collectivisation, were favourite sub-themes. In considering this material it would obviously be unfair to single out mere trash for discussion: one can hardly do better than to begin with a book which has often been described as a monument of socialist prose, and one which became a model for other work.

Mention has already been made[5] of Václav Řezáč, the eminent novelist who went as a government servant to the border areas; his intention was to write about the colonisation of the place by Czechs after the expulsion of the German-speaking inhabitants in 1945. This great plan involved the movement of millions of people, and the transformation of a whole sector of society. In its scope it evidently dwarfed such actions as the nationalisation of industry and the alteration of institutional arrangements in the Czech heartland. If indeed social changes were productive of creative literature, here at any rate we might expect to find a rich harvest. In fact a number of writers tried their hand at this theme,[6] but the intended trilogy of Václav Řezáč is among the most serious attempts. The first volume, entitled *Line-up*[7] was published in 1951.

The novel opens with a small group of Czech communists arriving in the border area where they are to work; the time is June 1945. There they meet their liberators, the Red Army men, and make friends with them. The newcomers settle down to constructive work at a textile and a ball-bearing factory. Their leader, the indomitable communist Bagar, soon realises the difficulty of his task. He meets the opposition of his class enemies, both German and Czech, who do not stick at violence to further their anti-social ends: at one point Bagar and his friends are rescued only by the timely intervention of the Soviet soldiers. The struggle against treachery and sabotage goes on, and a corner is turned when industrial production rises. Political success now follows, as a pro-communist administration takes over the affairs of the town. But treachery is still alive, and reactionary elements foster bourgeois prejudices among the honest, but sometimes misled, folk. The town certainly takes on some lifelike attributes of a frontier community: the moral principles accepted in a settled society are thrown to the winds, and the sexual licence and crude grabbing for money and power is described by the author with virtuosity and relish. A fair female spy (for the West) and a Nazi agent add human interest: the new community, shaken by doubts and prejudice, and assaulted by evil plotters, evidently stands in need of guidance. Happily the vigilance of Bagar and the Party succeed: the villains are unmasked and arrested; socialist virtue has triumphed. Their task fulfilled, the Red Army men leave, with the blessing and grateful love of the Czech settlers. The dragon of reaction is slain: another class enemy has bitten the dust.

When the book was published, it would have been politically impossible openly to criticise it adversely. The theme was exemplary: the treatment of character and situation could not have been better designed by the cultural planners themselves. And since Řezáč was a talented writer, the book was far from badly written. It was in fact hailed as a triumph of the new spirit in literature, and has remained as an archetype of the socialist Czech novel. But readers could scarcely help noticing that the book documented not so much the transformation of Czech society as the transformation of Václav Řezáč. He had won a deserved reputation as an exponent of the psychological novel and the exploration of the multi-layered reality which underlies overt human activity. In *Line-up* subtle problems of human behaviour and suffering had been swept away as by the wand of a socialist godmother. Reality had become one-dimensional: the human situation as susceptible of quite simple solution by application of a code not much more complex than that prescribed for boy scouts. There was nothing to worry about, so long as one adhered to the prescribed forms: the Party knew best, and if in doubt, the Soviets would always give guidance. Through the praise of critics a certain note of embarrassment could be discerned. Instead of characters, Řezáč had really portrayed types: the human situation had become a spectrum with each so-called character as a fixed point, each with a value rating, from the model communist Bagar at the top to the traitor Tietze at the bottom. If this was socialist realism, it was curiously *unrealistic*.

In 1952 Marie Pujmanová published the final volume of a trilogy begun fifteen years previously: the book was entitled *Life against Death*.[8] Unlike Řezáč she was not a recent convert to communism: hers was not the beginning of a new course, but the culmination of a life's work and belief. No one could suspect her of literary opportunism: in her youth her talent had won the admiration of the formidable critic Šalda; she had shown a consistent gift for sensitive observation, and an unswerving admiration for the quality of personal integrity.

The subject of her new novel was not the latest phase of socialist construction, but the hard days of German occupation – the wartime struggle which was the prologue, and promise, of socialist victory. Her field of action was rather wide; from the Eastern front to the home resistance; from the Partisans to the concentration camps. This width of cover presented certain technical difficulties to the authoress, and even sympathetic critics noted an awkward diffusion of interest. A successful focus of sympathy was provided by a major character of the trilogy, Helena, who seemed to approximate to Pujmanová's ideal of a person. Helena was a doctor. Her choice of vocation underlines the feeling of devotion to community service which is balanced by her social convictions. Her faith leads her to martyrdom, and she dies for the cause at the hands of the Nazis. Thus she combines in her own person something of the distinction of Madame Curie with the heroism of Julius Fučík. Helena is a worthy socialist heroine, grave, generous and self-effacing, untarnished by pretension or selfish ambition. In her own character she traces the line of ideal conduct leading from the doubts of *People at the Crossroads*, at the start of the trilogy, to the self-fulfillment and justification of *Life against Death*. The progressive ideas and the concern for humanity which she symbolises become, by an easy transition, identified with the cause of communism and the USSR, which then appears as a sort of life force. *Death*, which wears the swastika of Fascist imperialism, is the rotten core of bourgeois reaction. By a transition which might seem mysterious to Western readers, Fascism and war become identified with Western European and American ideas and practice. As in the case of Řezáč's book, there was a disturbing tendency to sketch characters merely as types or elements to illustrate the clash of good versus evil, approminating to political left-wing versus right-wing. In the later stages of *Life against Death* the novel takes on the semblance rather of reportage, with appropriate editorial comments. A symbolic ending of extraordinary banality was appended. The Czech hero Ondřej, who had earlier emigrated to Russia, improved his political education, and fallen in love with a Russian girl, inevitably is reunited with her when she appears on the Czech scene as a member of the Red Army liberating forces. This heart-warming happy ending, with its implication of sealing a political compact with the procreation of a new Czech-Russian generation, draws dangerously near to burlesque.

The years from 1949 to 1952 saw the publication of a large number of novels similar to each other in type: they dealt with the theme of building socialism, in particular by the raising of output. The hero is a familiar stereotype – young, presentable, of impeccably proletarian origin, and a dedicated communist. He arrives at a place of work where, for various reasons, production is lagging, or needs urgently to be increased. In *Louisiana awakes* by K. F. Sedláček[9] it is an old mine; in *Full Speed Ahead* by J. Otčenášek[10] it is a brick factory; in *Two Springs* by B. Říha[11] it is a village collective. In each case things are not as they should be. Apathy, absenteeism, even alcoholism among the workers mar the scene. In the village the peasants resist collectivisation; they are suspicious, prejudiced, and without proper understanding of the aims and possibilities of the new course. Politically uneducated and still labouring under the burden of the capitalist past, workers and peasants alike need, and respond to, the cheerful guidance of the dedicated hero. It is a hard struggle for their hearts and minds, but patience and exemplary behaviour by the Party local hero win their reward at last. Doubts give way to enthusiasm: so changed are the workers that they voluntarily raise their own norms and offer to work two, even three, shifts. The Plan is well on its way to fulfillment. But there is a dark side to this idyllic pastoral. In *Two Springs* a rich farmer Meztek, in *Full Speed Ahead* a malcontent Málek, in *Louisiana Awakes* the corrupt Director Berger, sabotage the plant: to achieve their ends they do not even stick at setting the place on fire. Marked out by their origins as enemies of the working class, they are beyond hope of redemption, and do not hesitate to stab their own people in the back for the sake of foreign agents of the West. Their end is predictable. Their removal seems to end the obstacles to the happy fulfillment of the Plan, and so to the advancement of socialism.

The firm planning which appears in such novels as an industrial phenomenon, has its counterpart in their literary construction. They seem often as based on a stereotype revealing only minor variations. The scene, environment, and source of drama, is a place of work, – a farm, factory, mine, or dam. The hero, endowed with some private feelings, is basically a symbol of leadership, industry, loyalty, and dedication: his private qualities and personal life outside his work are more or less incidental, an added grace, where they are not a positive hindrance. He is a true *hero of labour*. The central theme is industrial and political, with moral overtones. The reader's attention should be rivetted, his tension maintained, by questions like: will production rise? will the future of socialism be furthered? Yet tension is hard to sustain in a model where optimism is mandatory and suprises are unlikely: a happy ending is assured. Indeed the genre would have gained in interest enormously if only one of such novels had been enabled to end in the discomfiture of the socialist planners, and the triumph of the reactionaries. But such a book had no chance of publication.

The 'construction' novels of this period became a byword for banality and boredom. From the literary point of view they were a disaster. This was not due to a lack of talent on the part of the writers; nor to the lack of spontaneity with which they approached their subject. The best of the 'construction' writers were quite genuine in their attitude, and were glad to lend their talent to the service of a cause which was their own. Admittedly the genre posed some especial difficulties. Industrial output – no doubt of fascinating interest for efficiency experts – can be an unconscionably boring subject for other people. But this problem was not insuperable: Karel Čapek's *R.U.R.*, Galsworthy's *Strife*, for instance, had dealt with industrial problems, and with immense appeal and success. But in their case the industrial problem was studied not as a topic in its own right – as the centre of drama – but as it affected the lives of people. 'Construction' novels seem depressingly dehumanised: instead of industrial production revolving around humans, one gets the impression that the humans are themselves units of productivity, and a code of human conduct has given way to a code of industrial efficiency. But perhaps the worst feature of the genre was its gross simplification of human and moral issues. The cataclysmic events of recent times had revealed in fresh terms the appalling risks of the human condition; the wire-ringed camps of Europe, the desolation of Hiroshima, revealing the degradation of civilised man, had killed silly illusions of human perfectability or automatic progress. Man now appeared in his existential nakedness, balancing between hope and catastrophe. And amid this intellectual atmosphere Czech literature now purged from its pages all problems except simple puzzle-solving. Any critic could recognise the literary affiliations of the new genre. Stereotyped situations, symbols instead of characters, issues narrowed to the framework of a good-bad conflict, unquestioned acceptance of the correctness of ends, with no conflict of principle, the only query left open being the means of attaining the end. The formula was familiar in nursery literature for children, in so-called *Davy Crocket* literature, or Westerns for adults. There is nothing wrong with such literature as such, provided it does not masquerade as something else. A basic criticism of Czech 'construction' novels is that they masqueraded as serious philosophical literature, exposing deep human issues: worse still, instead of merely contributing to prose literary output, at one stage they almost monopolised it. The effect on Czech literature might not have been so bad if the Czechs had inherited a literary tradition of gay irresponsibility in which crazy modes come and go, and the reader can assuage his boredom or perplexity by the suspicion that the present fashion is in some way a throwback or a send-up. But the generally serious, socially committed, and self-consciously ambitious spirit of Czech prose forebade such ideas. Writers had to stand by what they wrote, then and later. The impression that gifted and privileged artists had misused their talents and betrayed literature, administered a shock from which the Czech literary world has still not recovered. It estranged the adult generation of writers not only from their public, but also from their juniors in the literary craft. Opportunism, betrayal of principle, guilt, and cowardice, gradually become associated with the profile of an author; the charges were the more deadly and irrefutable because they were, for the time being, not written, but whispered.

The artistic devaluation of the novel might have been borne stoically by the cultural bosses of the Party, provided that the work fulfilled its social function adequately. It aimed to engage the interest and sympathy of the reader; to persuade workers to identify with the positive types there depicted; to accept their social aims as their own; to sweep away their doubts and channel their efforts in a flood of constructive enthusiasm. Above all the novel, the press, poetry, drama, advertising, education, and open propaganda, had to convince the public that the aims of the communists were *right*, their means justified. The past must appear as an era from which one was glad to escape, and which had in effect been nothing but a preparation for the present age just beginning. The liberation of Prague by the Red Army in 1945, the assumption of total power by the communists in 1948, were the beginning of a new and happier era for the Czech people in general, and for the working class in particular.

It needs hardly to be stressed that such beliefs could hardly have been expected to survive the economic setbacks and general disillusionment which soon appeared as a blight on the new order. But the literary campaign seems to have missed its mark from the beginning. A first rule of propaganda is to hold the interest of the reader, and to this end concessions often have to be made. But concession to popular taste seems to have been totally overlooked in the culture plans. Escapism was ruled out by the socialist-realist Russian model; literature had to be based on the 'real situation'. No doubt some farm hands like reading about farms, and some factory hands about factories: but such people seem to be generally in a minority. Workers are not known for their interest in stories about raising production on the plant; in general they seem to be sick of the subject, and hope to escape it in their hours of leisure. In spite of this serious drawback, workers might still be coaxed into showing an interest, provided they could see the problems and characters of fiction as their own. Unfortunately the overdrawn characters of 'construction' novels, from the dehydrated hero to the evil saboteur were more akin to folklore than to real life. What was intended to be realistic literature certainly avoided escapism and entertainment; but it failed in realism. It is bad for a writer to travesty reality in a field which is comparatively unknown to his readers. To travesty reality in the very sphere native to them is to court disaster. And as if the authors had not taken upon themselves enough hazards, they embroidered their work with political and editorial comment, as if to make sure that the reader would not be allowed to forget that he was reading a work of moral uplift.

The effects of the new course in the field of prose literature were sad: but no less dismal were the effects on poetry. Spontaneity and personal involvement are qualities commonly associated with verse, which is an unpromising recruit for a campaign organised under any flag. The poster, the caricature, the parable, tale, or slogan, all are more readily convertible into organs of mass persuasion than lyric verse. Yet political poetry is certainly not unknown, nor is it necessarily condemned to banality. Under certain circumstances the poet may come forward as the spokesman of a cause in which he believes, and in which he inculcates belief among his listeners by the power of his art. Such a one had been Jiří Wolker in the 'twenties, and he had not been alone. In general poets appeal less to reason and logic than to emotion, imagination, instinct. A revolutionary cause needs few things so much as *faith*: and who best to express or kindle it than the poet?

In the period 1948-52 there were published plenty of verses full of revolutionary fervour. Some were literary exercises; others were

intended to be recited or chanted by demonstrators or orators. Looking back from a point outside the particular environment and situation
it is hard to evaluate them as literature – hard even to take them seriously for the most part.

Such poems were written not only by hack rhymsters but also by
talented poets. It was an ideological duty from which none who wished
to prosper in the new environment was excused. In spite of the pressure
on writers, poetry in the accepted sense did not immediately and irrevocably disappear. In 1949 the master, Nezval, published a new collection *The Great Clock*,[12] in which he included verses written during
wartime as well as recent work. As ever in Nezval's books, the poems
were of uneven quality, but the book contained personal lyrics in
Nezval's own, not unattractive style, proving that genuine poetry
could still appear under the new dispensation. But the reception was
ominous. As a great literary figure, an old Party member, and a
personal friend of men in high places, Nezval was not a figure lightly
to be assailed. Yet he represented, from his past, the very things which
Marxist critics were busy denouncing - surrealism, decadence, subjectivism, dalliance with private fantasies and unhealthy morbidity. *The
Great Clock* was criticised for its preoccupation with astrology, an
alarming implication of old-fashioned superstition. In any case the
book was insufficiently engaged with public issues to satisfy current
demands: it did not fall into the category of *construction* literature at
all. It was an anachronism which revealed that Nezval did not really fit
into the new course; he belonged irretrievably to a bourgeois world
whose time was over. Nezval, prophet of revolution, had become a
man of yesterday. The young aspirants of the future found his work
quaint and amusing. Two bright students produced a parody of his
work and achieved brief fame among the young. Unfortunately the
parody turned against themselves. The culprits were called to order
by Ladislav Štoll, an old friend of Nezval and now extremely powerful. It was said of *The Great Clock* that it was running slow: but the
students' clock was apparently fast: they were thrown out of the
university.[13]

Nevertheless Nezval took care to mend his ways, and to bring his
timepiece up to date. A born rebel to whom nothing was sacred, he had
been a master of debunking the old institutions and standards. In the
past the communists had at times winced at his bizarre experiments
and shameless licence; but his aberrations had been forgiven. His
destructive talents had suited them admirably as long as they were in
opposition: when he clowned, they grieved but applauded: when he

exercised his matchless gift of satire and abuse upon the bourgeois, they were delighted. But that epoch was now over. There was no place left for unorthodoxy or derision amid the resolute optimism of the new order. If Nezval wished to contribute to it, he would undoubtedly have to change his tune.

Ever resilient, Nezval plunged vigorously into the perilous waters of socialist-realism. In a burst of enthusiasm he promised to write a drama about the life of the communist hero Julius Fučík (an engagement which mercifully was never fulfilled). What he did produce, not without fanfares, was a long poem in honour of Stalin's birthday.[14] It has taken its place among the other courtly gestures of the time, gestures which belong more to political than to literary history. Nezval's poem is still read, as evidence for the author's career. It was no worse than a hundred others, and no less sycophantic. But it has a certain fascination as a document illustrating the fall of the poetic rebel whose wings had been clipped. Of course, during his varied career, Nezval had written scores of silly political verses; but in the past, they had often been an expression of mischievousness and effrontery. Now he who had respected nothing had become the court poet, falling into line with the regiment of hacks and yes-men.

In 1950 he published a quite ambitious poem in the new style. *The Song of Peace*[15] was written in simple ding-dong rhythm, in four-line stanzas, with a refrain whose uncomplicated expression was intended to drive the message home into even the thickest skull. It was evidently composed for recitation rather than study:

> That pilots may no longer find
> their bodies spoilt with gonorrhea
> or fly to devastate Korea
> bombing like robots, mad and blind,
>   I sing a song of peace.[16]

It was undoubtedly the old Nezval. Asked later how he had come to write such a stanza, Nezval answered that he could not resist the rhyme Korea/gonorrhea. A connoisseur of words, it had been his speciality to combine words of bizarrely disparate associations, in order to achieve odd effects. A rhyme of such striking vulgarity was quite in his style; except that in the past it would have been intended to amuse or shock. But in this case, he was evidently trying to be serious. Behind the stern mask of socialist dedication the clown involuntarily peeped forth. The poem was highly praised; and it was honoured with a Peace Prize. Needless to say it lashed the enemies of progress, including lords with fat cigars, the White House, Wall Street, and so on. The

defenders of peace were also a motley crowd; to show the internationalism of the cause they included Klement Gottwald and Charlie
Chaplin. The hero was of course Stalin:

> A song of peace, before us towers
> its generalissimo, his eyes,
> his face, most gentle, frank and wise,
> and shining with the light of stars.
>> He leads us into peace.

This, and other work of the time, may be read in the light of a later
remark, a discreet understatement by Nezval himself. He noted[17] that
'at a certain time the cult of Stalin's personality had taken on a uniform tone, and that undoubtedly in poems about Stalin, even by good
poets, there had been a tendency to bigotry, which was not merely
their own product, but a generally and officially encouraged phenomenon'.

The effects of the new course upon another talented poet may be
noted. The past of Konstantin Biebl in many ways resembled that of
Nezval; he had graduated from 'proletarian' poems to the avant-garde
school of Poetism and Surrealism. Widely travelled, romantic in
disposition, a cultivated and sensitive person, Biebl wrote much, but
published little. His support for the Party dated back to the days of
the alliance between communism and avant-garde art. In 1951 he
published his only post-war collection, *Without Fears*,[18] containing
poems written during the preceding decade. In this book one can therefore compare the tone of work composed during the war and during
lastest phase. Many of the older poems were nostalgic or romantic:
they contained echoes of the First World War (which Biebl was old
enough to remember), Arabs and minarets, caravans, jungle, and rice
paddies – scenes of his old Java days: there was also a 'Circus' section,
with Poetist motives. The Introduction (which seems evidently to have
been added last) and the final sections of the book represent the new
epoch. The poems here are very militant, and no doubt sincere. Biebl
is angry with the opponents of progress – with Mr Truman and
General MacArthur. Perhaps the most interesting piece in the section
is a poem entitled 'Manifesto to Nezval'. Here Biebl versifies a sort of
philosophy of socialist art. He warns would-be writers who find their
vocation in praising and lecturing workers and miners, in exhorting
them to fresh efforts, in embracing the tracks of railroads and exulting
in the smoke of factories. Far more subtle and rewarding is the place
of the artist in the new-born society; his role is to understand, to feel,
the triumphs and the anxieties of others, to interpret visions, and
crystalise the dreams of those who serve.

In this strange poem Biebl fired the first salvos in a campaign which was to grow against those who, in the name of socialist art, vulgarised and wrecked the literary effort of the new course. Biebl did his utmost to serve the Party, and for its sake he diminished his own stature as a poet. But to an increasing extent he was a target for the radicals. Like Nezval, he represented the decadent past; but unlike Nezval he lacked robust nerves and political protection. He endured a security check; but his clearance lent him no security. He felt persecuted and unsafe. At one stage he warned Nezval that the latter was under surveillance, and that all members of his family were being shadowed.[19] By his friends, and by those who knew him, Biebl was honoured for his talent and for the great heart which made him embrace the cause of the downtrodden. He survived the war, but not the liberation. In 1951, discouraged by events and embittered by persecution, he ended his own life.

Another member of the former avant-garde, Jaroslav Seifert, also ran into difficulties. In 1950 a number of works were published honouring the female Czech novelist Božena Němcová, on the one hundred and thirtieth anniversary of her birth: academician Mukařovský and that doyen of Marxist aesthetics, Zdeněk Nejedlý, both contributed books. Seifert, who had in earlier years addressed poems to her memory, on this occasion also published a long poem as a tribute to her.[20] His *Viktorka* had as its subject an incident from Němcová's best-known novel, *Grandma*. Viktorka, a peasant girl who had been seduced and abandoned by a soldier, drowned her own child: crazed by her experience and cut off from the normal life of the village, she took to the woods and lived like a wild thing until a lightning flash ended her tragic and tempestuous life. The story appears in the novel merely as an anecdote told by a forester; but *Viktorka*, like *Wild Barbara*, in another of Němcová's books, seems to symbolise her sympathy for the romantic outcast, who, seeming degraded, yet rises above the man-imposed restraints of society.

No-one could object to Seifert's poem as poetry: but his choice of subject outraged certain critics, who saw in it not only a dalliance with morbid fancy, but even an oblique attack on the present social environment. Seifert became the victim of what seemed to be an organised campaign, mounted by the younger Marxists against the older generation. One of the firmest denouncers of Seifert was the poet-critic Ivan Skála, who was building for himself a reputation for hyper-radical literary activity. Skála's criticism of the poem was the springboard for his denunciation of Seifert himself as one who, beginning as a proletar-

ian poet, had 'turned against his own class'. At the height of the financial crisis (in the thirties) Seifert had written verses of idyllic rapture. Now, 'in the true workshop of human happiness', at a time when all true poets strove to bear witness to the greatness of the time, and to help its progress, Seifert preferred to write verses of ruin, resignation, collapse: 'Today, when the flowers smell as never before, he writes:
     The rosemary smells no more as once it used to smell...
Seifert, between the lines of Viktorka, wishes to suggest to the reader that, in our world of new human fellowship, there is no love nor happiness. In one place he says:
     Man looks on man with evil in his heart...
'Seifert who, at a time when the people are victoriously realising their revolutionary ideals does not see these gigantic changes but sees only the mad Viktorka; he has no right to misuse the name of Němcová and Neruda; he has no right to misuse the honoured title of poet; he has no right to misuse poetry against the people, to ridicule all that is great and dear to our working people'.[21]

It seems strange to find a poet, as Skála was, using such shallow rhetoric. More astonishing is the lack of subtlety with which he reached his reckless and damning conclusions, potentially so dangerous for Seifert. It was, for the time being, the end of Seifert's literary career: he was silenced, and his name appeared only in the mouths of those who abused him.

Between 1949 and 1952 there was increasing pressure on writers to conform, and opportunities to publish what was aesthetically, (let alone politically) unorthodox, declined to vanishing point. As a result many established writers fell silent, in some cases because they were now excluded from publication, in others because they declined to write under such conditions. Of the older generation Zahradníček and Renč were now under the cloud of official displeasure. Of the middle generation Hauková, Hrubín, Kolář, Bednář, and Holan disappeared from the literary scene, turned to translation, or devoted themselves to the safer task of writing children's books. This trend proved to be among the most successful, though unplanned, results of the new course. After half-hearted attempts to ideologise children's literature, it was left for the most part free of pressure, and the entry of so many talented artists into the field led to an output of books, later of films, for children, of much charm and grace. The preoccupation with childish motifs, and the attempts to comprehend the aesthetic problems of children's art, were later in their turn to affect literature for adults.

It was hard for the apostles of socialist-realism long to sustain

style or conviction. But this was not the sum of their troubles. Before
the communists took power, reform or revolution had been supported
by the majority of writers because they felt themselves as the conscience of the nation. Arousing the social conscience of others, they had
won the admiration even of the so-called bourgeois class whom they
affected to despise. In 1946 František Halas wrote:

> We (writers) feel the future: that is why both rulers and the
> self-satisfied have always felt us disturbing.

Since governments do not welcome doubts as the rightness of their
policies, nor do they favour the assessment of practical measures
according to ideal principles, there is in most societies a perfectly
natural tension between writers and the so-called Establishment. The
tension is in fact an understandable extension of the tension between
artists and community standards generally, revealing itself in the
apparent eccentricity affected by intellectuals. Thus there was nothing
surprising in the support which the writers once had given to turbulent
left-wing movements against the pragmatic moderates who had for
long formed the governing class in Prague.

But the advent of the communists to power transformed the situation.
Once the communists took the reins, and formed their own Establishment, much less tolerant of criticism than their predecessors, the
writers found themselves on the wrong side of the fence. To be the
conscience of the nation, literature must reserve the right to oppose.
By demanding the support of the artists for their day-to-day- policies, the communists robbed them of their role as conscience bearers. Instead of stirring up doubts, the writers were now expected to
allay them, and stifle doubt in themselves. So, since the conscience of
the writers had been their greatest weapon as witnesses before the
people and as persuaders, once they forfeited the rights of conscience,
they were destroyed not only as artists, but also as persuaders. Their
contribution in fact became practically worthless. Once the artist
ceased to lead and agreed to follow, he lost his entitlement to speak in
his own name: what is worse, he lost his credibility and his respect.
Serving the commands of his masters, he harvested the contempt of
the masses whose teacher he claimed to be.

For years to come men were to speculate on the motives of the Czech
writers for acting as they did. Their apparent docility has been attributed to strict censorship, and to administrative pressure, including
threats to livelihood and liberty. Theoretically censorship did not
exist, in that no official body was empowered to confiscate, or forbid
the publication of any material. But in fact because all publishing and

printing enterprises were nationalised and all positions of influence were occupied by Party members, subject to Party discipline and direction, nothing was ever liable to be printed which contradicted Party policy. And since even Party members were subject to human error and ideological deviation, a veiled form of censorship operated through the Office for Press Review (HSTD), whose officers had the right to inspect material before publication, and to 'recommend' to editors the undesirability of publishing anything suspect: in any case nothing could actually be printed without the stamp of the HSTD officer.

But all this was merely a negative form of control: it could not in itself have produced such a flood of creative work designed to serve the Party line. It certainly fails to explain, for instance, the horrid gusto with which at least some authors celebrated repression, injustice, and blood-letting. The official Writers Union itself was tainted by association with the expressions of such support.

In the 'thirties leftist writers had nursed utopian illusions about revolution, and had used literature to propagate them. During wartime ultra-conservatives had reversed the trend and called for severe repression. After 1948 another turn of the wheel transformed the ultra-radicals into cultural guardians: having defeated the Fascists, they then took over their mentality, and ruthlessly eliminated what they conceived to be ideological opposition. The active support of writers for cultural repression cannot be entirely attributed to their servility, and susceptibility to corruption. Any study of modern politics will reveal the obstinacy with which apparently rational people will cling to illusions long after incontrovertible evidence should have convinced them of their invalidity. Some Czech writers allowed themselves to be corrupted by subsidies, privileges, appointments. Others held on to their fading idealism and supported the Party line at all costs, even through doubts and increasing disillusion. Perhaps, they reasoned, it was better to be wrong with the masses, than right against them. Then there was the lesson of the recent past. Although so much praise was given to the resistance against Nazism, it was well known how tragic and futile it often had turned out to be. Caution, guarded submission, a policy of wait and see, had become recognised as a sensible philosophy of survival. Czech writers submitted to communist policies because they saw at present no obvious alternative. Lastly there was the belief that a prime duty of Czech literature was to serve the nation. And from the idea of serving the nation, it was a short step to the idea of serving the Party. Had the latter been able to demonstrate over a long period that the interests of Party and nation coincided (and this was a main aim of propaganda), then the support of the intelligentsia would probably have been retained. But with the deterioration of conditions – social, economic, political – the idea became increasingly difficult to sustain, and the literary spokesmen hired to defend it plunged into further depths of disillusion.

The less spontaneous became the support of the writers, the more they were watched and harried. They proved the more vulnerable because they were organised; they had allowed themselves to be built into the political establishment. They not only relied on the government-owned network to market their books, and the official agency to deal on their behalf with foreign publishers. State prizes, sponsored lecture and study tours, organised literary campaigns, conferences, discussions, expressions of self-criticism, all helped to keep the writers in line. The organisation of culture down to the village level, in the new *Houses of Culture*, exposed not only the readers to writers, but also vice versa. The confrontation reminded writers that they were the servants of their public. The meetings were arranged by organs of the Party: ideas and criticism there expressed was naturally in strict accord with its guidelines: the occasion was an ideological exercise, which took place under the pictures of communist leaders and surrounded by the symbols and slogans of their political authority.

For it was no part of the plan to encourage free discussion. The literary consumer, at the end of a distribution chain, had no more control over production than had the consumer of industrial goods. The communists were proud that they had removed culture from the mercy of the market mechanism and the danger that artist, producer, or publisher might wish, for reasons of profit, to pander to the lower tastes of the public. Cultural production was geared to uplift and education. The question was: who should decide what was uplifting and educative, and what corrupting? The designated formers and upholders of taste held a key position in the pattern of culture.

It was taken for granted that the Party, as the source of authority and wisdom, must be the source of cultural policy. Since the USSR was the model of socialism everywhere, one might have expected that a Czech Zhdanov would have emerged as the authoritative arbiter of taste. Party officials and government ministers did not hesitate to lecture the artists on their tasks, but no Czech Zhdanov appeared. President Gottwald, Premier Zápotocký (who himself wrote socialist novels), Minister of Education Nejedlý, and of Information Kopecký, all appeared on platforms of writers' meetings. But their orders and exhortations were usually of a general character: the guidelines they issued were quite wide and open to interpretation. The interpreters, in effect the new taste-formers, were the critics: they included not only the writers of reviews, and readers for publishing houses, but cultural publicists, who spoke in the name of the Party. The critic was the key-stone of the literary establishment. He interpreted to writers the wisdom from above, and directed their efforts in the way they were to go: at the same time he expounded their work to readers, and gave the 'correct' – because official – evaluation of their work. Once trades union officials had represented the views of workers to management: now they passed the orders of management to workers. Now critics, who once had shown the reaction of readers to the work of writers, were set in a position above both: armed with an invisible, but apparently unchallengable, authority, they now instructed writers what they should write, and readers what they should read.

The role of the critic was neither easy nor safe: as a guardian of ideological orthodoxy he least of all could risk stepping out of line. And if the official line shifted, it was he, not the Party, who was blamed. Unfortunately for him, the pretence of free criticism was maintained, so he could rarely be absolutely sure what *was* official policy in literary matters. In 1949 the poet František Halas died. An old member of the Party, who had after the war entered the Ministry of Information under Kopecký, Halas was not the man to hide his feelings, and had quarrelled with the Party. He fell under the shadow of official displeasure, and was not a member of the newly formed Union of Writers. His work was criticised as decadent and existentialist; his death was ignored by the press. Then a letter of warm sympathy was received from the Russian writer Ilya Ehrenburg, an old friend from happier days. This evidently altered the position, and kind obituaries began to appear in the Czech journals. Then in January 1950 a slashing attack upon him was made by Ladislav Štoll at a working conference of the Writers' Union. Critics now dropped Halas, and reverted to a scornful silence about his work.

If writers were the engineers of souls, and critics the engineers of writers' souls, critics themselves needed help in their slippery task. Rather than risk their judgement, they looked anxiously for some authoritative lead as an insurance against error. Certain people in the literary field soon became known as 'reliable': they did not necessarily have to hold any official position, but it became accepted that their ideological, hence their literary, judgement was 'sound'. Among them were Jiří Taufer, Ivan Skála, Jiří Hájek, and Gustav Bareš (editor of

Tvorba). But none excelled in orthodoxy Ladislav Štoll, a heavy-handed martinet who became a sort of doyen of hyper-radical criticism.

Soon after the Communist take-over in 1948 he had figured prominently at the Congress of National Culture, where he had formulated the principles of literary rebirth and re-evaluation. In those days, when restraint was the order of the day, he had ridiculed the idea that Communism meant the regimentation of literature:

> How many times have we heard the enemies of socialism, under the pretence of protecting the autonomy of the literary sector from politics, declare that socialism will demand of the poet and artist that he betray his vocation. That he will be asked to versify political statements, rhyme political theses, to decline the word 'people' into all cases, to write, paint and compose propaganda, to put forward tendentious art made to order.[22]

Two years later, at a working conference of writers, Štoll presented a paper which was later published as *Thirty years of struggle for Czech socialist poetry*.[23] The book was to win notoriety as a handbook of marxist literary orthodoxy. Basically it was a retrospective sketch of Czech verse since 1918, with material selected and rigidly classified according to ideological criteria. Literary development was portrayed as a struggle between two trends - the healthy, socialist, optimistic work of S. K. Neumann and J. Wolker on the one hand, and of their opponents on the other: these were sometimes their natural class enemies, sometimes leftists with shallow roots in marxism, defeatists, men of little faith, or else anti-Soviet crypto-Trotskyists. Evil geniuses of the right were the critic Bedřich Fučík, the poet Kamil Bednář, and Professor V. Černý. The arch villain of the Left was Karel Teige, who had infected even Nezval with his Trotskyism. Those of little faith included Hora, Seifert, and Halas. The latter in particular came in for some harsh words. But all had long since 'parted company with Lenin': pessimism, morbidity, decadence, surrealism, existentialism, and intellectualism had estranged their work from the masses, and harmed the struggle for a higher social order.

Štoll's essay was a somewhat crude rewriting of literary history, with material arranged to lead to the climax of communist victory. Now that the inexorable laws of History had ushered in the new era of happiness etc. what was the role of the poet in the socialist society? Stalin had bidden poets be the 'engineers of souls': Gottwald had told them not to describe machines, but to 'sing of the loves and hates of our people'. Writers would need guidance, and they would find it from critics who were armed with scientific Marxism:

> We have seen how harmful – but how powerful – an influence was exerted in the past by misguided criticism. Incomparably greater and more powerful – and in this case of course, beneficial – will be the influence of our criticism, truly informed by Marx, Engels, Lenin and Stalin. But not only that. Our criticism will have to learn from the great Russian revolutionary democrats. It is they who, in a certain sense as creators of the new aesthetics, signify the last word in this branch... A true artistic portraiture of all that, with remarkable inevitability, takes place in the man of today, is impossible unless the writer's talent is continually imaginatively stimulated by the truest imaginative view of the world and life - Marxism-Leninism.

In his speech Štoll not only laid down the Party line on literary history, but condemned in authoritative terms living literary figures. There was, of course, nothing *illegal* in having been (or still being) an evil literary influence. There was also no law to stop any of the writers getting up and telling Štoll that his speech was stupid and misleading: but no one was rash enough to do so. The degeneration of the intellectual (and the political) atmosphere appears from the uncritical reception of his essay. Štoll had always been a man of wild words, and it was not easy to tell whether his condemnation of erring writers represented personal judgement or official threats. At any rate the condemned men found little comfort in them. Václav Černý had already been expelled from the university; Kamil Bednář was shunned, and excluded from literary life; Palivec, B. Fučík and Kalista arrested. Their fate was not necessarily caused by Štoll's verdict: but in the climate of the time, to be named a literary saboteur was equivalent to denunciation as a political heretic.

The Party could only discourage, but could not prevent artists from writing material of which it disapproved: some very good books were in fact drafted in the Stalinist period; but they could not be published. In most cases this was sufficient to stop writers, who had earn their living somehow, from composing anything likely to give offence. But the Party was not satisfied with regulating future literary production, the literature of the past – especially the recent past – was also subject to their anxious guidance. Libraries were purged of 'decadent filth'. The teaching programmes of educational institutions were brought into line. Teachers were subjected to security checks, and those who failed to give satisfaction were expelled. Even second-hand bookshops were brought under vigilant supervision, and restrictions were placed on the sale of books published before 1945: certain writers were placed on an Index, and their books were withdrawn from distribution. At the same time the theatre and film industry, which had made a promising revival after the war, were rigorously controlled. The writers themselves, organised through their Union, were reproved, rewarded, exhorted, lectured and generally told what to write. Such actions revealed the communists' conviction that literature and art were vital in the struggle for the mind of the Czech people.[24]

But as so often happens with planned campaigns, results did not accord with expectations. Now that the Party was entirely responsible for literature, and stamped its impression upon it, the new literature helped to form the Party's public image. As nothing could be published without the assent of the Communists, it was as though every writer spoke in the name, and with the authority of the Party. In cultural matters the Communists had in the past been associated with bold, outspoken views and daring experiment. The more chilling therefore was the impression it now gave of dreary mediocrity and tired rhetoric.

The communists must have been aware that a key to effective persuasion lies in awakening and sustaining the interest of the audience: for literary success an essential pre-requisite is readability. But readability is not produced by the constant and wearisome reproduction of orthodox formulae. Novelty, variety, paradox, originality of thought and treatment – qualities which the heavy hand of the controllers tended to eliminate – seem to be rather important for literature and art if it is to hold the interest of its audience; and all these qualities imply some freedom of action by the writers. It did not seem to have occurred to the culture bosses that the long-suffering public might eventually go on a culture strike against the provender dished out to them. Power apparently encourages authoritarian attitudes, and the controllers gave the impression of men who believed that people would read anything that their government judged to be good for them. In certain circumstances, with a captive audience, such an assumption may be true. Bible classes dutifully study the Good Book; children are instructed to appreciate prescribed reading; students frantically seek to master examinable material. In fact many of the books published in Czechoslovakia were as if part of a prescribed study programme, and much of the distribution was not by sale over the counter, but through the network of libraries, clubs, and factories. Czech literature began to bear an alarming resemblance to a *stint* – not recreation but formal and required instruction. And a common reaction to pre-scribed study is aversion both to it, and to everything for which it stands.

By its regulation of literature the Party did much to kill readership, and compromise itself. And since the basic aim of the cultural campaign was social, its failure was a social and ideological failure which cast discredit upon the Party itself. Once the communists had made them-selves responsible for literature, they were dependent upon its success, and every literary disaster was a blow which might be denied, but not concealed. Worse still was the increasingly obvious contrast between the idealistic theories of Marxism, and the reality of political life. The programmatic poems and novels were really advertising a political system in terms impossibly rosy, and as if conforming to the highest ethical standards. But politics, even in good times rarely seem to be conducted with high ethical standards. In political life men become accustomed to separating the practical from the desirable: what they do is not exactly in accordance with what they say. Policies, to be effective in this world, cannot always follow principles. As long as the communists had been in opposition, they could keep their princ-iples unsullied by compromise. But when they were in power the real world obstinately obtruded. Communist ideology, as a doctrine ex-pressed in literature, set up for itself high standards. Even if things had gone well, the gap between pretence and the reality would have been apparent. But at a time when almost nothing went right for the govern-ment, as it revealed itself as authoritarian and savagely repressive, the gulf widened between the idealised picture of communist society in literature, and the reality outside it. After six years under the Nazis the Czechs were schooled to hard times: but it was a senseless irritant to have the contrast officially driven home, so that in the end real life became almost a caricature of the life depicted in literature.

Declining economic conditions and increasing political repression alienated the masses and sowed doubts among the faithful. When things went wrong the communists did not question their principles, which were regarded as inviolable and outside discussion. Break-downs in the delivery of goods were blamed on saboteurs: for every major error a scapegoat had to be found. At first the scapegoats were taken from the class enemies, 'bourgeois remnants', and 'right-wing agents of imperialism'. But after the Jugoslav crisis, no charge became more dreaded than that of Titoism. Tito's old friends from the Comintern were in the highest positions in the Czechoslovak Communist Party; even they could have been infected. Only weeks before the break between Moscow and Belgrade an official Jugoslav delegation had been in Prague, its leaders photographed laughing with the Czech leaders: the heresy of an independent way to socialism had been official Party policy. Now no one was safe. A shudder must have gone through journalists when the editor of *Rudé právo* himself, Vilém Nový, was 'unmasked' and arrested in November 1949.

Earlier that year the Central Committee of the Party had discussed security measures to protect itself against saboteurs. Soviet experts were invited to Czechoslovakia, to advise on tougher methods. The following year, it appeared that the Czechs had not gone far enough. The Committee received from the Minister in charge of Security a Cominform resolution urging increased vigilance in the Party ranks, and the unmasking of bourgeois-nationalistic elements and agents of imperialism, *wherever they be hidden*.

The wave of arrests which followed, struck first at the leadership of the Slovak Communist Party, suspected of Slovak nationalism. Gustav Husák, President of the Slovak Council and the writer Laco Novomeský (Slovak Education Minister) were dismissed; they publicly confessed that they favoured 'reactionary tendencies'.[25] Their arrests followed. The Foreign Minister V. Clementis, a Slovak communist with a record of liberal tendencies, was in 1949 in New York, attending a session of the United Nations Organisation. He was recalled to Prague and arrested. One of the most talented and energetic of the younger Czech communist leaders was O. Šling. Among his greatest errors was a youth campaign in Moravia, with the slogan 'Youth leads Brno': its success seems to have alerted the Party leadership in Prague. Šling was arrested. It appears that such arrests still did not satisfy Stalin, who reasoned that Titoism had to be ruthlessly eradicated, and that its spirit was represented in the very heart of the satellite parties. In September 1951 Gottwald publicly noted that Slánský, General Secretary of the Party, had committed errors; the latter was removed from his post. In November he was arrested. A few days later, Gottwald publicly announced that Slánský had been unmasked as a traitor. With him fell an array of powerful communist officials.[26]

It is difficult to estimate the effect on public opinion of these extraordinary events. Most spectacular were the changes of fortune: one day a man was honoured, praised, held up as a model of communist virtue; next day he might be unmasked as a traitor, spy, saboteur:

yesterday's gaolers were today's prisoners. The Party seemed to be rotten with treachery: today's confident assurances might tomorrow be exposed as wicked lies. The effect on non-communists was less traumatic than upon the believers: the former lost jobs, money, houses; but the young communists stood to lose what was to them more basic, that is, their belief. One effect of the great purge was to produce a crisis of *faith* among the Party faithful. Propaganda may succeed in persuading people to believe things of which they have no direct experience; to persuade them to disregard the evidence of their own senses is more difficult. To suspend one's own judgement in deference to revealed truth, *faith* is needed: the more incredible the 'truth' the greater the depth of faith required. To believe what is apparently or demonstrably nonsensical demands an act of total faith amounting to mysticism. The supreme test of faith inflicted by the Czech communist rulers upon the faithful were the political trials in 1952. After their arrest, Slánský and his thirteen accomplices were kept under rigorous interrogation in preparation for a public trial in which the whole world would learn of their crimes from their own lips. When the hearings were held, the accused not only admitted every charge, some so incredible as to be laughable, but they eagerly demanded for themselves the severest punishment. The men in the dock were model witnesses in their own prosecution, and seemed anxious to expose every erring detail of their past. These men, who represented until their arrest the leadership of the Party, had, it appeared, for years been working devotedly against communism and for the forces of capitalism, fascism, and imperialism. Their crimes were illustrated in various ways. In the case of Clementis (until recently Foreign Minister) he had *questioned* the Party line in 1939 (in that he had openly taken up an anti-Soviet stand by objecting to the Soviet-Nazi Pact). Slánský, on the other hand, was guilty of *following* the Party line, when, in 1935 he had worked towards the Popular Front:

Slánský: I influenced the Party to co-operate with reformist leaders and with Beneš, who were agents of the bourgeoisie...

Judge: What happened about the Czechoslovak-Soviet Treaty (of 1935)?

Slánský: At the time when this treaty was concluded, I propagated the illusion that Beneš was an honest friend of the USSR, although he was an imperialist agent...

Judge: This means that in fact you assisted the imperialist agent Beneš?

Slánský: Yes, I personally assisted the imperialist agent Beneš.

Slánský also confessed his support for Tito in his 'counter-revolutionary' aims:

Slánský: Like Tito in Jugoslavia we tried to transform the Communist Party into an instrument for the restoration of capitalism.

Slánský's whole career had apparently been a masquerade, concealing his work for the class enemies.

Slánský: We were working for the aims of the Anglo-U.S. imperialists, the aims of the aggressive bloc of the U.S. and British imperialists, these aims being the restoration of capitalism and the preparation of a new war, which is today being prepared by the imperialists. The aim was to get Czechoslovakia, which freed itself from the imperialist sphere in 1945 back into that sphere, to make the country dependent on the imperialists, as under the First Republic (1918-38) to enable it to be exploited by the imperialists, to foil the building of socialism in ČSR and to enslave the Czech people again, so that industrialists, bankers, and landed gentry could exploit them once again, and so that foreign imperialism should profit from the toil of the people.

As the hearings went on, the accused outdid each other in their suicidal affirmations of guilt, all expressed in the formal, rather stilted style of marxist dogma. Among them was a prominent communist journalist Andre Simone (formerly Otto Katz), until recently an editor of the Party daily *Rudé právo*:

Simone: I am a writer, supposedly an architect of the soul. What sort of an architect have I been, I who have poisoned men's souls! Such an architect belongs to the gallows. The only service I can still render is to warn all who, by origin or character, are in danger of following the same path to hell. The sterner the punishment... (voice falls so low as to be unintelligible).[27]

Simone, who had spent the war years in Mexico, was an old friend of the author A. Koestler. Simone's 'confession' here was a quotation (as close as Simone could recall it) from Rubashov's fake confession in *Darkness and Noon*; which Koestler had modelled on Bukharin's confession at his show trial in Moscow. One must assume that Simone deliberately used the words as a camouflaged message to advertise the falsity of the confession: he knew that Koestler at least would recognise the message, and perhaps trusted that somehow he could avoid his fate. In fact no move was made to save him: if the left-wing intelligentsia in the West even noticed, they took no action. Only Koestler has gone on record as having reacted with shock to the transcript of Simone's last words.[28] It was an interesting and melancholy instance of the inter-relationship of literature and life. A rehearsed confession by a doomed man in Stalin's Russia had inspired a literary passage, which then had been turned back into reality in a Prague court, itself to become the material for future literature.

Years later it was officially confirmed[29] that the evidence was fraudulent, and the methods used to obtain confessions were illegal. That was fairly obvious at the time, but it was a mystery how men as tough as Slánský could have been driven to incriminate themselves in such an obliging way. Later the survivors explained. All were in various ways broken, and forced to sign confessions. Then they were given good treatment, assured of leniency, and rehearsed until they could recite their confessions word for word. Before the actual trial, judges, counsel, prisoners, all went through elaborate rehearsals so that the performance would be perfect. The teams that had worked on the prisoners vied with each other in the excellence of their preparation: during the hearing accusers and accused met in the corridors, congratulating each other on their performance. Of the public, for whom the show was provided, some no doubt believed the stunning revelations; they could only conclude that the Party, built and led by such men, was rotten with subversion, and that many of the solemn pronouncements made in its name (including the present?) were lies. Other people shook their heads and suspended normal standards of belief. Others, idealists among them, reached the depths of disillusion and despair. The trials seemed like a nightmare world lying behind the facade of normality. From the absurd confessions to the childish recitations they were a spectacle of unreason and unreality: the final macabre stroke was the verdicts, and the hanging of all but three of the accused.

Just as the communists used poetry, novels, drama, films as a form of propaganda and public relations, so they used the courts of justice. All genres were made to play their part in proclaiming the power and virtue of communism and the Soviets, and denouncing their enemies.

The crude and cynical use of the courts for temporary Party ends had terrible results in undermining the legality of the state apparatus and demonstrating the communists' own violation of law and human rights. The trials also advertised an aspect of communist practice hardly reconcilable with its theory of scientific materialism.

The trials were not genuine or traditional hearings, in that the guilt of the accused was accepted from the start, even by the prisoners themselves. They went through the motions of defending themselves, just as the judge went through the motions of judging the issue, and the prosecutor went through the motions of establishing guilt. But the entire co-operation of the troupe, and the ceremony which accompanied the macabre performance made it appear less like a court hearing, and more like a *ritual*. This was itself a spectacular, blown-up, version of a routine becoming familiar throughout the Party. As the accused were mercilessly interrogated and humiliated, so the rank and file were subjected to loyalty tests, their past background exposed, and their present beliefs examined. As the accused confessed for the benefit of the public, so the ordinary members were called upon for regular *self-criticism*. The judgement and retribution of the courts upon the unfortunate Slánský was repeated in milder or varied form in myriads of cases outside the courts and as part of normal ideological discipline: error, confession, retribution was the routine. As the Party exercised its stern inner discipline by its own methods, so, for wider effect and to an international audience, the courts of the state were appropriated to do the same. Holding its doctrines inviolate and its judgements infallible, the Party had become like a religious sect which forces upon its members the idea of *sin*; which tests their faith, convicts them out of their own mouth, purges, forgives, or punishes their transgressions. The ritual demanded *scapegoats*, who were made to suffer in gaols and camps; or were killed, some physically, some symbolically, when they disappeared from society, and their names, works, and memories were erased. An ultimate test of omnipotence is the power to raise from the dead. Even this was symbolically accomplished by the Party, when in years to come, men who had long been forgotten, returned as from the grave, were legally reborn, declared to be retrospectively innocent, and were officialy *rehabilitated.*

The principles of social justice, and cultural and material progress, had been for long associated with the Communist Party in the minds of much of the public, and many of the writers. It was because they conceived it as the party of conscience that their efforts had been so liberally engaged in its cause. But within five years of their accession to complete power in Prague, the communists had succeeded in destroying their own public image and the faith of so many followers. Through the hard years of struggle, especially in the deadly work of the wartime underground, they had been prepared to sacrifice themselves to their principles. Now they were themselves the ruling group, they did not shrink from sacrificing others. Indifferent to present suffering because of their view of future, they applied increasing force to a public 'ideologically unprepared'. Aiming officially at a goal of justice, love, and peace, they violated their own laws, and stirred up mass fear and hatred. Proclaiming the truth of their cause, they advertised their own lies, and so encouraged doubt and disbelief in every statement they made.

As they sank deeper into deception, their facility for distinguishing truth from lies seems to have become blurred, and belief at any cost was demanded of their followers. At the same time they made such belief impossible for rational men. The witch-hunts and political trials were like a crazy drama acted out in public life: public justice was exhibited as a sham — a public show played out 'with a real hanging as the prize for the loser. It was the trials above all which illustrated the contrast between the utopia of the programme and the horrid reality of the present. As repression increased, and rumours of the victims' dreadful fate ran through the streets of Prague, there were gay processions and dancing in the streets, as if to emphasise the macabre unreality of contemporary life and the gap between pretence and truth. The more the Party violated the principles of justice and freedom, the more they boasted of their implementation. Factory workers and students put their names to petitions asking for the execution of their own acquaintances – as if the aim of the Party was to incriminate as many as possible in the liquidations. Literature, urged to write realistically, enshrined the lies, proclaiming the imaginary triumphs of the new tyranny in books which would return like ghouls to plague their authors in years to come.

Contemporary Czech literature did not, and could not, portray the real situation: reality had itself become taboo. Yet the atmosphere of the time had been caught in Prague literature of thirty years previously. Those who knew the work of Kafka (and the suppression of his work by the communists helped to widen its cult), could but marvel at the prescience of its author. The *Castle* appeared to Kafka, as to Czechs in the early fifties, as an impenetrable sanctum guarded by faceless bureaucrats, and symbolising a code of behaviour incomprehensible to outsiders. The *Trial* had described with uncanny realism the bewilderment of accused unaware of what crime they could have committed, and feeling the more guilty on that account. Doomed unless they found the right path in accord with the will of the Master, they had no way of finding it. Whether they sought the path or hid from it, their fate was the same. Tried without knowing for what or by whom, they were executed without contact with justice, and unable to make any sense of their judgement. Even so, in 1952 men saw those who opposed, or seemed likely to oppose, the will of the Party arrested; those who (like Slánský) had supported it with all their heart, were arrested too. It was not merely that truth, freedom, justice, were perverted. When idols fell, when jailers became criminals, Security meant peril, and Information lies, salvation seemed no longer attainable by rational means. Life had become a bureaucratic nightmare.

What Kafka described was the enforcement of a code to which men lacked the key. The Master of the *Castle* was the more terrifying because his will was a mystery. In the Prague of 1952, an act or word applauded one day could be grounds for treason the next: in such circumstances men could do little to influence their own fate. One is bound to enquire why Kafka's nightmare was so realistic: why did the communists make it come true? And here one may note that Kafka was not alone in his prescience. In *The Good Soldier Schweik* the situation occurs of Czech soldiers marched off to the shambles with no idea of purpose, and on muddled or nonsensical orders: when they had no rations, they were given pictures of the Austrian Emperor to raise their morale. In similar fashion, years later, when the Czech workers were confused, and short of essentials, they were given bound copies of Gottwald's speeches. Hašek and Kafka differed in language, style, and theme, but both, with deadly accuracy could describe the effects of a bureaucracy unrestrained by humanity. What Hašek in lesser, and Kafka in greater, degree reveal, is the alienation of a ruling group from its subjects.

While writers were being urged to write realistically, this, the increasing alienation of the Party, was a reality which was felt, but never could be mentioned. Party policy still dictated that the writers should direct their work to public issues: but the day might come when public issues were so inflammable, their truths so confused with retractions and revisions, that even the Party might decide it better for literature to move into less turbid and perilous waters.

IV

The Eyes of Children

A sort of wisdom:
before the Council kneeling low
confess to the Cardinals your transgressions!

Better to kneel than perish at the stake,
better to thrust the truth down deep below;
and let it sleep where it won't awake;
then, reassured, feel you've convictions none can shake.

Hey, Comrade Galileo,
a sort of wisdom, eh?

Yes, wiser far the liar than was he,
the fairytale lad who rashly dared to state
and shout what no one was supposed to see –
the Emperor was naked there.

L. Novomeský (tr. J. Lindsay)

Critics of post-war Czech literature find general agreement in placing the worst phase of literary Stalinism in the years 1950-52. There was a natural time-lag between the results, as they appeared in publishing programmes, the release of finished work, and their reception by the reading public. By 1952 the socialist-realist literary line, proclaimed with bombast and enforced with rigour, had delivered its sad harvest. As examples of its disappointing results may be cited the poetic diatribes of the younger generation of poets – S. Neumann, M. Sedloň, I. Skála, and V. Školaudy. If socialist-realism, and the conduct of literature 'in the public interest', was to be judged by such work, little was to be hoped for: nor indeed was much to be expected from it that could not be obtained more economically in a primer of Marxist sociology. Less immature, but even more depressing, because buttressed with a securer technique, was the work of serious and established writers like Nezval, Řezáč, and Pujmanová. Their talents were known, and admired: now they were giving what presumably they hoped was their best, in the cause which was their own. The failure of the new communist literature would have been more understandable if its advocates had been able to mobilise only the fringe of literature to their policies: in fact they had on their side many of the best living Czech writers. Yet the fruits of socialist literature were tasteless and bitter. Nothing condemned them more than the terrible contrast between the living style they portrayed, vibrant with resolute optimism, and the desolation of fear and suspicion which haunted real life. It penetrated the literary sphere itself, leaving a trail of banned journals, suppressed publications, silent presses, and writers denounced, intimidated, or arrested.

The unreality and basic falsity of the officially encouraged literature must soon have become evident even to those who encouraged it. The position was deplorable; and at no stage do the Party leaders seem to have been happy with the literary scene. But the faults were naturally attributed not to defects in the Party guidelines (much less to the system itself) but to the writers themselves. They were charged with bourgeois attitudes; with having but shallow roots in Marxism; and (in the case of the younger writers) with immature extremism and a reluctance to learn from the Marxist classics.

The cultural aims of the Party were practical and utilitarian: it was therefore logical that practical criteria should be used for estimating the value of the literary effort. Its value could properly be measured by its social results. The acid test of books and poems praising the regime was in the extent of improvement to the regime's public image. If the novels of collectivisation were successful, surely their success would be evidenced by increased enthusiasm for the collectivisation campaign. Socialist literature could be judged by its success in persuading people to change their views: it could also be judged by its success in harmonising public opinion, and reducing social tension. It is a traditional function of literature – especially of Czech literature – to act as a repository of hopes and aspirations of the group, to link their past to their future by the recreation of legend; and, by offering a core of remembered, shared, experience, to lend some unity of purpose to the community. How well was socialist literature facing up to this exalted role? The communists, holding in their hands both the control of literature and the means of measuring the public response to it, were in a position to attempt some realistic measurement of its social impact. They could, and perhaps they did, ask themselves how far the novels, the drama, the poetry, were establishing in the public consciousness a socialist ideology, which was itself the projection of a new living style.

From the comments of Party spokesmen, and from subsequent changes of cultural policy, it seems clear that communists soon realised the failure of literary policy, at least as it was implemented in the early years of the administration. Perhaps the nightmare atmosphere of public life and ferocity of the regime's social measures precluded success for any literature with such aggressively optimistic overtones: the lack of realism was patent, and the contrast absurd. But even under more favourable conditions a literature based on stereotyped formulae, characters, and situations would have had a poor chance of sustained popularity. Its natural domain is a captive audience – a school or congregation: its predictable response from a free audience is boredom, apathy, and finally disgust and resentment. And although writers, publishers, and distributors could be controlled, audiences could not. The early fifties have left a record of books published in huge imprints, the mass distribution of literature through clubs, associations, and factory libraries, but of declining interest on the part of the public. The common reaction to regimentation was resentment, distaste, and finally hostility. An example was the treatment of the work of the veteran communist poet S. K. Neumann, who had died in 1947. He had always enjoyed a warm following, even among the ranks of his political opponents. In his book *Thirty Years of Struggle* Štoll had taken Neumann as the model of a progressive and gifted artist, one by whose measure other lesser men could be assessed. Štoll's verdict was dutifully echoed by other critics: at the same time a great campaign was mounted to spread enthusiasm for the poet, and bring his work forcibly to the notice of the young. Neumann's poetry was expounded in a somewhat simplistic, not to say bombastic fashion. There were numerous open discussions of his work – exercises in public relations which helped to turn literary criticism into a farce; for there could be no frank exchange of views where issues had been authoritatively expounded, and where literary views could be regarded as tests of political loyalty. This one-sided exposition of the work of a complex artist could do nothing but harm to his reputation, as well as to the literary programme. Neumann, that restless, lively rebel, was converted into a tedious relic of the past, stylised and dead. His poems had become a stint to be avoided; his name a symbol of cultural authoritarianism.

But if the campaign to mould popular taste failed; its failure did more than damage the memory of the writers whose works were being plugged. Since the favoured writers were now identified with the regime, a literary failure was, in its own way, a political failure as well. Having engaged literature overtly in politics, the Party found it had harnessed to its chariot a very temperamental and unpredictable animal. The Party had put itself in the position where it was responsible for the success and popularity of literature; and not even the most ferocious administrative measures could guarantee success, much less popularity. By 1952 modern Czech literature had reached probably its lowest ebb, and regimented output encountered a wall of public apathy.

A cure for the apathy, and the unpopularity of 'official' literature, lay readily available, if only it could be used. All that was required was the freedom to apply to the current scene the method of realist criticism which was recommended in theory. As a matter of fact books were being written at the time which did subject conditions to critical examination – there was a great hunger for social, if not socialist, criticism. An example was Jiří Mucha's *Cold Sunlight*[1] a book of reportage from the punishment camps. But there was of course no chance of such realist writing, even on much less sensitive issues, being published at the time. Indeed the possession of such a manuscript could have been represented as seditious; all such writing had to be concealed, to await possible publication in happier times. The application of *realist* criteria to current social issues was the last thing the Party vigilantes were likely to permit. Claiming realism as a working method, they exiled literature from any overt attempt at its attainment. The paradox of literary politics was complete.

No less sour were the fruits of literature as the propagator of ideology. Amid the intellectual disintegration of past years, and especially amid the disorientation of the post-war period, political ideology had for many people assumed the traits of a possible new unifier. Beyond the narrower loyalties of family, of class, or even of nation, socialist ideology appeared almost as man's last hope; like a new church, harmonising the aims of nations and peoples in a common set of social aims for the betterment of mankind. The cruel realities of political life and international rivalry had severely damaged such an idealistic conception: but in 1948 many communists, and communist sympathisers had still believed in it. In 1952 such people could ask themselves how ideology had fared as a social harmoniser. In fact, under instructions from Moscow, the 'class struggle' had been deliberately intensified: class had been set against class; the intellectuals had been divided from the masses; Czechs at home had been set against their fellow-countrymen abroad: most unexpected of all, the generations had been divided by politics. The old-guard communists repeatedly found themselves denouncing the young for their apathy, suspicion and hostility, when they were not denouncing the fanatical young communists for their immaturity. The generations were again divided, and at times Party leaders seem to have suspected that communist and non-communist youth were drawing together against them. Increasingly the leaders were assuming the role of a ruling oligarchy, backed by and subservient to a foreign power, and in confrontation with their own people. Instead of becoming the unifier, ideology had become the divider. Amid this atmosphere of increasing alienation, intellectuals who once had supported the Party seemed to be drawing away, if not to outright opposition (an impossible position to admit), at least to a neutrality which was itself a form of silent condemnation.

For the unsatisfactory situation in cultural life scapegoats were needed. In February 1952 the cultural daily *Lidové noviny*, edited since 1948 by the novelist Jan Drda, ceased publication. It was replaced by the weekly *Literární noviny*, an official platform of the Union of Czechoslovak Writers. A week later came the end of *Tvorba*, the Party's own cultural journal, which had been the platform from which official denunciations of 'unsound' intellectuals had been mounted. It had hitherto been regarded as the mouthpiece of the Party in cultural matters. Its editor, Gustav Bareš, now disappeared from public life.

The evil influence of Slánský was alleged in every aspect of Party activity, and the charge of Slanskyism was as serious as that of Titoism. The charges against Slánský and those associated with him, were, in general, charges of sabotage and espionage in the interests of the West. In his 'misinterpretation' of official communist policy he was branded as a *right-wing* adventurer, or deviationist. However in cultural affairs the charge of Slanskyism seems to have been of the opposite nature. The influence of the Slanskyists in cultural life was denounced as an *ultra left-wing* deviation. He was accused of pushing the communist line to insane lengths, alienating community feeling, and so sabotaging communist policy:

> The influence of the former secretariat, led by Slánský, had unfortunate effects upon Union activity and upon the whole development of literature. Instead of general care and help, certain of his associates interpreted the leading role of the Party in such a way that from time to time they decreed various moves in a bureaucratic and authoritarian fashion; or they initiated in the press attacks on certain writers; they crudely interfered in editorial policy, in their leftish way preventing or impeding the publication of famous works of our literature. In this way they encouraged in us feelings of naive conceit, with which we sometimes looked at non-Party writers, and at artists who often were painfully fighting for their own further artistic development.[2]

While errors in other sectors of public life were still being blamed on lack of vigilance, and on bourgeois leanings, in the cultural sphere it was lack of tolerance, dogmatism, and heavy-handed repression which seemed to be the culprit:

> Until recently there were serious and dangerous obstacles for writers. To put it plainly: it was the half-educated, sectarian, and vulgar criticism... Writers were subjected to unfeeling criticism, unsocialistic and hostile, which failed to take into account the internal struggle for rebirth which so many artists undergo.

In July the Minister of Culture himself, V. Kopecký, entered the fray:

> It seems that the poets tried to carry socialist-realism to absurd extremes. They assume that it is enough to string together, without form or harmony, currently used words such as *shockworkers, brigades, conferences, national committees, tractors, combines* etc... and then call it poetry, poetry with a trend, poetry in the socialist spirit. But socialist-realism requires art to be, like science, a highly intellectual way of interpreting reality – reality of life, of nature, of the processes of existence, including the interpretation of sensual and emotional phenomena...

By the end of the following year Kopecký, in biting (and not unsuitable) language was venting his ministerial scorn upon the cultural revisionists, who had, of course, only been trying to follow what they conceived to be his own guidelines when he had been Minister of Information: he denounced

> all utterances of schematism, vulgarism, superficiality, and grayness, which still appear in literature and other arts... The so-called 'dry biscuits' think the advent of socialism means that people cease to have normal joys, longings, passions predilections and claims on life, and become mere mechanisms which can be wound up at liberty... They think the only good socialist works are those with ideology scooped up by the bucketful, and discussions of socialist problems like newspaper editorials.[3]

It was not surprising that Slánský's influence should be blamed for the failures in the cultural sector, for he was blamed for more or less everything else. What was at first sight surprising was the grounds for the attacks upon him. It was true that creative work had been stifled, artists destroyed, and sensible criticism rendered impossible by dogmatic interpretation and violent attacks on dissenters. These were in fact the methods which the Czechs had taken over from their Russian models, in particular from Zhdanov. They were the methods canonised by Štoll and other official spokesmen, such as Kopecký himself.

In choosing to identify Slanskyism with dogmatic attitudes and crude enforcement of cultural guidelines, it appears that the Party was giving notice of a change of cultural policy. What caused the change is not altogether clear. The depressing nature of the cultural harvest was a factor. The suicide of Biebl, who had complained of harassment by over-zealous Party members, was a shock to his old friends. Kopecký, who answered to the Politbyro for cultural matters, had a soft spot for artists whom he had admired in his youth. Brash young critics who in 1950 saw themselves as the voice of a new age, treated the pre-war avant-garde with contempt as both passé and tainted with bourgeois decadence. But writers like Biebl, Halas, Seifert, and Nezval were linked by generation and background to the present leaders. By 1952 the latter apparently decided they had heard enough denigration of their old friends. A member of the old avant-garde, Adolf Hoffmeister, returned from a diplomatic assignment in Paris. Unaccustomed to the cowed attitudes which had developed in Prague in his absence, he answered criticism with a candour which had become unusual, accusing the young critics of ignorance and conceit. Encouraged by the improvement in atmosphere, other writers came forward in their own defence; Nezval stepped into unblushing heresy by defending Cubist art. For the first time for several years a vigorous discussion sprang up in the press, and writers whose names had not been heard for some time, began to appear once more in print. The young critics now found themselves at the receiving end of the abuse; so-called Slanskyists were accused in the press of 'denigrating gifted people who as citizens had shown right attitudes, even if as artists they had formed groups with formalist or decadent programmes. Such people had been subjected to insults and humiliation, encouraged by literary saboteurs.'

A change of course in cultural matters may have been decided because of the peculiar situation of the Czech scene. But external factors were also involved. Since the Jugoslav heresy had been exposed, it had been clear that the only safe way towards socialism was a rigid application of the Soviet model in every aspect of administration.

Whereas before 1948 communists had claimed that they inherited the truest Czech traditions, after 1948 spokesmen vied with each other in affirming their adherence to the Soviet example. This simplified the problems of critics: they were safe if they followed their Soviet exemplars. But in 1952 certain doubts arose in the minds of Czech critics about their understanding of Soviet criteria.

Since 1949 Czech critics had generally condemned the work of Karel Čapek, the friend and biographer of President Masaryk, and the author of an embarrassing essay entitled 'Why I am not a communist'. After 1949 Čapek's plays were no longer performed; his books were not reprinted; as a figure of the pre-war bourgeois Establishment he was consigned to oblivion. But in 1952 a horrid doubt set in. A selection of Čapek's works had been published in Moscow, with an introduction by the Soviet critic Nikolsky. Naturally Nikolsky's essay was translated and reprinted[4] in Czechoslovakia. In the essay Čapek was portrayed as a stern critic of capitalist society (*R.U.R.*); as one who foreshadowed the catastrophe which naturally attends on the capitalist system (*Krakatit*); and as one who spoke with the voice of the people in the class war (*Matka*). Čapek, it was claimed, had admired Soviet culture and had stood on the side of revolution. By his anti-Fascist and humanist stance he had won the hearts of Soviet readers.

This curious tribute to a Czech writer currently denounced by Czech communists was a shock for critics, and a source of spiteful amusement for their readers. It seemed very unfair that, just when the Czechs were valiantly striving to echo the Soviet line, the rug should be pulled from beneath their feet by a person who, being Russian, was beyond their own criticism. Their position was the more embarrassing because of the pretence of free speech. Nowhere had the Party or government issued any edict directing that Čapek or anybody else should be attacked as a writer. Because Štoll, Taufer, etc. made statements which led critics into certain attitudes, this gave the latter no alibi when their own comments, following what they believed to be the official line, were turned to ridicule by a pronouncement from Moscow.

A further shock was administered when the Czech poet Ladislav Fikar published in 1952 a translation of verse, *Love Stanzas*, from the pen of the Soviet writer Shchipachev.[5] A favourite contrast in Czech Marxist criticism was between 'civic', and 'personal' or 'subjective', art. Civic art was 'objective', i.e. it reflected the socialist construct of reality; thematically it was involved with such vital issues as the conduct of the farm or factory, the peace struggle, and the ideological fight against imperialism. 'Personal' or 'subjective' poetry, involved with love, flowers, nature, and such like, was a retreat from reality into the childish world of dreams, idylls, and self-indulgent sentimentality. Love poetry had not disappeared in Czechoslovakia, but it was in disrepute. Shchipachev's love lyrics were not exactly startling by Western standards, but their publication added confusion to the Czech literary scene. At one stroke they rehabilitated a type of literature which the stern disciples of soc-real doctrine had thought to extirpate. Worse still was the phenomenal popularity of the book with the Czech readers. The first edition was sold out within days, and the Youth Publishing House brought out a second edition of 10,000 copies. Within two years the translation went through three reprints before popular demand was satisfied. There was general satisfaction that modern Soviet literature was at last achieving popularity; but from the ideological point of view it was the wrong kind of literature. Its success effectively disproved the claim that the Czech public desired nothing more than what had been hitherto the typical products of the soc-real style, that is the ideologically orientated, constructivist type. Its publication in Moscow likewise revealed that the Czech critics had only imperfect understanding of what constituted 'socialist literature'. In any case they did not spare their praises for the book. 'We are enchanted by the touch of something pure, noble, honourable, and true. A new feeling, a new attitude to the world breathes from the poems. Only a *new* man could have written them – a Soviet man. And we long to become such...' Another critic discovered that a poem, while expressing socialist feelings, need not do so by reference to tractors and such things. 'Love poetry also can express the *new relationships of socialist society.*' The book became a springboard for some tactful homilies: 'An idea had grown up among us that under socialism man ceases to feel the touch of sadness; or if he does, there will be no place for such feelings in poetry. This view is confounded by Shchipachev's book.'

In retrospect the cultural thaw which has been generally identified with the post-Stalinist period, seems to have been anticipated in Prague. In 1952 the excesses of the critics were curbed, and writers who had been silenced returned to public life. An anthology of verse, *The Poetic Almanac of 1953*, which in fact was collected in the previous year, is significant in its content. Not only is Seifert restored to a place of honour, but one finds again the names of Kamil Bednář and the ex-surrealist Ludvík Kundera. The Introduction (dated to June 1952) was written by Závada, who touched cautiously on current problems of criticism:

Together with our whole society our poets are passing
through a stage of rebirth, in ideas and in art. They no longer
concern themselves with their inner problems, but live to the
full amid the life of their people and their native land. In contemporary Czech poetry the life of our people is reflected in its
many-sided complexity... From our journals have disappeared verses which instead of pure human feelings produced
merely general phrases... The struggle for a truthful and fine
poetry is far from over. Our poets need to portray more deeply and truthfully our people's heroic fight for a happier future;
they need to develop still further their ideological and artistic equipment. We must get rid of the last traces of formalism
and naturalism. We must avoid cheap optimism and idyllism,
garrulity and preciosity... The prime aim of the editor of
Poetic Almanac 1953 has been to acquaint the reader with the
whole broad front of our poetry. In it therefore there appear
the names of some writers who have not been publishing
recently, and whom we need to mobilise for future work...[6]

Závada's words express what he conceived to be the new middle-of-
the road policy for literature – a rejection of schematism, and a general closing of the ranks. An unintentional touch of irony was his use of
the word 'mobilise' in a literary context. In fact so much of the Party's
cultural programme, with its drumfire of propaganda, its violent
slogans, its use of intimidation and appeals to mass hatred, had given
the impression of a *campaign* in a contrived civil war situation – a recreation of the post-revolutionary period in Russia.

The silencing and intimidation of the pre-war socialist writers had
been one of the cruder excesses of the Stalinist period. The correction
of that excess, the rehabilitation of non-communists like Čapek, and
the widening of the concept of socialist literature, could be interpreted
as evidence of a milder line in cultural affairs. They did not however
imply any relaxation of Party control over literature; and while a
milder tone was adopted towards those regarded as basically friendly to the regime, the 'class enemy' was treated with undiminished
ferocity. Recent events and pronouncements had produced a certain
confusion of criteria. It was time for the Party to spell out its policy in
clear terms.

What appeared to be the new, officially approved, guidelines appeared in a joint article by Taufer and Štoll in *Literární noviny.*[7] In the
article Slánský was accused of having divided the left wing; of under-
estimating the strength of reaction; and of failing to identify the true

class enemies. In the Syndicate of Czech Writers in 1947 there had been men like Peroutka, B. Fučík, and J. Knap, 'a nest of counter-revolutionary feeling'. Now that Slánský had fallen, it was time to put an end to this cosy, apolitical, chumminess among the literati. The enemy was to be found in Catholic, agrarian Fascists of the former literary periphery. Compromised even in pre-Munich days as traitors, voices of reaction and racism, they were still continuing in their pro-Fascist line.

> After Palivec,[8] behind whose "pure poetry" there lay concealed the filthy mentality of a spy, we have encountered before the People's Courts people like Kostohryz or V. Renč,[9] who in pre-Munich days called Karel Čapek an enemy of Czechoslovakia.

The article posed the question on which side of the barricade each stood. The critic's duty was to determine from the general attitude of a writer whether he was with the communists or against them; and not to aim shafts at men on his own side. The article went on to exhort critics to liquidate the remnants of Slanskyism in literature; by which was meant apparently ultra left-wing attacks on the pre-war avant-garde and other pro-communist writers. On the other hand Taufer and Štoll warned fiercely against any turning towards liberalism, or tolerance of the unprincipled products of bourgeois literature. There must be no underestimation of the importance of ideology in art, nor weakness towards wrong opinions, or any idea that the decadent trends of bourgeois art had any claim to be called progressive. Finally the article sharply criticised *Literární noviny* itself for airing incorrect views and tolerating a revival of formalist and decadent trends. The rejection of the *sectarian* (i.e. ultra-radical) views of Slánský must not be followed by a revival of *liberal* views. A danger of the latter was seen in a recent pronouncement by V. Nezval: while rebutting the extremist attacks on art by Slanskyists he had been wrong to defend the style of cubism in painting.

Such were the limits of the cultural thaw, as laid down by the Taufer-Štoll team. While checking the antics of the doctrinaire radicals, it flatly rejected any deviation from the official line. Ideological conformity was still to be the basis of literary criticism: the schematists had gone wrong, not primarily because of their schematism, but because they had unmasked the *wrong enemies*. The Party thus reaffirmed its faith in the crude attitudes of the past, but pointed out to the critics a safe target. The writers of the Catholic, so-called Ruralist, school were revealed as an acceptable scapegoat. They had already been hounded out of literary life; they were now treated as traitors and saboteurs. They were arrested for complicity in a fictitious conspiracy, and sentenced to savage terms of imprisonment. The group included the poet Zahradníček, novelists J. Knap and F. Křelina, the critic Bedřich Fučík, and the poet-historian Z. Kalista[10]. In years to come their innocence was officially established, and some survived their terrible ordeal to tell of their experience. This cynical liquidation of a whole literary school was among the most repulsive crimes of literary Stalinism in Prague.

The last months of 1952 were a time of doubts and disarray in the Czech cultural milieu. Officially and ostensibly all was optimism. Administratively advocated, extravagantly praised, socialist-realism dominated the scene: minor deviations, even from Moscow, could not shake its authority. But behind the front of unity there was no little confusion. Most ominous for the future of Czech literature was the deep distrust which had grown between writer and public – a gap which corresponded to the increasing alienation between government and governed. The Party professed zealous interest in the welfare and purity of literature, but in fact their energies were urgently required elsewhere, for Czechoslovakia was now facing a real crisis. Since 1948 the country had made impressive progress in heavy industry, contributing notably to the frantic re-armament drive of the whole Soviet bloc. But the progress had been at the expense of consumer goods and transport. The Czechoslovak economy had been driven much too hard by the Russians, and the resulting havoc showed itself in wide and hardly veiled dissatisfaction. All shortcomings were officially blamed on the victims of the purges; and the tempo of terror accelerated. Amid this bizarre atmosphere were paraded the slogans of grotesque optimism: LIVING IS BETTER: LIVING IS MORE JOYOUS. Winter closed in upon a city plagued with transport break-downs, coal rationing, and production failures through lack of fuel.

Before the Spring of 1953 arrived, Stalin and Gottwald were both dead. As Malenkov announced a new course of co-existence with the West, Tito was on a state visit to London. The strange kaleidoscope of events was enlivened by a Moscow announcement reversing one of Stalin's final paranoic gestures, the arrest of the Kremlin doctors. At the same time came the first hints of a purge within the Russian Security apparatus. Complaints were aired of illegal practices by the Soviet secret political police. The position of Beria himself was shaken: within three months he disappeared from public life, and the report of his arrest for treason followed.

The death of Stalin seemed like the end of an era – perhaps the end of the cold war itself; perhaps even the end of the great terror which had held Eastern Europe since the end of war. Internally the curb to the power of the secret police in Russia, externally the movement towards co-existence, raised the possibility of new genuinely liberal course. In Prague there was uncertainty: grown accustomed to instructions from the Centre, all awaited the next move. If the new Soviet government were to liberalise its relations with the satellites, and purge the guilt of the Beria agents, it could be the end of the authority of the Soviet 'advisors', especially the Security group, who had organised the show trials, ordered the arrest of Czech communists, and set up a ruling cadre outside and above the official Czechoslovak organs. Slánský and his associates had been dead less than six months; three members of the group had escaped the death penalty and were serving their life sentences. The attitude of the government to the Slánský trial and to the survivors, who knew the whole story of the faked evidence and forced confessions, was crucial. A kind of paralysis lay on Czech public life while the decisions about the future of the Party and the country were made in Moscow: today's prisoners might well be tomorrow's leaders; and vice versa. But as the weeks passed, hopes of a great change began to fade. There were changes in Soviet personnel, but the Soviet presence in Prague remained: there was no rehabilitation, and no exposures of malpractice. In May a new series of political show trials began. At the same time the Czech government introduced drastic measures to meet the financial crisis: a currency reform was carried through which had the practical effect of wiping out savings above a certain level. The public response was hostile; strikes broke out at Prague and Ostrava. In Pilsen a riot situation developed, with workers and Security police facing each other in ugly confrontation. In East Germany the situation was similar, and the world heard for the first time of workers rising in armed conflict against the government which ruled in their name. The risings were crushed without difficulty: the workers proved helpless before the overwhelming power at the disposal of their political bosses. It seemed that nothing had been achieved, and a new era of repression was commencing. Yet, in the cultural field, a fresh wind was blowing.

In Moscow there had appeared signs of open discussion quite alien to the Stalinist epoch. The delicate question of the writer's freedom was raised in article by Ilya Ehrenburg, 'On the Work of an Author'. He remarked, among other things, that a writer is not a piece of machinery; nor does he write merely because he has been elected a member of the Writers' Union: his work is an expression of himself, and holds up a mirror to the world as he himself sees it.[11] It seemed that the Party's right to lay down literary guidelines was being called into question. At a conference of Soviet critics the view was expressed that the work of writers had been hindered rather than helped by directions from above. The literary journal *Novy Mir* became a centre of lively discussion, and its editor, Alexander Tvardovsky was identified with a liberal approach to literary problems in general. In December *Novy Mir* printed an essay by V. Pomerantsev 'On Sincerity in Literature', which went further in pressing the case for freedom of composition. In effect Pomerantsev claimed that an author's first duty was fidelity to his own inner convictions: a prime criterion of value in a literary work was the degree of frankness with which it was expressed.

Such heretical utterances provoked as much uncertainty in Prague as in Moscow. During Stalin's lifetime the Czech communists had learned that if there was any safety, it lay in an unquestioning acceptance of the Moscow line. But now the problem was to know exactly what *was* the Moscow line. In the cultural field there could hardly be a rigid enforcement of policy when no one was quite sure what the policy would turn out to be. In the meantime a greater freedom of manoeuvre was possible. The Russian debate was followed attentively in Prague, and the unorthodox views of the Russian comrades were dutifully reprinted in the Czech journals. Under their safe cover it was possible for the Czechs too to question the value of bureaucratic interference and enforced conformity.

In an officially approved attempt to liven up the Czech literary scene, there had been a mild revival of satire; the targets were of course limited to those in official disrepute. Satire now began to turn on less orthodox objectives. J. Marek, hitherto known as a fervent exponent of literary orthodoxy, pictured the plight of the critic, desperate for some guidance about what he was supposed to say:

> In the old days, he pondered, the situation was clear. There were papers which praised everything and papers which did the reverse. It was easy to write then. But today there is such uncontrolled *freedom*. What am I saying? Freedom? Anarchy! Write something, and you are in trouble[12]...

After 1948 the critic had been exalted to a high position: as the vigilant mentor of writers and the guide to readers, he had been the key to Party control of literature. Now, bewildered, abused and ridiculed, the critic was becoming a figure of fun. A conference of Czech literary critics was held, but no firm conclusions or easy solutions appeared. The old practice of replacing literary comment by political denunciation was explicitly disowned. But the arch exponents of the technique, Štoll and Taufer, were too high to be criticised themselves. If there was to be a reform, it would be imposed from above. The conference solemnly affirmed its adherence to the literary principles bequeathed by Klement Gottwald!

For those who looked in vain for a clear lead from Moscow, the uncertainty must have been agonising. Fortunately for the dogmatists the interval of doubt was of short duration. Early in 1954 *Pravda* began to call for stricter control over the artists. Pomerantsev's article came in for bitter attack, and the Ministry of Culture took time off to rebuke him. Ehrenburg was adversely criticised; Tvardovsky denounced, and dismissed from his editorial post. The hard-liner Surkov came forward as the spokesman for a policy of renewed toughness towards the dissidents. In April four Soviet writers were expelled from the Writers' Union. The hope of genuine liberalisation seemed to have died when Surkov supported the application of the notorious Zhdanov decrees, which had laid down the guidelines of Stalinist art.

After this, the time was ripe for the 'normalisation' of the Czech cultural scene. The Central Committee of the Writers' Union met, and recorded its official disapproval of both Slanskyism and the new wave of liberalism, subjectivism, and sentimentality detected in recent work. The influence of Pomerantsev was noted with sorrow, and blamed for a movement in Czech writing away from objective to subjective criteria, from civic to personal poetry, and towards a 'misguided' stress on spontaneity in literature. The meeting reaffirmed the unbreakable bond between sound ideology and artistic value. Later, at the Party Congress held in Prague, the lesson was driven home to the erring writers. In particular Kopecký and Novotný flayed the satirists,who were accused of bad taste, vulgarity, and an underrating of the people's class consciousness. Under no circumstances would they tolerate efforts to slander and ridicule the Party and its glorious role: such slander could benefit only the Reaction.[13]

It seemed that the interval of semi-freedom, or of exploration, was over: communist literature had returned to its blind alley. But the impression was misleading. No purges followed; there were literary scandals; but less intimidation. The regime in Moscow, and consequently that in Prague, was moving with caution. Externally the USSR was anxious to improve its image, and had no intention of stepping up tension or outraging world opinion. In spite of its stern rebukes to erring artists the Czechoslovak Communist Party took no overt action against them: the writers were left to settle their own quarrels. Perhaps it was felt that the role of creative literature in moulding public attitudes had been over-estimated. Now that the terrifying figure of Stalin had been removed, men like Kopecký, who had his lighter side, and Zápotocký, who had literary aspirations, felt they could afford to look with more indulgence on the idiosyncrasies of the artists.

In any case books had been written and published during the interval and their influence could not easily be eradicated. Ehrenburg's novel *The Thaw* was perhaps the most striking relic of the period, outlasting it and keeping alive the hopes which accompanied its creation. In Czech literature it was verse which led the way in deviating, first cautiously, then more boldly, from what had been the officially enjoined style. Personal lyric became more common, more self-expressive, and in some cases more challenging. A landmark of the period was a collection of verse by the young poet Milan Kundera, entitled *Man, a wide garden*.[14] It was socialist writing of a bold programmatic type, but with a difference. Its socialism was closer in spirit to that of the early 'proletarian' poets of the 'twenties than to the versified sloganry of the 'fifties: it was a return to what has been termed 'socialist humanism'. Kundera's themes were the personal problems of individual cases. Hostile critics noted the immaturity, the lack of *objectivity* of the work, and dismissed it as an irrelevant throwback to the old lyric of personal drama. Kundera however was far from being an ivory tower dreamer. Undaunted by the threatening atmosphere of the recent past, he used his poems to give back to the Stalinists invective in their own style:

> gloomy priests who shut themselves in Marxism
> in the cold citadel...

Kundera had no objection to using art as a platform of social action; but to the general surprise, he seemed to be turning official theses inside out:

> 'The new morale' you said
> 'Pioneering élan'!
> Parading on the First of May
> Arms waving
> Like a windmill

In one dreary, mournful cantata.
Sails turning
Precisely as the wind prescribed.
A mill. A wooden mill.
Each time my woman's eye would seek to catch your human voice
I heard the creaking sails.
Crying? What is there to regret?
I'm leaving... the wind blows on.
Keep turning! Turning![15]

Kundera's outbursts were somewhat ahead of his time. As the rein over literature tightened again, such programmatic gestures were rare. But the shift of interest from the monumental to the human dimension, from abstract constructs to personal expression, went on. When one looks back at the products of that time, they seem less important aesthetically, but necessary, as a way back to genuine realism. In conditions when values are perverted and criteria confused, the touch of normality and sanity can be a liberating experience.

Officially, the old politically committed literature was still heavily favoured, and critics penned severe comments on 'unhealthy' trends in contemporary writing away from ideology and social principle, and on 'spineless, unprincipled aesthetes who tolerate writing estranged from, and alien to the working folk': such trends were liable to lead 'to the underrating of civic poetry and militant literature'.[16] There were always critics and writers ready to oblige with examples of the right way about things: a good example of officially approved art of the time was a monumental volume by many hands entitled *Stalin is the Life of the Future!*[17] It came appropriately at a time when the government was earnestly commemorating the great dictator with a gigantic statue of unbelievable ugliness overlooking the centre of Prague. The commemoration, both in words and in stone, were soon to become an unexpected embarrassment.

The shifts and uncertainties of official policy, the diminished vigilance of the Party towards creative literature, helped towards a greater differentiation in literary production. Books of the pre-communist era were republished: new novels of socialist construction were still appearing; but so was a fresh harvest of lyric verse quite alien to Stalinist norms. It was well received by the reading public, and its popularity was no doubt aided by aversion to the heavy diet of officially inspired, wearisomely didactic, work. But the popularity of lyric with a wide section of the community suggests that it responded to a genuine cultural need. Czech literature – acknowledged as the voice of its people, the embodiment of their language, the scrapbook of their past and future – had lost its way. It was as if the threads of tradition had been broken, and only the delicate hand of the poet could resume them. After a great catastrophe it is sometimes necessary to return to first principles: writers, seeking a fresh beginning, instinctively search for the motifs which are familiar, because very old. They can speak again to their audience through themes and shared recollections which will strike up answering vibrations. In seeking to overcome the alienation of writer and reader, the poets had to begin in what had become almost a foreign language, deformed by falsity and known deceit. Every image and phrase was an exploration, an attempt to resume contact on uncertain ground. It was natural that the ground chosen should be that of human feelings, the world of nature, of folklore and of children.

In the darkest days of Stalinism a first tentative beginning had been essayed, and by a poet of whom one might least have expected it. V. Nezval, official poet of the regime, had left his desk at the Ministry of Information in 1950 after a heart attack, and returned for a prolonged convalescence to his native Moravia. There he had composed the long poem *From the Home Country*[18], a title intended to revive memories of Smetana's symphonic poem. There was nothing ideologically unsound about the book, which looked at the past of the toiling village through the eyes of the socialist present. But in retrospect the book has significance as an untopical offering - a turning back from civic programmatic poetry to the idylls of the land. The poet of the barricades had come back to his roots. The woods and the cherry orchards of his Moravian home, the old ways of village life, were for Nezval the first step back to a resumption of his career as a lyric poet.

After the First World war the Czech Expressionist poets had begun again by adopting the styles of children: to see the new world it was necessary to look through the eyes of the very young, whose sight was not warped nor feeling deformed by catastrophe. So too in the early 'fifties, Czech artists drew from the children's art, where so many of them had found refuge, the inspiration for a fresh start. The style of writing and illustration of children's books remained mainly conservative: children's art was inextricably connected with folklore and the oldest traditions of Czech culture. Written in simple style by the most sensitive poets, illustrated in traditional colours and styles, the children's books of the 'fifties remain a touching monument to the continuity of Czech cultural tradition. It was from here that a fresh beginning could arise.

Dogmatic formulae, dehumanised models, false optimism, which had disfigured common literature, had left writers with the guilt of conscious deception. By contrast children's art seemed like an island of peace and truth. If literature were ever again to fulfill its social function. of holding up a mirror to society and challenging its conscience, first it must purge itself of lies, and win the trust of its readers. Children's art can present its own truth – obliquely expressed, but no less effective for that. The vision of the adult world through the eyes of children is rather disturbing at the best of times. The angle of vision is strange, and the perspective unfamiliar. Adult literature may accept as the natural order an arrangement of functions around a centre of power. The children's world has an inverted order; for there the centre is the child – symbol of weakness and vulnerability, facing menaces larger than life. In stories and poems where the reader's sympathy is drawn to the animals, insects, and flowers, and the enemies are giants, or wicked adults, one detects a perhaps unconscious social allegory. All the massed power of the incomprehensible system is ranged against the hapless individual: but his weakness triumphs over the force of ogres. In a world where the cult of materialism was officially propagated; where the tractor and the factory were the symbols of human progress; it was left to children's art to keep alive the belief in miracles, the realm of dreams, irrational hopes, and escape into harmless mischief. But the fantasy of children's literature is accompanied by its own brand of realism; for there things are called by their real names, without false associations: it is the eyes of children which detect – because they cannot comprehend – the deception of the Emperor's new clothes. Qualities native to child art – humility, trust, belief – appeared to Czech readers the more precious by contrast to the bombast, deception, cynicism, which breathed from the officially praised products of socreal literature.

Among the established writers who made for themselves a new reputation as the authors of children' literature were F. Branislav, F. Nechvátal, Kamil Bednář, and Nezval himself. A poet who stepped out of literary politics and for ten years devoted his talents almost exclusively to child prose and poetry was František Hrubín. His work and his stance won him great popularity, and he came to be regarded as the type of artist, silenced by faceless bureaucracy, who found his own way to speak to the people via personal lyric. Between 1947 and 1956, when he returned to the literary stage as a straight lyric poet, he published twenty five books for children, and in 1953 was honoured with a state prize. Hrubín's verses were in the tradition of Czech folk art; in some cases actually inspired by paintings in the folk style. Seifert, in his book *A Painter Went Humbly out into the World*,[19] did something similar, though intended primarily for an adult audience. In 1954 he produced a new book which was soon acclaimed as a classic of modern Czech literature. Entitled simply *Mother*[20] it combined the elements of traditional art and return to the world of childhood. In itself it summed up a whole trend of literature away from the monumental to the humble; from public themes to private; from the pseudo-reality of political slogans to the known reality of Czech home life which was the product of its past.

The trend was set by older writers, men of calibre and reputation, who had played no part in the degradation of literature by schematism. It was a trend which was welcomed, because needed, in the circumstances of the time; and younger writers followed it; often with disastrous results. Homely motifs and simple themes are among the hardest to manage, and require for success a mature art: artless forms can appear merely silly: appeals to the heart can be offensively *heartwarming*. Critics dismissed the swarm of love ditties, nature poems, and folksy songs as trivial and sentimental. Others defended them as inspiring, patriotic, and a reaction to Slanskyist *cosmopolitanism* (a feared term of abuse at the time). At any rate the trend seemed politically harmless: the Party culture bosses might well be relieved, after the failure of the programmatic, committed literature that it was at least steering into waters quite disengaged from current problems. Young rhymsters, old opportunists, such as are found on the periphery of any literary world, now churned out romantic pieces with as much facility as they had recently inscribed socialist hymns. As might be expected, the trend was short: once it had served its necessary purpose of clearing the ground and providing a springboard to new work, it passed away, leaving few books of value contributed by the younger generation. A not unconvincing relic of the time is *The Czech Dream*[21] by Josef Kainar. In his earliest post-war period a poet of existentialist absurdity, Kainar had plunged into the dangerous waters of political verse, not entirely without success. Turning to child art he had produced an attractive puppet play (*Goldilocks*).[22] Playwright, satirist, composer of pop lyrics, Kainar belonged to the Moravian tradition which had once produced the composer Janáček. Together with Milan Kundera and Jan Skácel he belonged to a group with local affiliations and disinclined to be dazzled by the dominance of Prague in cultural life. In *The Czech Dream* Kainar confronted the difficult days of the present with the nation's crises of the past. The Czech dream, not a utopia or a sociological construct, appeared as a communal experience, a memory which was also a hope. It sprang from a cavalcade of history, linked by imagination and expressed by poetry. Kainar's grasp of tradition enabled him to handle the demanding task of recreating the past. His book recalls the literature of the Munich period or of pre-war, setting the trials of the present into the perspective of previous times. Now, as before in Czech art, its immense reserves of national feeling and tradition were being tapped to provide momentum for a fresh start in a new Spring.

By the summer of 1955 it was clear that the worst period of cultural Stalinism was over. There were no more purges: literary questions could be debated without evoking charges of treason or the intervention of the secret police. Government spokesmen appealed for the co-operation of all sectors of the intelligentsia, irrespective of political or religous creed. A partial amnesty was proclaimed, and emigrés were encouraged to return to their homeland. A mark of relaxation in Prague was the reopening of cafés and restaurants which had been closed in the hard times as relics of a discarded way of life. The iron curtain began to dissolve, and cultural contact was resumed with heretical Jugoslavia and bourgeois France, traditional centre of Western culture for Czech artists.

In 1954 Nezval, now officially styled a National Artist, went back to Paris for a brief visit. For him it was like stepping backwards twenty years: they had been years which had swept away friends, hopes, and illusions. The Paris of his pre-war Surrealist days was still there, but Paul Eluard was gone. The poems which Nezval wrote during his French stay were naturally published in Prague. Far from rhetoric, from optimism, and from any idea of soc-real constructivism, the poems, with their elegaic, almost openly decadent, languor, set the seal of the Master on the return of lyric unencumbered by political overtones. The poems were published as a collection entitled *Cornflowers and Towns*.[23] In the book Nezval reaffirmed his stature, and found his way back to the public which had admired him. In Prague the era of mandatory optimism and Stalinist culture was over. It was the lyric poet who had led the way in the struggle for more artistic freedom: now his right to be *himself* was openly asserted, and, by default, conceded.

The thaw was gathering pace among Czechoslovakia's communist neighbours; and the cultural exchanges fostered in Stalinist days to ensure ideological uniformity, were now spreading dissident views. In 1948-9 when the Czech communists might have preferred to go more slowly with the class-war, and the tightening of authority, they had been pushed along by the examples around them. The trial of Rajk in Hungary, and the unmasking of Titoists elsewhere, had been the mandatory model of their own trials and repression. Now, when in Prague the Party was tolerating, and cautiously regulating, a policy of relaxation, they were again overtaken by the wilder actions of their neighbours. In Budapest, at the annual meeting of the Hungarian Writers' Association in 1954 its President P. Verres openly declared the worthlessness of all literature based on lies. The thaw was being encouraged by the New Course leadership of Imre Nagy; but free discussion exposed the alarming hatreds which had been aroused by Stalinist policies. The situation was getting out of hand, and in 1955 following the resignation of Malenkov in Russia, Nagy himself was replaced by the hard-line Rakosi. A policy of open repression followed, and the intelligentsia was ranged against the Party. Unfortunately for Rakosi, the new regime in Moscow lent no support to a neo-Stalinist policy, and Rakosi himself fell, after the rehabilitation of Rajk, and the exposure of the hideous chicanery of the trials. Shame, shock, mutual accusations, followed. The New Course was restored in Hungary, leaving a situation more critical than before Rakosi's crude attempts to stifle the truth. From Prague all this was being closely followed. The extraordinary sequence of events had exposed the insecurity of the Party's control, and the terrible secrets waiting to be divulged. The demand by Hungarians to know the truth inevitably affected the Czechs, who remembered that this was the regime with which their own government had walked hand in hand.

Meanwhile in Poland political events had been overshadowed by literary scandals. After some hesitation the policy of cultural relaxation had been accepted by the ruling front (P.Z.P.R.), but the Party apparatus was finding it increasingly difficult to keep proper control over the airing of grievances, and the correcting of past errors. In literature it was lyric poetry which in Warsaw, as in Prague, led the way towards the exposure of the truth. Adam Wazyk had been regarded as a fanatical Stalinist in the early fifties, completely subservient to the Party, a Polish poet who had sold his soul to communism. When the truth began to emerge, and Wazyk felt himself a victim of deception, he turned his anger on his deceivers:

> The nation was working and
> philosophical scoundrels attacked us;
> they have stolen our brains bit by bit
> and left us merely belief.

A man on stilts taught us the art of walking,
blind men were lifting torches
a deaf man was searching conscience at the market place
ascetics bred crimes.[24]

He was sent to the new industrial complex of Nowa Huta to write about this triumph for socialist construction. The result was a series of sketches published together as *Poem for Adults*. A theme is the inversion of truth, exemplified by the terrible contrast between the idea of a workers' paradise and the squalid truth of Nowa Huta:

From villages and little towns they come in carts
to build a foundry and dream out a city,
dig out of the soil a new Eldorado...
the great migration, the twisted ambition,
with a string on their necks – the cross of Czestochowa...
the huge mob, shoved suddenly
out of medieval darkness: inhuman Poland
howling with boredom on December nights...

                              * * *

It's true!
when the brass trumpets of boredom
jam the great educational aim,
when vultures of abstraction eat out our brains,
when our language is reduced to thirty magic formulas,
when the lamp of imagination dies out,
when the good people from the moon
refuse us the right to have taste,
it's true,
we are in peril of ignorance and stupidity.

                              * * *

All this is not new. The Cerberus of socialist morality is old.
Fourier, the dreamer, charmingly foretold
that lemonade would flow in seas.
Does it not flow?
They drink seawater,
and cry:
Lemonade!
returning home secretly
to vomit.
to vomit![25]

Poem for Adults was published in Poland in August 1955. It was the most open expression of anger, disillusion, and despair yet to appear in print behind the Iron curtain. Bitterly attacked in the Party press, the poem converted Wazyk, once an object of hatred, into the hero of the hour. The poem was translated, and its fame quickly spread beyond the frontiers: by the end of the year it was already circulating in Prague. It was a strange experience to see in print what many had thought, but none had published. It ended a period when the limit of an artist's hope was for some toleration and indulgence from above: for the first time the message was of rebellion, and implied a demand for retribution.

The summer of 1955 saw the unveiling of Stalin's statue in Prague. Above the swelling doubts and infectious dissatisfaction the statue towered in all its imposing grandeur, symbol of a monolithic power impervious to assault. While Stalin stood, the Czech communists could feel that the reins were still firmly and unchallengeably in their hands. But the crimes and the lies of the past were not forgotten, and could not be undone: truth exists in the minds of men, and cannot be forever concealed by massive structures of words or stone. While men looked up trustingly, or apprehensively, at the great statue above them, the explosive was already being prepared which would blow it to atoms.

V

The Flowers of Evil

'Let a hundred different flowers bloom!
Let a hundred different ways of thought contend!'

Mao-tse-tung

In February 1956 the XXth Congress of the USSR Communist Party was held in Moscow: it was attended by Party dignitaries from the satellite states, including Novotný from Czechoslovakia. Apparently they were inadequately briefed about the thunderous revelations which were to come, for up to the eve of the Congress they were still making laudatory references to the memory of Stalin. As the Congress proceeded, from the unwieldy and unreadable bulk of the Soviet leaders' speeches emerged a realisation that a new line radically different from that of recent years was being laid down. The policy of co-operation with non-communist parties, and of a parliamentary road to socialism, were restored from the limbo of heresy. Old Bolsheviks long dead were ceremoniously rehabilitated. The policy of peaceful co-existence on an international level was to be pursued with increased vigour. Above all, and as a symbol of an end to the old ways, Stalin was flayed with a ferocity which became apparent only when the 'secret' speech of Khrushchev was leaked. The self-erected idol, the symbol of Soviet leadership and communist dedication, was exposed as a blood-thirsty tyrant, obsessed with imagined threats, cynically ordering the deaths of faithful followers for imaginary conspiracies.

The conclusions to be drawn from the Soviet change of policy were not at all clear: one thing which was apparent was that Stalinism, as a way of government, thought, and administration, was officially taboo. One of the features of Stalinist policy had been the development of a form of Soviet imperialism towards the satellites. The leaders and the people of the latter might well ask themselves whether the new Soviet course involved an end to such imperialism. The intentions of the Russians were awaited with mingled hope and apprehension – with hope by the majority who looked for relief from external pressure and internal repression, with apprehension by those whose jobs, power, and privileges seemed threatened by any change of policy which was likely to eliminate the favourites of Stalin. In these circumstances they proceeded with the utmost caution, feeling out the intentions of Moscow, avoiding internal scandals, and seeking maximum co-operation both within and also outside the Party. The powers of the Security police were curbed and a relaxed atmosphere was encouraged. Political prisoners were released with a minimum of publicity; it was impossible to make public restitution and admit that the great purge had been a conspiracy between Party and Security, because the present leadership was involved in the guilt. Compounding the deception, they put the guilt on Slánský himself, who had allegedly corrupted the Security service and fallen in the trap he had laid for others. Thus the Czech leadership rode out the storm, blandly avoiding fuss, and calming the demands for reform with a fresh crop of soothing lies. The Kafka image of government persisted; nothing was shunned more resolutely than truth and reality. The Russians made no move towards interference; nor did they offer any obvious guidance. Through the Spring and Summer of 1956 in Prague there prevailed a mood of uncertainty – about the intentions of Moscow, the attitude to be adopted by the Party, and the extent of the thaw in both international affairs and home policies. The field for manoeuvre was greater than at any time since 1948, and the risks were less. For those hardy souls who sought to reconnoitre the permitted limits of cultural freedom, no better opportunity was likely to arise.

A Congress of the Czechoslovak Writers Union had been fixed for April 1956. It had been intended to discuss various organisational matters and questions of common interest, and to digest the wisdom divulged at the Soviet Writers' congress held at the end of 1954. There was every expectation that the Czechoslovak Congress would take the form of a public relations exercise for the régime. Greetings from the Party, addresses of welcome, formal speeches, and previously approved resolutions, would advertise the solidarity of the literary front to the Czech public and to the world at large. Of course, any meeting of artists is likely to throw up a few wild statements and attitudes; but the leadership of the Union was in trustworthy hands, and no serious attempt to challenge its authority was contemplated. To make it quite clear that a Party line on literature was still in force, and that no challenge to it would be tolerated, the President, Zápotocký himself, had laid down the line in a statement to the writers before Christmas 1955:

> We cannot retreat one step from our principles: we are building socialism, and intend to finish the job. We will subordin-

ate everything to this basic principle, even literary and artistic work. Our artists are all for socialism, but they keep saying: 'Give us freedom, so we can do anything we want.' In reply I say: 'We will not give such freedom to our artists, because if we did, we should be unable to build socialism... Artists must realise this, especially those who dream of unlimited freedom for art, those who dream of art for art's sake.[1]

But between the planning of the Congress and its realisation fell the Soviet revelations, and the official dethronement of Stalin. It was the Czech Party leaders who were now on the defensive, and the writers met in atmosphere of exhilerating uncertainty, quite unforeseen by the original conveners.

A lively discussion was afoot in the literary journals during the weeks preceding the Congress. Previous aims of the agenda were already out of date: the chief task evidently was to apply the lessons of the Soviet XX Congress. Its relevance to literature was obvious: in Moscow no less an authority than Sholokhov had stressed the disastrous effects of Stalinism on Russian literature and cultural life. The Writers' Congress in Prague was a golden opportunity to follow the Russian example in rooting out of cultural life all *non-Leninist* methods. What were these methods in the Czech milieu? Writers in the journals obligingly provided a comprehensive list. To begin with, there was the centralised and bureaucratic control of literary activity by the Writers Union itself. There was a record of inattention to the feelings of rank-and-file artists, and especially to the tastes of readers. Literary judgement had been replaced by authoritative political pronouncements: in fear of committing mortal error, writers had looked to the guidance of the infallibles set above them. The relationship between art and politics had degenerated to a state when art had surrendered its autonomy, and so made itself unfit to carry out its proper function in society. The crude limitation of cultural freedom was to be seen best in the case of so-called literary criticism, which had become merely a system of petrified dogma. Of such engaging frankness were the comments addressed to the coming meeting. It was taken for granted that an access of freedom would be permitted, and speakers anticipated it in their public discussion.[2] Suddenly the atmosphere was freer than it had been for years; and hopes soared for the results of the Congress.

It was held in Parliament House, Prague, from April 22 to 29, that is, in the days immediately preceding the official 1956 May Day celebrations. The awesome surroundings, the official setting, and the pomp of the opening proceedings were such as to discourage any thought of wild protests or stormy scenes. President of the Republic, Zápotocký, read out to the assembly a message from the Party Central Committee. It was taken as a matter of course that the direction and tone of the Congress would be regulated by the Party, which would decide what measure of liberalism it would tolerate. The thaw, if any, would be no less closely dictated than the repression to which it was responding.

Zápotocký's message was meant to be encouraging. It commended writers who had, despite obstacles, sought out new ways for themselves: it sternly warned against pomposity, pseudo-military jargon, and schematism: and it touched on the problem of artistic freedom in a socialist society:

> The Party has never prescribed, and never will prescribe to writers their literary work. We have always been against the regimentation of literature and the stifling of creative powers. We believe that the writer must enjoy full freedom, that he must march on alone in his artistic development... The Central Committee considers you to be the foremost helpers of the Party in the great cause of creating socialism in our society.[3]

During the first two days of the conference all seemed to be proceeding in accordance with official expectations. The Chairman Jan Drda read a long speech in which he touched cautiously on the changed atmosphere in public life: he acknowledged that some justifiable dissatisfaction had arisen through officials distorting the Party line, as well as through misplaced zeal on the part of inexperienced comrades among the writers. One of the early speakers was V. Nezval: his position of safe privilege, his erratic record, and his recent signs of literary unorthodoxy all suggested that he, if anyone, might be the spokesman of a new liberalism. But this elder statesman of revolutionary literature revealed a becoming caution in his criticism. Drawing attention to the positive achievements of Soviet poetry, he singled out Mayakovsky, Jesenin, Shchipachev, and above all his friend Boris Pasternak as praiseworthy examples. Nezval defended the persecuted Czech poets of his own generation, Biebl, Seifert, and Holan, and put much of the blame on younger critics like Ivan Skála. This technique, of shifting the blame on to minor figures who could not hit back, was recognised by listeners as one which belonged as much to the bad old days as did the excesses which Nezval was condemning. Nevertheless he managed to include an analysis of the 'personality cult' as it had been manifested in Czech literary life, and concluded that it was basically anti-artistic, and anti-intellectual: he spoke with scorn of the 'sergeant-majors of poetry', and suggested that Drda was himself not without blame.

Nezval seemed to have correctly gauged the extent of the freedom which the Party was prepared to offer: there would be less overt interference in literary work; for the harm done a few scapegoats would be offered, and these might include Drda himself, who seemed to have become expendable. Very little would be changed, and no tremendous revelations were to be expected. By the third day attendance at proceedings was falling, as interest waned. Then a minor revolution took place when, on the proposal of a rank-and-file member, the assembly voted to take routine reports as read, and leave more time for open discussion. Perhaps encouraged by this harmless victory František Hrubín, himself one of the recent victims of official displeasure, took the floor. His words were directed to the central problem for discussion, the present state of Czech literature:

> It was an unhealthy and degrading thing for Czech literature that in past years it has been impossible to discuss its problems openly. Now the possibility exists. I think it is my duty to express myself publicly on certain questions... Answers must be sought by us all, by us non-Party writers, as well as by communists... During the last few years I have, among other things, been studying the work of the so-called Accursed poets, Poe, Baudelaire, Verlaine... For weeks I tried vainly to translate Mallarmé's sonnet on the Swan.. What drama is contained in those verses on the agony of the swan condemned to the icebergs, and unable to extricate her frozen wing from the ice! How much more tragic has been the fate of Czech poetry in recent years! It, the heir to Mácha, Neruda, Bezruč, was likewise consigned to the ice. It was not in the likeness of a swan, but of a hunted and exhausted doe. Its blood, racing with the pursuit, did not congeal; the ice did not melt; poetry, driven frantic, faced the callous front of ice-cold dogma... I ask you how many talented people saw their wings frozen! how many perished in the icy crust!

Hrubín underlined the role of the poet as one who, seeking freedom for himself, helps to achieve it for others. Freedom he defined as the liberation of man from the chains of superstition, not only that transmitted by old beliefs, but new orthodoxies deliberately inculcated from without. Not long ago Fascism had inculcated its superstition; in more recent years writers had been found to lend their talents to shameful campaigns. Persecution had killed Biebl; isolated and ruined Kolář. Cruel, but true, were the words of poet Závada:

> Splendid are the funerals we can devise:
> but we are burying the living...

Hrubín ended his speech with a reference to Hans Andersen's story of the Emperor's New Clothes. The voice of the child who exposes the fraud is like the voice of the poet: he does not open the eyes of the people – they already see – but he opens their hearts; for he is their voice.[4]

As he ended his emotional speech, the audience rose to its feet, and gave him a standing ovation. The mood of the conference seemed transformed; and speaker after speaker came forward to express their views in frank terms. There were complaints of bureaucratic interference with literature, and crude regimentation: names began to fall, including that of the Minister Štoll. An unexpected development was the reaction of the younger writers who had been expected to carry the blame: Skála and Školaudy hit back at the older generation, exposing the crude hypocrisy of Nezval: he who now presumed to judge others, had himself, together with Jiří Taufer, usurped authority in the Union of Writers, and waged a reign of terror over his opponents. M. Sedloň asked when were they going to hear how exactly cultural policy *had* been made, i.e. who really was to blame:

> The people best qualified to explain are comrades V. Kopecký, Štoll, Hendrych, Taufer, Bareš, and the rest. But they are silent. The only people at whom the finger is pointed are those who have already lost their positions... I suppose we are not going to believe that it was Skála, Štern etc. who brought in these Draconic methods...

The meeting seemed to be getting out of hand. But an even more serious note was injected by Jaroslav Seifert. Himself a victim of the purge, a former communist, and a writer of tremendous popularity, he was in a strong position to demand a reckoning. Gravely he reverted to the idea of the writer as the conscience of his people:

> I am afraid we have not fulfilled this role for many years: we have not been the conscience of the many; we have not even been our own conscience... If an ordinary person is silent

about the truth, it may be a tactical manoeuvre. If a writer is
silent, he is lying...

Seifert recalled some of the injustices done to Czech writers, and claimed that it was their duty to rectify these injustices. That meant inviting
back to the literary field all those who had been unjustly silenced and
excluded, even as Seifert himself had been excluded. Secondly there
was the case of the writers actually in prison. If members present
admitted their errors and guilt, and these explanations were considered acceptable, then the errors and guilt of the imprisoned writers must
also be reconsidered. Seifert ended his speech with a request that the
new committee to be elected should take *immediate* steps to right the
wrongs done.

The tantrums of minor writers might be ignored as irresponsible;
but Seifert's detailed demands were too much for Zápotocký, who
replied for the regime. Acknowledging the poetic talents of Hrubín
and Seifert, he rejected their claims. As far as the rest were concerned,
Zápotocký could at least claim that he had stuck to his principles,
whereas it was increasingly obvious that some of the writers in the
room had revealed total inconsistency, not to say hypocrisy in their
change of front. On the final day of the conference elections for the
new officers were held. Chairman Drda saw his position of Chairman abolished. Two of the unpopular hard-liners, Taufer and Řezáč,
failed to secure election to the committee. The new First Secretary
was a 'safe' choice, Jan Otčenášek. Hrubín and Seifert were elected to
the committee; but so were Nezval and Drda. Delegates had let off
steam; and in some cases there had been statements which would not
lightly be forgotten. But the Party had the situation in hand.

When the excitement of the congress wore off, the heated words and
rebellious gestures seemed to have achieved very little. A test of their
effectiveness might be seen in the treatment of the imprisoned writers,
specifically, Zahradníček, Palivec, and Kalista. Seifert had more or
less demanded their release, or at least a review of their position. They
were not released; nor was any known review undertaken. It seemed
that the structure of power was impervious to words.[5]

But the subsequent course of events did not support such a view.
The writers' stand in 1956 could not be elminated from the record:
many times during the following years it was recalled; and historians
are agreed in regarding it as a decisive moment. One may ask why
Hrubín's reference to the Swan of Malarmé was so impressive in its
effect upon the audience. Poetry, symbolised in the bird whose graceful wings are meant for freedom, was pictured as trapped in an element

that lacked even the human association of chains. Who could not recognise, in the image of the bird, the fate of the whole Czech nation? Art, officially regarded as the moulder of public opinion for the regime, was now proclaimed as the latter's victim: by implication literature, together with its public, were ranged against its rulers. The antipathy was driven home by the startling implied comparison between the communist and the Nazi regimes. In calling writers the conscience of the people, Seifert had re-affirmed the ethical function of art, as Marxists had always believed. But by his half-veiled accusations of guilt in high places he disassociated the nation's conscience from that of its rulers. In their different ways Hrubín and Seifert both indicated the gulf which had arisen between governors and governed. Both implicitly rejected the role of spokesman and apologist for the regime – a role which had become institutionalised in the last few years. Dis-associating themselves from official guilt, and rejecting the patronage of power, the dissident writers appealed straight to the people: and at one stroke they crossed the gulf which had alienated them.

It had not been expected that a conference devoted to literary problems would take up the question of the political trials. But the dissident writers boldly linked the fate of literature with the political oppression whose glaring proofs lay in the trials. In dwelling on the question of *guilt* they forestalled the suggestion that all could be made well by a few gracious gestures on the part of the leaders; or by the demotion of minor figures. Justice demanded that the guilt be sheeted home to those who owned it. At this stage it was impossible to say openly, what all knew intuitively, that the guilt lay with the top men of power. Redemption, later to be called *de-Stalinisation*, could come only with the demasking of the real culprits, the political leaders. The message could not be expressed; but it was understood.

During the eight years which had elapsed since the communists took power, they had eliminated or rendered harmless all social and cultural structures which could offer an alternative to themselves. As a matter of course they spoke authoritatively in the name of the nation; and demanded, or assumed, that the nation identify itself totally with the regime. The further they drifted out of touch with the common man, the more unreal became this identification; but it could never be quest-ioned openly. In 1956 the writers who revealed themselves as an op-pressed group, identified themselves with the oppressed masses, and by implication crossed over from the protection of the official ranks to the people, abandoning their patron for their audience. Literature – courted, bullied, paid, and corrupted by regimists, now asserted its separateness from them. Declining to share the guilt of association, the writers made freedom their goal: artistic freedom was demanded not only in its own right, but as the symbol of political freedom. It was, after all, the communists who had asserted that art and politics were inseparable.

Another disturbing feature of the conference was the open admission, on the part of younger writers, that they recognised a generation gap between themselves and their elder colleagues. It was a group of poets who came forward as the spokesmen of the younger generation – Milan Kundera, Jiří Šotola, Karel Šiktanc, Miroslav Florian, Miroslav Červenka, Miroslav Holub. Apart from Kundera, whose home was in Brno, all these people were associated with the journal *Květen*. All had begun their literary career after the war, and had been exposed to communist influence all their adult life. They were the first wave of writers who were the offspring of the new era: and because of their youth none had any responsibility for the administrative crimes of the Stalinist period; the worst fault with which they could be charged was that they had uncritically accepted the lead of their elders. Even if they had been without doubts before, the recent revelations and undignified somersaults which they witnessed would have encouraged an attitude on their part of critical disillusion. At the Congress the young poets came forward with a common programme of their own. It was evidently easier for them to indicate what they were trying to avoid than exactly to define their own goals. They explained their aversions – bombast, false heroics, varnished positive heroes and uncomplicated situations of 'construction literature', ringing declarations and monumental pathos; vague generalities and bloodless abstractions. They did not reject engaged art or ideological motivation, but, as Šotola pointed out, they wished not to manifest their convictions but to *realise* them. They rejected the image of the poet as a teacher or the spokesman for a campaign. In search of realism – a word recently so terribly misused – they tried to bring down art from the clouds to the earth: instead of all-embracing concepts and revealed truth, they preferred to go their own way in a search for humble reality. Their literary programme was in fact rather vague: evidently it was against all declarative or manifestation art, and looked for reality at the grass roots of life. Thus they coined the term the *Poetry of Everyday*.[6] It was exemplified on the pages of *Květen* in the short pieces, humdrum scenes, and unprettified cameos of the poets – in detail consciously unpoetic, and in form adhering to the norms of everyday speech. The art of the everyday took as its subject-matter

the whole complex world of modern man, unvarnished, unsimplified –
it abjured the poetic world of golden sunsets as well as that of political
blue-prints. It was clearly influenced by current Italian neo-realism,
and sought to return literature to the unromantic atmosphere and the
vernacular forms of the modern world. It was more than a mere reaction against the closed forms, and the closed ideas, of the recent
literary phase; it was an attempt to widen the range of art by avoiding
what had become trite and conventional, and by exploring for new
responses. For Holub especially it meant bringing into poetry the
strange new world of science and technology, and reinforcing poetic
insight by the observation of the pathologist:

> Here in the Lord's bosom rest
> the tongues of beggars,
> the lungs of generals,
> the eyes of informers,
> the skins of martyrs,
>
> in the absolute
> of the microscope's lenses.
>
> I leaf through Old Testament slices of liver,
> in the white monuments of brain I read
> the hieroglyphs
> of decay.
>
> Behold, Christians,
> Heaven, Hell, and Paradise
> in bottles.
> And no wailing,
> not even a sigh.
> Only the dust moans.[7]

Holub was not alone in seeking to link poetry with medical science.
The poet E. Petiška, who had for ten years withdrawn to the less
controversial field of children's literature, returned in 1957 with a
collection entitled *Moments:*[8] his theme was the stream of recollections
and associations of a hospital patient:

> Across the slopes of night the fever climbs.
> Upon the bed beside the door the patient
> clutches at the sheet; he fights
> to hold the balance of the spinning room.
> From shadows comes the sound of shuffling,

> the click-click-click of slippered feet –
> partings, partings, partings...

An almost forgotten older form had returned to Czech poetry – stream -of-consciousness verse, with its aim to uncover reality by penetrating the walls around men's innermost feelings and instincts.

A leading spirit in the poetic movement, and an editor of *Květen* was Jiří Šotola; whose book *Our Daily World* appeared in 1957.[9] Šotola wrote from a Marxist viewpoint, though his art was clearly directed towards the problems of individual self-expression rather than towards the more abstract aims of social realisation. The poems were set in low key, and specialised in paradoxical juxtapositions. He was interested in exploring the gap which exists between the person as he appears in outward expression - his social gestures, often according with a social expectation or convention - and the unseen conflict within him. Social forms seem to draw into a community individuals whose real life, the drama within themselves, makes them strangers to each other:

> Through Prague they walk bemused in sleep –
> blonde girls whom love has visited with pain,
> a man behind a blind; a washerwoman; aged folk;
> all kept alive by a longing not to isolate;
> to sew together veins of the punctured earth;
> to sketch a new design,
> create a meaning
> from stars, and rain, and birds –
> the whole revolving world.

Šotola is an incorrigible optimist: the barriers between men can be broken down by compassion, and a feeling for exploration as bold as that of Columbus – Šotola's symbol of man's restless search for a new home. The human alienation which he depicted, became the *leitmotif* in Milan Kundera's *Monologues*.[10] The human relationships of which he wrote were those of love - conventionally the closest and most delightful in man's experience. But his love poems were highly anti-romantic in tone: their atmosphere was of suspicion, disappointment, and disillusion. The form of the poems was like a little dramatic sketch, a telephone conversation of which the audience hears only one side: the lovers reveal themselves as tired and sardonic. As a sharp antithesis to the stylised lovers of Stalinist verses they show signs of physical and emotional disfigurement. In a prefatory poem which became famous,

Kundera warned that the poet's task was to be uncompromising, to go to the very bottom of human doubts, hopes, passions, and despair. Absurdity and physical disgust are among the commonest features of his poems. They include a few simple narrative pieces: an uncomplicated soldier, estranged from his familiar village life and sweetheart, uses his well-oiled rifle to shoot himself. An office worker seeks escape in the arms of his wife from his wretched existence; and in his meaningless job he seeks escape from his boring wife. Kundera's poems accorded with the current mode in their ironical, consciously casual style, and because he drew his material from the trivial round. But they carried a harsher note of disillusion. Kundera is undoubtedly one of the most talented and original of living Czech writers: pretence and hypocritical orthodoxy are anathema to him. But his own literary beginnings have moments which painfully recall the Stalinist era; (his second book had been an epic poem on the communist Czech hero, Julius Fučík). Kundera's dissatisfaction with his own work, which at times mounted to a physical aversion, soon persuaded him to abandon poetry altogether: but his literary career was only just getting into its stride.

The years from 1956 to 1958 saw a great renaissance of Czech poetry, and a great revival of public support for it: the poets had won back their alienated following. Florian, Šiktanc, and Červenka contributed with distinction to the style which was associated with their journal *Květen*. Older critics noted how curiously it resembled a style of poetry which had been popular fifteen years before. In wartime Prague the poets Blatný, Bednář, Orten, and Hauková had likewise shunned false heroics and theatrical gestures to write of the confined and fragile world of down-at-heels Prague with all its shortages and austerities. Rhetoric, sentimentality, and ideological gestures had been repulsive to the young poets of that time, as now. The hard days of war had driven them to find meaning only in people, and on the streets. It was striking, and rather chilling, to note the similarities in the two eras, and the similar reaction to it by literature. It was a harsh commentary upon the resolute optimism which was still being officially propagated, and a significant, because unintended, reaction by the poets. Writers of an older generation were now returning to a literary climate more congenial than for several years. Jiří Kolář, and Jiřina Hauková; Hrubín, Seifert, and Mikulášek, all contributed to the literary revival with new work of mature quality.[11]

Czech poetry seems generally to react more quickly and sensitively to changes of taste and atmosphere than does Czech prose. At the

Writers Congress the (ex-Stalinist) critic Jiří Hájek voiced concern over the state of the contemporary Czech novel, and asked when writers were going to take serious note of the consequences of the 'personality cult' on literature. Other literary commentators noted that creative prose was lagging in its reformation: the events of the past era had frightened away the novelists from serious work, or maybe had permanently deformed their literary judgement:

> ... writers saw the world askew; they did not judge or weigh facts, but expounded them with the aid of dogmatic formulae, instead of scrutinising them by real life standards. In fact they did the reverse. It was real life that they tried to adapt, trimming it in accordance with those false dogmatic formulae that are the death of art. Not only that. Instead of trying to master life, facing up to reality and boldly grappling with it, they became mere narrators of events and illustrators of dogmatic theses. They did not *discover* the world in all its complexity, its varied, often subtle, shades: they feared to look into the human mind because of the feeling they might find there something not in line with the theories blazoned out and forced upon them from all sides. The result was the disappearance not only of the psychological novel, but, even worse, of psychology itself.[12]

The author of the comment, Bohuslav Březovský, was himself a serious novelist who knew what he was talking about. The so-called psychological novel had been rather a successful feature of Czech creative writing, and its elimination was a well-chosen example of the harm done to it by political interference. The exploration of the human mind by the writer, exposing split motives, divorced loyalties, unusual or paradoxical human relationships, had been officially discredited as morbid and unhealthy, a typical product of bourgeois decadence, quite unbecoming to the healthy, uncomplicated world of the socialist 'construction' novel. Yet by 1956 the first in a new wave of psychological novels had already appeared – cautious and tentative in its approach, but definitely a revival of the genre. It was *Citizen Brych*[13] by Jan Otčenášek, the author of the earlier construction stereotype *Full Speed Ahead*.[14]

In theme and form *Citizen Brych* resembled the socialist epic novels of the early fifties: as in them the personal drama was played out against a background of the events of 1948 and thereafter. But it differed in that it portrayed in detail the intellectual conflict within the chief character, and sympathetically discussed the independent role of the intellectual at a time of social struggle. In the novel Brych's personal problems develop in step with the political crisis. After 1948 his boss defects, and he has the opportunity of promotion. But he declines to forward his own career on such terms, or to identify himself with the aims of the communists:

> He seemed to have awakened from a soothing dream and to be facing a rough wall. He had not imagined it like this. Threats, dictation, the workers' committees! Fear and hate! Revenge! Listening to their radio. Reading their news sheet. Odes to socialism, all in unisen. Mass cowardice swelling like an ulcer. People fired, and more reliable substitutes appointed... Is this really socialism? The rule of the workers?

Brych is disgusted with the prejudice and crude propaganda he sees around him. He stands aloof from the race for power, and from the mutual venom: preaching tolerance, he practises non-involvement. But amid the growing tension of the class-struggle the communists will not accept his neutralism, and press him for an answer – With us? or against us? Caught in a conflict of loyalties Brych tries to stand above the struggle, and is condemned for bourgeois objectivism. Unable to abandon his principles he finds the only solution in flight. He leaves Prague for the border, and spends a night of self-examination in the company of his fellow defectors. At this moment of personal crisis he sees through the selfish motives of his companions, and realises that this course of action offers no hope. He returns to Prague, and to communist society. His motives in pursuing tolerance and neutralism were pure; but as a living style it is inadequate. The novel gave scope for some pungent comments on the sins of the bourgeois, as well as the vulgar excesses and careerism of the Stalinist period. But it was a new thing for a novelist to set up as his central figure an intellectual weighted with bourgeois scruples and moral doubts: it was certainly a departure to treat the theme of the defector in this sympathetic way: (it coincided with a drive by the Czech authorities to coax the defectors back home). An usual feature was the method of narration, revealing events not in the objective epic style, but as viewed through the eyes of the chief character. The novel was no longer attempting merely to mirror events, but to give them subjective treatment.

When it first appeared in 1955 *Citizen Brych* seemed to be a daring experiment. But times and taste were changing so quickly that it soon came to be regarded as belonging to the pre-reform era. After the stormy debate at the Writers Congress the election of Otčenášek as Secretary was welcomed by the authorities as well as by the writers: his reputation was that of a safe, middle-of-the-road man. He had updated the socialist novel, and made it more palatable to contemporary taste. Others followed his example. Březovský himself published *The Iron Ceiling*, a novel similarly set against an industrial background, containing a study of character and inner conflict, but ending with the death of the would-be neutralist. Bourgeois, or any other sort of 'objectivism' was still out of official favour.

But in 1956 had appeared a novel much more subtle and original, and little tainted with the defects of the 'construction' era. It was *Follow the Green Light*[15] by Edvard Valenta, a veteran writer and journalist, who thus achieved his first major success at the age of 55: maturity was a feature of the work, and its action was viewed largely through the eyes of an older man. Its scene was set not in the contemporary socialist world, but in wartime Czechoslovakia. Where Otčenášek had tentatively demoted the positive qualities of the hero, Valenta produced the first fully fledged anti-hero. The central figure of his novel was one, Professor Šimon, an elderly and ailing recluse. From the danger and tumult of wartime Prague he moves for safety to the rather dreary milieu of a tiny Czech village: in this hideout he contemplates his own fate and the human situation: he is wrapped up in himself, and shows no inclination to engage in the titanic conflict of the day, nor to assist others: a complete individualist, he realises, and philosophically accepts, his alienation, regarding it as typical of the human condition. Ironical, pragmatic, sceptical, he is without any pretensions to heroism, and sees the motivating force of his own life as fear. It was fear that prevented him from opening his wife's letter when she left him, or his daughter's last note before she committed suicide. Fear almost compelled him to work for the Nazis: and fear has brought him to this present retreat. A failure in personal, and in social affairs, he is the reverse of the masculine figure heroised in communist novels, and canonised in the person of Julius Fučík. Yet by a strange combination of circumstances it is this figure who achieves what would be generally regarded as heroism. In the closing stages of the war the woods around his cottage are full of partisans. A sick woman is brought to him for shelter, and he takes her in, because he lacks the courage to refuse. His death is only a question of time: he is shot by the Germans for actions which were against his will, and contrary to his convictions. Ironically, his sacrifice comes at a time when it has become no longer necessary. The time is May 1945.

In the stereotype of socialist novels, the hero is socially validated by his ability to set an example, to lead, and to be at one with the masses. Professor Šimon is an individual at tension with society, and a failure in all his relationships. If he achieves nobility, it is in spite of all his efforts: he is a study in alienation. When the novel appeared, the poets were writing of men's inner conflicts; and Šotola in his verse was fond of contrasting the social gesture of a man with the turmoil within him. Valenta in his novel explored the inner drama, and underlined the strangeness of its contrast with the actions expressed.

Valenta's novel was striking as the first full psychological novel: it was also a fine piece of work in its own right. The story was told on two levels: apart from the direct narration of events, there were interludes in which Šimon wrote in his own person. He was himself writing a novel, and in this secondary narration we have the reflections of the author at one remove, and at a different point of time. As a novelist Šimon considers the atmosphere of contemporary Czech society under the Nazis; the analysis contains features alarmingly applicable to the later period of Stalinism:

> I am often dissatisfied with the development of the characters whom I myself have created, and to whom I have assigned prepared courses of action. Dissatisfied because suddenly they stop acting as I intended. Of course there is nothing new in a writer's characters turning against their creator. But I try to discover why they suddenly lose their individuality, even when, true, it is only a form I imposed on them myself; and why actually they keep changing into misty outlines.
>
> It isn't difficult to see the answer. It is... the inability to maintain one's own face, and the need to assume that of another, frequently the face of an impersonal mass, which does not want to be outstanding or different in anything; that wants to lose itself in required conformity. It is controlled by the rule of fear. Destruction, devastation, towns laid waste, the killing of millions of innocent people, contempt for the truth and the most basic laws of conscience, the denial of everything which had been considered precious, unprecedented ferocity, and the matter-of-fact daily occurrences of the most horrible injustices – in a word all these commonplaces of the Hitler era, an era marked by terror, have succeeded in destroying our souls.

Unending fear of almost everything evil, from lack of bread to a martyr's death, has been moulding our former qualities into a depersonalised slime of bitterness, hope, resignation, defiance, selfishness, despair, and faith: it gradually changes us so that in the end we too would be capable of betraying everything we so far have believed in, if we knew for certain that the cost of courage will be death...

Dignity, and the right to live as an individual, are ridiculed, depreciated, and destroyed, just at the time which has thrown up, as the exact reverse of contemptuous rejection of the individual, a new cult of self-exaltation. It is a new perverse *romanticism*, a new veneration of a personality detached from the mass, not responsible to them, and thinking for them – or rather, *not* thinking for them. I make bold to say that the main feature of this era is not brutality, nor ignorance, nor arrogance nor lies, but romanticism. All its main constituents have been restored to life, with one difference; that today's hero will be regarded by posterity not as absurd, but as gruesome...

I must not forget the situation into which I set my characters. Five years ago they could not have dreamed that one evening the radio might announce to their dear ones, sitting uneasily at their meagre supper, awaiting their return from office or workshop, that they had already been executed... My characters must, in accord with reality, take for granted the possibility of a sudden martyr's death. I say to myself, too, that if my turn came, and they gauged out my eyes and tore out my tongue, I should be not entirely certain whether I was the victim of injustice or not; whether I had not *merited* this punishment merely by reason of my existence, because I am what I am.[16]

In his analysis of Nazi rule, Valenta touched a chord familiar to his readers. By putting the reflections in the mouth of Professor Šimon he led the reader to the implied comparison of the writer in wartime penning his views of the regime, and the present writer likewise commenting on contemporary conditions. The similarity between the Hitler and the Stalinist period could not be mistaken:

In the formation of a new political man, people often twist, or conceal the obvious truth that the masses can have a common, united, and powerful belief only when it is pressed upon them by a strong personality; for there is no other way to lead the masses to accept one belief. For this hidden truth... we have now the cruel witness of Adolf Hitler. He has proved to us the danger that arises when the tongue of a strong personality, who alone is permitted to think, is more prized than his heart or understanding. Hitler, a romantic and 'I' man, was put into the saddle by the crowd: for that he promoted them to be the decisive judge, instigator, and inciter; and at the same moment he anulled them – just as he promoted and simultaneously annihilated his 'I'. I can hear the all-powerful, and powerless, crowd shouting out from the loud-speakers its rhythmical chorus of applause and consent. I see the forest of arms outstretched to take on the fetters of unanimity, the ear-splitting sound of whistles, and the beating of drums, the thundering rhythm of endless marching ranks... Millions are invested in the thousands of kilometres of flags, in gigantic platforms, the most varied uniforms, and the other ritual symbols... all this goes on so that we can see the power of the German crowd which, enslaved itself, tries thus to prove the power and the infallibility of one man. Hearing and seeing this, in fear we ask ourselves whether the crowd rejoices and marches and gives unanimous thanks because it is really convinced of the leader's greatness, and the justice of the beliefs and actions in whose name men march and die; or whether these cries issue through teeth clenched in anger and despair; in the knowledge that *not* to rejoice, *not* to march, *not* to thank, would be useless; that a cry of rebellion, or even a proud silence, is pointless; because the collective, the political face has been smashed as effectively as the face of the lonely individual.[17]

Valenta's book was only one of a group which turned back for its material to the war years. After 1955 came a second wave of war novels comparable to that of ten years before. But the treatment was different. In the later period the theme of war was a safe one for writers returning to the literary arena, and the theme lent itself to realistic treatment by writers who drew on their own direct experience. But where the first wave of novels had tended to deal with the theme of courage, self-sacrifice in a common effort, and the triumph of the right cause, identified ideologically as that of the communists – the new novels dwelt more on the plight of hapless, innocent, and often unwilling victims.

Arnošt Lustig is a Czech Jew who during the war had suffered in Nazi concentration camps, escaped from a death transport, and lived in hiding in Prague. Later he had worked as a journalist, and had covered the 1948 Israeli-Arab war from the Israeli side as a correspondent. During the Stalinist era he had fallen under official displeasure, and he returned to the literary arena only after the improvement in atmosphere. In 1957 he published a collection of short stories *Night and Hope*, and in the following year *Diamonds of the Night*.[18] Lustig's literary technique was quite out of character with that of recent Czech prose. Instead of the wide canvas and epic-type narration which had been general, Lustig's stories were almost plotless. Action was described through the eyes of characters, and his themes were intensive studies of their inner lives. Situations were chosen for their outwardly humdrum character: pretension, heroics, flamboyance were all shunned. As if to emphasise the vulnerability of humans before power, Lustig's favourite characters were children, or the very young. The darkness which features in both titles, is the darkness of German persecution: its hapless victims are the Jews.

The persecution of Jews under Nazi rule was also the theme of Otčenášek's most successful novel *Romeo, Juliet, and the Darkness*,[19] a book which seems to owe much to *The Diary of Anne Frank*. In Otčenášek's book a Prague student, Paul, meets a Jewish girl Esther, who is on the run from a death transport, and has nowhere to go. Although not at all anxious to get into trouble, Paul finds himself unable to walk away and dismiss her. Without quite knowing why, he accepts responsibility for her safety, and hides her in his little den behind his father's workshop. While she is concealed there, Heydrich is assassinated, and Prague falls under a reign of terror, immensely compounding the dangers of the position. To save his parents from anxiety, Paul has to deceive them; as he draws closer in spirit to the girl, Esther, so the barriers rise between Paul and his father. To save Esther from fear, he conceals from her the new perils of the situation. So the private room, where he has played out the fantasies of his later childhood, becomes a symbol of their isolation from the outside world, dominated by the darkness of Nazi terror. Police searches, boots kicking down closed doors, informers, arrests, shootings, anger and fear fill the darkness outside the enclosed space of the tiny uncomfortable cell which is their only refuge. So a strange love affair is played out, struggling to exist against the whole weight of a world aimed to crush it. The tragic end has an air of inevitability. To save her lover, Esther runs into the streets when they are filled with soldiers: she races through the alleys and dark passages, seeing at their end a square of daylight which, in her tormented mind, she confuses with the familiar remembered daylight of her childhood. A bullet cuts her down as she reaches the light.

It seems appropriate that, in the second half of the 'fifties, Czech writers should have been drawn to the theme of the Jewish persecution under Hitler. As the victims of an organised, official purge, the Jews presented a striking symbol of the fate of deviant minorities in conditions of brutal intolerance. The allegory with the recent persecutions – specifically that of Jewish victims of the Slánský trials – was obvious: but this interpretation of the writing would be superficial. The old novels of socialist construction had demanded of the reader that he identify with the system; that he find moral assurance in its power and its reigning ideology. The new literature showed the *victims* of ideology and power: it called the reader to participate in the fear experienced by the hunted, the little people crushed between powerful conflicting forces. Symbolic of construction literature were the regimented factories, the banners, slogans, drums of mass parades. Typical of the new literature were bewildered, lost people, the humble ghetto, or the tiny secret room where Paul and Esther acted out their tragic romance. As the selected backdrop for drama this room differed from the factory or the Red Square not merely by its humble insecurity, but because it was a private world, an escape from the collective movements outside it. One is reminded of Winston Smith's secret hideout, in Orwell's *1984*, where lovers find a brief, and doomed, respite from the overwhelming pressure of public life outside. Love is pre-eminently an expression of man's inner, private being; it is appropriate that it should be linked, as a theme, with the search for escape from the horrors of a totalitarian regime.

Valenta, Lustig, and Otčenášek differed from earlier writers in their treatment of the war theme; but in one respect at least their attitude was similar. Looking back in anger or compassion they treated the memory of events with grim seriousness. By contrast, the most successful Czech novel on the theme of the First World War had been comedy – *The Good Soldier Schweik*, that classic send-up of military muddle. So far Czech writing on the theme of the Second World War had produced nothing comparable. The events seemed still too recent, too grim for humour, especially in the iight of their aftermath. The whole subject had been more or less taboo for parody, and no event was more sacrosanct than the liberation of the Czech lands by the Red Army. In these circumstances a novel entitled *The Cowards*,[20] by an unknown writer, Josef Škvorecký, fell on the literary scene in 1959 like a bomb-shell.

The events of the novel take place in a small Czech town during the week in May 1945, which saw the entry of the Red Army, the end of the war, and the start of a new epoch. In the novel the epoch-making events are viewed through the eyes of Danny, an at first sight surpris-ing choice for a hero. A young and typical product of the Protectorate years, he is bored with life, politically naive, without illusions, and quite lacking in civic responsibility. His energies are concentrated on a less than successful chase after a girl friend, Irene, and on his main love, jazz. There is a strange contrast between the sanctity of the back-ground events – the May revolution and the liberation – and its devas-tatingly realistic treatment. Danny is both the narrator and the real subject of the novel. Being clearly incapable of evaluating the historic events unfolding before him, he merely relates them, without varnish, superlatives, or enthusiasm. His style of narration is characteristic of his generation; its unliterary quality and its authentic diction, and reportage in the first person, make the novel at first seem a kind of *Real-life Confession* story in an illustrated magazine. The essential triviality of his life-style and his aims in life – girls, jazz, dodging trouble – make Danny an outrageous and convincing choice as a witness.

It was Danny's lack of respect for higher things that helped to spoil his chances with Irene. He seemed to regard nothing as sacred – and not out of moral conviction, or on any sort of principle, but because his limited experience had not so far presented to him anything that did seem sacred. He could not see anything heroic in the behaviour of his elders; and he noted without surprise their cautious obsequious-ness, gross self-seeking, and shameless somersaults of loyalty, which were the background for their expressions of patriotism and self-sacrifice. The reader, who might well recognise himself or his fellows in this dead-pan stuff, might regard the novel as a parody of Czech heroism and of the treasured events of 'glorious May'. The actions of the novel's characters reveal without the need of comment that behind their claims to patriotism lay an ordinary (and understandable) cowardice. On the stylistic level we find a contrast between the pre-tentious language of the 'leaders of the resistance' and the unemotional slang of the narrator: by implication the pretentious speeches and chest-thumping claims are seen as simple hogwash. Even before the great events begin, Danny feels it will all be useless:

Flags were hanging from the church and the bank: it looked like October 28th at dinner time. The flags made me feel fed up. It was as if I could smell roast goose coming from the houses. That's how it is. They will roast them all right. That's how it goes. Fear, glory, the brass band, speeches, and a cut off the joint and two veg. It'll be the same all over again. Not a thing changed. A few days of excitement, then the mixture as before – just the same sticky, glutinous mess.

The earth-shaking events do not effect any great change in Danny's character. It is not that he is insensitive, but he makes little sense of them, because they hardly touch him personally. Through his eyes we see the entry of the victorious Red Army:

I was just thinking; then suddenly a funny noise came from the distance. It was like the rattling of many wheels, and it drew nearer. There was a sound of whips cracking; and then, in the opening of an anti-tank barrier there appeared two battered prairy horses, and behind them a Russian on the box. The Russian swung the whip over his head and sang. The horses galloped along and the wheels of the gig rattled on the cobbles. I looked at the Russian, then there was a second gig, then one after another they came leaping past the anti-tank barrier, and poured along the road through the Square towards the West. The place was full of their rattling and the cracking of their long whips. They jogged along, one behind the other in a quick-moving, smelly procession at a wild gallop, with the red-cheeked Russians jolting high above the battered backs of their horses, singing Russian songs. People stared at them from the pavements. The gigs raced along at a crazy pace, and the tiny horses tossed their manes. An endless stream of them. The air was full of their smell, a kind of tundra smell; and I began to soak it up, and I stared at those beaten-up faces, and it seemed impossible to believe that they really existed – these people who knew nothing about jazz, and maybe about dames either: they rattled along with revolvers on their greasy behinds; unshaved, with bottles of vodka in their pants, all lit up, drunk, victorious, not thinking of the things I thought of, absolutely different to me and terrifically alien, but still fascinating. I looked at them in wonder – so this was the Red Army! It raced on, dusty, wild, not stopping, sweaty, barbaric, and me staring at them and

thinking of Blok, that somebody lent me during the war; and
I didn't know whether this really was the beginning of something, some revolution, and whether it had anything to do
with me and my world. I didn't know. It all rushed past me,
as though it was all wasted on me...

Danny is depressed by his sense of estrangement: he cannot honest-
ly say that he feels much interest or enthusiasm for the things that seem
to be regarded as important. The pitiful boasting of his elders and
betters, the brutality of Czechs beating up German prisoners, are
repulsive. Even to join in a celebration of victory is embarrassing:

When they stopped singing, one of the Frenchmen called out
to me from the dance-floor, 'Vive la France! Vive les Soviets!
Vive la Paix!' and he smiled at me. I smiled back at him, and I
wanted to yell something back, but I was suddenly embarrass-
ed. I would have liked to shout something as crazy as he had,
but I couldn't. I just grinned and waved my hand, and felt
mad that I didn't know how to shout like that, and now my
pleasure had been spoilt. I couldn't shout 'Long live Czechoslovakia' or anything like that. I just couldn't. Maybe because
Czechoslovakia is such a damn big word... I'd never been able
to shout and yell at parades and holler 'Welcome' and all that
sort of stuff. It was OK – but for Christ's sake if only they
would leave me alone!

The Cowards was received by critics with a storm of anger which at
times approached hysteria: its hostile reception can only be understood in its historical context. The novel was regarded as an affront;
not only because of its irreverent treatment of sacred events, but also
because it described them in the slangy vernacular of the youth group.
The very fact that a novel should be written in the recognisably authentic
language of the young was a kind of challenge to those taste-upholders
who authoritatively claimed to speak for the younger generation. By
its radically different style the novel implicitly proclaimed that a
generation gap existed.

Danny's slang was the language of his generation; its symbol was
jazz, the true outlet for its self-expression. In wartime, jazz had become
a means of escape from the regimented world of Nazi occupation. It
cheered young conscripted Czech workers through the long hours of
enforced labour in German factories; and it provided a link with the
outside world – Dixieland, swing, the American style. After the war

it remained a treasured memory, the first love of the generation grown
to manhood in the Protectorate. Accepted as the symbol of youth
doing its own thing, it later became a symbol of protest against another
form of regimentation. The socialist style imposed on art and life after
1948 was stern, ascetic, dedicated, demanding, pretentious, schematic:
jazz was a symbol of everything opposed to this: its relaxed and improvised methods, its sweet, sentimental themes, its spontaneity, its
lack of pretence, and its untraditional forms – all this set it apart. It
was unpolitical at a time when politics dominated everything; and
above all it was American-orientated. By their stern discouragement
of jazz, and other 'bourgeois trash', the communists ensured that it
should become a symbol of protest against themselves.

The Cowards was the first great Czech novel based on the theme of
jazz: to the discomfort of Škvorecký the book was interpreted as
definitely anti-Establishment. The impression of authenticity hung
like a millstone round its neck; for by espousing a style so unlike
traditional soc.-realism, it exposed the latter's *unrealism*. Like the
poets of 'everyday art' Škvorecký had brought literature down from
an imaginary Valhalla of monumental heroics and abstract ideological
patterns to the familiar rich vulgarity of the real world. But perhaps
Škvorecký did more than this. There are times when systematic lies,
pretentions, and self-deception can hypnotise public opinion: certain
ideas, though hardly supported by common experience, are relegated
beyond criticism. Of all the communist mythology nothing was more
untouchable than the legend of the liberation. When Škvorecký
portrayed the events through the eyes of Danny, he violated a taboo
in a seemingly unexceptionable way. Danny became the modern
equivalent of Hans Andersen's child who exposed the sham of the
Emperor's new clothes. Like the child, Danny was protected by his
innocence: he broke the taboo because he had never heard of it. There
are times when literature can itself be an act of liberation, merely by
calling things by their right names. The Cowards was an important
novel not only because of its intrinsic literary merit, but because it
acted to *demystify* what had become holy writ.

Demystification is a feature of post-Stalinist literature. Negatively
it operated (as in Škvorecký's case) by the debunking process of clearing away humbug and exposing self-deception: positively it clarified
and drew attention to real, instead of imaginary, issues. The process
was illustrated in both prose and poetry, by a shift of focus from the
grand and sacred to the ordinary, real, and familiar: people and
situations were portrayed for themselves, and not as mere illustrations

of political doctrine. It might thus seem that the aims of cultural policy were frustrated, and this was the view of many Stalinist critics. But in one sense the reverse was the truth. Cultural bosses had intended literature and the arts to lead public thinking, and to act as a form of social co-ordination and social diagnosis – but the alienation of literature from reality had prevented this. When literature regained touch with familiar reality and won back its audience, who at last could identify with what was presented, literature regained its lost social role as a mirror in which the society could examine itself.

Any examination of Czech creative literature of the 50's confirms the impression that the year 1956 was decisive for change, though the ultimate direction of change was as obscure in the cultural, as it was in the political field. Individual groups of writers, like the young poets around the journal *Květen*, planned their limited programmes, but the literary harvest as a whole represented no programme, but rather a general reaction to the atmosphere of the preceding period. The commonest features of the new literature were a self-questioning, a feeling of moral anger, and a desire for freedom to tackle the disturbing problems which had become apparent. The attitudes which the writers expressed, as far as they were permitted in their published work, seem very much to have reflected public feeling. Consequently the same attitudes tended to appear in other forms among other thinking groups; in particular those concerned with higher education. The Writers' Congress had hardly finished when the Prague university students revived a traditional May Festival procession, which turned into a demonstration with unexpected tones of irony and dissent. At the same time it was revealed that student groups in a number of centres had formulated a programme which included the demand for democratisation of public life, an end to the jamming of foreign broadcasts, more contact with Western influences, less regimentation, and more independence from the Party-controlled Youth Union.[21]

Dissatisfaction on the part of the students was echoed by sections of the teaching body: here dissent came from an unexpected quarter. Among the Party's contribution to the reform of higher education had been the establishment of Departments of Marxism-Leninism at tertiary institutions. But the bright and dedicated young Marxists appointed to these key jobs were among the first to become disillusioned. Brought by the nature of their work into direct contact both with the students and with the institutional effects of their social theory, they were in the best position to note the tragic gulf between theory and practice, and the results upon the new generation whom they were teaching. In 1956 a group of Marxist theoreticians at the Prague School of Economics actually began to formulate a programme of political reform, intended to clean up the Party and give it a second chance. Their efforts did not get very far, and we know of it more from the official condemnation of their efforts than from their own formulation. They asked for changes in the highest bodies of the Party, a rethinking of the aims and definition of socialism, and as a first step, the convening of an Extraordinary Party Congress to consider these, and other similar proposals.[22]

Party hacks who had become accustomed to regard as natural their claim to authority and wisdom, had hardly recovered from the shock of this rebellious impudence when they discovered that dissent was rife in other Social Science Departments of the universities. In search of relevance and indoctrination, the teaching of philosophy had shifted its stress from ethics and metaphysics to social philosophy. But instead of hammering home simplistic formulaic propositions to their students, the social philosophers were indulging in rash speculation on such subjects as the nature of political dogma, the possible development of differing models of socialism, and the deleterious effect of bureaucratic rule on public behaviour. This might not have mattered so much had the debate been confined to seminars within the campus; but the young philosophers, of whom two, Karel Kosík and Ivan Sviták, became especially notorious, showed an alarming tendency to extend controversial discussion into the public arena. Perhaps the most serious challenge of all was posed by attempts at public discussion of juridical principles by Prague's academic lawyers. They brought into question the validity of certain current legal assumptions, including the class interpretation of legal administration: their relentless discussion of theory and practice in fact threatened to expose the illegality of Party action, for instance in the field of censorship. Their insistence on the letter of socialist legality could hardly be faulted; but a consequential campaign for civil rights was bound to bring them into head-on clash with authorities.

In the Spring of 1956, when the Party and government leaders were still hesitant what course of action to adopt, the spectacular upsurge of energy and questioning among the Czech intellectuals seemed capable of provoking great changes in public life. But luck was against the would-be reformers. In Czechoslovakia, unlike Poland, there was little close contact between the intellectuals and workers' movements, and in spite of official protestations to the contrary, no little antipathy and suspicion of intellectuals by workers. At any rate in 1956 the latter made no overt sign of active support for a reformist campaign. The idea of reform was in the air, and great changes were expected, but given the institutional framework, it seemed that change could be initiated only from within the Party itself.

The possibility of the leadership reforming itself was evidently slim. In Poland and Hungary the party reformers could call on leaders who had themselves been victims of Stalinism, and by their imprisonment had avoided responsibility for excesses in public life. But in Czechoslovakia the ferocity of the purges had eliminated any possible reformist leadership from that quarter (if indeed they had escaped the gallows, Clementis, even perhaps Slánský himself, might in 1956 have come forward as 'liberalisers'). The existing Party leadership was composed of men who were demonstrably and directly responsible for Stalinism; it was nonsensical to expect them to eliminate themselves.[23] A reform of the Party might have come from a challenge from within the hierarchy, utilising a ground-swell of popular feeling. In fact there were signs of alarm and confusion within the Party during the Spring and summer of 1956. Questions were being asked, doubts aired at Party meetings: even *Rudé právo* conceded that the question of the day was *Who to believe?*, only to suggest the clever answer *Believe the Party!* But grassroots feeling posed no real threat to the leadership: the political structure was expressly designed to ensure control from the top. There seemed to be only two real threats to the leaders – a dissident element within its own ranks, or else a decision from Moscow to remove the present Czech leaders. Both threats were very real; but neither eventuated. The ruling group maintained its solid front; and Moscow, divided and unsure in its own leadership, did not, for the time being, attempt to exercise the authority which Stalin had held over the satellite governments. As Spring gave way to summer, the Czech leaders gained in confidence, and began a counter-attack upon their opponents. There was some perfunctory acknowledgement of blame, chiefly for 'misunderstanding' the Jugoslav situation, and for excesses in the field of justice. But the blame was laid at the door of the Slánský group, who, being dead, could not answer back: the fault of the purge which destroyed Slánský, was attributed to his own efforts.[24] The official press began to use language of increasing menace towards serious criticism: those who dared to advocate change, or even discussion of change, were dubbed as irresponsible elements, class enemies who had infiltrated into Party ranks: it was made clear that such 'irresponsible attacks on those who refused to open the gates to anarchy', would not be tolerated.[25]

By the middle of June, that is, before the Polish and Hungarian crises, the Czechoslovak Communist leadership had already weathered the storm begun by Khrushchev's revelations. The only serious threat to the power of Novotný and associates seemed to lie in the unpredictable attitude of Moscow; and this was bound up with the latter's rapprochement with Tito. It was decidedly awkward that the Czech communist leaders had liquidated rivals in the name of eliminating Titoism – a charge hardly likely to be forgotten in Belgrade. But during the first half of 1956 Khrushchev followed a policy of general conciliation; he was ready to be friendly with everyone; and the world was treated to the odd scene of the Russian leaders dining with the Queen of England in London.

For the time being the Russians made no gesture of disfavour towards Novotný; and events soon made them appreciate the value of such an obliging ally. For the relaxation of tough tactics brought its own nemesis elsewhere. In Poland the reformist movement showed signs of an unmistakably anti-Soviet nature. Then, in June at Polish Poznan, a local strike erupted into open violence. Moscow read the signs correctly, and gave evidence of a change of course. Officially the unrest was attributed to foreign provocateurs and imperialist agents. Prague's anti-reformist line was being vindicated, and the charges were echoed with enthusiasm in the Czech press. The Czechoslovak Party sent a delegation to Warsaw to show its solidarity. The subsequent admission by Polish leaders that the strike had been spontaneous and caused by genuine grievances, was received with shock and anger in Prague; and the official Polish announcements were censored out of the Czech newspapers. In Poland the reformist process was speeded up, and Gomulka returned from official disgrace to lead the Workers' Party. As Khrushchev, now thoroughly alarmed by events, flew to Warsaw with the Soviet top brass, Russian troops began to move on Warsaw, and Polish forces were deployed to confront them. But the crisis passed without bloodshed. A non-committal communique was issued by the two leaders, and the Russian troops were pulled back. For the time being the Polish right to national communism was vindicated.

Immediately a second crisis blew up in Hungary, whose virtually free press had been carefully following the Polish developments. In Budapest a rally of students, writers, and intellectuals turned into a mass demonstration outside the Polish Embassy. As Imre Nagy addressed the crowd, elsewhere in Budapest the great statue of Stalin was brought crashing to the ground. So the Hungarian revolt began, with the Hungarian Security troops and Russian occupation Forces under heavy attack. By the beginning of November it seemed as though Hungary had won its freedom, when the fighting was called off, a new liberal-communist government formed, and Soviet forces pulled away from the capital. But the impression was illusory. Within a few days Russian troops began a military operation on Budapest. After heavy fighting, during which an astonished world saw Hungarian workers resisting Russian tanks, the shattered city was retaken; and the reformist leaders arrested by the Russians. The Czech government, which had consistently denounced and opposed the Hungarian reformers, could congratulate itself that its warnings against liberalism and against national movements had been fully justified.[26] It seemed that the dangerous flirtation with liberal communism, with Titoism, and with co-existence in the international sphere, was over. Novotný could rub his hands over the vindication of Stalinism. In December at a meeting of the Party Central Committee he welcomed the 'stabilisation' of Hungary, and criticised the attitudes revealed by the Polish and Jugoslav comrades in the crisis. The events of Hungary had confirmed the views of the Czechoslovak leadership that so-called national Communism was merely a screen for *foreign imperialism*: those who beat the drum of anti-Stalinism were furthering *the ends of US policy*. In January the Czech leaders paid an official visit to Moscow, and on Stalin's tomb they laid a wreath properly inscribed 'To the Great Leader of Socialism'.

In the time of testing, the Novotný leadership had indeed proved their total dedication to the Soviet Union. They could pride themselves that they were now Moscow's most trusted ally; and in June a visit to Prague by Khrushchev and Bulganin gave the seal of official Russian blessing upon the Czechoslovak leaders. The period of vacillation which had followed Stalin's death now seemed to be over: the Leader was dead, but his policies, suitably up-dated, lived on. It remained only to clean up the remnants of mild rebellion which had manifested themselves during 1956. As the intellectual opposition posed no serious threat to the stability of the regime, a few stern warnings would seem to suffice. A minor incident in December revealed which way the wind was blowing. The novelist K. J. Beneš incautiously suggested that the Hungarian tragedy had certain moral lessons for the Czechs, and that the mistakes of the Rakosi regime, which had provoked the crisis, were related to excesses by Communist regimes elsewhere: they too in some way shared responsibility for the tragedy.[27] At once Beneš was called to task by the Party daily *Rudé právo*, which held him up as an example of a confused intellectual who had allowed himself to become the dupe of enemy propaganda. In April 1957 Minister Bacilek reported to a Party meeting that ideas of Polish and Hungarian intellectuals had influenced some Czechoslovak writers. In June at a Congress of Journalists, the press was criticised for the crime of objectivism, and accused of servile admiration for the West. During the same month at a meeting of the Party Central Committee Hendrych stressed the need for ideological work, and the struggle against not only dogmatism but also *revisionism*, which had by now become the term used for all reformist endeavour:

> We shall not tolerate the hostile campaign carried out under the slogan of the fight against so-called Stalinism, which is an attempt to liquidate the revolutionary foundations of Marxist-Leninist teachings... Advocates of revisionism have used as a pretext for their activities the conclusions of the CPSU Congress, in particular its criticisms of the personality cult. They have tried to distort the conclusions of the Congress in an opportunist, capitalist way, to falsify and exploit them for a general attack on all basic principles of scientific Socialism. In this they were aided by a collection of reformist and Trotskyist renegades... The revisionists not only pose as Marxists, but as the only revolutionary and creative Marxists... They lump their attacks on the principles of Marxist-Leninist teaching under the heading of the fight against Stalinism.[28]

Kopecký addressed his remarks specifically at the writers:

> Anyone who thinks the Party will allow literary journals to be misused for the publication of revisionist, nationalistic, bourgeois liberal opinions and for advocating an opposition policy, is mistaken.

After this the onus was on the writers themselves to declare their 'anti-revisionist' attitude. At a session of the Writers' Union the secretary, Otčenášek obligingly came forward to criticise the rebellious words spoken at the 1956 Congress. Otčenášek associated himself with the Party leaders' criticism of the Congress; assured them that the writers stood firmly behind the Party; and urged all writers to oppose revisionist tendencies. He strongly disassociated himself from the stand taken by Hrubín and Seifert last year, in particular to Seifert's claim that the writers were the conscience of the nation. Hrubín himself declared that nothing he had said was directed at the Party: the editors of *Květen* and *Literární noviny* which had come in for severe criticism, admitted their errors, and the editor of *Literární noviny*, Jan Pilař, was replaced. The main cause of Pilař's downfall was perhaps his decision to print the speeches of the Second Writers Congress in 1956. The new Secretary of the Writers Union was Ivan Skála, whose one-time attacks on Seifert had long since marked him out as the embodiment of literary Stalinism.

Between 1956 and 1959 the Czech writers were lectured, exhorted, harassed, and threatened; but literary life did not return to the savage atmosphere of the early fifties. Restraint was the order of the day: the attitude of the authorities to the writers seems to have been one of suspicious tolerance. There was little attempt to force writers into political engagement; it was enough if they avoided political provocation.

The uncertainty of the controls exercised is apparent from a study of the publications of the time. The Writers' Union weekly, *Literární noviny*, followed the Party line, but with some restraint: the journals of the younger writers, *Květen* and *Nový život* continued their rambling debates on literary matters, revealing some divergence of interpretation within the permitted spectrum of Marxist ideas. The Writers' publishing house, *Československý spisovatel*, actually improved its list of titles, including in its programme the work of talented authors like J. Mucha, O. Lysohorský, and J. Hauková, who had been in trouble with the regime, and whose work was well outside the guidelines of Marxist aesthetics. The firebrands of the 1956 Congress, Seifert, and Hrubín, were still published, and their talent acknowledged.

Much of the credit for the high standard of publishing may be given to the head of the Writers' publishing house, Ladislav Fikar: but his downfall came in 1959 after he authorised the release of Škvorecký's novel, *The Cowards*. The month when the book was launched (December 1958) revealed in its advertising brochure an interesting range of titles, including essays by Lunacharsky, Brecht, Fedin, Šalda, and Stendhal; and *Readings from the Kralická Bible* by Ivan Olbracht. Škvorecký's book was introduced in the brochure by a sympathetic interview with the author. After publication, it actually received a favourable review, in the Prague evening newspaper *Večerní Praha*. A week later the storm broke. The book was taken out of circulation; library copies were put under lock and key: the reviewer J. Lederer was sacked; and the editor, Jan Zelenka had to apologise for the incautious praise. Škvorecký was removed from his job in the journal *World literature*; Fikar and several of his staff were fired from the publishing house. His place was taken by Jan Pilař, who had earlier been pushed out of his job in *Literární noviny*. Škvorecký was called upon to explain his actions to the Writers Union, and was for the time being ostracised from literature.[29]

In June 1958 at the XI Communist Party Congress in Prague a decision was taken to 'complete the building of socialism in Czechoslovakia': as part of the programme the whole cultural establishment was expected to rally round the Party in a campaign to root out all vestiges of revisionism. As the existing organisations had shown less than total dedication to this task, a new Committee of Socialist Culture was appointed: it was headed by the former Minister for Education, and author of the notorious *Thirty Years of Struggle for a Socialist Poetry*, Ladislav Štoll. His appointment seemed to be an official re-enthronement of cultural Stalinism. It occurred at a time when Khrushchev had eliminated all his rivals in the Kremlin; when Tito's Jugoslavia was once more the object of abuse from the new Commonwealth of Socialist Nations; when Gomulka's Poland seemed to have fallen back into line; when the Russians were celebrating the execution of Imre Nagy and other 'traitors'; and the satellite governments were welcoming the news with expressions of exaggerated and sycophantic joy. According to all the signs, the period of wavering, and of attempts at reform, was over.

In September 1958 the Czech daily *Rudé právo* opened up its heavy guns on *Květen* accusing it of 'cosmopolitan humanism', and bracketing it with bourgeois literary manifestations. Members of its editorial board were described as under the influence of Jugoslav and Hungarian revisionists. The future of the journal was clearly in doubt, and in their efforts to stave off the blow, the editors narrowed still further the range of comment, practically eliminating anything which could be regarded as provocative. In January 1959 the journal made its own self-criticism: a long article conceded that errors had been made: it also noted that the era of Everyday Poetry was over. The fate of the journal was finally decided at a Writers' so-called conference held in March. The main speaker was Štoll, assisted by Hendrych and Koutský, from the Ideological Section of the Party's Central Committee. From the start the tone of the pronouncements was authoritarian and repressive: evidently it was intended as a public exercise intended to wipe out any remaining legacy of the 1956 Congress, with its dangerous implication of tolerance towards revisionism.[30] A blast of criticism was aimed at both the journals *Květen* and *Nový život*, which were accused of providing a platform for ideologically false statements, not far removed from *revisionist* tendencies: also the young writers had been erroneously claiming that the role of literature was to criticise, to accuse, and to bear witness. To save them from further heresy the two journals were closed down.

In June was held the *Congress of Socialist Culture*, a mass demonstration attended by almost a quarter of a million people: within the framework of the rally, meetings of all the cultural organisations were held, to 'discuss' political and ideological questions: foreign guests included Shostakovich and Paul Robeson.

The main address was delivered by Štoll, who made clear that he intended to present a balance sheet of developments in the cultural field since 1948. He admitted that during the years there had been criticism of the strong tactics taken by the Party against 'foreign bourgeois and revisionist' (i.e. liberalising) ideas. Experience however had taught that

> making concessions and leaving things to chance causes real damage, this means retreating before the enemy, giving him opportunities to extend his influence. The strength of our ideology lies in the fact that it is not a weapon of defence but an offensive weapon...

Štoll recalled the impact of the XXth Congress of the C.P.S.U. which had, among other things 'settled accounts with dogmatism and with the cult of the individual'. This however had been mistaken by world imperialism as a sign of weakness:

> Thus in the autumn of 1956 there occurred a co-ordinated attack by international reaction against the united socialist camp and the international Communist movement, the counter-revolution in Hungary and the armed struggle against the national liberation movement. This crude attack was accompanied by a shameful ideological campaign in which international revisionism played a revolting role.

Nowhere did Štoll define the arch-enemy, revisionism, except by association with the forces of opposition:

> ... the ideological defenders of capitalism and bourgeois interests... together with the revisionists have strengthened their attacks, presenting old theories patched up as new,

against socialist literature and art because it consciously serves the great, humanistic ideas of our age. If we tear off the external mask of various aesthetic theories which argue the social non-commitment of the poet, which argue the harmfulness of joining ideology with art, aesthetic and political theories directed particularly against socialist-realism and Soviet art – we see that these attacks are nothing more than part of the march of reactionaries against the working class, against the lands of socialism and communism.

One notes the unblushing reversal of logic whereby Seifert's assertion of the poet as the conscience of the nation had become equated to the social *non-commitment* of the poet: more sinister was the implication that all forms of protest against the Party's manipulation of literature were part of a political campaign against socialism, and consequently a form of sedition. Štoll insisted, however, that no real talent, no truly creative force, could feel any lack of freedom under a socialist system. Those who declared that they did feel such a lack revealed that they belonged to an outmoded bourgeois ideology, and had an outworn class mentality, that of the old privileged castes which tried to stand above the people. Štoll's conclusion was comforting:

In the past period we have noticed in criticism and theory an inability to distinguish the qualities of the new socialist realism from primitive naturalism which approaches reality without enthusiasm, without burning conviction, without deep personal experience. Many other shortcomings were also evident which deserve to be criticised. Basically, however, the mighty stream of our art, born under the impact of the great historic events of May, 1945, and February, 1948, was healthy, and contributed lasting values to the culture of our nations.[31]

By 1959 it was clear in Prague that the cultural thaw had run its course. The Ideological Section of the Party had once more completely taken over control of literature and art, and the values they were preaching were hardly distinguishable from those of the early fifties. The suppression of the young writers' journals in Prague was a symptom of the revived hard line in cultural administration. In Moscow Boris Pasternak had been forced to decline the Nobel Prize, after an officially inspired campaign of calumny and vulgar abuse. From Poland the rebellious novelist Hlasko, who had epitomised the revival spirit in literature, had withdrawn into exile.

In Czechoslovakia's northern and southern neighbours the reform movement had failed; and the Czechoslovak leadership could pride themselves on their part in the failure. It was they who had held the line for Moscow, and averted a danger of ideological revision or imperial disintegration. Through the tense period the Czech masses had looked on, and had made no attempt to assert their influence. Within, or outside, the Party, the rank and file were weighed down by a sense of helplessness: the inevitable Forces of History – the unavoidable dictation of the great powers over small – the lesson of failure, and the need for submission – all this had become part of national consciousness. What terrible reality lay in the seemingly nonchalant words of Škvorecký's anti-hero in the *Cowards*:

> "I caught my breath in pain for everything that had happened – for the SS Men that they had killed, and for poor Hrob who had fallen... and from the orange and saffron sky to the West I felt the movement of a fresh, and freshly futile, life. But it was fine; and I raised my shining saxophone towards it, and sang: and I said, through its gilded frame, that I accepted it; and I accept everything that comes; because there is nothing else that I can do..."

The Politics of Illusion

'The censored press has a demoralising effect. The archvice, hypocrisy, is inseparable from it; and from this, its basic vice, stem all its other weaknesses, which indeed lack any disposition to virtue - its vices of passivity, which even from an aesthetic standpoint, are detestable... The government only hears its own voice; yet acts under the illusion that it hears the voice of the people; and demands from the people to accept this illusion as true. So the people for their part sink partly into political superstition, partly into political disbelief, or else withdraw completely from civic life, and become a rabble interested only in its own affairs... Since the people must look on free writing as illegal, they get used to thinking what is illegal as free, and freedom as illegal, and that what is legal is unfree'.

Karl Marx

By 1959 it had become clear that the harsh measures used by Moscow to reassert control over the Socialist bloc did not mean that Khrushchev had abandoned hope of a détente with the West. At the XXI Congress of the CPSU he held out the prospect of a Russian consumer society with a butter-before-guns philosophy, and claimed that by 1970 the USSR would be out-producing the USA. Competition was evidently to be peaceful; and Khrushchev implied that Russia faced no more serious threats from the West. The problem of the refractory socialist states seemed also to be in hand; and the refusal by the USA to aid Hungary encouraged the belief that a form of grudging coexistence was common policy to the super-powers. Thus a fresh start could be made in seeking such arrangements with the capitalist states as would permit a reduction in war expenditure, and a consequent increase in investment directed toward consumer satisfaction. A regalvanised programme of peace missions followed, and Khrushchev himself expanded in the atmosphere of Camp David and the presence of his arch-enemy Eisenhower only two months after the latter had inaugurated Captive Nations Week. The two leaders discussed plans for disarmament, a new start in friendly co-operation, and a programme of cultural exchanges. The new policy meant opening wider the doors of Eastern Europe to Western influence, and a kind of cultural competition: this in its turn implied a renewed de-Stalinisation policy in cultural affairs.

In fact the Union of Soviet Writers had held its Third Congress in

May 1959 in such a mild good-humoured atmosphere as to make it clear that the time for a new thaw had arrived. Khrushchev himself rolled up to the Congress, and in a mainly conciliatory speech suggested that the writers themselves be left to settle their own differences without outside interference.

In Prague the new line in Soviet cultural policy was watched with attention, and no doubt with no little perplexity. Relaxation of control from the communist Centre, however welcome in theory to the satellite states, was bound to complicate life for their leaders, if only because it meant an absence of firm directives, i.e. the possibility of doing things which might subsequently be denounced from the Centre as terrible mistakes. The best policy was to take no decisive step in any direction, to wait and see – a policy which accorded well with Czech national tradition. If there is one consistent element in Czech official policy in the years between 1959 and 1963, it is ambiguity and hesitancy, harsh words and little action, a lack of clear direction and a paralysis of decision.

The Writers Press (Československý Spisovatel) was now headed by the dutiful Jan Pilař: when its publishing programme for 1960 was announced, the contents were as depressing as the guidelines:

> The Writers' Press by its books wishes to serve the people, socialism and peace. In closest co-operation with the Union of Czechoslovak Writers it advances into the new decade conscious of the tasks which have been imposed on all workers on the ideological front by the XI Congress of the Cz. C. P. and the recent Congress of Socialist Culture.[1]

Dr. Pilař's military metaphors were continued by Bohuslav Březovský, speaking on behalf of the Czech writers:

> On this fifteen years' journey there have inevitably been victories and defeats. There have been writers who shut their eyes to the present and retreated to the past. There have been periods of errors and dubious paths on to which writers have been lured by theories of conflictlessness, by schematic interpretations of class struggles and lifeless theorems which persuaded authors to shape their work to the models of dry theoreticians of life. On the other hand there was a period of uncritical criticism and irresponsible gaming, even of dangerous liberalist and objectivist tendencies...

But readers could take fresh hope:

> The contemporary village and its outward change, and the
> inner conversion of its inhabitants, the people working on
> the big dam constructions, the new relationships which are
> born from today's deep social change, the unique technical
> advance, the conquest of the universe – how could a writer
> worthy of the name ignore them? And it is gratifying that they
> are not. Let us look into the writers' studies and glance over
> their shoulders at their manuscripts. Here is Pavel Bojar. He
> is writing the third volume of his trilogy on the village of Ros-
> nov, its people, and their common efforts, difficulties and
> victories. Likewise Brno's Ivan Kříž, inspired by the fortunes
> of a village in Southern Moravia...[2]

How many readers must have winced to hear that the village novel of
socialist construction – the epitome of literary Stalinism – was to be
taken out of its wrappings, and updated for the sixties! It is well to
begin with such works, revealing as they do both their legacy of the
past, and the contrast with what was to come. Pavel Bojar published
(together with his wife Olga) the novel *Harvest* in 1961: Ivan Kříž
published *The Great Solitude* in 1960: in the same year was published a
third novel of this type, *Green Horizons*, by an author, Jan Procházka,
whose career was to be one of the surprises of the sixties.[3]

The first two volumes[4] of Bojar's trilogy about life in a South
Bohemian village during the post-war period had appeared in 1952-3.
Since then time had brought its own harvest of crises in Czech literature,
as it had in Czech agriculture: a comparison of the third with the preceding volumes might be expected to show what development had
taken place during the intervening years. In this case the comparison
has its surprises. Stylistically, as contemporary critics noted, there
was no development at all, unless perhaps the narrative technique
could be said to have moved further towards the slow, naturalistic
style of the Czech XIXth century village novel. The literary thaw of
1956 had drawn attention to the schematisation of character in soc-
real novels; and here fruits of the criticism were apparent. The Bojar
characters, though resurrected from the earlier volumes, seemed to
have undergone a metamorphosis. Hero of the trilogy was the hearty,
horny blacksmith Dolista, chief of the village Party organisation (and
now boss of the tractor station). A dedicated family man in earlier
episodes, he had suffered a regrettable moral decline: having seduced
the village teacher, he oscillates between his wife (now expecting her

third child) and his mistress, in time-consuming mental anguish. Nor is the ethical inadequacy of Mr. Dolista out of keeping with the morale of this once enthusiastic rural collective. Spite, dishonesty, chaos, mar the idyll: the new leader of the co-operative supplies only a focus for the common hatred. Hope seems to lie in a woman, Květa, the coming leader. But alas! her morals are also not without blemish. Worse still, she compounds her fault by the political error of an emotional liaison with the son of a kulak family. A critic of the novel commented that it contained passages which were ready-made for recitation in a political orientation course for collective farmers.[5] So unpromising were the results of six years development! No future for creative literature could be found in this direction.

Less depressing was Ivan Kříž's *Great Solitude*.[6] The setting is similar, a co-operative farm whose atmosphere is poisoned by personal discord. Martin Souček, a dedicated communist and army officer, returns to his native village for a holiday; he decided to settle there; and gives up his army career to become President of the farm. This (like Czech agriculture in general) had reached a desperate state: neglect, idleness, drink, and theft, form a realistic pattern of disorder. It is a formidable task, and the hero tackles it manfully in a way for which his military training had prepared him. Unfortunately, he does not realise how far his own background has alienated him from the villagers, who show little comprehension, and less enthusiasm, for the new Spartan ways. Driving himself on, Martin becomes indifferent to the needs of rest and food, and even to the attentions of his sweetheart Ann: she is understandably annoyed, and the romance seems headed for the rocks. The dedicated communist finds himself alone amid the collective, ridiculed and shunned. *The Great Solitude*, which is the village's name, has become Martin's human situation. Now that he is surrounded by the angry silence of his fellows, his own morale begins to crack: he takes to drink, and leads a double life; a model citizen outwardly, inwardly bankrupt. Socially he has achieved complete success; in his private life he knows failure.

There is undeniable irony in the situation, though it is spoiled by the novelettish ending when all the misunderstandings are cleared up and happiness prevails.

Construction novels of the early fifties had pushed human relationships into the background so that the foreground could be filled by problems of building socialism. Kříž had taken the model, and in following it had highlighted its inhumanity. Solitude, or rather alienation, is to be expected of a course which sacrifices human relationships to social duties: this is the reverse of the old assumption that man finds his personal achievement and satisfaction in a common social effort. A tendency in 'thaw' literature had been to move away from political and social themes to private worlds and psychological studies. A new synthesis seemed to be the traditional soc-real model together with an in-depth study of the central character, whose overdeveloped social side and underdeveloped emotional side revealed him as a deformed human being. The novel might have been denounced as revisionist if it were so interpreted. On the other hand it had much in common with the Stalinist type, both because of its schematic design – the whole plot was really a clash of types and causes – and by reason of the mandatory and deplorable happy ending, which was quite out of character with the rest of the book.

In 1960 appeared the novel *The Green Horizons* by Jan Procházka, hitherto known mainly for his work on film scenarios. Unlike most writers he was active in public life. As a leader in the Youth Movement he had headed a working drive in the Western border area of Bohemia, and his novel was regarded as semi-autobiographical. The Writers Press had established a new series, intended for work of a true-life, or reportage, nature; and Procházka's novel was chosen as the opening title in the series.[7]

Just as Martin, in *The Great Solitude* had left a promising army career for the rigours of life on a farm, so in *The Green Horizons* Ondřej abandons a comfortable career in research to become chairman of a depressed collective farm in the Bohemian borderland area. While he slaves to rescue the farm from its deplorable situation, he finds but poor co-operation from the farmers. They prove to be either indifferent, or actively hostile to this dynamic intruder into their world of rural apathy. As he cannot do everything by himself, Ondřej is forced to drive the farmers harder, so antagonising them further. In this unpleasant atmosphere the tension mounts; and a not surprising climax is a fight, in which the unfortunate hero is severely handled by three bad characters. He is taken to hospital, where the farmers visit him; are reconciled; and praise his sterling qualities.

Certainly the novel's plot seems crude – a Stalinist construction novelette crossed with a Wild West romance about manly pioneers. But superimposed on this social frame is what is almost a second novel, dealing with the inner life of the hero, who seems at times more concerned with the depressing progress of his love life than with the equally depressing progress of the farm. It is hard to say whether the social action is merely a background for the private characterisation or vice versa. At any rate the two are not very skilfully blended. It is as if Procházka had accepted the old collectivisation novel, and grafted on to it features of the psychological novel, revived during the thaw period. As if to draw attention to the dichotomy, the author employs two styles. The action on the social plane is recorded in flat, impersonal reportages; ('I wrote it just as it happened.' claims Procházka in the Foreword): on the other hand the problems of Ondřej's private life are related in a semi-autobiographical personal fashion. Part of the time the reader is escorted on a literary tour of the collective farm, with a guide pointing out the problems: part of the time we see the same society through the eyes of its hero, who is also its victim.[8]

The harvest of constructivist novels had in common both the theme of work, and the fact that the hero attained heroism by his leadership in farm or factory: the theme was the social validation of a man in his work setting. The neo-Stalinist novels modernised the stereotype in various ways, chiefly by attaching some human interest to the main characters. The novels could be called realist, because they publicised a contemporary issue which not only involved Party policy, but also engaged people's minds at the time. But the reality they showed was a mirror-image of reality. At a time when people were flooding from the country into the towns, from the chaos of the collectives into the hardly less chaotic, but more sheltered, life of industry, the positive heroes moved in the opposite direction. Their motivation, like their characters, belonged less to the contemporary world of Czechoslovakia, and more to the wish-fulfillment world of its rulers. The crux of the matter was the happy endings, which even enthusiastic contemporary critics found a bit far-fetched. But with all their faults the neo-Stalinist wave was at least an advance on the original article. In their books both Kříž and Procházka show interest less in the *act* of collectivisation than in its real results on the human victims and their relationships. When the hero tries to put ideals into practice, his reward is alienation – at least until the final improbable conversion of his opponents. One is reminded of the alienation theme in contemporary Western literature. But the isolation of the Angry Young Man in the West was a result of choice: the man of integrity flees from society to protest his aversion and defend his integrity. This was an attitude to become associated with young Czech intellectuals too: but the isolation portrayed by Kříž and Procházka arose from different reasons. The Western protester escaped to isolation as an act of self-projection: the Socialist hero found isolation in his rejection by society – it was an exclusion which he faced for the sake of his principles, but from which he longed to escape. But whether as an ordeal to be endured, or as a refuge to be gained, alienation as a theme was to haunt Czech literature for years to come.

The theme was treated with subtlety by a young writer, Jiří Fried, in his first novel *Stress of Time*.[9] The central figure – he is hardly a positive hero – is Miroslav Klička, a chess professional. He has lived for some years in Prague away from the scenes of his childhood, and has not realised how far he has moved away from its world. While his mother lived, she was the bond which connected him with his past: her death, and his return for the funeral, brings about his personal crisis. One notes certain features common to Fried's novel and that of Kříž and Procházka. The hero returns to a simpler world where he is a stranger: his ordeal is estrangement from the ordinary folk around him: the solution is renewed relationship. The scheme may be similar, but the treatment and angle of vision is very different. In *Stress of Time* isolation from the collective is not an ordeal externally imposed upon Klička, and from which he is fated to escape and rejoin the crowd. His isolation is a fact of life, the result of an almost unsurmountable gap in experience, tastes, and intellect. The climax of the novel is not any action by Klička, but his discovery of a real situation. As in the tradition of classical drama, tension centres on the hero's recognition of where he really stands in the human condition. In the novels of Kříž and Procházka the gap between hero and public is more or less the result of a misunderstanding, which is cleared up in the trivial endings. Basically the leader and the led are one: the theory of the system can permit no recognition of the loneliness of power as a fact of life. In Fried's book the gap is natural and necessary; it arises from the human situation. There is a rather obvious symbolism in the physical separation of Klička's two worlds – the homely small-town life and that of sophisticated Prague. The apparently uncomplicated, well integrated, busy extraverts contrast with the intellectual who works and lives apart: even in Prague there is a wall between him and his fellows:

> Conversation with my friends in Prague is above all an art of *avoiding* contact. To be, like now, alone in my room, as far from the world as the moon, is my basic living style. I am constantly somewhere other than I ought to be: everything is going on somewhere else.

The author compares his fate to that of a Jew in wartime, confined permanently to one room which he dare not leave for fear of his life; or to the fate of a cripple, physically confined and incapable of movement. The intellectual is cut off from life; his world is a living death. It is the anguish of this discovery which is the central motif of the book:

> I saw before me the series of dreary years which lie before me: and they were impersonal and vague as the hotel rooms I sleep in... 'Will it be really so?' I ask myself with horror! 'For ever? No change at all? And must it be like that?' My future lay before me, and it was like my mother's poor corpse.

The intellectual longs to link up again with the stream of homely life to which he has become a stranger. But this life turns out to be not so idyllic as one might expect. A brother who married in anger, lives on in settled matrimony: but it is a reconciliation with the unavoidable. A sister who went out into the wider world in rebellion, has returned to the closer confines of her home town with little to show for her quest. The less gifted also know discontent: their wisdom, and their apparent peace, lies in their acceptance of life's limitations. Their secret is resignation: to them life and work is a self-sustaining process. But the intellectual by his greater awareness is condemned to permanent discontent: unreasonably, insatiably, he seeks a meaning in life. The death of his mother, which brought the knowledge of his alienation from his past, has merely revealed to him a crisis of values. Now the past is seen as lost, and the familiar landmarks swept away, life's futility is shown in all its frightening clarity. Hence the feeling that the years have run through his fingers like sand – time has brought its sad and meaningless harvest of knowledge. Klička finds as the focus for his feeling of futility his occupation. Chess, the utterly *unproductive* game of pure reason, has become a symbol of a wasted existence. Intellectual excellence means human isolation: but the hand and the brain are linked by the heart, and in human relationships man finds his reconciliation.

The loneliness of the intellectual, at tension with society, is familiar in modern literature: it had been effectively explored recently by Valenta in *Follow the Green Light*. But Fried's novel was a portrayal of life in a *communist* society, where theoretically such an estrangement would not arise. The hero was himself a communist who had found his appointed place in the new society, and had served it with his talents. Now he was questioning the value of his life and work. The novel suggested a solution; but it amounted to little more than resignation – the same solution as that found by the less complex characters. The problem of the intellectual in contemporary communist society was one of which the writers had ample experience: it was encouraging, but

strange, to see it aired with such terrible, if veiled, reality. Paradoxically it was its familiarity which made it exotic. As in the story of the
Emperor's New Clothes, the revelation of what all knew, but none had
dared openly to say, was itself an act of liberation.

Human relationships in the socialist epoch were to become a subject
of increasingly realistic treatment. One novel of the time deserves
mention, although originally published in Slovak, and then translated
into Czech. It was *The Nylon Moon* by Jaroslava Blažková.[10] Thematically it was, or should have been, a love story: but its presentation
was anti-romantic and anti-poetic. The romance had a background of
public life and constructive work. The heroine Vanda is an architect,
as is also her lover. Life and conviction seem to be always at half-
pressure. For one who builds the future Vanda's outlook is strangely
disinterested: 'I live only for this day and maybe tomorrow. After that
- it means nothing to me.' Love - traditionally the central human
relationship – is a mere shadow of the grand passion. The lovers part
without tragedy, without real commitment to each other. At the end he
lights a cigarette and looks up at the moon: down upon the man-made,
the artificial, the second-best, world shines the nylon moon. Yet the
world contains at least one genuine character, the devoted communist
functionary, familiar to all readers of socialist novels. He is old and
tired; his life has become a struggle against the weariness which over-
whelms him amid the crushing responsibilities and boring routine of
his existence. His ideals survive through a mist of smoke-filled rooms,
and a legion of irritating frustrations and trivialities. No romance is
possible from this quarter: the hint of intimacy between him and
Vanda disappears into familiar frustration. The world portrayed is
one of sad scepticism, of tragi-comedy, of gentle but sad irony: the
relationships exist, but there is a deformation within them. The book
achieves the atmosphere of idiotic boredom so well captured by
Italian neo-realist films of the 'fifties. The popularity of the novel
indicated that the days of glamour and heroism in Czech literature
were numbered. Readers and critics welcomed the arrival in literature
of a world tired and ersatz; and yet genuine, and endearing in the truth
of its image of contemporary Czechoslovakia.

In the deglamorised pictures of run-down Prague one notes a reaction on the part of the authors from the varnished world of Stalinist
literature. In the interests of truth there is a correction from the poet-
isation of life. Poetry itself had to some extent been de-poetised by the
'every-day' group of poets, and the trend was not lost: a glimpse of
shabby realism is captured by Ivan Diviš:

Leaning against the wardrobe, bemused at three in
   the morning,
disbelieving her eyes glued to his reeling steps –
the old knight had deigned to return...

   she stands, a fairy torn apart
in her one cheap flannel nightie, limp
with the corpse of hair about her face
   clutching her wreathing veins, sickened,
and weeps, in the final pangs of love
   buried in unbelief...
Only something –
a tattered remnant, strip of a once gay flag,
a fibre of wilted stalk of gentleness
he had lavished on her when they were one,
   in spite of everything peeps through his dissipation...[11]

Other poets took the reaction against glamour and optimism much
further: for the first time for many years pessimism, decay, and a
morbid dalliance with death became common motifs of modern
poetry. Prose writers were still working on the theme of the last war,
and the possibility of the next:[12] 'the officially encouraged peace movement ensured the ideological acceptibility of such themes, and continuing atomic tests and international crises likewise maintained their
topicality. But the war motif was treated by the poets with an obsessive
horror and irony that recalls the baroque period of Czech literature
and its revival in the 'thirties. Karel Šiktanc returned to the theme of
Lidice, the Czech village annihilated by the Nazis:

The dead are funny like clowns
you can step on their feet
you can knock off their glasses
the dead cannot defend themselves
You can steal their ring
monocle, cuff-links, medal, watch,
pull the shoes from the smith's feet
and boots from the police...[13]

Josef Kainar was a poet who, even in the hard times, had somehow
preserved his integrity while continuing to publish, and had become
known for his command of grotesque humour. In 1960 he published a
new collection *Lazarus and the song*.[14] In the poems, Death, in the
shape of Lazarus, surveys the world around him: his killing touch

rests on a child and pram, the innocent and lovers, blighting hope and death:

> O how I pity you, daisy baby!
> But all of us are carried in different prams;
> One with blankets full of ash
> and fire eternal. And your tiny eyes, squirrel,
> do you know how their diamonds cut a groove
> in the glass of purest frost of utter death?

The book collected the confessions of tragic heroes, who revealed the secrets of their darkest hour. It was too much for some critics, who saw in it a mirror held to contemporary society and its social conscience:

> It seems to meas if some of these cruel fates are touched by the breath of Lazarus... that new-born, cruel and polished being who walks through the key poems... that materialised ghost of bourgeois emotional aridity and emptiness, indifference and resignation, lies, and mechanised thinking, the embodiment of everything inhuman... cunningly attacks the defenceless denizens of our life...[15]

It is significant for contemporary literary taste that this book, over which many critics shook their heads and used words like 'existentialist gloom', 'feelings of futility', 'demonic predestination', ran into a second popular edition of 24,000 copies.

Jiří Šotola, in *Cemetary Street*,[16] added his contribution to the funereal scene:

> And I will rot
> And I will turn to dust
> With painful
> Fragrant
> Dirt of the world beneath my head.

And his former colleague from the journal *Květen*, Miroslav Červenka:

> ... Silent dejection of pavements. A beret
> cemented into foundations of waterworks. Sobs under
>   neon lights.
> Thresholds of flats, worn round by heels of generations
> that leave every morning

and, tired at evening, wipe from soles
the sand of foundries, mud of graveyards,
dirt of crushed leaves from autumn alleys[17]

The *fin de siècle* atmosphere that descended on Czech poetry at the end of the 'fifties was primarily a reaction against the ghastly, forced optimism of the Stalinist era. But the trend was also influenced by a revival in the popularity of Halas, and of Vladimír Holan, the surviver and most eminent representative of the pre-war baroque style in modern poetry. Holan, after 1949 condemned by critics and rejected from literature as a decadent formalist, had long shunned the contemporary scene. Shut away in his gloomy house on the Kampa island of the river Vltava, he lived as a recluse amid the relics of the past. He was still writing, though he published little, and gradually a fascination gathered around this aloof, invisible artist. Journals began to print excerpts from his work, though literary rumour said that his latest poems were inexplicable, laid in the borderland of the mind, a dialogue with the dead. (His new book when it appeared in full, was *Night with Hamlet*.[18]) Holan was an attractive model for the young, for he was without guilt of complicity in the excesses of recent times: he was a living victim to whom atonement was owed; and above all he epitomised in himself and the whole style of life (or rather, non-life), which he had adopted, the non-conformist outcasts, the lost ones. Withdrawal, defiance, a deep and tragic irony, were dominant feelings of the style which briefly ruled Czech literature at the turn of the decade.

In retrospect this interlude of pessimism seems to be remarkable less for itself than for the reaction which it involved. As in painting, so in literature, darkness and light serve each other by their contrast: a common reaction to fear and horror is a heightened sense of life. In earlier Czech literary history the tension of the First World War had preceded both the grotesque, mad, humour of Dada, and the vitalist movement of the poets. The poetry of the early 'twenties had seen a remarkable cult of the simple, earthy, elemental joys of life. Writers and painters had gone right back to first principles, starting afresh to end the old ways, and return art to its simplest forms: *Life* had been their cry. In the late fifties there were already signs of a new vitalist phase, and in none was the contrast life/death, tragedy/exaltation, developed so well as in the work of the Moravian nature poet Oldřich Mikulášek. In his book *Convictions and Pardons*[19] he developed the contrast of life and death in some detail and in various forms. Death is anthropomorphised in the person of the Crier, who proclaims the possibility of escape from the burden of living:

He spoke in the name of grubs and worms,
of the white and rosy nakedness of earth:
Who goes to them
will be eaten to the bone.
Then turn to them with trust!
He said too: Weeping will be no more,
only silence wafted over the secret places...

Elsewhere he stresses the moment of intense experience, when all the
senses are heightened; life and colour are enhanced by their background of destruction;

... the Spring passed by.
The trams seemed redder,
and from the holes,
the bullet holes in walls,
for the raids of love
sparrows took off
from their tiny hangars...

The contrast is extended to unexpected corners of the human situation:

A tiny glimmer of light burst through...
A moment such that makes the condemned
forget the waiting rope.

Together with vitalism came the cult of childhood. In fact so many
poets had avoided contemporary issues by writing for children that it
was not surprising that the motifs and symbols were carried back into
adult literature. In his poem *Cemetary Street* Šotola effectively used
the language of infantile play to point the lesson of earthy decay: in
The Toy Mill[20] František Gottlieb pictured in the broken toy the whole
world of his past. But the younger poets went further, writing in the
style, and as if through the mouths of children. The familiar horrors
figured in their verse, but all was seen as through the eyes of the
innocents. Master of the style was a new name to Czech poetry, the
young and gifted Josef Hanzlík; his first book of poems was *The
Lamp*.

Before my father went to sleep
he always put on the lamp.
Quietly he would lie
in the shy and steady presence of the light.

My father was blind,
he did not see the light,
knew only that it was near,
knew the switch told him light existed,
he sensed its dry electronic taste
and the feel of light was for him the feel of the living world.
My father had no eyes
he could switch on and off,
but what people think they see behind closed lids
he also saw.
Grave and motionless he lay
and beneath the skin
his body pulsed to the tides of blood and flicker of
nerves.
The lamp was shining.
The light touched my father
and my father breathed the light,
drew it in by mouth and through his pores
and the light ran through the tangled arteries and veins
flowed into the heart
flooded the hot darkness of the brain.
And then he saw things as the eye sees them
in their raw tormenting shapes and animal reek.[21]

In 1948 Hanzlík had been only ten years old: all his youth had been
spent in the era of communist rule. He summed up in himself more
than a decade of socialist development, and was its most eminent
product to date. To his impeccable upbringing he added the study of
modern Russian literature, and translated with grace and distinction
the work of Voznesensky and Jevtushenko. Hanzlík did not differ
from his older Czech contemporaries in his choice of themes. In the
poem *The Lamp* are to be found familiar motifs – war and man's inhumanity, the suffering of the innocent, labour and human fellowship.[22] But there is something different in Hanzlík's poems. Perhaps
it is summed up best in the obvious absence of *guilt*. In the art of the
'fifties nothing is so pervasive as the sense of guilt: accusations, denunciations, judgements, confessions, penalties, reprieves, remissions
– the attributes and the atmosphere of legal assassination and ideological inquisition haunt the work of the writers. Hanzlík, and others
of his generation seem to lack the automatic guilt reflex to which the
elders had become conditioned. He writes of atrocities with com-

passion, but without accusation (that was to come later). Gravely and sensitively he reacted to the world as he found it. But the gap between the generations appeared clearly, and he wrote from the point of view of the child regarding the father. Others, perhaps more obviously than Hanzlík, acted like men who hung on to their childhood as if reluctant to enter the tainted world of their elders.

In 1960 the Writers Press published a collection of verses by young poets. Entitled *Young Wine*[23] it was technically a beautiful production, and revealed the importance which the Press attached to the work of the newcomers. The book contrasted pleasantly with another production about that time by the same Press, entitled *Fifteen Mays*.[24] The latter was intended as an official tribute to the post-war, socialist era which had followed the liberation of Prague by the Red Army. Produced in gaudy colours, it carried a frontispiece of a Czech peasant embracing a Russian soldier, and a mass of peace signs in the form of hearts. The poems, in Czech and Slovak, were mainly from the old guard, and included such pieces as *Song of Peace, Honour to the Red Flag, Lenin, Workers' Quarter*, and so on. It was the swan song of the old programmatic verse, and already seemed incredibly out of date. By contrast the anthology of young poetry was touching in its simplicity and directness, and impressive in its quality. The collection showed that Hanzlík was one of a whole new wave of gifted youngsters: Ivan Wernisch, Jiří Gruša, Petr Kabeš, and Jiří Pištora were among the contributors who were soon to make their mark on Czech literature. Their work was varied in its scope: but one thing that made this group remarkable was their absence of pretence, and (unlike previous generations) their lack of any common programme.

No less direct, but more programmatic, was the work of Miroslav Holub, the scientist who had made a late debut as a leading exponent of the 'poetry of everyday'. Carrying into poetry the rational and sceptical approach of his calling, he was with the neo-realists in his aversion to false heroics and sentimentality. His style was naturally austere, and his approach anti-romantic. In Holub one sees the exact reverse of a style which had prevailed in the early 'fifties, a style characterised by stirring declamation, and would-be heart-warming pathos blurred with tears. Where Hanzlík shamed such stuff by his terrible simplicity, Holub punctured it by his wit and heavy irony. Where Stalinist odes sought to sweep away the listeners in a wave of unreasoning emotion, Holub's poems appeal directly to the intellect. Depoetising poetry, he at times gives an impression of an art almost mathematical: life becomes an equation with plus and minus quantities. It is like the schematism of Stalinist art, but with the values turned on their head. Holub's aversions range from the earth's great ones, mindlessly destroying for power, to the smug and conceited, those who are indifferent to the issues of life, or close their ears to the cry of distress which is part of life. In *Polonius*[25] we recognise Shakespeare's unctious moraliser in modern guise:

> He slinks up the stairs,
> oozes from the ceiling,
> floats through the door
> ready to give evidence,
> prove what is proven,
> stab with a needle,
> or pin on an order.
>
> His poems always rhyme,
> his brush is dipped in honey,
> his music flutes
> from marzipan and cane.
>
> You buy him
> by weight, boneless,
> a pound of wax flesh,
> a pound of mousy philosophy,
> a pound of jellied
> flunkey.

But Holub's favourite confrontation is that of high and low, the would-be heroic and the patient struggler. In his book *Achilles and the Tortoise*[26] Holub developed the theme which he himself described as that of 'immortality and the historical value of every honest human existence and every positive act'. In the famous paradox of Zeno, the swift-footed Achilles can never catch the slow-moving, patient, and stumbling tortoise. Even so, the powerful ones of the world, for all their pride and glory, may threaten, but never catch or understand, plodding humanity, as it inches forward, painfully but inexorably on its weary pilgrimage ahead. The trail of progress is littered with the sacrifice of those who see too clearly for their rulers – Socrates, Archimedes killed at his calculations, Galileo condemned by ecclesiastical authority. The ruthless possessors of power confront their subjects, who though powerless in worldly terms, yet carry within their obstinate questioning minds the hope for struggling humanity. The analogy with the present political situation was such that few could miss it, and none would declare it.

For any regime which operates a command plan for culture, the theatre, both live and film, presents a special problem. Propagandist material can be printed in mass editions, distributed to clubs, libraries, and captive audiences, so that even if it goes unread, an air of success can still be maintained. But in the theatre the work is brought face to face with its audience, who will pass verdict upon the play, if only by staying away from it. Empty theatres are a very cogent comment by the public on the planners, and on the writers who serve them. Consequently the theatre was always more responsive to popular taste than other branches of crative art. When the cultural freeze descended on Prague in 1958-9, an attempt was made to reimpose the spirit of Party orthodoxy on live theatre. The result was the worst season since 1945: public response was so deadly that the experiment was abandoned, and the theatre led the way in relaxation. Initially the trend was set by imported works, in particular, a fair crop of 'progressive' Western plays. The Party's cultural hawks seemed either to drop their guard, or show a rather vague idea of what really was 'progressive' in Western literature. At any rate the Czech stage could only profit from the resulting productions, as Arthur Miller, Priestley, Anouille, Sartre, Dürrenmatt and others became familiar to Prague audiences. A predictable result was that such formidable competition, which carried the exotic whiff of forbidden fruit, forced off the stage drama of the old-fashioned Stalinist type. A contemporary critic could complain that all writers of the Stalinist period were indiscriminately condemned as unsophisticated vulgarians, and that the bourgeois element which had been driven out of politics was returning to the theatres to snigger or cheer from the safe cover of darkened auditoriums.

Western plays, already screened for political acceptability, were still liable to drastic cuts, in order to remove any possible threat of heresy. But the sophisticated theatre-goers of Prague were so suspicious of political interference, and so skilled in reading between the lines, that they rapidly discovered in any Western play oblique reflections upon their own social conflicts. Arthur Miller's play *The Crucible*, when staged in the USA, dramatised the issue of the McCarthy-type political witch hunt. But when staged in Prague the play took on fresh, and even more sinister, associations. In this case critics openly discussed the play's bearing on the issues of Stalinism, and no-one could miss the application of the work to the contemporary scene in Prague:

> If we have to look for the meaning of this play, which is very
> timely for us all in the present situation of the world, I see it in
> this: in Miller's desire to shake man out of his inability to
> resist the forces of the powerful, and to resist any form of
> darkness, demagogy, and hysteria, which keep reappearing in
> the world in so many guises...
>
> The topical value of the play lies in the fact that it demon-
> strates how just and important it is to liquidate the cult of
> personality, some signs of which are clearly to be seen in the
> play...[27]

By their insistence on the social function of literature the communists
ensured that it would be scrutinised for its social and contemporary
implications by the public. It seems that once it is accepted that current
issues are to be discussed through a code, i.e. that behind the overt
drama lies an implicit implication, then the public will expect to find
secret political issues in almost everything presented to them. When
open and frank discussion is not permitted, and certain questions are
taboo, every allusion or hint may become magnified in importance,
and literary criticism becomes the art of decoding a puzzle.

Among the theatre productions of the period one new play is of particular interest as an example of the portrayal of contemporary issues
through creative writing. The play was *Antigone and the Others*[28] by
the Slovak writer Petr Karvaš, and was presented in differing versions
in both Bratislava and Prague in 1962. It was one more modern adaptation of the classical Greek tragedy, the *Antigone* of Sophocles. In the
classical play the king Kreon forbids under pain of death the burial
of the dead rebel Polyneikes: the king's authority as ruler intersects
with his personal feelings, when the order is defied by his own niece
Antigone, who acts in the interests of a higher duty. In the classical
tragedy two valid principles clash – the rule of law (the highest civic
principle), and obedience to an older, divinely ordained morality.
Modern adaptations have generally interpreted the clash of principles
as between individual conscience and civic authority, or tyranny.

In Karvaš' play the scene is set in a Nazi concentration camp: the
time is near the end of the war, when the approach of the liberating
armies has been temporarily checked and victory seems far away. The
hopes and morale of the prisoners are low: to break their spirit the
camp commandant gives them a terrible object lesson. The communist
leader of the camp resistance (a German) has been caught and executed;
his mangled corpse is set on display as an example to any would-be

resisters: the power of Nazi terror seems irresistible. At this point the leader of the Slovak resistance group among the prisoners decides that at all costs a dramatic gesture must be made. The stealing and burial of the corpse will be the best way to reveal to the whole camp that defiance continues. Understandably his friends object that the gesture is senseless and will bring terrible consequences on the whole camp. But an unexpected ally appears in Anti, an unpolitically minded girl from the camp brothel: she offers to do the deed, but she needs the help of others. There is an allied air-raid on the camp, and in the confusion the corpse disappears. It is not made clear exactly who carried off the body; but the prisoners as a whole suffer the consequences, and the SS prepare to liquidate the camp.

Among the changes which Karvaš made to the original thematic material two are especially noticeable. The clash of valid principles, on which the classical tragedy rests, has been replaced by a mere struggle between good and evil. Secondly, the individual defiance of Antigone has been replaced by a *collective* resistance (Anti and the others). An effect of both changes is to make the piece seem less a tragedy and more like a socialist morality play. It is interesting to compare the theme to that of Kundera's *Owners of the Keys*.[29] In both plays the choice of action is between passive resignation and active resistance, which involves the destruction of innocent bystanders. For a communist hero the choice is obvious: he must take part, at whatever cost to himself or others. When trees are felled, the chips fly (as was said about the victims of the Slánský trials). The aim of resistance justifies the unfortunate cost. In the case of Kundera's play there is a note of scepticism, almost of parody. In the case of Karvaš' *Antigone* there is no hint or suspicion of such critical treatment. Irrespective of the consequences, resistance is justified by its effect on morale: only by action can faith and co-operation be maintained.

When one surveys the literary harvest of the years from 1959-62, it is clear that the gloomy predictions of a cultural recession were not justified. Stalinist influence continued, writers were harrassed, publication was restricted, Party vigilance fitfully maintained: but the darkness of the Stalinist period did not return. Among the most encouraging and surprising features of the cultural scene was an improvement in literary criticism, which at one time seemed a lost art. At least two excellent books were published in this genre, both concerned with the pre-war Czech avant-garde. One was Milan Kundera's *The Art of the Novel*,[30] on the work of the novelist Vladislav Vančura. The other was *Bedřich Václavek and the Development of Marxist Aesthetics* by K. Chvatík.[31]

The latter work was distinguished not only by the scholarly treatment of this pre-war communist writer, but by the fact that Chvatík reprinted, in a long Appendix, a series of literary documents from the pre-war period which, by reason of their authorship or controversial character, had long been unobtainable. Although a normal approach by Western standards, this was radical in Prague, and seemed like the opening of a new and freer epoch in literary life. The practice continued of Party spokesmen misusing the role of the critic by merely using the review as a means of keeping writers in line, or warning them against ideological impurity. But side by side with this political moralising a separate literature of genuine criticism developed; so that readers of serious journals began to find reviewers openly disagreeing about the worth or the interpretation of a new publication: the voice of an 'official' critic no longer sufficed to end discussion. In 1960 appeared a popular-type handbook *Fifteen Years of Czech Literature*[32] by Jan Petrimichl, completely orthodox in its treatment, and authoritative in its judgements, as befitted the Party standing of the author. This 'official' literary balance sheet of the years 1945-60 was then itself subjected to criticism. The following comment is from the pen of Milan Kundera, who reviewed it:

> It is a book very typical of a certain method of thought which has generally prevailed in Czechoslovakia in recent years. New Czech literature is analysed in detail in total isolation from its international context. Apart from an obligatory condemnation of an unnamed Jugoslav revisionist there is no serious consideration of world literary practice or theory... To be honest I must admit that the author is aware of his own limitation. In the Introduction he writes: 'We will trace the general curve along which our literature moves in the fifteen post-war years. It is apparent that this curve runs parallel to that of our economic and political life. Literature appears before our eyes as a sensitive reaction, more or less, a mirror, to all the revolutionary changes which have gone on around us.'
>
> It is incidentally quite typical of the author's *a priori* method that instead of placing questions at the beginning of his work, he puts conclusions, so that his study becomes a mere illustration of its final theses – theses which incidentally are self-contradictory. If the author at one point claims that the development of our literature was parallel to our economic and political life, it must follow that literary develop-

ment was significantly marked by the dogmatic errors of the
personality cult, which played its well-known part in our life.
But if so, how can the author be right when he claims that
literature was more or less a mirror of reality? For the era of
the personality cult produced such conditions as to rule out
the possibility of the personality cult being understood as the
personality cult, or dogmatism being taken as dogmatism, i.e.
of reality being exactly and fully reflected in literature.[33]

In such pungent and casual style did Kundera expose not only the
defects of Petrmichl's book, but of his whole method, which was, of
course, still the official method of literary evaluation.

Ever since 1948, when the Communists had taken over the running
of the country, they had unashamedly used their control of the cultural
sector to win the allegiance of the nation to their political cause. Although totalitarian control enabled them to dominate the sector and
make the rules of the game, experience had shown that this was not
the same as controlling the minds of either writers or public. To keep
tightening the screws was not, it appeared, the answer; and the early
'fifties had shown that repression beyond a certain limit could prove
counter-productive. The co-operation of writers was essential, and
this had seemed to be forthcoming. But repression had turned willing
supporters into grudging servants or disillusioned opponents, and the
latter category now included a majority of the most talented writers.
Politically appointed hacks with heavy hands and poor judgement had
regimented and antagonised angry or panic-stricken artists. The
result, in the early 'fifties, and in the brief re-Stalinisation period of
1958-9, had been a literary harvest which was rejected by the public
and brought nothing but discredit on the regime. On the other hand,
when softer tactics had been tried, and writers flattered, paid, and
cajoled, they had showed signs of impudently speaking their minds,
and ungratefully biting the hand that fed them. It was a dilemma for
the cultural planners – repression and relaxation both had their perils.
In retrospect the years between 1959 and 1962 seem like a period of
transition. A paralysis of indecision lay over the cultural sector, as it
did over economic life: the situation had drifted on without any firm
policy: writers and rulers circled around each other, feeling out some
relationship which would satisfy the minimum requirements of each.
No one doubted that the trumps lay in the hands of the rulers, if they
chose to use them: for there was always the ultimate sanction of force.
But as time passed, this ultimate sanction grew less and less feasible,

through developments out of the control of the Czechs. When Khrushchev pushed ahead his policy of international détente, he expected, as a matter of course, that the satellites would fall in line: and international détente implied internal relaxation, or at least no obvious return to the ways of Stalin. It must be conceded that Khrushchev's policies were hard to follow, and at one stage in 1960 it looked as though he might be about to revert to the cold war. At the same time there was a hardening of the cultural line in Moscow, with open attacks on Ilya Ehrenburg and the liberal journals *Novy Mir* and the *Literary Gazette*. But in 1961, it became clear that détente and de-Stalinisation were to proceed. In October at the XXII Congress of the CPSU Khrushchev delivered a speech which in effect spelled out the end of a policy of political absolutism: this time the denunciation of Stalin and his policies was evidently irreversible, and was followed spectacularly by the symbolic gesture of removing Stalin's remains from the Kremlin mausoleum.

The symbolic re-burial in Moscow indicated to the world that the old ways were ended, and would not be revived: police terror was no longer acceptable as a standard means of government in the Soviet bloc. Thus in Prague the final sanction of the cultural planners was removed. Across the whole range of social policy de-Stalinisation meant a retreat from the idea that all social and most private activities were subject to direction by Party leadership and supervision through Party cadres. In the cultural field it implied abandoning the attempt to run culture merely as a system of public instruction and indoctrination. This did not mean cultural freedom: but it did mean that political interference in cultural life would be limited to cases where the rulers felt it to be necessary. As the communists themselves interpreted their own guidelines, there was still a wide field for repression and coercion. But the official attitude was defensive rather than aggressive. The writers would not be forced into any positive programme: provided they left the regime alone, they could write more or less what they wished. On the other hand the communists had reason to expect that more tolerance would bring dividends in the form of willing co-operation from the less incorrigible artists. The Czech communists had generally attached importance to culture. At the present time a good public relations scheme might be very thing to restore the Party's rather tired image, and close the rift which had opened up between rulers and ruled.

Even though the ultimate goals of the communists changed little through the years, great changes are evident in their methods; and the

shift is well illustrated in cultural policy. In the early 'fifties the cultural
orchestra had been conducted in a symphony extolling the glorious
achievements of communism: its tone had been aggressive, assertive,
confident: its eyes were fixed on an assured future. In the early 'sixties
the tune was muted, and claims more modest. The message was defensive. Stalinist absolutism was a past myth: perhaps it had never
existed in Czechoslovakia: anyway it would not recur.[34] The Party had
never forfeited its right to lead. Power was in the best possible hands: if
things had gone wrong, the wicked men were dead or impotent. De-
Stalinist messages sought to explain the past and justify the present.
But by implicitly admitting a need for justification it limited its claims,
and replaced the grandiose arrogance of Stalinist days with a more
human appeal.

VII

How To Put Things Right
Without Changing Anything

'To tell you the truth,' said Schweik, 'you're in a bit of a mess. But one mustn't lose hope, as Gypsy Janeček said at Pilsen – how it still might turn out all right, when they were putting the rope round his neck in '79 for a double murder. And he was right. They took him off the gallows at the last minute; because they couldn't hang him because of the emperor's birthday falling just on the day he was going to be hung. So they hung him the next day, after the birthday. And by a stroke of luck a reprieve came for him the day after.'

J. Hašek *The Good Soldier Schweik*

'I enjoy a circus. Because we live in one.'

Pavel Kohout *August*

In the year 1962 brighter days seemed to have arrived for Czech cultural activity. Some good new material was reaching publication; the literary journals revealed a wider range of discussion; and the Czech film industry in particular was showing golden promise. The mess in cultural life had been caused primarily by crude bureaucratic interference; if this were muted, and the writers were allowed to get on with their job, there seemed good reason to suppose that a rapid improvement could result. After the gloomy experience of the past the writers were hardly likely to use their increased elbow room to seek active confrontation with the authorities if they could avoid it. Of course, greater freedom for writers, by widening the front of criticism, always carried a potential threat to authority: but cultural, unlike economic, controls could be tightened or loosened without disastrous side effects, and in response to immediate developments. Greater freedom for literature was regarded as an act of generosity by the Party, not a right won by the writers; any move in an anti-dogmatic direction was naturally accompanied by a simultaneous move of heightened vigilance to contain any serious questioning of the structure of authority or the correctness of the current Party line.[1]

The pace of the thaw was being set by the USSR. It reached a high point with the public recitals of anti-Stalinist poetry in Moscow; the globe-trotting of the 'angry-young-man' Jevtushenko; above all with the publication of Solzhenitsyn's *One Day in the Life of Ivan Denisovich*.[2] Under Khrushchev's leadership the Russian communists seemed to be set for an ostensible break with the past, as though emphasising the Party's right to rule by virtue of its *contrast* with Stalinism. In a Preface to Solzhenitsyn's novel the poet Tvardovsky wrote: 'An honest probe to the end into the remnants of that which casts a shadow on the past, is a guarantee of a complete and irrevocable break with all that was evil in it.' In Czechoslovakia the more friendly attitude towards the writers was expressed not only in a more relaxed publishing policy, but also in official pronouncements. It was recognised that the harassing of artists had driven an unwelcome wedge between them and the people, a wedge which 'suited anti-socialist elements'. The Party 'trusted the artists... and had made clear its decision to put an end to the remnants of methods belonging to the personality cult period, methods which had raised a barrier of distrust between public and artist: it was a welcome sign that the writers should now be engaged in active discussion of their role'.[3]

Officially the more indulgent line towards the intellectuals was regarded as a sign of increased confidence on the part of the regime, which could now afford to be generous towards its more erratic subjects. In actual fact the weakness of the regime was becoming increasingly evident at a number of points. During 1962 the economic position had deteriorated alarmingly: results, including power breakdowns, food shortages, and queues for essential goods, were too overt to be ignored in public announcements, and eventually compelled the government to abandon the Third Five Year Plan. At the XIIth Congress of the Czechoslovak Communist Party, held in December 1962, the existence of serious social problems was acknowledged. The public was assured that they would be tackled with resolute measures; and that the days had passed when the Party would accept face-saving assurances and dogmatic assertions as a substitute for practical diagnosis and action.[4] But even more serious than the economic situation was an increasingly overt rift within the Party leadership itself. During the year an ominous development had been the dismissal, followed by the arrest and imprisonment, of the Minister of the Interior, Rudolf Barák. The official grounds for his punishment – economic offences – were popularly regarded as a cloak to conceal what had been a struggle for power within the leadership. At the same time the Slovak wing of the Party was showing obvious signs of a move towards putting pressure on the Czech leaders to get a better deal for Slovakia. The still uneradicated symbol of discrimination against it was the fate of the Slovak communists purged in the treason trials of the '50s, and convicted of 'Slovak bourgeois nationalism.' They included the Foreign Minister V. Clementis (hanged), the fiery Gustáv Husák and the poet L. Novomeský (both imprisoned). When they had been subsequently released, and by implication acquitted of the charges falsely laid against them, the cause of Slovak nationalism was also openly resurrected, and the full rehabilitation of the martyrs became a matter of honour to Slovak communists. Both Husák and Novomeský had great influence and enjoyed much popularity among their people; nor were they the kind of men to let past injustices be forgotten. It was decidedly awkward for Novotný. As he himself, together with his closest associates, had been involved in rigging the trials, there could be no question of a full and open enquiry. The cover-up had to be maintained at all costs: but the Slovak pressure for the truth was growing, and commanded as a platform the Slovak wing of the Party itself. As a concession to pressure, yet another commission was set up in September 1962 to investigate the trials (the Kolder Commission). In the following April it was announced that the (secret) report had been handed to the Supreme Court; in May the matter was declared officially closed. Not thus however could the cause of the Slovak victims be fobbed off.

In March 1963 Josef Urválek, President of the Supreme Court and formerly chief prosecutor in the Slánský trial, resigned his office: his presence had become an embarrassment to the regime. Early in April a meeting of the Party Central Committee accepted the resignation of the Slovak C.P. First Secretary, Karol Bacílek, who had been in charge of State Security in 1952-3. In spite of his high Party position, and his uncomfortable closeness to Novotný, he was sacrificed – a scapegoat for the betrayal of Slovak interests to Czech Stalinism. The move could be regarded as a victory over the wishes of Novotný himself. Stalinism, which he himself symbolised, was still under pressure in Moscow, and the Slovaks could press their advantage. Bacílek was replaced by a younger man untainted by the scandals of the fifties: neither wild nor nationalistic by reputation, he was regarded as a safe choice who would cause no trouble. His name was Alexander Dubček.[5]

The issues at stake between the Czech and Slovak wings of the Party were national and personal: they revolved around the distribution of power and privilege, and involved problems of planning and investment. There was no argument about Communism as such, nor about the Party's right to monopolise authority. But the past errors of the Prague Stalinists were a powerful weapon in the hands of their rivals. To cover their past, the Czech leadership was forced towards a policy of reform, and the Slovaks found common ground with Czech reformers within the Party. Before things could be put right, it was obviously necessary to find out what had gone wrong in the first place: thus from the Spring of 1963 work began to be published which subjected the Party's record to close scrutiny. In an ominously entitled article *The Cult of the Plan*,[6] the economist Selucký drew an analogy between deformations in public life caused by the 'cult of personality' and those in the economic field caused by the cult of planning for its own sake. The aim of Selucký and other modern communist economists, to urge a more pragmatic approach to current problems, was acceptable to the Party leadership in general terms; and had Selucký confined his arguments to economic problem-solving, there could have been no objection. But the positive and sensible side of communist theory required experts to explain their ideas to the masses; thus it was right for Selucký to publish his views to a wider audience than that of the professional economists. But it was a surprise to find in the popular press such views, criticising a tenet of communist policy and saying openly what others thought, but left unsaid. Everyone knew that the country suffered from the cult of planning; but the truth had hitherto been regarded as taboo. It is a vital principle of any socialist state to apply to society a command plan, and as a matter of fact the recent C.P. Congress had emphasised the need to 'strengthen the plan' as part of de-Stalinisation. Crudely simplified, and stated out of context, Selucký's views were heretical. As such they were especially welcome to the literary rebels; for it was by the regime's command plan for culture that it controlled the writers, claiming the inalienable right to do so by reason of the Party's 'leading role' in society.

Criticism of the cult was carried further by a Slovak philosopher Jan Rozner in an article *On Mysticism*. Rozner, taking as his brief some comments on a recent poem, discussed the state of mind, or the mindless psychosis, which had produced Stalinism. A 'cult', as he said, is a form of worship: its object is approached with reverence to which reason, or sceptical examination, is anathema. Its power depends on the *faith* of its worshippers: a cult mentality is essentially opposed to rational thought, and involves a rejection of it. Stalin had moved from a position of being a statesman and theoretician to an incarnation of wisdom, justice, and virtue. In the days of the cult, it was not enough to support socialism; the acid test was one of *faith*. Whoever lost faith in Stalin, was himself lost for communism. Belief was demanded even for the most improbable claims; whoever doubted them, showed the inadequacy of his faith, and thereby damned himself. In that atmosphere doubt became a crime; critical thought became treason. Statements emanating from Stalin were not subject to discussion, but were accepted as *revelation*. Since the revelations were of a higher order than the truths of science, they were applicable to all fields of human life, including linguistics, biology, and palaeontology. The results were often disastrous; but the truths remained; for they were dogma, untouchable by logic, irrefutable, and irreversible, save by him who had spoken them. To reverse them was impossible, for thereby he would have proclaimed his fallibility. De-Stalinism could be achieved not merely by changes of policy or personnel, but by a total rejection of the *mentality* which had produced the dogma. Not faith, but sceptical examination; not trust, but a determination to subject every proposition, every taboo, to relentless examination – *this* would be de-Stalinisation.[7]

This was too much for certain people, and an angry reply began a detailed discussion conducted through the pages of *Literární noviny*, a discussion which only served to publicise the issue further. At the same time M. Hysko was publishing similar heresies in Bratislava. Drawing attention to the quasi-religious attitudes of the 'cult' period, he rejected any criterion except that of truth perceived through reason, and went so far as to express doubt about the infallibility of Party policy itself.[8]

On April 22nd 1963 the Slovak Writers' Union held its congress in Bratislava: it was preceded by a wave of articles in which the question of rehabilitating the Slovak martyrs was linked with a programme of wider demands for reform.[9] Novomeský returned to print; appropriately it was with an Ode to the executed Slovak Minister Clementis; (in Prague *Plamen* took the hint and also published a poem by Novomeský[10]). In an unusual anticipation of Party initiative he was openly and demonstratively rehabilitated at the congress by readmission to the Slovak Writers' Union. It was a symbolic gesture. Novomeský addressed the assembled intelligentsia gravely, with dignity, and pride. He spoke as one acknowledging not a favour, but a merited and long-delayed victory, and deliberately he set his own case in a wider context:

> Now it has been decided to repeal the verdict by which I was expelled from the Union of Slovak Writers twelve years ago, it

is fitting that I should above all acknowledge those friends, comrades and non-comrades, known and unknown, who resisted that decision, and who, alarmed and indignant, sought its annulment... But the verdict we saw annulled today was only a minor part of something much bigger, much more monstrous and terrible, something that no one here present has the right to forget or avoid... In the 'fifties it was not just one name struck off the register, and other names blackened. No. Much more grave and tragic events took place, events which, for those involved, can never be undone. And with these events the trust, confidence, understanding, even the loyalty of many thousands was wiped out! I believe that what we have to do now is to restore the attitudes in the mind of the nation... communists and non-communists alike... No price we may have to pay is too high in this endeavour. No price that will expose the truth, unembellished and unrestrained. The truth is the only currency for which the people will be willing to exchange their trust in us, in our books, our articles, our novels and poems, in our indisputably high aims – socialism and communism.[11]

Novomeský concluded his emotional address by recalling the last letter written by Clementis, 'our comrade and friend', shortly before he was hanged. The brief message, affirming Clementis' belief in the ultimate vindication of the socialist cause, was like a gruesome echo of the message of Julius Fučík before he was executed by the Nazis.[12] Novomeský's appearance and his speech were the highlight of the conference; his words were echoed by speaker after speaker; a whole campaign for the correction of injustice had been mounted. In this case it was the literati who put into words sentiments backed by the Slovak nation and by the Party. It was appropriate that the feelings of the day should find expression in a poem. On April 15 Michal Chorvath published *A Toast, on the occasion of a friend's birthday:*

The May moon beats on the window pane,
It pulls you from the radio,
A curtain drawn between reality and chaos.
Where lies the truth? Where lies the truth?
Behind the unreal tissue reality of strife,
Ahead the smell of blood,
On the whet-stone, sound of sharpening knife,

A rope that tightens on the neck,
The ribs that crack,
Death rattle in the throat,
Teeth chattering in fright,
The stammering words of fear...[13]

A month later the Union of Czechoslovak Writers held their own Congress. After the experience of the last meeting in 1956 and the recent fireworks at the Bratislava gathering, the authorities might well have anticipated trouble. But this does not seem to have been so. Any large meeting of artists is bound to carry some risk of rash and defiant gestures, but the crack-down after 1956 was thought to taught the Czech writers an adequate lesson, and the wild men among the Slovaks were not expected to export their rebellious attitudes to Prague. An admittedly ominous note had been sounded by Mňačko, who replied to a pre-Congress questionnaire on 'Truthfulness in literature'. In the course of his answer, which was published in *Literární noviny*,[14] he remarked on the apparently inevitable disagreements which arise between writers and authority; these he attributed to the natural tension between the writers' interest in change, advance, experiment, and authority's tendency to canonise, stabilise, and petrify an existing condition, i.e. its inbuilt *conservatism*. What made Mňačko's remarks so tactless was their evident truth. But with a few minor exceptions, the atmosphere preceding the Congress was far from lively: its expected theme was the overcoming of the remnants of dogmatism in literature. But as the present regulation of literature was regarded by the writers as only marginally less dogmatic then before, the theme suffered from the familiar lack of realism, and at some stage the Party secretary in charge of cultural affairs, C. Císař, seems to have become exasperated with the boredom and cynical apathy which he scented in the writers. At a pre-Congress conference he told them to wake up; not to be afraid to speak their minds; and to inject some ginger into the proceedings.

In the opening address by V. Závada, there was a special word of welcome for Laco Novomeský on his return to the ranks of the writers. Even had the latter not spoken, his presence was a reminder of wrongs which had only begun to be righted: in fact his words were very practical. Recalling Císař's invitation to speak up without fear, he recalled that this is what they had done in 1956; but on that occasion frankness had not paid. 'Remembering this,' said Novomeský, 'I am now cautious what I say.' The theme of the 1956 Congress and its aftermath was taken up by other speakers, who pointed out that the foreshadowed de-Stalinisation had never happened. Instead there had been a new wave of administrative interference in cultural matters: dogmatism had returned, only changing the slogans and phraseology of its policies. Examples of literary repression were cited: the reprisals on Škvorecký and the banning of his novel; the victimisation of critics who had praised it; the liquidation of the journal *Květen*; the ostracism of the poet Holan; the prevention of writers from making contact with the literary life of Western Europe; and the childish falsification of literary history in text-books for students. The leadership of the Writers Union itself came in for criticism; it had shown little energy or resolution in protecting the interests of its members. Ivan Skála, Ladislav Štoll, and Jan Petrmichl were named and more or less openly identified with the policies of dogmatism. Some telling blows were delivered by younger writers. Anton Hykisch suggested that their elders envied them their *clean hands* ('None of us younger people has ever caused anyone to be arrested, falsely incriminated, or imprisoned'). Jiří Gruša told the older generation they should not be shocked when their sons asked the question: "What sort of people really were you? *and are you now*?"[15]

The proceedings were taking a disconcerting turn, and at one point Jiří Hendrych intervened to remind the writers of their position, as 'the Party's assistants in the ideological sector, entrusted with the tasks of forwarding the communist education of the people and confronting the assaults of bourgeois ideology.' Members of the old guard who felt themselves under attack, defended themselves as well as they could. But the older bluster was missing; in face of unusual provocation they were restrained and defensive.

When the brave words were over, men wondered what really had been achieved.[16] The results of the elections to the committee brought into it a fair representation of the rebels; but Skála was re-elected Secretary: the writers had not yet taken over control of their own organisation. Yet the cause of genuine reform had a strong base in the Union, and, as it turned out, Skála's leadership was not to last very long.[17] The fact that the speeches were published was a clearer indication of renewed freedom than the speeches themselves. Once the principle of open criticism was accepted, the reformers could hope to put their case not only within the Party, but to the general public as well. The pressure on the unfortunate Štoll did not end with the Congress. His book *Thirty Years of Struggle for a Socialist Poetry*, regarded as a kind of text-book of literary dogmatism, was now subjected to a severe review in *Literární noviny* by the young critic Jiří Brabec, who in particular attacked the false criteria which Štoll had spread by his book, and which he had never abandoned.[18] Štoll naturally hit back with vigour, and gained support from published statements by Hendrych, and by the Academy (L. Štoll was Director of the Academy's Institute of Czech Literature). In past days such big guns would have sufficed to silence any critic, and effectively dissuade anyone else from publicly taking his part. But in the new climate of opinion Brabec stood his ground; and the Union of Czech Writers joined ranks to affirm his right of criticism.[19] It was surprising to see a confrontation between Union and Academy, both subject to Party direction, and each in its own way representing Party policy. It seemed that the authorities had no intention of intervening in such a dispute, but were content to hold the ring, allowing the contestants to settle their own differences. It was a sign of real advance that a public argument should not be settled by appeal to authority.

On May 27 1963 the Slovak journalists held their own Congress at Bratislava. The role of the press in stirring up mass hatred during the purges of the early 'fifties had not been forgotten: at a time when the cause of Slovak rehabilitation was being pressed, the Congress offered an opportunity for the journalists to put the record straight by sheeting home the blame where it belonged – to the authorities who had regulated the hate campaign. A minute's silence was held for Clementis and other victims; then speaker after speaker rose to demand justice for the victims and their inquisitors. The most sensational address was from Miro Hysko, ex-journalist, professor of Bratislava University, and high official in the Slovak Communist Party. Deliberately dating the period of active Stalinism as from 1949 to *1962*, he accused the leadership of actually reinforcing 'dogmatism' at the time when they had pretended to be reforming it. Illegal police methods had continued; reprisals had been taken on those who dared to criticise them; victims of the political trials had been held in prison *after* their innocence had been proved; a hysterical campaign against the so-called bourgeois nationalists had continued practically to the present day. Hysko's denunciation of the guilty men was violent and specific: he mentioned by name Široký, still, at the time of speaking, Prime Minister. In a choice passage Hysko suggested that reports on the Slovak victims prepared by the Party Central Committee differed from those of the medieval inquisition only by reason of their socialist terminology. His speech was printed intact in the Slovak C.P. daily, *Pravda*.[20]

This extraordinary attack on recent Party leadership under Novotný, and the naming of his closest associate Široký, amounted practically to a challenge to the present leadership. According to the conventions of the time, by authorising the printing of the speech the Slovak communist leaders had associated themselves with its sentiments. It was a most serious situation for Novotný: he travelled to Slovakia, and in a speech at Košice on June 12 he defended the Party leadership, reiterated the charges of bourgeois nationalism, and bitterly criticised *Pravda* for allowing itself to serve as a platform for violent attacks on the Party itself.[21] In an unexpected, but astute, move Novotný also put his case to a world audience by giving an exclusive interview to the special correspondent of the London *Times*. While naturally avoiding mention of any intra-Party conflict he defended his record across the whole field of policy, including the handling of the Slánský case, economic policy, de-Stalinisation, and relations with the USSR.[22] Novotný was able to summon to his aid the influence of the Party hierarchy; firm expressions of support for him, and criticism of Hysko, appeared in both Prague and Bratislava: Dubček also joined his voice to the supporters, criticising not only Hysko but also *Pravda* for printing the speech. In Prague Hendrych accused Novotný's critics of supplementing the arsenals of hostile foreign propaganda: he referred to the Writers Union and the Slovak Journalists Congresses in threatening tones.[23] Novotný averted the threat to his position; but his attempt to save Široký failed. In September he was dropped from the Premiership and the Presidium. In spite of tough talk by the Party bosses the critical voices had been vindicated. With the removal of Široký the door was opened wider to reform.

One long-standing point of agreement between communists and non-communists had been the traditional Czech view that it was a proper function of literature fittingly to represent the national culture to the outside world. By its power of selection over what was published the communist command plan for culture had been at one time expected actually to improve the national image. Not only had this naive expectation been grievously disappointed, but the restriction on contacts with abroad had resulted in a painful isolation and consequent provincialisation of Czech culture itself. One cause of the tension between writers and officials was the desire of the former to widen, and of the latter to limit, cultural contacts with Western Europe. This limitation was officially defended on the grounds of protecting the Czech reading public from Western commercial trash and hostile ideological propaganda: in practice it limited the horizons of Czech culture and prevented writers from projecting a fitting national image abroad. This disturbed officials less than the discovery that a policy of cultural isolation had serious practical effects on economic development. While contact with the industrial nations of Western Europe involved a mild risk of ideological infection, isolation put Czechoslovak technology in danger of obsolescence in the rapidly changing climate of ideas and techniques. Attempts were made to combine cultural isolation with limited scientific co-operation, but results were disappointing. Apart from the disinclination of Western nations to go along with such a policy, the distinction between scientific and humanistic disciplines had become increasingly blurred. We live in an age when research combines incomprehensible specialisation with a complex interfusion of concepts and techniques: calculations in the field of pure linguistics influence the work of acoustic engineers; the abstract research of logicians affects the development of computer technology: cultural isolation is a dangerous policy for any developed nation which does not wish to be left behind. It was the final, resigned recognition of this fact, combined with the general reaction against the practice of Stalinism, that moved the leadership inexorably towards a policy of lowering barriers and relaxing the guidelines of cultural control. The extent of relaxation was a matter of compromise, a kind of battlefield on which reformers and conservatives gained or yielded ground; the permitted growth, or the reduction of contact, was regarded *inter alia* as a measure of progress towards reform, or temporary regression towards neo-Stalinism.

In July 1962 J. P. Sartre had used an invitation to a Peace Congress in Moscow to express publicly the theme of the indivisibility of true culture, and the need for the Socialist countries to break down the cultural isolation to which they had subjected themselves. As an example of how the policy had served to impoverish Russian culture he cited the work of Franz Kafka, still virtually unknown in the USSR. Sartre's speech was subsequently translated and published[24] in Kafka's home city, Prague, the recognisable original on which *The Castle* was based. After 1945, as his work had won wide international recognition, it also had become a point of dispute in Czechoslovakia, with the division drawn along ideological lines. While the communists dismissed his work as bourgeois, negative, and decadent; to critics of the communist system Kafka's world became identified with that dominated by the mindless machine of totalitarian regulation. While Marxist critics had dubbed his work anti-realist; to their opponents the effect of his work was terribly realistic. In 1963 critics could argue a comparatively simple question of the need to accord belated recognition to a great writer who had been condemned on ideological grounds, and according to guidelines which no longer found acceptance among the Party intelligentsia. In this case the fact that it was a Western Marxist, Sartre, who had raised the issue in Moscow made the rehabilitation of Kafka a test for the policy of opening the windows to enlightened currents from Western Europe.

But Kafka was much more than an unjustifiably neglected writer. There was firstly the circumstance of his Prague home and his status as a German Jew. But what made him such a suitable test-case for the policy of literary relaxation was his general identification with the theme of alienation – the vision of the individual lost in a world of administrative chaos and futility – the world which, to readers, anticipated the Stalinist police-state. The atmosphere of *The Trial, The Castle,* or *In the Penal Colony* struck too vivid a chord to be permissible reading in a real police state. Readers could find a fascinating familiarity in the petrified irresolution of the surveyor who was prevented at every turn from carrying out his work by incomprehensible prohibitions; the absurd plight of an accused man unable to identify his judges, lawyers, accusers, or even his own guilt; the anguish of one who recognises there is no security in official justice, and a victim who knows that whatever he does, he will be condemned. The atmosphere of symbolic nightmare in Kafka's books had an uncanny realism in Prague: the impact of his work was potentially explosive in a society where his allegories were so closely attuned to the recently remembered realities of life. Early in 1963 a conference was held on problems of contemporary prose, at which Eduard Goldstücker and Karel Kosík raised the question of Kafka's status, the neglect of his work in Prague, and his relevance to the present day. Kosík compared Kafka's work to that of Hašek, both dealing with a world of soulless and meaningless bureaucracy. Kosík's remarks on Schweik (Hašek's comic hero) were daring in their topical significance:

> At times when there are passionate arguments about whether two and two are eight, or seven, or ten; and whether it is more advantageous and informative for two and two to be five, or seven, or ten; then the trivial and banal remark that two and two make four has a revolutionary impact... If Schweik appears one minute as an idiot and the next as cunning, one minute as a servant and the next as a rebel, etc., though he always stays what he really is, then his indefinable and changing

aspects arise from the fact that he forms part of a system that is inverted and inverting, a system based on the general proposition that people pretend to be something other than they really are, a system whose central characters are the swindler and the controller, a system which contains as an organising principle *mystification*... whoever takes things seriously and literally, uncovers the absurdity of the system, and by his action himself becomes absurd. It is a system whose upper crust is convinced that the subordinate elements are twisters, scroungers, malingerers, and traitors; whereas the ordinary people see, through the mask of official gravity worn by their superiors, figures which are merely comic. It is a system where basic human relationships revolve around the mask, around masking, and demasking.[25]

In 1963 the rehabilitation of Kafka's work became an important test of de-Stalinisation in Prague: as so often when the communist intelligentsia faced a test of policy, it was decided to hold a conference to discuss the issue, in this case a conference of Czech and Soviet critics, with some Marxist participants from elsewhere. It was held on May 27-8 at Liblice, a recreation centre of the Czechoslovak Academy.[26] In the event the Soviet critics did not attend; but critics from France, Austria, and Germany did. On the face of it the occasion was merely a meeting of academics discussing esoteric questions of literary criticism. In fact the participants were aware that behind the academic questions lay issues of current cultural politics. The international implications were made evident by the stature in the communist movement abroad of some of the participants, including Roger Garaudy of France and Ernst Fischer of Austria.

It was appropriate that the Czech convenor was Goldstücker, himself a recently rehabilitated Jewish victim of the political trials. No one could miss the symbolic significance of the occasion: in restoring to Kafka his due position the conference was ceremonially annulling the literary policies of Stalinism. The tone of the discussion was generally scholarly; the political inferences were implicit. But several speakers, commenting on the theme of alienation, noted that it could not be regarded as peculiar to the capitalist system: under socialism too the individual could fail to identify with the values of the system, and could experience the feeling of tragic absurdity characteristic of those, who by their inability to relate to society, seek in vain to establish their own identity.

But the most radical contributions to the discussion came from philosophers Ivan Sviták and Alexej Kusák. Sviták referred contemptuously to 'the aesthetics characteristic of the recent past in Czechoslovakia, which had banished Kafka from its deliberations in order to maintain its own distorted ideology.' He declined the label of 'existentialism' for Kafka, since almost all human philosophy is a variation on the theme of the human condition; the label became therefore meaningless (observers might reflect that the term 'existentialism' had been one of the most recklessly used labels used by dogmatists to vilify intellectually challenging work). Sviták paid high tribute to Kafka not only for his splendid grasp of poetic technique, but for his ability to incorporate the inexplicable into expressed reality: in spite of its refusal to approximate to an identifiable world, his world remained hauntingly convincing:

> Perhaps the way he probed the fathomless abyss of our existence precipitated the controversy between him and the proponents of the shallow rationalism which likes to pass itself off as a scientific philosophy, because it is determined to turn a blind eye to the irrational in man... Kafka's stories are merely the codes and tools of transcendence, an attempt to interpret the chaos of existence... The symbols are an integral part of the enigma, a code for the uncommunicable... Kafka's reality communicates in code and the only way to understand the message is to decode it...

While Sviták spoke in terms of abstract philosophical conceptions, Kusák applied Kafka's legacy to the Stalinist situation, openly comparing the bureaucracy described by Kafka with that of the communist state. In his words, the Kafka situation was the model of certain situations well known in the socialist countries at the time of the personality cult; the process of subjugating the individual to absolute institutional authority had made the absurdity of Kafkaesque experience an everyday phenomenon:

> *The Trial*, a word which for twelve years has left its mark on our lives, is for me the cornerstone of Kafka's writing... *The Trial* is for me a basic probe into the social reality of the modern world.

The open expression of such bold sentiments must have been disturbing for the organisers of the conference and the Party watchdogs present. Pavel Reiman, then Director of the Institute for the History of the C.P., had been for some years a defender of Kafka against his denigration by the dogmatists. At Liblice he changed his position, perhaps thinking the debate was going too far, and compared Kafka to a mouse caught in a trap, running helplessly to and fro and collapsing into final exhaustion. Reiman's critical view was supported by speakers from the East German delegation, who returned to the interpretation of Kafka as a decadent symbol of a dying society, one who had nothing to say to the new world of socialism.

The colloquium had exposed a significant difference of opinion among the delegations, and it ranged most of the Czech critics on the side of Western Marxists against their East German colleagues. Garaudy was not the man to hide his feelings, and he published his views in *Les Lettres Françaises* in an article *Kafka and the Prague Spring,*[27] welcoming the turn of events as a step away from the subjugation of the mind to Stalinist schematism. This was not a very pleasant way of summing up a difference of views with a fraternal colleague, who was thereby put into the Stalinist category; and Kurella angrily replied in the journal *Sonntag*, published by the Cultural Union of the G.D.R.. Ernst Fischer likewise entered the fray, condemning Kurella's methods of argument and his tendency to regard any disagreement with his views not merely as mistaken, but as actively hostile, i.e. an attitude which belonged to the Stalinist past. The debate across the journals had publicised the Liblice conference, and made the interpretation of Kafka an international issue between the Parties. In Prague *Literární noviny* then found it suitable to print Kurella's article, together with answers by Garaudy, and a general comment by Goldstücker (5/10/63), who regretted the sharp differences, but left no doubt that he stood with his French and Austrian colleagues against Kurella and the East Germans. The basic grounds of dispute were various. At the most overt level was the offensive parallel between Kafka's world and that of neo-Stalinism. At a more theoretical level was the dispute on the nature of realism. To liberal Marxists like Garaudy, realism involved the ability to penetrate the human condition to the core, exposing the hidden cancers of alienation and dehumanism before others could consciously express them; consequently the truly realist writers were tragic outsiders, like Brecht. Such a notion of realism contradicted the basis of officially propagated soc-realism, which held art to be a mirror of society. The rehabilitation of Kafka in Prague implied not only the opening of a door to Western liberal influences, but also the open rejection of imposed

conformism in aesthetics. The rift with the more conservative East
Germans was now in the open, and the Czechs could congratulate
themselves that, in the cultural field at least, Prague was a centre of
anti-Stalinist reform. In a late comment on the conference a Czech
critic wrote:

> It is natural that in this situation the discussion (at Liblice)
> took on the form of cultural politics. It became a demon-
> stration of the determination of reviving Marxism to take up
> a new, more sensitive attitude – not only to the work of Kafka
> but also to those products of world literature of the last
> decade which have been lumped together under the crude
> label of modernism or decadence.[28]

The Liblice conference and the publicity which followed it brought
into public view the problem of the neglected, because officially ostracised, writers. Kafka, who had been a matter of vital interest to a small
minority, suddenly became a household word in Prague. His works
were published in large editions: the literary journals, radio and television programmes, examined his legacy: and there was talk of staging
The Trial and *The Castle*. On his birthday an official delegation honoured his grave; and in 1964 a Kafka exhibition was held in Prague and
opened by his friend Max Brod. When the play *Who's Afraid of Virginia
Woolf* was staged in Prague, the title was rendered as *Who'd be afraid
of Kafka*. It is safe to say that in 1963-4 Kafka was far more popular in
Prague than he was in London or New York. It would be absurd to
pretend that *The Trial* is an easy book to read: its popularity was due
to its symbolic significance. Even those who never read the book saw
in it an allegorical anticipation of the world of Stalinism, and regarded
the official acceptance of Kafka as a genuine sign of de-Stalinisation.
The fixing of the Kafkaesque vision in print, and its publication in
communist society, ensured that such a world was no longer tolerable.
Once the world of Kafka became real in literature, it could no longer
be maintained in life.

In retrospect the year 1963 seems to have been a turning point when
the Prague communist leadership began to yield serious ground to the
pressure for reform. Because underlying issues – the guilt of Novotný,
and the destructive record of the Party leadership – could not be aired,
the debate between reformers and conservatives went on via the code
and the allegory. For five years literature, the theatre, film, and cabaret
formed a stage on which symbolic issues were debated and their sig-

nificance understood by writers and audience, trained by experience in the art of disguise and unspoken recognition. In such circumstances the serialisation of Solzhenitsyn's novel; the publication of a long poem on *The Death of Stalin* by Šotola; an article by Mňačko on the need to rehabilitate the word *conscience*; all performed the function of political parables.[29] A heightened significance returned to literature, where ideas were ventilated, gestures made, and the limits of permitted freedom were probed.[30]

During the sixties a familiar motif in literature became the confrontation of reality and unreality, truth and the masquerade. A new play by Ivan Klíma, entitled *The Castle*, advertised its affiliation to the spirit of Kafka by title and atmosphere.[31] In the play the castle's walls enclose a bizarre fellowship of pseudo-intellectuals – a non-writing writer, a non-thinking philosopher, a scientist who has long abandoned science – together with a group of others who serve and watch them: they include a former standover man, now appointed Commissioner for the Delimitation of Statues. The sole activity of the savants is pretending to be active; their only interest is the protection of their privileged and sheltered position (the castle walls have the double function of keeping in the inmates as well as keeping out the real world). Self-deception and sloth, suspicion and fear, the unrelenting betrayal of intellectual and moral values characterise the inverted world of their ivory tower.

The action of the play opens with a scream. A younger Fellow recently admitted to the group and not yet corrupted, lies dead. As if to take his place, a new young member enters from without: it is Josef Kahn, son of the surveyor (Kafka's J. K.). Plunged into this sterile world of illusion he is still intellectually and morally alive, though uncertain, and incredulous of what he sees. A chance quotation on his part from the dead man, '*We have no other faith but reason*', freezes his hearers, who recognise his dangerous sincerity. An investigating magistrate reconstructs the crime, and J. K. plays the part of the murdered man. The whole society of the Castle is endangered, not by the crime, but by the investigation of it. The play ends with the shutters of the Castle closing on the new victim. Nothing must be allowed to pierce the veil of falsehood; or violate the holy sanctum of illusion.

For the audience Klíma's castle had an uncomfortable association with Dobříš, the chateau which the regime had thoughtfully assigned to the Czech writers in the 'fifties as a quiet place wherein to pursue their socially valuable labours. In the play the pompous and self-deluding sentiments of the writer Aleš were only too reminiscent of the remembered pronouncements of real writers. The play appeared as a grotesque travesty on the modern treason of the Czech intellectuals, corrupted by state patronage, betraying the principles they professed to uphold, sheltered from any breath of reality by the alienation to which their efforts had brought them. It was perhaps this interpretation of the play, as an attack on the writers, which recommended it to the authorities, and enabled it to be staged.[32] The interaction of reality with grotesque masquerade was the theme of J. Topol's play *The End of the Carnival*,[33] set in a backward village where Party officials, against a harsh setting of social planning, local resentment, and personal alienation, are just eliminating the last traces of traditional freehold farming.

In differing ways and against different settings Klíma and Topol staged the theme of social break-down in a small community: in both plays the death of an innocent victim is the culmination of a deterioration in common understanding, a lack of common purpose among people who have become strangers to each others' inner life. In thus exploring the alienation theme in tragic theatre the Czech dramatists had some common ground with the Western theatre of the absurd. The latter however was distinguished not only by its irony, but by its revelation of the nonsensical base of popular institutions or assumptions, and by a pressure on the audience to admit the falsity of current illusions. In any socialist state there was a ready-made subject for absurd theatre in the bureaucratic machine, and this was the daring subject of Václav Havel's play *The Garden Party*.[34]

Havel is not only a dramatist but also a poet of visual forms; in his poems impact is produced by typographical arrangement of the same phrase, repeated *ad nauseam*: meaning is conveyed via words which by repetition have become meaningless. He applied to the stage a similar technique. There is a folk saying that clothes make the man, rather than *vice versa*: in the bureaucratic world of *The Garden Party* it is the cliché that makes the official; and the *phrase* that organises the world. Although the play is regarded as a satire on planning, Havel does not at all challenge the right of the planners to plan; he merely explores the logic of their approach, and carries it to disarming extremes:

Secretary: You can yourselves participate, provided that you have sent an exact text together with a health certificate and permit from the Head of your Section to the Secretariat of Humour, and to the Ideological Re-Organising Committee at least two months before the date of the garden party.

Clerk: Provided you get a permit from the Organising Committee you can dance, i.e. in the area of Large Dance Floor A between 11.30 and 12 p.m. and between 12.45 and 1.30 a.m.. Large Dance Floor A is reserved until 11.30 p.m. for the Liquidation Method Section, and between 12 and 12.45 a.m. for the People's Commission and the Delimitation Sub-Commission...

Hugo: Excuse me, but Small Dance Floor C is clearly smaller than Large Dance Floor A. Why not move Self-entertainment together with Aids to Amusement to Large Dance Floor A, and the dance of Sections to Small Dance Floor C?

(Clerk and Secretary exchange meaningful glances)

Secretary: At first sight there is logic in the suggestion.

Clerk: Unfortunately this kind of logic is purely formal...

The object of Havel's satire is not Stalinism, but the de-Stalinisers:

Plzák: There are two camps at the Inauguration Section; old dogmatic phrase-mongers and we young chaps with a sense of humour... I refuse to work with paper abstractions; one mustn't pour out the *bath-water with the baby* you know. I'm an enemy of cheap optimism – mustn't be afraid of contrary opinions. Everybody interested in the common good ought to have at least 1-3 contrary opinions, as was so well put in the resolution of the 23rd Inauguration Congress...
I personally sort of fancy art. I think of it as the spice of life.

Secretary: Absolutely. At the next meeting of the De-limitation Sub-Commission I propose to recite a few lyric-epic verses...

Plzák: It's good you're influenced by questions of art. Mind you, one mustn't one-sidedly overrate art and sink into unhealthy aestheticism profoundly hostile to the spirit of our garden parties...

Hugo: ... The pseudo-familiar inaugurational phraseology hiding behind the routine of professional humanism is a profound dilution of opinions which finally and necessarily led the Inauguration Service into the position of one who undermines the positive endeavour of the Liquidation Office towards consolidation, and the absolute historical necessity of this is expressed in the wise act of its liquidation.

Director: I couldn't agree more.

The horrid familiarity of the language, and the imbecillic convolutions of situation, produced on the stage a crushing effect of realism: the dialectical rituals of planning advance by a self-sustaining momentum into an area outside the real environment of society, yet still connected to it by the logic of the Plan. Attempts to put right the errors of the 'old dogmatic phrase-mongers' serve only to add pleasingly to the bureaucratic muddle; for the outlook and methods of the 'young chaps with a sense of humour' are identical with those which they are supposed to reform. Social problems are hard of solution; but problems of planning can always be resolved by compromise. In the play Hugo finally persuades the Director to combine the actions of the Liquidation Commission and the Inauguration Commission by setting up a cross-functioning complex wherein both can contribute to the common advantage.

Hugo: The best would be if we organize both trainings at the same time: The inaugurators will be training the liquidation officers, while the liquidation officers will be training the inaugurators.

Director: And will it then be inaugurated by a liquidation officer trained by an inaugurator, or by an inaugurator trained by a liquidation officer?

Hugo: Another training will have to be organized: inaugurationally trained liquidation officers training liquidationally trained inaugurators, and liquidationally trained inaugurators training inaugurationally trained liquidation officers.

Director: And will it then be inaugurated by a liquidationally trained inaugurator trained by an inaugurationally trained liquidation officer, or by an inaugurationally trained liquidation officer trained by a liquidationally trained inaugurator?

The Czech literature of de-Stalinisation rarely achieved the impact which might have been expected, except when something quite novel succeeded in arousing an official storm which bathed the work in unwelcome publicity. The weakness of most de-Stalinist books of the early sixties derived from the fact that they appeared to play the de-Stalinist game from what had become the new Party position.[35] Once the Party tolerated (and so, in effect, encouraged) 'revisionism', then revisionist works lost their function of protest, and became an expression of changing orthodoxy. In the case of Havel however, his work could not be classed as revisionist or orthodox; for he portrayed Stalinism and anti-Stalinism on the same level of absurdity. He simply did not play the game of revisionism versus Stalinism at all. His plays might therefore be called apolitical; and yet in one sense, which was for him perhaps fortunately hard to define, they were essentially political.

In Lewis Carroll's book *Alice through the Looking Glass* Alice walks into a world which is completely determined; without choice; and governed by laws comprehensible, but alien, to Alice. She quickly learns to run quickly in order to remain on the same spot, and to reach a place by walking away from it. The organising principle is the chess game, whose rules are known to Alice; she realises that the recurring and inevitable fights between the Red Knight and the White Knight are not due to any difference of opinion or clash of temperament, but are part of the game; and proceed in accordance with its rules. As a pawn, she can only move in one direction and her vision is confined to the next square: the superior pieces can move backwards and even sideways, though their vision is equally limited and they can only carry out their assigned moves. But although Alice can adjust her behaviour to the laws of Looking-Glass world, she retains her capacity for normal reasoning, and so has an immense advantage over the automated figures around her. Unlike them, she can refuse to play; and since she remains uniquely human, she does not need to take the rules of the game seriously. In Havel's *Garden Party* Hugo Pludek (whose favourite pastime is playing chess against himself) likewise masters the rules of bureaucratic Looking-Glass world; and being aware of the game, is able to manipulate it to his own advantage. What is more he, like Alice, discovers that *words*, which the uninitiated regard as passive objects, are really powerful creatures, able to live a life of their own, and eventually to dominate those who thought to manipulate them.

Havel followed his success of *The Garden Party* with a play, *The Memorandum*,[36] which explored the relationship between language and power. The scene is the office of a public enterprise manned by clock-watchers who get through the day gossiping, making coffee, dashing out for snacks, discussing the quality of canteen food, etc. The Director, Mr Gross, receives a memorandum written in a new, artificial language, Ptydepe. Behind his back his deputy has introduced the compulsory use of the new language for all office communications. Gross of course cannot read the memorandum, nor can he discover what it is about; as no translation from Ptydepe can be made without authorisation (written in Ptydepe) given by the methodician appointed for that purpose. A new office has been set up in the building, and a Ptydepist is installed there; however Gross finds it impossible to communicate with him, as the Ptydepist constantly drops into Ptydepe; and anyway he requires a fresh set of documents before he is willing to sign any authorisation for translation. The Director realises that he is trapped; the whole organisation of the enterprise obviously depends on a knowledge of the texts, whose meaning is inaccessible to him. He is tempted to discipline his deputy for gross insubordination; but he realises this would be unwise, as he fears the exposure of his own guilty past; (he not only had allowed his child to play with the office rubber stamp, but also, to save time, had bought a new notebook out of his own pocket and authorised its use as office property). Compromised by his past, he decides he has no alternative but to resign, and to clear himself by self-criticism:

Gross: I'm sorry, Mr Ballas, but the circumstance I've allowed myself to point out is simply a fact.

Ballas: What of it? We won't be bullied by facts![37]

(*Long pause.*)

Gross: (*in a quiet, broken voice*): I plead guilty. I acknowledge the entire extent of my guilt, while further realising the consequences resulting from it. And I wish to enlarge my confession by the following self-indictment. I issued an illegal order which led to the fraudulent authentication of my own, personal notebook. By this action I abused my authority. I did this to avert attention from the fact that I'd appropriated a bank endorsement stamp improperly for my private use. I request for myself the most severe punishment.

The Deputy, who has now become Director, magnanimously allows him to remain in the enterprise in a lower position. Gross takes the place of the office spy, who sits in an interior spy-hole and observes the clerks through chinks in the walls. (The spy-hole was not designed in the building, but was a space left over, due to miscalculation by the socialist architect). Villainy seems to have triumphed; but the cause of justice is about to prevail. It becomes clear that the authorities 'up there' had never given the green light to Ptydepe, and in fact had never heard of it. Anyway Ptydepe is a failure because no one can under- stand it; worse still, it turns out not to be so totally depersonalised as was hoped: as soon as it is used, it has a fatal tendency to take on aspects of *human* communication. Gross is hauled from his spy-hole and reinstated; he and his deputy resume their positions in the firm: to take the blame a minor scapegoat is found and sacked. The society of the enterprise is thus cleansed of its past dogmatic errors; made wiser by experience, it proceeds to the introduction of a new synthetic language, different from Ptydepe, and taught by the same teacher.

Behind Havel's satire on modern communication theory was clear- ly visible the rather terrible allegory of a power game whereby indi- viduals maintain or exchange their positions in the hierarchy not in accordance with their talent or probity but by blackmail and bluff, based on their manipulation of secret knowledge. The authorities, like arcane religious groups, maintain their power by constant re-interpreta- tion of sacred texts whose sanctity ensures that they remain in the exclusive possession of specially trained priests, and are kept incom- prehensible to the masses. Those who, like Gross, operate the system in its middle echelons, can only guess at the intentions of the unseen group 'up there'. Constantly vigilant to cover up any real or imagin- ary indiscretion in their own dossier, they seek only to avoid trouble for themselves, hence to avoid any possible action based on values, ideas, or principles which might lie outside the working of the closed, depersonalised, and nonsensical System.

During the sixties Václav Havel worked as literary manager of a small experimental theatre in Prague, *Divadlo Na zábradlí*, (the Theatre on the Balustrade). It was one of a group of such theatres which had sprung up since 1959, a movement which grew out of improvised sketches and musical features at popular night-clubs. Gradually small groups, formed on the basis of personal acquaintance and common interests, found their own modest venues and floated their own productions: they quickly established a recognised style whose features were improvisation, a combination of jazz, witty dialogue, light satire, and above all, an intimate atmosphere before a small audience. Their style was unconventional as a matter of course; they operated with minimal equipment; and they relied for effect on mime, optical illusion, surprise, contrast, and word play. It was their youthful spontaneity above all which made the small theatres seem so incongruous in Czech cultural life, which had been for so long organised, controlled, and approved by officialdom. No official had called them to life; and they fell into no plan. The singers and actors, by their clothes, slang, hair styles, and jazz could easily be identified as a part of Western decadence which had served as a warning and a foil to a constructive, puritan, socialist morality. Though lectured, warned, threatened, and rebuked by its elders and self-appointed mentors, youth had at least found for itself an exclusive place in creative culture; and it was in spite of, and demonstratively apart from, the official stream. Nor was their influence confined to drama. For as the so-called Small Forms acquired the traits of an unofficial youth cult and a centre of non-conformist expression, painters and artists who were ignored or ostracised by the official arbiters of taste, began to exhibit their works in the foyers of the theatres. It was as if they had become a liberated cultural area amid a domain of sterile ideology. Their phenomenal popularity must have been a source of pain to the cultural planners. When the officially supported orthodox theatres were facing a crisis of falling attendances, there were queues before the small theatres. They could not be ignored; to suppress them would have been a stupid provocation to public feeling; and their improvised style and easy relationship with their audiences made them difficult to control. Their disengagement from politics and ideology was seen itself as a political gesture – of boredom, apathy, and contempt towards the officially propagated mainstream. They showed up by contrast the failure of a whole cultural programme; and by their success they innocently provided an indictment of those who had presumed to impose a cultural plan in the name of the people. The comparison of relative popularity between orthodox and non-conformist theatre was a verdict on the cultural planners as clear as if, instead of the drama, the Plan itself had been called before the audience to face public judgement. Literary historians realised that in this way Czech theatre was resuming a path it had trodden before. Thirty years previously avant-gardists had also provoked a conservative Establishment. Then however, it had been the communists who had represented popular unorthodoxy: now the same group, grown old, corrupt with power, but still calling themselves *revolutionaries*, were shown as a mirror image of the conservatives they had once attacked.

Such were the theatres of the small forms – Semafor, Apollo, A.B.C., Paravan, Evening Brno, and others. With Havel on its permanent staff, the Theatre on the Balustrade provided a natural home for the Czech equivalent of the theatre of the absurd, and is most closely identified with it. It was no doubt Havel's affiliation to the Western absurd theatre that helped theatre audiences in London and New York to understand his plays, and to make him internationally the most famous living Czech dramatist. His work was certainly influenced consciously by Beckett and Ionesco;[38] and yet in one sense is as unlike them in spirit, as he is in background. The absurdity he portrays seems more a product of a political situation than of the existential human condition; and the sense of total impasse and chronic irresolution, so familiar in Western way-out drama, is alien to Havel, as it is alien to Czech literature generally. It is as if the difficult conditions of publication provided a constant, but not an impassive, barrier upon which the writers flexed their muscles. Havel did not enter the lists against an ideological adversary (though his work has suffered from that interpretation); but his satiric portraits naturally took on characteristic features of the contemporary scene, which, like Alice, he observed without submitting to its rules. His work, like that of Topol and Klíma, belongs to the category of social satire, of a more or less fantastical nature.

Much more overtly political, and more scandalous in its time, was a new play by Milan Uhde entitled *King Vávra*.[39] The theme was drawn from the repertoire of children's fables. The King of Ireland suffers from a distressing deformity – donkey's ears. To maintain a credible degree of gravity and wisdom appropriate to his high office, he naturally conceals the truth about the ears, whose non-existence becomes a crucial political issue. The public (played on the stage by a single actress) suspects the horrid secret; but naturally conceals its suspicion; and the king is of course suspicious that his subjects suspect the truth. The deception is mutual: the monarch and his conformist subjects live in a conspiracy of reciprocal pretence. But with the passage of time the pretence becomes merely formal and the unspoken 'secret' is accepted as a fact of life: within the framework of a 'reform programme' the King is pleased to admit the fact. What matters is not the existence of the donkey's ears, but the persistent refusal to draw from them the obvious conclusion, i.e. that the King is an ass. The philosophy of the society is made explicit: it is not important what one *sees*; what matters is getting the correct *viewpoint* from which to observe it. The play ends with the stage in darkness: then the same action begins all

over again. The revelation of the dreadful secret had made no difference: the system (like that of Novotný's Prague) was capable of absorb-
ing harmlessly even the most startling truths from the outer world of
reality.

It says something for Novotný's self-control that the play, with its
outrageous personal implications, was not stopped, but continued to
be performed to enthusiastic audiences. A rival for its political provocation was an imported stage success, Jarry's *Roi Ubu*, in which the
Czech audience could not mistake the significance of Ubu as a king of
slaves who accept prison as a refuge from any sense of responsibility.
In a scene of delicious topicality two American-type tourists[40] are
permitted by the greedy, repulsive, but obliging, Ubu to step behind
the bars for a while so that they may see things *from the other side*.

For the Czech stage the 'sixties was a period of intense vitality when
Prague theatrical productions attracted international acclaim for their
originality and technical excellence; and a wide selection of modern
European drama was allowed to compete for audiences with the new
wave of Czech writing. Satire has been singled out for notice here, and
in fact it attracted most attention at the time, not only for its quality
but also for the intensely political atmosphere which the situation had
developed. One notes that it was stage satire, rather than satiric prose,
that set a trend in cultural life: the confrontation with a living audience,
the close rapport with it across the footlights of the Small Forms, and the
traditional comparison of audience to jury, all gave to contemporary
drama an appellative function, and fitted it pre-eminently to take the
lead in social criticism.

The years were also rich in creative prose: the spectrum of fiction
was wide, and ranged from near-straight reportage to absurd fantasy.
In the first category may be placed a book which claimed to be entirely
factual, except only for the change of characters' names. The book
was *Overdue Reportage*[41] by Ladislav Mňačko; a collection of episodes
which had already been published in the Slovak newspaper *Kulturný
život*. A Czech translation quickly appeared; the book sold 300,000
copies, and changed hands on the black market at a scarcity price.
Mňačko was already the author of a best-selling novel *Death's name
is Engelchen*,[42] but his flair was for political journalism. For part of
1964 he was chief editor of *Kulturný život*: his wide circle of powerful friends; his Party status; and his reckless and violent personal
manner made him a formidable opponent to the Press censors.
Mňačko's name became a byword for outrageous non-conformism,
and it was his influence among others that made *Kulturný život* a head-

ache for the controllers, and a forum of intellectual challenge to the Establishment in Prague.

Mňačko prefaced the book with an essay explaining its purpose.

> Against the remnants of the cult of personality it is no use struggling by resolutions, speeches, motions... This book seeks to be a warning, a reminder that no injustice will remain hidden, that it is senseless to rely on people's short memories or on the idea that 'time heals all wounds'... In case these errors should recur, we must have no excuse that we lacked experience; that we trusted to the wisdom and honesty of an individual or group; that our only sin was blind faith... My aim is to document what went on in those unhappy years.

The collection comprised eleven cases of people who had been victims of legal injustice under the communist system; some of the material referred to the late 'fifties, i.e. well into the Novotný era. They presented a fair range of personal tragedy and public malpractice, including bureaucratic tyranny, crude careerism, dishonesty in high places, and the political manipulation of the judicial system.[43] Mňačko's stories present the Stalinist era in Prague in rather a matter-of-fact way that carried conviction: it is neither a Kafkaesque nightmare nor a time marred by the errors of a few individuals, but a whole way of life whose features included lies, corruption, and deceit on a big scale, the victimisation of the weak, and collaboration with victimisation.

Mňačko's book had no trouble with the censors, who accepted it as a document of de-Stalinisation by a devoted communist. It was the most spectacular example so far of the official policy of restoring the image and honour of the Party by revealing the truth about the past: by de-Stalinising, the Party reasserted its right to lead.[44] But this was an argument which was hardly likely to find understanding in the West. In January 1964 the *Deutsche Zeitung* printed a translation of one of the stories, *Garden of Pain*, under the title of *Der Rote Foltergarten*, (*Red Torture Garden*), and labelled Mňačko optimistically as leader of a democratic opposition in Czechoslovakia. The West German publishing house Hegner Verlag then brought out a pirated version of the book, entitling the book *Verbotene Reportagen*, (*Prohibited Reports*). Mňačko then sued the publisher and forced him to withdraw the book from circulation. He also refused permission for the book to appear anywhere abroad, or even be reprinted in Czechoslovakia. 300,000 copies had already appeared, and this, he suggested, was enough to make his point.

The incident had an interesting sequel. In Slovakia there had been a move to stage Rolf Hochhuth's new play *Der Stellvertreter* (*The Representative*), but Hochhuth refused the Slovaks permission on the grounds that he did not wish his play to be misused as a weapon against the Catholic church in conditions where the Catholic viewpoint could not be openly defended. There was thus something of an analogy between the attitudes of Mňačko and Hochhuth on opposite sides of the ideological gulf. In an open letter offering a public discussion of basic cultural and political questions between East and West Mňačko suggested a dialogue. Hochhuth never took up the challenge to public debate; but he answered with a published letter entitled *The power and freedom to revolt*.[45] He took rather a hard line with Mňačko, and attributed the gulf between them mainly to the Party's claim to speak with absolute authority and thus to be beyond the control of criticism. No serious writer should accept the view that a political party could be the arbiter of truth. 'It is inconceivable to me', said Hochhuth, 'how anyone can support a situation in which one party, one religion, or one race dominates all the others... *We Germans have experienced it...*' Mňačko's reply was weak: he denied any conflict between the will of the Party and the claims of truth, and turned the argument towards the misdemeaners of the West, Vietnam, etc., all the crimes which the Western intellectuals for all their claimed freedom had failed to prevent. The dialogue thus faded out along familiar doctrinal lines; but from the Czechs' point of view there was one gratifying sequel. Hochhuth's letter, together with Mňačko's reply was published in full by *Kulturný život* (2.1.65): in a surprising aftermath some of Hochhuth's views were later defended in the same journal by a surviving victim of the Slánský trial, Evžen Loebl.[46]

Mňačko's book of reportage on the theme of Stalinism was one of a number of such works submitted, but not always published, at the time. More important from the literary point of view was Jiří Mucha's diary from the punishment camp, *Cold Sunlight*. But it found less favour with the authorities, and had to wait another four years before it could be published.[47] There was also a great deal of writing which spanned the genres of journalism and fiction – the spectrum runs from thinly veiled reportage to pure fiction laid in an authentic atmosphere and background. Jaroslav Putík was, like Mňačko, a journalist who graduated to creative writing with a strong feeling for historical authenticity. His first such work was a sixty page novella *The Wall*.[48]

A communist survivor of a Nazi concentration camp lies at death's door. The war is just finished; the ordeal is over, and the survivor conducts with himself a running dialogue, seeking the answers on the nature of idealism, guilt, heroism, cowardice, collaboration with evil, and the justification of the right way. Like a man drowning, he relives past experiences, and examines the values by which he has lived. To what end were the sacrifices and risks? One of the few beliefs left to him is the idea that evil will be punished. But even this belief is shaken by experience. The victims die; the scoundrels live on. Maybe, when the storms of anger have passed, all will return to the same bad old ways. One notes the contrast with the Fučík stereotype – the happy ending of the hero who died cheerfully that others might live. Now the hero lives on; he is, so to speak, *condemned* to live with his doubts. Instead of shallow heroics there is humility; in place of blind faith there is a groping for something like common humanity. The book had unmistakable ideological overtones: the ordeal through which the victim had passed was that imposed by Nazi occupation; but its implied transposition to Stalinist Prague was obvious, and provided the basis of its contemporary realism.[49]

In the case of Ivan Klíma's *Hour of Silence* we have a work of serious fiction set in the authentic environment of Eastern Slovakia in the post-war period.[50] Certain features of the book recall the 'building of socialism' novels of the early 'fifties. Its action concerns the aftermath of German occupation; the changes in village life brought by the advent of a socialist order; the actual and symbolic struggle to contain the threat of natural catastrophe, in this case the floods which threaten to engulf the villages. One expects the building of a dam, and a hero to build it. In this case however, the man who, having lost other beliefs, believes in the dam, is the loser. The dam, symbol of the better life to come, breaks, like other faiths and illusions.

The construction of the novel is complex, and its basic theme philosophical. Action takes place on different time levels and in parallel situations. The priest who, under unbearable pressure from the Germans, compromises with his values and loses his faith, has his fellow in the Communist who loses his ideals. The new social faith, remorselessly propagated by political agitators, crumples at the touch of reality, even as the much more hallowed faith had crumpled. The political belief which had determined his career for the engineer Martin, was also the common factor underpinning his marriage; when belief falters in the hour of test, it exposes the flaw in the personal bond.

The action begins as war ends in Slovakia; the stereotypes of a war situation are revealed – the collaborator, the informer, the partisan, the naive and the indifferent. All are scarred by the fear and hatred which is a legacy of the occupation. When the Russians come, they bring a political ideal which promises a new world, to rise like a phoenix from the ashes of the old. The engineer Martin Petr, is of the new generation which will bring it to life. But with experience comes doubt. His friend David is arrested: there is concealed corruption on the site; the villagers obstinately oppose the reforms intended to assist them. He fails to persuade the villagers to join the collective, and sees others apply firmer treatment. As they 'voluntarily' sign away their land in submission, he realises a terrible thing. The treatment meted out by the authority which he himself represents, is intended deliberately to humiliate the villagers: *that* is the real point of the exercise: to show people that they are powerless, and must submit. Thus is reached the final act of 'liberation': its expression is the angry silence of the village, covering the enforced assent to a new burden of suffering laid upon the victims: 'Anything that happened is better than this silence that covers life and hate and love and lies...'. All the clatter of processions and slogans is drowned by this deathly silence. The shadow of ideals once untarnished falls on this scene of loss and betrayal; and there can be no life until the people find voices to speak again.

A feature of the old 'construction' novels of the 'fifties had been their offhand treatment of the common man, in whose name the Party claimed to rule. The tendency had been to treat him more as a unit of production, or an object whose well-being was the subject of a technical problem. De-Stalinisation literature of the 'sixties showed greater interest in him, as a victim of the system and its deformations. But the tendency remained to see him through the eyes of the leading group, not to see *them* through *his* eyes. The reportage of Mňačko, like the novel of Klíma, is written from the viewpoint of the builders of socialism: the plight of the commoners is important as a sting to their public and private conscience, and a spur to their efforts to atone. There is an analogy here between the fictional heroes who, by enlightenment and compassion, justify their position; and the Party which, by reforms imposed from above, sought to vindicate its claim to rule. The soldiers of Herod weep for the slaughtered innocents: now Herod is dead, and his successors proclaim themselves the protectors of justice. But what if the innocents themselves demand to speak? It was a further stage in de-Stalinisation literature to show the situation through the eyes of the victims, and to invite the audience to identify with them against massed authority. The heroes of a new wave of writing in the sixties were not only the strong who had learned wisdom, but the weak who endured despite; the disadvantaged, unable to claim their basic human rights; ignored and excluded from participation in the social process. At first such books described the situation obliquely, using parallel instances. In the modern Czech literary tradition there was already a ready-made stereotype of a harmless, persecuted minority, the Jews under Nazi occupation. It was this apparently threadbare subject which was chosen by a young writer, Ladislav Fuks, for his first novel, *Mr. Theodor Mundstock*.[51] Its non-hero is an aging, shabby, almost comic figure who wears the Jewish star; patiently and obediently sweeps the streets; and awaits his summons to the death camp. Mundstock never thinks of active resistance to the occupier: he accepts that he is totally powerless to avert or even to postpone his fate. His problem has become very limited – how to go ´ ´iving with impending death without dying prematurely of fear. .íis whole life-style is reduced to an adaptation to fear.

There are certain features of this novel which link it securely with its time: the atmosphere of mutual and accepted deception, where the truth is taboo; the destruction of human rights, not through arbitrary violence but as a regular system; the attempt to go on living amid an atmosphere of total alienation. The novel shows life in conditions where nothing is left but the will to live; in Mundstock we have the sympathetic portrait of man as a helpless and unresisting victim of utter humiliation.

For the post-war generation there was poignant significance in the image of the Jew as a victim of power: until very recent times the Jewish race has been regarded as the type of passive, non-resisting, non-violent victim, talented with an endless capacity for suffering outrage in silence. But in the biblical story the innocent objects of Herod's violence are children, equally helpless, but with the added refinement that they cannot comprehend the existence of the evil which strikes at them. It is children who supply the stereotype of suffering in the work of the younger generation of Czech writers. The poems of Ivan Wernisch, Petr Kabeš, and Josef Hanzlík are filled with the images of childhood. It is a world that lies as if under constant threat: over the defenceless, the naive, the unprepared children lies the shadow of absolute power in all its potential brutality: their inability to grasp its menace makes them seem the more helpless and threatened. In the poem *The Black Merry-go-round*[52] a crowd of children is whirled on the senselessly revolving roundabout as war explodes around them. Probably Hanzlík's best-known poem is *Clap Hands for Herod:*[53]

We
little children in shifts
with the bloodstains
long since washed clean
have gathered here
as we were told
and are waiting to welcome King Herod
For us murdered innocents
a special place was set aside in Heaven
There are woods here
full of bushes and deer
and grey caves to hide in
We the smallest among the dead
believed in our ignorance
that King Herod
was a wicked man
who had us killed
out of sheer brutality and heartlessness

But now we have been told:
Look at the woods you live in here
even the tiniest singing birds
fatten on insects all colours
of the rainbow
to end up in wild cats' jaws
little snakes gulp down mice
and big ones rabbits and game
the wolf that devours the sheep
falls sick and is torn to pieces by his brethren

And even the flowers and the bushes
strangle each other's growth
each seizes his share of the sun
But far far worse is it
among men
who besides their animal malice
hate one another
and have the cunning
to perfect their power to kill

That is what they told us
and we pale little angels
gulped in horror
and crouched even lower among the tree roots
grateful
that in our bloodthirsty woods
we were not really alive
and they went on:
There is no love among men
nor anywhere else in the world of the living
Only King Herod
loved you spotless white little humans

above all else
and freed you from the toils of life
only to save you
from its infinite horrors
Thank your deliverer
and if he comes to see you
greet him with songs and applause

There were some among us
who cried out then
that there is love among men
the palms of their hands still remembered it
and King Herod
was a foul murderer
who ought to be drawn and quartered
with a butcher's axe
and the pieces thrown
to the wild beasts
but there were others among us
who stopped their mouths for them
for we were filled with joy
and gratitude towards the king
and we listened eagerly to what came next:

Give thanks that you have been delivered from the world
the valley of tears
where the name justice is given
to a blind girl with a pair of scales
who has turned all the openings in her body
into wells of the plague

give thanks to King Herod
who has saved you in the greatness of his love

and we wept
with tears of pity for the lies and slanders
we had been led to believe before
and we lifted up translucent hands
in gratitude for the truth revealed to us

and now we have gathered here once more
around the sacrificial altar
and are ready to burst into song
and are longing to clap our hands
for Herod

who is coming to kill us again

The helpless innocence of children, and the menacing world created by their elders, seems like an obsession with the younger writers of the time. The finger of accusation was pointed at the source of guilt, always the older generation, in an obvious political analogy. Other cultural genres portrayed the same gesture in their own way. One of the screen successes of the day was a trick film, superficially a fairy tale for children, actually a social fable for adults, *When the Cat Comes*.[54] The scene is a traditional Czech town, set around a cobbled, medieval square. The town has fallen on evil ways: the atmosphere is polluted by the wickedness of the burghers. Above the town in a high turret lives a magician, aloof from the corruption below. His daughter, a beautiful girl dressed in black tights, is the owner of a black cat with magic powers: through his spectacles human beings change colour in accordance with their concealed vices. The town is emptied of its children, driven out in disgust when they perceive the greed, dishonesty, and utter hypocrisy of parents and teachers. The cat has brought the moment of truth to this strange community: the children will not return to their desolated home until their elders change their ways and become worthy of the image which the children have of them. The social parable was charming, and struck at the audience with its topical realism. Youth with its clean hands, the middle generation with its chameleon-like changes of colour, the linking of hands between oldest and youngest to accuse the guilty intermediary – all this belonged to a consistent pattern.

The writers of the old *Květen* group were now active, and a good deal of the new writing recalled the neo-realist style which had been associated with them. The conscious de-glamorisation and de-poetisation of their work set them apart not only from the old soc-real writers, but also from the 'magical-wonder' verse of the younger lyric-ists. Poet of the 'everyday verse', Miroslav Holub, wrote in 1961:

> There are some poets – metaphysical poets I would call them – who create (or think they create) by their verses a new land, a new reality – some kind of miracle or magic. That is what I would call a naive approach to art. I am not concerned with creating a new world, but with discovering the real one.

While other writers explored their indignation in biblical parables or utopian satire Holub remained empirical and matter-of-fact. While other poets assaulted the emotions with the mystery of images, he exposed deceit and false sentimentality with cold precision. Here is a poem of his which recalls, with unexpressed irony, the 'heart-warming' pseudo-optimism of the old socialist-construction pieces:

On the Building site of a Hostel
Among pools of earth,
in a chain reaction of bricks,
between the decaying milk-teeth of concrete blocks
has just been hatched
a grey, two-phase
coffin.
                   (Wipe your feet)
Enter a dignified museum
of the gall stones
of emptiness
                   (Quiet please)
Fingers of piping explore the hollows
and the Monday morning howl
is everywhere
                   (No spitting)
Above the bunk
a single bulb rages
suspended
from a concrete sky.
And on a nail
driven into flesh

shipwrecked socks and brassieres
are drying.
                              (No sliding in the corridors)
We met
staring girls' eyes,
wandering like bugs over the plaster
and we asked,
what is love
and
shall we soon be young?[55]

Holub's austere scepticism in the field of social engineering may be compared to the less austere, but no less sceptical attitude of Milan Kundera to the field of intimate human relationships. Kundera's first book of fiction was a collection of three short stories entitled *Ludicrous Loves*,[56] each an episode of emotional failure and ridiculous futility. In each case the narrator is of an intellect which sets him well above his surroundings and enables him easily to penetrate the cheap facade of petty deceit. Nevertheless his cleverest schemes founder on the human element, and the unpredictable frustrations that lie close below the surface of life and love: they are stories of deformed relationships, in which the pursuit of romance is one more illusion, leading into a trap. In his second collection *A Second Volume of Ludicrous Loves*[57] the ritual of courtship reaches still further depths of irony and disillusion. An awareness by the lover that the game is a futile exercise does not affect his willingness to continue it; but rather exemplifies the truth that pointless activity and empty ambitions constitute the natural condition of man.

The stories contain characteristic motifs; an individual is caught in the emotional trap which he has unwittingly devised; through the mask-mentality which arises from the game of deception and self-deception identities become confused. One more example from contemporary fiction may be noted, illustrating the fascination of the theme of lost identity. In the story *I am not sure*,[58] by Ivan Vyskočil, an important official Otto Zabel, on holiday with his wife, receives a telegram, recalling him to duty. His wife objects to his departure, and when she cannot persuade him, she spitefully forces him to deliver some jars of jam for her to an unknown address at the place where he has to change trains. Reluctantly pushed into this idiotic position, he tries to carry out the assignment, but the taxi driver takes him to the wrong address. Suddenly he is arrested by two men who question, confuse, and threaten him. To his horror he finds that he can give no rational explanation of what he is doing at the house; his story is ridiculed and disbelieved. He is shoved into a cellar; locked up; completely disorientated and frightened; so that he begins to behave like a lunatic in primitive reaction to his nightmare experience. During the night he is visited by a woman, first sinister, then comic, who carries on a seduction game in the darkness to win his confidence. But instead of him confessing to her, she begins to confess to him. Next morning he escapes without difficulty, and everything returns to normality. The story continues with the author's critical reaction to his own composition: he decides to vary the ending. In the first variant Zabel, after his escape tells what has happened, but no one believes him. At first they think it is an excuse to cover his absence; then when he sticks to his story, they come to the conclusion that he has gone crazy, and lock him up. Finally Zabel, realising that telling the truth has got him into the madhouse, accepts that the whole thing was imaginary. When he finally comes to believe that he really was mad, i.e. that he *did* imagine the whole thing, he is regarded as cured. This variant does not entirely satisfy the author, who seeks yet a third alternative. Perhaps the whole incident was not a mix-up, ending in a misunderstanding, at all. Perhaps it was a complex plot, devised by a whole group of people to implicate and liquidate this high official, who, once he loses his identity, ceases to *be* a high official. So in one sense he *was* a different person; and his captors were right to lock him up and disbelieve him. After all, there are more things in heaven and earth...

In this story, as elsewhere in his work, Vyskočil combines a bizarre situation with a rational approach, and leads the absurd contradictions to their logical conclusion: it is a kind of philosophical fiction, in which the logic of the method makes the absurdities seem all the more grotesque. The logic is of general validity: the situations are closely connected with the current situation and ideological context. The fantasies are like metaphors expressing motifs, familiar in other literature of the time: social alienation appears as a loss of identity; disorientation as the desperate search for a way out of a trap which cannot be defined or comprehended:

A man travels round the world, seeking a place which could not be found on any map; he is searching for NOWHERE – he looks for the road to NOPLACE. The car owner can go 'anywhere'; but he wants to be 'somewhere else'. In a place that's more *right* for him. Like our young enthusiasts. Like them, he has the possibility of choice, and cannot make up his mind. He wants someone to step into the car and indicate a direction and a goal: but his passenger also knows only a negative direction; she knows that she wants 'to get away'. When he tries to carry out her wishes, she is alarmed, and prefers to turn back, choosing the past; memories; recriminations; the illusion of memories and recriminations; travel in a circle. The owner of the car drives full speed into a wall.[59]

Disorientation and the search for an identity in a hostile, incomprehensible world are motifs of a general, existentialist type, familiar in the contemporary literature of Western Europe, and not confined to any ideological climate. They are brought directly into contact with local political issues and nailed to an actual situation, in a novel first published in Slovak in 1956, and revived in 1963. The novel was *The Demon of Assent* by Dominik Tatarka.[60] An intellectual, Bartolomej Boleraz, is returning by plane from a writers' conference with his companion, a high Party functionary, who has for long been his watchdog, his overt persecutor, and his secret admirer. In a storm there is a crash; and a heavy bag full of Party documents splits the writer's head open; the brain of the functionary pours into it. Boleraz, whose mental identity has now become rather obscure, in a sort of posthumous life tells his story, which constitutes the main body of the narrative:

> Lots of our contemporaries think, like I do now after my death, with an alien brain... They think that they have reconstituted their brain and piously convinced that with this reconstituted organ of thought they take in the world in a more enlightened way than they would using their own heads. Dissatisfaction with one's own brain is actually a rather progressive trend: lots of my contemporaries are fairly bursting with eagerness to reconstitute and intermingle their brains with a borrowed brain. So, by their good efforts, they mix up and knead together a pure paste.

The flash-back reveals that this strange transplantation metaphorically sums up a personality confusion dating back some years. As a writer, and a 'bearer of the nation's conscience', Boleraz had been subject to unusual pressures during the period of the personality cult. He was pulled one way by his personal conviction of his innocence, and in the opposite direction by objective evidence that he was really a traitor. Feeling that his very reason was threatened by the dilemma, he decided to save his reason by conceding that he *was* a traitor. He accepts the working principle of *guidance and assent*. The test of his loyalty comes when his own wife and son are accused; he passes the test well by demanding the death penalty for them. Unfortunately he finds that he has destroyed himself, both as a writer and a person. At last he rebels, and at a writers' conference he renounces his demon of assent, and dares to claim that *black is not white*, and that 'artificial flowers have no smell'. By the unanimous vote of his fellow writers he is disowned and denounced. His reason collapses, and he is confined to a psychiatric clinic. Later comes the revelation of the 'cult of personality'; and he is unanimously hailed as a hero by the same writers who had denounced him. After this final bizarre turn comes the plane accident which returns the reader to the starting point of the story.

The irony of Tatarka's story was compounded by its real-life background. In the early fifties Tatarka was one of the Slovak writers singled out for especial persecution. His books were supressed; if anything of his appeared, it was received with contempt and hostility: he was condemned and shunned by his fellow writers. The story *Demon of Assent* was therefore founded on very personal experience; and the phrase used by Boleraz at the writers' conference, that artificial flowers have no smell, was actually used in a conference speech by Tatarka himself. But the true irony was still to come. When the story appeared in 1956, it (like Boleraz's words) was hailed with applause by the writers who had previously persecuted Tatarka, and was regarded as a fine example of de-Stalinisation literature. But when the Party line changed again, Tatarka once more became an object of suspicion: his *Demon of Assent* had become a damning proof of his *dissent*. The republication of the story in 1963 was one more sardonic turn of the wheel: once more Tatarka was a hero. History had repeated itself; and the trenchant irony of his story had received a bizarre confirmation by its reception in the real world of Czechoslovakia.

Tatarka, like Škvorecký, Novomeský, and Holan, is among the writers who re-emerged in the sixties from official ostracism. Together with the return of the old came a wave of the new, in theatre, in film and in creative literature. Among the discoveries of the time is a writer whose work is outstanding for its originality and popular appeal. It was Bohumil Hrabal, who was not a young man (he was born in 1914) but was new to the reading public. After studying law, and after surviving traumatic upheavals to his career during the period of war and post-1948, he had worked his way through a giddy sequence of unskilled and semi-skilled jobs, and rubbed shoulders with a wide spectrum of human types, including many of the gossips, dropouts, and oddbods who were to appear in his tales. His first book had appeared in 1954 in an edition of only 250 copies.[61] A second book of his was seen through the press, but then banned.[62] Only in 1963 did he burst upon a surprised public with his *Pearl at the bottom*,[63] which ran quickly into three editions. It was followed in 1964 by his best-known book *The Crazies*[64] then by *Dancing Lessons for Seniors and Advanced*.[65] Probably Hrabal is known best in the West for his least characteristic work *Closely Watched Trains*,[66] which was filmed, and won an international award.

Czech readers tend to associate Hrabal with the characters in his *Crazies*. The title is a neologism in Czech, and its meaning gains definition only from the stories. One common features of the crazies is that they are all individualists: unencumbered with any vestige of ambition, malice, respect, or conviction, they lack possessions, goals, or the desire to obtain any. They show a tremendous interest in life, and great capacity for coping with it; in spite of the fact that their lowly self-chosen position at the bottom of the heap exposes them to attacks, humiliations, the wrath of upstanding citizens, and an endless series of mind-bending disasters. They live in a state of muddled but genial anarchy; and are quite oblivious of any creed or ideology. They accept the most diverse tribulations with undiminished interest and goodwill; their philosophic attitude and dead-pan reaction is enough to drive their betters into a frenzy.

Hrabal's stories are more or less plotless dialogues, or monologues (the whole of *Dancing Lessons* is in one sentence). The stream of words carries a relentless surge of gags, anecdotes, stories: usually they include hideous mischances, and are marked by paradox and gross incongruity. A female butcher hangs her daughter on a meat-hook and absently slices steaks off her: a family talk affectionately about what a muddler their Dad is, how he always falls off the roof, pokes the blade of a sickle through his head, so they fairly burst with laughter at the sight. A girl hangs herself in a public lavatory; in an interesting discussion over the corpse a man relates how his own wife is always trying to commit suicide, but always botching the job. The crazies are usually tremendous liars ('Better to tell lies, because they sound more like the truth.'). Two old failures lie next to each other in hospital; a hack journalist and singer. On their death-beds they relate their life stories: the one how he rocked the world with his stories; the other how whole theatres rose to applaud him. The hospital barber listens with indignation to all these (entirely false) claims. When he is wheeling their corpses off, he meets a patient who mistakes him for a doctor in his white coat: he begins to tell his own lies... A jeweller crawls under his daughter's bed to hear her 'contribution to a European renaissance' with her boyfriend. A spring slices through his neck: his shouts of agony are drowned by his daughter's squeals of delight above his head. A typical extract:

> Our parson got himself in a mess when he caught a boy doing a girl by the church one night, at first he got a shock that it was the curate, but still he had to report it and some missionaries came, as morals were going down in the district, and four footballers came, that's how the four missionaries looked, they had habits with belts round the waist and in the end they so improved the morals of the place that the police had to intervene, because the social democrats kept putting provocative questions about man coming from the monkeys, and then they quarrelled about where does the chicken come from? From the egg! And where does the egg come from? From the chicken! So the free-thinkers and the missionaries howled at each other for two hours until they shouted with their last ounce of strength And where did the first egg come from? and the free-thinkers shouted From nature, and the missionaries said it was God, and they bashed into each other and the police intervened because the women went round for them and said the heathens were insulting God's sons, then the women started throwing stones at the free-thinkers and hit two of the policemen, because you can't mess around with God...[67]

When Hrabal's work became popular, people asked why it had had to wait so long for publication. It seemed difficult to object to it on political grounds since it was demonstrably apolitical. But in conditions where all cultural life is politicised, the apolitical becomes, by a Hrabalian paradox, itself political: by ignoring the official line, it protested against it. Hrabal's stories are so far removed from the official style of the old official literature as to constitute an opposite pole to it. It is instructive to compare his characters with the heroes of the soc-real novel. While the latter tended to be stern, humourless, respectable, ascetic, disciplined, highly motivated and impersonal types; Hrabal's characters are relaxed, cheery, vulgar, indulgent, feckless, anarchic, unheroic and very individualistic *personalities*, without any consistent motivation except to keep going: they are the off-people of society, who seem paradoxically to typify it. Soc-real novels had placed at the centre of interest the solving of some problem of social engineering – the eradication of a harmful influence; the construction of some useful piece of work – and the humans seem little more than the instruments which complicate, or help to solve, the problem – an elite manipulating, or a mass manipulated by, social forces, ideology, History. By contrast Hrabal's stories are all concerned from first to last with people, and their private lives: where social movements or ideologies touch them (viz. the free-thinking social democrats and the church in the extract above), it is only as a background; an irritant to be endured; or a source of innocent fun. The polarisation which applies to character and content applies also to the formal organisation of the books. The soc-real novel, like the ideological creed it echoed, was organised according to a fairly strict pattern. There was a hierarchy of components in accordance with their social importance, their contribution to the solution of the problem, and their capacity for uplift. Space was rationed; whole chapters might be devoted to exploring the technical ingenuity of the engineering project, or the invincible optimism of the Fučík-like hero: personal friction merits space only for its social implications: aimless trivialities and fruitless daydreams are ignored or curtly dismissed. By contrast, Hrabal's stories seem to lack any organisation at all: the style is flat; they are rambling and discursive; there is no detail too trivial to engage the interest of the narrator; nor any feature so emphasised as to organise the jumble of anecdotes into a hierarchy of importance. Recent writing had shown a tendency towards looseness of construction, as exemplified e.g. in the distaste for a 'happy ending' or any neat tying up of the threads: Hrabal took the tendency to its limit. In soc-real literature in its purest form every element was eliminated which did not fit into the pre-ordained pattern. With Hrabal it is the pattern itself which has been eliminated.

The result was a Hrabalian realism so vivid as to expose by dreadful contrast the monumental pretentiousness and false values of the schematic literature which was its opposite pole. Of course soc-real literature had long gone out of fashion; but it was only with the advent of Hrabal that the dynamite below its pedestal seemed finally and irrevocably to have been ignited. The popular impact of his books was comparable to the impact of Hašek's *Schweik*: overnight Hrabal's crazies became a national type, setting a style for off-beat living. Fears were expressed that the whole of modern Czech literature was likely to become Hrabalesque.[68]

Future historians will no doubt attach to Czech writing of the sixties the title of 'de-Stalinisation'. But the category requires some modification. Mňačko's *Reportages*, Bublík's *Spine*, and Klíma's *Hour of Silence* are all against Stalinism, and by implication call for the reform of the system. In one sense therefore they are the reverse of the old Stalinist literature. On the other hand they, like it, echo the current line of the Party; like it, they are concerned with problem solving and with social planning; their heroes, though less schematic and more human, are also highly motivated by social goals, and tend to find their highest satisfaction in a reformed past or a better future. History has placed Stalinists and de-Stalinisers on opposite sides of the fence, yet they shared many attitudes, including a desire to use creative literature for the purposes of political exposition and moral persuasion. Both groups of writers wrote socially engaged literature, and in this they were at one. It is not surprising to find that some of the keenest de-Stalinisers were themselves ex-Stalinists.

But if one turns to the work of e.g. Havel, Milan Kundera, or Hrabal, one finds oneself in a different world of literary aims and values. It explores territory far beyond the confines of soc-real literature; it does not aim at any particular form of uplift or persuasion; owns to no criteria outside creative art; and does not attempt to play the political game of *pro* and *anti*. In general it is concerned with the individual, not with the collective good; and with the present, not with the future (like the Stalinist builders), nor the past (like the de-Stalinising reformers). Man appears in his alienated isolation, in his naked absurdity, or in his individual irrelevance. He may accept or avoid responsibility, but the one thing he never does, is to hide behind a collective will or a collective guilt.

Czech literature, art, and theatre became much more variegated in the sixties. Probably it won widest international acclaim by its new wave of films; but the dramatic improvement here was in keeping with a general advance in almost the whole cultural sector: live theatre flourished, and foreign entrepreneurs competed for Czech companies to fulfill engagements around the world. The international barriers were falling: as Czech artists and writers travelled abroad, so their foreign counterparts were visiting Prague and taking part in open and freely reported discussions on cultural policy. One result was a widening of cultural horizons at home, reflected in a more cosmopolitan literary taste. A further result, hardly relished by the cultural watchdogs, was the greater opportunity for intellectuals to express unorthodox views merely by associating themselves with, or even by not dissociating themselves from, the less inhibited comments of visiting Marxists like Sartre and Garaudy, who were themselves privately encouraged to explore the permitted limits of freedom on behalf of the home team. By linking up with their natural allies abroad, Czech intellectuals gained a marginally safer base for dissidence. At the same time the tendency at international gatherings for hawks to group together with hawks, and liberals with liberals, gave more room for manoeuvre, and broke up the appearance of a monolithic front presented by the Union representing all 'recognised' Czech writers. In September 1962 Aragon visited Prague to take an honorary degree at the Caroline University; and the public address which he delivered must have given great joy to his friends among the Czech writers. Among other contemptuous snubs aimed at literary schematism, he commented on the absurdity of cultural theoreticians dictating to writers what they ought to write, instead of basing their theories on what actually was written.[69]

One can examine the progress of literary de-Stalinisation by observing the changing role of the theoreticians and the critics. In the de-Stalinisation phase when only the message was changed but the direction from above remained, the position of the official critic was high: a critic or theoretician in name, he was still in fact employed as a *task-master* to the writers. But as new work became increasingly divorced from any official line or viewpoint, as in fact the writers began to take over the literary province and were able to publish what appealed to them, the task-masters dropped out of sight. If they objected to new work (as they did), their comments were printed, and ignored or contradicted. Critics like Štoll and Taufer no longer spoke with authority; the Party evidently did not choose to reassert its influence via such men. Its more liberal wing could rejoice that a freer policy towards the artists had paid handsome dividends: writers had regained their readership, the theatre its audience. The public image of the regime had improved at home and abroad: it could be argued that more freedom for criticism had actually increased the authority of the regime by raising its prestige. But there was another side to the picture. Criticism once let loose, is liable to get out of hand: it was hard to separate attacks on past leadership from oblique criticism of the present. Novotný might congratulate himself on his own forbearance, but his patience was far from inexhaustible. In any case there had been some unsettling developments in the communist movement abroad, and the leadership in Prague showed signs of some insecurity. The screws had been loosened on cultural expression, and they could be tightened again;

there was no intention of letting helpful criticism or harmless satire develop into open defiance or an encouragement to rebellion. Having for so long regarded culture as an administrative sector, and writers as naughty and temperamental, but easily manipulated, children, it was hard for the leaders to imagine that they would not respond readily to a few quiet words of warning. But conditions had changed since the fifties, and a graduated series of warnings and threats was to gradually entangle the regime in a situation where writers faced rulers in a confrontation carrying the gravest consequences.

VIII

Stalinism with a Human Face

'Don't shoot, there's people there.'
J. Hašek *The Good Soldier Schweik*

Within the context of de-Stalinisation in public life there developed in the mid-sixties something more positive and organised which subsequently became known as the Czechoslovak reform movement. It began with very limited aims, and was originally directed primarily at correcting some disturbing symptoms which had appeared in the national economy. What ended as a movement for wide political, social, and cultural reforms started as a set of proposals designed to promote improved efficiency, balanced economic growth, and a better use of the country's human and material resources.

Since 1948 the Czechoslovak economy had been subjected to a series of crises and re-adjustments. Ruthless industrialisation and the imposition of the Soviet model had produced rapid, but unbalanced, growth in the '50's. The transfer of labour from less productive sectors (especially agriculture) to more productive industries had produced tremendous dislocation without achieving the degree of economic improvement which might have been possible in a country starting from a less developed base. By the mid-fifties gains were marginal, and the strategy was proving counter-productive. At the same time Czechoslovakia, much of whose industry was dependent on international trade, was suffering badly from the political effects of the Cold War and the economic isolation of the Soviet trading bloc. The results, in the form of obsolete equipment, chronic shortages and breakdowns, was blamed officially on sabotage, the efforts of the class enemy, foreign agents, etc. But since 1956, amid the atmosphere of international détente, such crude explanations had been muted. In any case popular exasperation found more satisfying targets in the Party leaders, the bureaucracy, the ideological basis of managerial appointments, and the rigid system of central directives. Economic difficulties were always the greatest source of public dissatisfaction with the regime, and the cause of gravest concern to its leaders.

In 1958-9 a concerted attempt had been made to tackle the problem in a rather fundamental way. It consisted of a series of measures aimed at freeing the central planning authorities from operational involvement; strengthening the influence of grouped productive units over decision-making; and encouraging the individual enterprises to participate more actively in the planning process, by paying more heed to their submissions and providing more incentives for efficiency. This programme of limited reform arose from the climate of de-Stalinisation of the 1956 period; but by the time it began to be implemented, the climate had changed again. At any rate this cautious attempt at modifying the Soviet model seems to have run into difficulties from the start. The results were disappointing: instead of improvement, there was an actual decline in morale and efficiency. By 1960 the situation was so serious that the experiment was called off, and there was a move towards re-centralisation of control. By 1962 the economic situation had become critical, and the country was entering a period of economic recession. In 1963, instead of rising, the national income actually fell; and the Third Five Year Plan had to be scrapped.[1] The extent of the crisis seems to have taken the political leaders by surprise, and left the planners in a quandary. Among Party intellectuals it had long been felt that simplistic political decisions, based on ideological presuppositions, had for too long usurped the role of realistic programming; their views were confirmed by events, and now at last the leaders were more inclined to take the advice of the experts. During 1963 an Economic Commission was at work, chaired by an accomplished Marxist theoretician, Ota Šik. Its report was presented in January 1964; after intensive discussion and amendment it was endorsed by the Party Presidium in the following September, and by the Party Central Committee in January 1965. During that year a select group of enterprises tested the proposals by pilot projects; and various preparatory modifications were introduced into the legal and administrative system to enable a changeover to take place. Beginning from 1966 the reforms became operative: their implementation was a gradual process over the next three years. Considerably modified from the original proposals of the Šik Commission, the programme became known as the New Economic Model (N.E.M.).[2]

The Czechoslovak reform movement, which attracted world attention in 1968, was much wider than the N.E.M., but the latter can be regarded as its starting point. N.E.M. was the first major organised action of a revisionist nature permitted and encouraged by the regime: unlike the previous efforts of individuals and small groups, it was able to organise wide support and co-ordinate a reform strategy. The economic model had definite implications of a political, social, and cultural nature: its success depended on reactivating the participation of the general public and the intelligentsia in the social process.[3] Some decentralisation of control had been an aim of the earlier experiment; but the new model aimed to carry it much further; indeed the reformers seem to have persuaded the leadership that the previous experiment had failed because it had not gone far enough. Details of the N.E.M. proposals, and the degree to which they were ever implemented, are readily available: here it is sufficient merely to indicate certain general features. The intention was evidently to secure a greater democratisation of economic life by reform at various levels of policy-making. At the grass-roots level self-management bodies were to be set up in the individual enterprises; at the top level the central planning authorities were to be made more responsive to popular wishes and ideas. The central authority was to relinquish price control over a sector of the economy, and limited price movements could take place, reflecting the market trends of supply and demand. To that extent the structure of prices would reflect realistically the actual state of scarcity and popular demand, and the public as consumers would directly influence the structure of the economy.

The model implied a radical revision of certain *political* principles. The enhanced role of the market mechanism as a modifier of economic decisions (or rather, as an indicator activating economic regulators) meant transferring some power of initiative from the Party apparatus and allowing the plan to respond to pressures which were self-regulating, not regulated. The loosening of central controls meant that the authorities had to be prepared to surrender some power, at least in the economic sphere. But since economic and political planning was integrated (e.g. economic manipulation was a vital component of political control) the logic of the new model implied an across-the-board liberalisation of public life. Great significance attached to the proposed self-management committees with their power to formulate production policies, conduct negotiations and generally co-operate with other similar bodies on an enterprise-to-enterprise basis. This apparently harmless provision cut across what had been a basic principle of communist rule, namely that 'correct channels' existed whereby orders were passed downwards, and submissions upwards, through a rigidly maintained vertical hierarchy of command. The system (which is of course not confined to the communists) is in direct opposition to a horizontal system of arrangements whereby individuals or bodies with similar interests voluntarily form themselves into pressure groups to press for their own ideas or advantages. The proposed loosening of the vertical system of control implied the possibility of voluntary groupings and pressures forming at various levels, with the hope of eventually modifying economic, and perhaps political, policy at the highest level. If it was to work, such a democratisation of policy-making necessarily implied a guaranteed freedom of speech and negotiation in order to allow the free competition of ideas and programmes. The Party would retain its leading role; not as a source of all wisdom and initiative, but rather as an arbiter of pressures, and a guarantor that the framework of socialism would be preserved.

The proposals of the N.E.M. were radical enough, but the philosophy behind them was much more so. Czechoslovak communist policy, which had taken its cue from Soviet Stalinism, had tended to absorb into the state apparatus all societal activities and organisations, including the Trades Unions, the churches, youth and educational movements, and *even the Party itself.* The philosophy of the N.E.M. implied a reverse trend. Not only did it seek to involve the public once more into active participation, but also to re-activate organisations which had become merely levers of governmental control. The reformers were later to be charged with undermining the leading role of the Party; but the charge had substance only in so far as 'leading role' was a euphemism for monopolistic power. By shedding some of the controls it had acquired over society, the Party could have regained its role as a political party wedded to reform.

The hopes raised by N.E.M. seem in retrospect rather utopian. At the heart of the problem lay the anomaly of a regime whose control rested on a monopoly of state authority, proposing to put into operation reforms designed to end that monopoly. As a result, the reformers met a constant barrage of suspicion and obstruction, both at high Party, and at managerial, level; and this forced them into a series of delays and compromises. It is to be noted that the divisions of opinion, the discussions, lobbying, and negotiating within the Party produced a *de facto* condition of political pluralism such as had not been evident for many years. The reformers might well feel that as the economic model gradually came into operation, even with serious modifications, the logic of its development would eventually bring about political liberalisation which would allow the model to function to maximum advantage: economic would bring about political democratisation. But at some stage there came an awareness that the process might have to be reversed. Instead of economic change effecting political democracy, it might be necessary first to reform the Party leadership in order to give the reforms a chance to work. Thus what began within the Party as a lobby advocating economic change, gradually began to take on the dimensions of a widely based political reform movement, which required support from the media to spread its views. Within the Party some measure of reform seemed inevitable: opinion was divided only on the extent of the reform and its political implications. Radicals and conservatives looked around for allies to bolster their cause – organised labour, the Slovaks, the intellectuals. As usual the trump cards lay in Moscow; and a decision from that quarter could have settled the argument. But in 1964 the wishes of the Kremlin had again become obscure. In August Khrushchev with Gromyko had spent ten days in Czechoslovakia, attending celebrations of the Slovak rising, giving out medals, and lending benign support for Novotný. The visit was featured by the foreign language journal *Czechoslovak Life* in the October issue, together with happy photographs of the smiling leaders. Unfortunately, the release coincided with news of Khrushchev's fall. Once more the Czech leaders had been caught napping. Brezhnev's intentions towards the satellite states were in 1964 not at all clear; and from the example of Rumania it seemed that more independence might be tolerated by Moscow. At any rate the Czechoslovak leadership did not join in abuse of the fallen leader, and Novotný is said to have expressed his official regret at the decision to fire Khrushchev. A certain coolness became evident in Czech-Russian relations, and neither government did much to disperse it. For the time being Moscow's influence on Czechoslovak internal affairs rested in abeyance; and Novotný's position seems to have been strengthened locally by the impression that he was championing an independent line. In Prague the talk was that after a heated telephone conversation he had actually hung up on Brezhnev. During 1964-5 the political situation in Prague was unusually fluid: arguments about the extent of the necessary reform could be settled among the Czechs themselves.

How far economic reform was felt to be necessary by the rank and file, and how far it was acceptable to the ruling elite, depended on the acceptance or the rejection of some rather basic ideas. Was economic progress possible without increased flexibility? Could the regime survive in its present state if it accepted genuine democratisation? Would the fruits of liberalisation outweigh the risks? What did freedom really involve? The discussion about the implications of reform became so open and wide-ranging that it involved a reconsideration of Czechoslovakia's whole orientation. Because the issues were so very wide, historians, philosophers, and creative writers were all involved. It was no longer a question merely of what had gone wrong; although this question, as it was now posed, probed deeply into the past of the nation. The question of the day was: Whither Czechoslovakia? By what path should she move? What were the essential values which would govern her choice?

The search for a new orientation, together with a sharp scrutiny of the past, led naturally to a re-examination of national values and traditions. It was as if Czechoslovakia were seeking to resume a broken continuity: and it was here that the role of the writers was important. Traditionally they had been regarded as the standard bearers of national ideals. Although corrupted by conformists and collaboration, they had nevertheless been the first to raise a voice of open protest in 1956. They had themselves suffered, and they had represented the sufferings of Stalinist victims: in 1963 they had been again among the first to awaken from the Stalinist spell. Ideas were their province: and in any case they were important because they were in direct contact with the general public via the media. The writers' journal *Literární noviny* opened its New Year issue in 1965 with an essay on *The Tradition of Humanism and our Era*; and returned to the theme repeatedly through the year.[4] It was natural that writers should seek to link the rejection of Stalinism, and all its associations of tyranny and crude materialism, with a reconsideration of the humanism regarded as traditional to Czech history since the time of Hus, and in modern times associated with T. G. Masaryk. It was only a question of time before the comparison should be openly made.[5] The new economic reform was by implication a criticism of the Soviet model which had been imposed on Czechoslovakia; and the reform movement involved a departure from Soviet style in general. National differences between Czech and Russian ideas were now more or less openly admitted.[6] To be generally acceptable the new orientation would have to be more in keeping with Czech national temperament and tradition.

Disillusion with the restricting effects of the East European bloc led naturally to a desire to return to the European mainstream from which Czechoslovakia had moved in 1948.[7] It was in cultural life that the trend was most evident. The Kafka conference with its international implications had been an early move in this direction. Closer ties were fostered with the French and Italian Communist Parties. Both Garaudy and Pasolini visited Prague and led open discussions there in 1965:[8] the views of Sartre and Togliatti found ready coverage in the Czech cultural press.[9] Intellectuals from West Europe, including writers, artists, film and theatre critics, were now common visitors in Prague, attracted by the freer atmosphere and by the reputation which Czechoslovakia was winning in the realm of films and live theatre. Among the Czech critics there was intense discussion of the literary avant-garde of the 'thirties, whose ideological orientation had been communist, but whose inspiration had come not from Moscow but Paris.[10] The leading theoretician of the movement, Karel Teige, in the 'fifties denigrated as a Trotskyist, now returned to a posthumous popularity, and his essays were handsomely reprinted.[11] At the same time critics turned their attention to the non-communist literary legacy, and to more recent writers whose names had been taboo.[12] In the *Dictionary of Czech Writers*[13] published in 1964 reappeared the names of writers living in exile abroad – Egon Hostovský, Jan Čep, Ivan Blatný – together with objective assessments on their work. Even more significant was the return to publication of those who had never left the country, but had descended into an inner exile more bitter than a physical migration. Václav Černý, who in the 'forties had set out in words, and represented in his own person, a case for a Western orientation for Czech culture, now resumed publication.[14] The work of Catholic writers Durych and Zahradníček became once more available. Authors long kept on the fringe of literary life as ideologically undesirable – Jiří Kolář, Kamil Bednář, A. C. Nor, Jiřina Hauková – reappeared on publishers' lists.[15] In Prague popular culture flourished, and for a brief spell it became known as the Hippie capital of Europe. The American off-beat poet Ginsberg was crowned King of the student festival – then he was arrested on a narcotics charge and deported. Tourism from Western Europe was booming, and it became a two-way process. In 1965 the Czech Parliament had affirmed the right of Czechoslovak citizens to a passport for foreign travel.

It seemed a hopeful sign of greater tolerance in high places, and of enhanced respect towards Czech Catholic traditions, when a debate was opened at a philosophical level between Marxist and Christian thinkers. Archbishop Beran of Prague, for long detained and forbidden to practise his office, left for Rome, where he took his place as a Cardinal. In the cultural field a sign of return to tradition was the staging in Brno, then in Prague, of the baroque Passion Play *A Comedy on the Crucifixion and Glorious Resurrection of our Lord and Redeemer Jesus Christ.*[16] Its success with the public was extraordinary, and the play was well received by the critics: the theatrical event of the year 1966 was provided by this revival, with its naive and poetic art, its allegory of renewed life through suffering, and its appeal to old associations of past history. It was part of a revival of interest in the whole epoch of Czech baroque, once written off as a dark age of peasant oppression and Catholic bigotry. Now at last it seemed that the time had come for a general healing of wounds, and of escape from ideological provincialism.

The current trend towards international détente, the increasing dialogue with West European intellectuals, the open discussion of reform, – all these were encouraging signs that Czechoslovakia was at last heading towards a happier and more relaxed future. The progress was real: but it was the product of a situation with less reassuring features. The pleasant feeling of change was itself a sign of instability which could have unpleasant consequences.

The re-programming of economic life gained such support as it did from the Party hierarchy in the expectation that by increasing efficiency the regime would strengthen itself. Evidently there were men at the top who were prepared to relax controls, at least temporarily, if this was a necessary condition of improvement. For this they needed the technical experts, men like Šik, Selucký, and Mlynář, whose loyalty to the Party was accepted. But these men lacked real power; they could only influence the men who had power. The experts explained with great patience the wider political implications of the desired reforms: but whether their explanations were taken seriously by the rulers is open to question. The latter had become so accustomed to necessary changes being publicised under false packaging that they could be excused for some scepticism. The reforms would be allowed to continue just as long as they paid off in efficiency: if a ground-swell developed which really looked like taking the initiative out of the hands of the men above, that might well be the end of the reforms. The leaders differed in their attitudes, and in their readiness to accept a modicum of change; but there is no evidence to suggest that they were other than united in the determination that nothing in the reforms should be allowed to challenge the political authority of the Party. And since they identified the Party with their own authority, that meant that they would tolerate no threat to themselves. Men like Novotný and Hendrych, limited in their intellectual and educational background, could hardly be expected to follow the complexities of the programmes put before them; and it is highly unlikely that they even found the time to study them. But however limited academically, they were shrewd enough politicians, and backed their own judgement in estimating how far to let the experts have their way. To outside observers it might seem that the pace of change was self-sustaining and inevitable. This was evidently not the view of the leaders, whose whole future rested on the need to keep the situation well in hand. Change, in other words, implied increased vigilance. The faster the vehicle of reform moved (and in fact the programme of economic reforms was slowed by an apparently endless series of compromises), the greater would be the need to keep the foot on the brake. Freedom was 'given' by the Party: the more generous it was in this regard, the more necessary it became to ensure that it was not 'abused'. The greater the degree of public relaxation, the more intense became the surveillance upon it. One possible danger was that the reformers, when they could not get what they wanted from the authorities, might try to pressure them by appealing directly to the public via the media, as theoretically, they had every right to do. An extreme possibility, was that the reformers in despair might one day try to enlist public support *against* the Party leaders. The danger of Party intellectuals trying to get their way by reactivating forces *outside the Party*, had still to be kept in mind. All this added up to a difficult situation for the media. It was there that the first symptoms of danger would appear. There was no harm in economists like Selucký and Šik airing their views in the literary journals, (as they did); nor in the latter opening their pages to debate on the political and social implications; for it was an axiom of cultural policy that literature should *engage* itself in the social process. But the situation was carefully watched; and from 1963 the writers found themselves even more than before an object of suspicious scrutiny. A paradox of the reform period was that the natural tension between writers and regime, instead of decreasing with the enhanced relaxation, actually increased, until it assumed the characteristics of a confrontation.

Since 1953 a Central Agency for Press Supervision (HSTD) which was controlled by the Ministry of the Interior, had operated preliminary censorship of all published material.[17] An Orwellian piquancy was added to the situation, in that the institution of censorship was forbidden by the Czechoslovak constitution. Necessarily therefore the controls were authorised by a government decree which was itself confidential; the censors were not called censors; nor did they possess any legal power whatever. They merely 'advised' editors. To begin with, the relationship between editors and censors was co-operative; the latter read the material and made suggestions. In case of continued disagreement over the inclusion of an item, the matter could be referred to higher authority, normally the relevant Ministry, or the Party secretariat. In some cases the editor even got his way: a phone call to some competent official would be sufficient, and the censor would obligingly affix to the page proofs his stamp, without which nothing was accepted for printing. Eventually the Central Committee of the Party took over responsibility for arbitration in such cases of dispute; but it became increasingly difficult for an editor to find any official prepared to listen to him. Although the HSTD man had no authority to confiscate any material, by merely withholding his stamp until a decision was given, he effectively limited what went into print. As censorship was illegal, one of the censor's jobs was naturally to cover up all traces of his own existence. If material set on the proofs was held up or withdrawn, no tell-tale blank spaces could be left (as had been the case in the pre-war period). The spaces must be filled with emergency material - a rule which added to the harassment of editors, forced to retain reserve material for this purpose. The overall result was the growth of a system of censorship which had no legal existence and covered up its own activities. How freely information could flow depended on the attitude of the HSTD men (who were not even consistent with each other), and the Central Committee, whose attitude shifted in accordance with their interpretation of Party policy and the leaders' wishes, and with the conditions at a given time.

About the time of the XII Congress in 1962 a fairly free flow of information was permitted, as appears from the ventilation of angry comments on current economic hardships. The era of 'guided liberalisation' was beginning. But the freer flow did not mean that supervision was looser, only that more material of a critical nature was permitted by the censorship. Such criticism, expressed either in general terms, or addressed to minor officials, did not touch the Party itself or its leadership: all 'negativist' or 'unsuitable' material was censored out as hostile to the spirit of socialism.

Censorship is of course an entirely negative way of influencing public opinion: while it suppresses unwelcome evidence and criticism, it does little to form or manipulate the attitudes of the public. The 'educative' aspect of culture was a constant aim of Party policy, and methods varied with conditions. Into the mass media was fed a diet of suitably processed material. The mechanics of control presented no problem. Since all newspapers and journals were nationally owned, all journalists were public servants. But with the creative writers and creative literature the situation was always more complicated. The failure of the cultural command plan in the early 'fifties had shown that the arts do not lend themselves easily to the uses of indoctrination.

Over the years the creative writers had won ground in a campaign to disengage literature from ideological propaganda. By 1963 a reasonable degree of literary autonomy had been achieved. Provided that the writers did not provoke the regime, the permitted range of publication was wide. In effect art was more or less excused from direct participation in any politico-cultural plan: its duty of social engagement was interpreted loosely. But from that time the writers themselves, drawn by the ferment of the reform movement, showed renewed signs of involvement in social issues. This attitude should have pleased the leaders, as it was apparently what they had wanted the writers to do. But the latter, in their contrary and irritating fashion, seemed to be interpreting reform in a way less than helpful to the authorities. Given the limited field of possible readership for anything printed in Czech, and consequently the limited number of writers it could sustain, it was natural for the professions of journalism and creative writing to overlap: journalists wrote novels, and novelists published their views on current affairs. During the reform period it appeared that the degree of independence that creative writers had won in the literary field they were now carrying over into the field of journalism.

In Czechoslovakia the so-called cultural journals enjoyed a surprisingly wide circulation by Western standards. In 1964 the combined sale of the weeklies *Literární noviny, Kulturní tvorba*, and *Kulturný život* was over a quarter of a million copies, representing an estimated readership of over a million in a country of fourteen million inhabitants. During the period of wide-ranging debate over the reform programme these journals, with their impact and prestige, together with the comparative independence of their contributors, were a source of deep concern and suspicion to conservatives in the Party hierarchy. A document which sheds light on this concern was the report of a subcommittee set up by the Central Committee of the Party in 1964 to study the role and conditions of the cultural journals. The report, discussed on 17. 2. 64 by the Ideological Commission and on 24. 3. 64 by the Party Presidium, was published in full in the Party theoretical journal *Nová mysl.*[18]

The document commented favourably on the space devoted by the journals to discussion of social problems, but stressed the need to maintain a view in harmony with that of the Party, as formulated by its highest representatives. The journals had shown commendable zeal in their campaign against the remnants of the personality cult: on the other hand the reform ferment was at times presented in a very *one-*

sided fashion: editorial policy was showing political weakness and ideological confusion which needed correction. The journals seemed to be taking up an autonomous line, interpreting Party policy according to their own ideas. Evidence lay in the large number of examples of work whose publications had had to be stopped by administrative action.[19] Treatment of past events had been negativist, with a tendency to blacken the role of the Party in such a way as to confuse readers: the Party line itself was apparently regarded at times as 'conservative' and the term 'progressive' was given to subjectivist views of doubtful validity. It seemed that editors were so afraid of being thought dogmatic that they swung to the opposite extreme, adopting attitudes of exaggerated tolerance to nihilistic or confused ideas. An example was a recent article in which a writer, while ostensibly attacking dogmatism, actually brought into question basic Marxist principles: in opposing the idea of class-war, he was expressing views which were frankly *liberalist* and *revisionist*.[20] In fact the journals had lent themselves to publication of views irreconcilable with Party policy. Over-reaction to the personality cult had resulted in Party discipline being thrown to the winds, and to a trend towards anarchy. Treatment of current work in the social sciences had also been unsatisfactory; e.g. Löbl's revisionist attitude towards economic planning; the extravagant praise of Kosík's *Dialectics of the Concrete*, the description of Party ideology as 'a system of mystification' and a 'form of modern mythology'; the revisionist views of Ivan Sviták etc. The journals had also published some unhelpful articles on the question of the struggle with hostile ideologies; in fact a recent discussion in *Plamen*, in stressing the need for friendly discussion and the frank exchange of views, had tacitly accepted a policy of co-existence between Marxism and bourgeois ideology.[21] This was quite wrong; there could be no compromise between *lies and truth*. Peaceful co-existence in the political field did not lessen the need to take vigorous action against ideological diversion and anti-communist policies aimed at political disorientation.[22]

It was right to provoke discussion, but it must not be *one-sided*, and it must be guided to the *right conclusion*. The independent line taken by the journals showed a distrust of Party policy and a denial of its leading role: the impression given was of opposition towards Party policy. In questions of creative art the same attitudes were evident: once more the social function of art was being queried; ideological criteria were opposed; there was chaos in criticism, for which the editors were responsible. The Party line was clear – it supported socially engaged art, and rejected art which was self-orientated, esoteric, socially neutral, or content with aping bourgeois fashions. It was for editors to see that the Party line was carried out – the Party had the right to demand discipline from its members; *there must be no toleration of hostile ideologies.*

From the fact that this document was passed by the Central Committee and the Presidium we have the right to conclude that it was an authoritative statement of Party cultural policy. An examination of the document yields depressing conclusions for those who would identify de-Stalinisation with the relaxation of central control over publication. There are repeated assertions of the Party's absolute right and duty to control the expression of such views and criticism as the Party itself deemed necessary in its own interests: and the Party accepted no interpretation of its rights, or the correctness of its course, outside itself. The right of the Party to control, meant in fact the right of the upper hierarchy: the viewpoint of the Party meant the views of the leaders at any given moment: those were the views which the cultural sector had the duty of spreading, or at least the views with which it must harmonise its expression of opinion. Once the Party line was set, the editors, as responsible officials in the cultural sector, were bound to select material for publication with a view to carrying out the line and strengthening confidence in the Party, (which meant confidence in its current leadership). It was right to withhold from publication views and criticism which were *unhelpful* (i.e. unwelcome), or liable to *confuse* (i.e. ask awkward questions). Since material which might be unhelpful or confusing could be in the form not only of opinion but also of fact, the implication was that unwelcome *information* must also be suppressed (as the record shows, and subsequent testimony confirms, that it *was* suppressed).[23] It is important to note that suppression did not rest on the claim that such information was *wrong*: while it might be objectively correct, it earned the right to suppression by reason of its putative effect of the readers. In effect the general guidelines to editors on what they could and could not publish stemmed from the principle: *nothing must appear which might be harmful to the Party's public image.* And since the Party leadership was the sole acceptable judge of what was likely to be harmful, a second principle followed: *nothing must appear which was not licensed by the authorities.*

The document repeatedly stressed its rejection of past 'dogmatism'. De-Stalinisation was still the official goal of cultural policy. The question arises: in what way did views expressed in the document of

1964 differ from the Stalinist official viewpoint of 1950? At both times the Party claimed an absolute right to control the formulation and expression of views and the dissemination of information: the right was exercised by ensuring that all positions of responsibility in publishing remained in the hands of reliable Party cadres; that there was a close scrutiny of publication; and that the interpretation of what was harmful, misleading, liable to cause doubt etc. was so wide that it could cover almost anything. In 1964 the permitted range of opinions was wider than in the earlier period; but the principle of control was the same. Freedom meant not the escape from harness, but a longer rein, and a less ferocious treatment of deviationists. Since such "freedom" was within the gift of the authorities, to be granted or withheld in accordance with their current views and interests, the screws which had been loosened could be tightened again as the situation required.

A person reading the document for the first time might well be puzzled at the singling out of Ivan Sviták for special attack. He was neither politician, political commentator, nor specially concerned with public affairs. As a highly intellectual philosopher who mixed mainly in academic circles and addressed himself to abstract problems, it seems strange to regard him as a dangerous threat to the Establishment. But his fault, like that of other philosophers and social scientists, was his concern with *principles.* He challenged in various ways not the Party's right to suppress any particular opinion, but its right to suppress opinion at all. The Party was strong on action but weak on principle. It claimed truth for all its statements and justification for all its actions at any given time. In permitting and sponsoring a de-Stalinisation programme it conceded that mistakes had been made in the past. On the other hand it is hard to find any admission that the *Party* had been wrong, and that those who opposed the Party line in Stalin's time had been right. Policies and conditions changed, but somehow the Party, since it "based its actions on scientific Marxism", was always right. Had it conceded that it had been wrong before, the possibility might arise that it was wrong again. The Party was right now (1964) in its determination to end the "remnants of the personality cult" (to de-Stalinise): yet since in one way, it had never been wrong, its present policy did not involve any revaluation of principle. With one voice it proclaimed that its policies reversed those of the past. With another it proclaimed their continuity. Whatever the Party policy was at a given moment, it was correct; *even when it contradicted the correctness of past Party policy.* In effect the Party claimed infallibility for its views, and philosophers like Sviták had to challenge this absurd assumption if they were not to appear to themselves merely as court fools, and as "clowns with diplomas". Unfortunately it was by reason of its claim to truth at all times that the Party claimed to license truth. Once it conceded the possibility of its own error, that its policies and views were still negotiable, then its claim to cultural control went with it. The anxiety of philosophers like Sviták and Kosík to discuss principles, was rightly seen by ideologists as an assault on their central position.

One depressing, and revealing feature of the document is the patronising and arrogant tone adopted towards the intellingentsia in general and the writers in particular: it is a tone which speaks volumes for the true relationship in which they stood to the authorities, now constituted as their *de facto* patrons. One gets the impression that the cultural sector was still regarded as a minor area of government, containing officials at the higher, and writers at the lower, level. The latter received the guidelines handed down to them: their duty to obey the guidelines was regarded as self-evident. Nevertheless the document restricts its attacks to work on current affairs, criticism, or theory. Although the cultural journals also carried creative literature, the latter is not the subject of hostile comment. This confirms the impression given by publishers' lists; that while control on theoretical or documentary work was strict, the rein on creative literature proper was loose. In spite of their non-communist affiliations and their records of detention, a poet like Ivan Diviš and a novelist like Jiří Mucha were now free to publish again. But Mucha's documentary of the camps, *Cold Sunlight*, would have to wait nearly four more years before it could appear: freedom in the field of creative literature and art was a positive gain: but writers who proposed to carry that freedom into the area of reportage or journalism had better beware!

The document was intended as a warning; and it was followed by action against two selected targets from among the persons criticised. Ivan Sviták was fired from the Institute of Philosophy; expelled from the Party; and eventually banned from publication. The other victim was Milan Hübl, Vice-Rector of the Party Academy, and a prominent historian. He was dismissed from his position at the Academy, and eleven of his colleagues left with him.[24] A tighter control was placed over the cultural journals. The chief editor of *L N* was traditionally selected by the Writers' Union, but the appointment was subject to confirmation by the Party Central Committee. Jungmann's appointment never was confirmed, and for three years he carried on the job under threat of removal at any moment, so that he was made to feel under constant watch. The paper was the subject of criticisms, threats, and proddings from the Party centre; and there was a high rate of interventions by the censors. By January 1965 the Party Journal *Život strany* was calling for still stricter control over literary publication, and complaining of liberalist, opportunist elements at work in the cultural field. In February 65 the editor of *Kulturný život* was replaced. During that month the editors of all the cultural journals were summoned to the Presidential palace to hear Novotný personally lay down his views.

In June the Writers' Union was to hold a plenary session; it was preceded by a meeting in the office of *L N* during which the rising tensions were discussed, and a gloomy view of prospects was taken by Goldstücker and Kundera.[25] At the plenary session V. Havel sharply criticised the unreality of past planning, revealing how deplorably the prophets had misread the shape of future developments. As an example he cited the fate of the journal *The Critical Monthly* which had been liquidated after 1948. Havel took the excellence of this journal to be a matter of general knowledge; but its true appreciation of Stalinism was the cause of its liquidation. Now the position was that after official acknowledgement of past errors, the journal was still liquidated, but the Stalinists were flourishing; in other words, present cultural policy promoted Stalinists, but disadvantaged those who had opposed Stalinism at the time. (This part of Havel's remarks did not appear among the minutes of the meeting as published by *L N*, his words became publicly known only when they were angrily attacked in the Party journal by official ideologue F. Havlíček.) In so far as Havel was calling for the redress of a wrong committed by the literary Stalinists, his voice could properly be called the voice of de-Stalinisation. In the threatening reply of Havlíček, published with the authoritative backing of the Party journal, we see the reaction of authority.[26]

These were straws in the wind: so far the authorities, while scattering warnings, had been cautious in action. The first victim to feel the full weight of the Party's displeasure was a recently founded journal of the younger writers. It had been planned in the reformist days of 1963, and duly appeared the following year under the auspices of the Writers' Union, but run by an autonomous editorial group of young writers. It took its name *Tvář*, (*The Face*) from the title of one of Halas' books. The gesture indicated a source of inspiration acknowledged by the young writers – not only Halas himself, but the men of the thirties who had once been the literary avant-garde. In choosing to acknowledge this link with the past, the young of the mid-sixties

by implication had avoided affiliation with the generation which immediately preceded theirs. *Tvář* soon became regarded as the organ of
the generation *with clean hands* – dissociating itself from an era which
it regarded as an unfortunate and irrelevant chapter in the history of
Czech culture. At a time when anti-dogmatism was officially encouraged, it was anti-dogmatic in an unorthodox way, subjecting to
ruthless criticism reformist, as well as Stalinist, views.

In the spirit of the thirties *Tvář* made conscious efforts to bring together contributions from the genres and the arts: its spectrum of
interests was wide, and fell within the framework of no obvious literary programme; it also resumed contact with the stream of pre-war
Catholic literature. As the atmosphere deteriorated in the cultural
sector, *Tvář* received increasingly unfavourable notice from authority.
At the same time its open and sometimes tactless criticism of the
preceding generation did nothing to endear it in their eyes. The *Květen*
group, now in their forties, had regarded themselves as the harbingers
of reform and the champions of those rights which the young now
seemed to take for granted. It was galling for writers like Šotola and
other *Květen* stalwarts to find themselves now regarded as passé, and
identified with the very era against whose enforced standards they
had themselves rebelled. Stung by the airy and reckless attacks of the
young writers, Šotola voiced his displeasure on the pages of *L N*[27] Šotola was not alone in his criticisms; the journals carried comments on
the disappointing contribution that *Tvář* was making, the limitations
of its positive achievements, its lack of profile, etc. At the same time
rumblings were heard from more official sources. *Tvář* was accused
of propagating mysticism and spiritualism, of rubbishing the achievements of socialist art, and of providing a platform for openly anti-
Marxist views.[28] By the second year of its existence *Tvář* was drawing
fire from both reformers and unreformed Stalinists. Nothing annoyed the reformers more than the willingness of the young writers
to lump together dogmatists and anti-dogmatists as equally buried
in the mire of the past, locked together in a futile love-hate relationship, and still stuck in the irrelevant quarrels of the 'fifties. Obviously the men around *Tvář* were not much impressed with a reform movement which was guided by people whom they identified with the bad
old days.

As 1965 drew to its close, there began to appear some ominous signs
about the future of the journal. In *L N* Trefulka wrote bitterly of the
abnormality of a situation in which authors and journals which
adopted any but a strictly Marxist stance became threatened by ad-

ministrative action: it was a situation which recalled a not too distant past.[29] In December *L N* revealed, in the minutes of a Union committee meeting, a plan for founding a new youth journal, but disassociated *L N* from rumours of a coming liquidation of *Tvář*. The 1966 New Year issue completed the sad story. The Union had offered to underwrite *Tvář*'s financial losses on certain conditions, including increased prices, retrenchment of staff, etc.: part of the deal was a reshuffle of the editorial board required by the ideological Commission of the Party, which had the right to confirm such appointments. On behalf of the editorial board of *Tvář* J. Nedvěd had declined to accept the offer, thus concluding the existence of the journal.[30]

The aftermath of this sorry episode is worth noting. In the same issue of *L N* which announced *Tvář*'s demise was printed a comment from Jan Trefulka. He used the opportunity of rebutting a personal attack upon himself to express his public regret at the fate of the journal, and compared its suppression to action in the 'fifties against men like Holan and Seifert; i.e. he noted a return to Stalinist methods in the field of culture. The second incident concerns the fate of the editor Nedvěd. He was made the subject of a spiteful personal attack in the official Party journal *Život strany*, and was accused of twisting the line of *Tvář* in conflict with the interests of socialism; of using the journal to disseminate bourgeois philosophies; and of refusing to abide by Party discipline. In consequence Nedvěd was expelled from the Party and excommunicated from free literary life.

The suppression of *Tvář* and the action taken against selected dissidents, although mild by Stalinist standards, seemed to confirm the impression given by the threatening tone of the Party Press towards all expressions of unwelcome opinion. Kremlinologists abroad noted the rehabilitation in Moscow of Zhdanov, the embodiment of Stalinism in the cultural field. At the same time it became known that some of Stalin's works were to be reissued. In March 1966 came the trial of the two Russian writers Daniel and Sinyavsky in Moscow. The publicity given to the trial by the Soviet authorities was like a warning to all contemplating intellectual activity contravening the wishes of authority. It was accompanied, in Moscow and in Prague, by rumours of the arrest of suspected Russian dissidents, and forcible commitment of selected victims to psychiatric clinics for 'mental treatment'. The trial had one surprising aftermath. On March 15 the Italian communist paper *L'Unità* published a report that a delegation from the Czechoslovak Writers Union had been sent to Moscow to protest to the Union of Soviet Writers about the sentences. The report was denied the next day by the official Czech news agency. On April 9 there appeared in *L N* a brief note on the Union's activities, which included a laconic mention of the visit of a three-man delegation for discussions in Moscow. Privately Czech writers conceded that a protest had been conveyed: it was further claimed that an approach had been made to the Party at the highest level to take up the matter with the Soviet Party leaders. The hope remained that even if the USSR reverted to Stalinism, and this was the Brezhnev line, the Czechoslovak C.P. might still pursue its own form of de-Stalinisation, and thus, like Rumania, attain a level of independence which was certain to improve the Party's image at home and to strengthen Novotný's hold on the leadership.

A great question now hung over Czech Party policy, and as the Spring of 1966 gave way to Summer, the ambiguity persisted. The choice for Novotný was complicated by uncertainty about the intentions of Moscow, about Brezhnev's feelings towards the Czech leadership which had rather identified itself with the Khrushchev policies; and not least about Brezhnev's own prospects of survival. If Czechoslovakia decided to back what appeared to be the Brezhnev line, and call off what was left of the de-Stalinisation programme, the change of policy would be first signalled in the media. While observers anxiously scanned the journals for evidence of the choice - a renewed liberalisation drive combined with an independent line, or else a new repression - the authorities characteristically maintained the ambiguity of their policy and kept their options open for as long as possible. There were threats and warnings to intellectuals; editors were harried; selected victims were demoted or fired; the writer Havel, after accepting an invitation to attend an international P.E.N. conference, had his passport confiscated at the last minute. All this was ominous, but not irrevocable – a sort of contingency plan for neo-Stalinism. At the same time Prague was full of foreign visitors; discussion was open; publication in the field of creative literature had rarely been freer. The XIII Congress of the Czechoslovak CP adopted a sensible resolution on cultural problems, but no action was taken to implement it. Interminable speeches of suffocating boredom, rhetoric, clichés, threats, encouragement, stylised ambiguity, all helped to make the Congress a non-event, foreshadowing anything or nothing.

Then suddenly in August 1966, at the height of the holiday season, when Prague seemed to be at its most relaxed, the blow fell. The young writer Jan Beneš was taken into custody on a serious offence. He was known to have taken a leading part in the campaign of protest against the writers' sentences in Moscow, and was regarded as among the most militant of the younger writers. He was also suspected of maintaining contact with Pavel Tigrid, the editor of the emigré journal *Svědectví*, published in Paris. It was the first arrest of a writer for cultural-political offences since the 'fifties. The deep anxiety aroused by the move was not confined to Czechoslovakia. At the request of intellectuals abroad concerned with cultural freedom and human rights, Amnesty International took up Beneš's case.

Another indication of the hard line came in October, with the promulgation of a new law providing for the censorship of all published material by a Central Publication Board (UPS). Thus, for the first time, censorship became legal, although it was still technically incompatible with the Czechoslovak constitution. The grounds on which material could be suppressed were the generally accepted ones of official secrets, industrial techniques, etc. But an additional clause empowered the Board to draw the attention of editors to material which might conflict with 'other interests of society'.

Even at this point official policy could be said to be ambiguous. The open institutionalisation of censorship pointed to the likelihood of renewed repression. On the other hand the legalisation of what had been a surreptitious and arbitrary arrangement might mean a cautious move towards a more open system: under the new law there were some safeguards for journalists, and editors had the right of appeal against censors' decisions. The law could be interpreted as evidence of both re-Stalinisation and de-Stalinisation. Obviously everything depended on the spirit in which the law was administered, particularly on the interpretation of the clause on the protection of society's 'other interests'. We know in fact that interpretation was left in the hands of the Party apparatus; consequently the law had the practical effect of handing control over the press and the whole cultural sector into the hands of Party officials. Thus the Party was left in a position to deal more efficiently with any symptoms of disagreement with its policy.

The new bill contained a clause the significance of which only appeared later. In an apparently liberal gesture, it did away with the need for the *licensing* of new journals; they only needed to obtain *registration*, and the Ministry of Culture was bound to register them provided they had satisfied the normal requirements. All existing journals were also required to register; but no sign of urgency seemed to be implied by this formality, and journals went on publishing for months to come without bothering to register their existence. The effect of the new clause was to be made apparent only in 1967.

Meanwhile much of the newly published creative literature was still

actively concerned with problems of the Stalinist past in Czechoslovakia. Bohuslav Březovský's novel *Eternal Lovers*[31] contains the
retrospection of a historian who, at the age of 50, looks back on the
sorry record of his life – the fears, the compromises, the failure of his
hopes and ideals, the self-delusions, the suspension of his own judgement and repression of his own conscience for the sake of an imposed
orthodoxy which had turned out to be a hollow deception:

> How enviously I remember the times when my heart was still
> sensitive and uncorrupted!... the times when we lost almost
> everything, we atheists who could not live without a faith, we
> believers in reason, who are now incapable of comprehending
> or explaining, we, with a heart like a torn, dry rag in our
> hands... looking back we realise with horror that we have
> judged without right, we have murdered in thought and in
> reality, we have ourselves been murdered a hundred times...

Březovský's novel is an interesting representative of a new genre –
the retrospective exploration of the Stalinist period as seen through
the eyes of a committed Party intellectual.

More subtle, and of greater literary interest, was the first novel of
an established journalist, Jaroslav Putík, whose literary work admirably reflects the overlap between creative art and the mass media.
Among his earlier books had been *Conscience*, a study of the American
atomic scientist J. Robert Oppenheimer.[32] The book was a case study
of the intellectual confronted with the pressure of authority and the
voice of conscience: there was an obvious analogy with the problems
of Putík's own society. His new novel was *Passion Sunday*.[33] Its basic
theme reflects a moral and political dilemma. At times of stress should
one join the battle, with all the consequences that follow? or draw
back, and allow events to take their course? The heroine, Lucy, had,
like Putík in real life, chosen the way of commitment – wartime resistance; arrest; the camps; post-war political activity on behalf of the
Party. Like Putík, she had become a successful journalist. Then
comes her attempted suicide! The question which her case poses to
society is this: why, when she has accepted the risks and attained
success, does she choose to demonstrate her sense of failure in this
dramatic way? The investigation of her case is handled not by a professional psychiatrist, but by a scientist dedicated to the methodology of
the electronic brain and the idea that computerised science can uncover all secrets of the human heart. It is he who becomes the narrator
of the story; his research succeeds in exposing him to the reader,

whereas the inner life of Lucy never yields its mystery. The search into her past leads him back into the life of the concentration camp and the tensions set up by the stress situation there. Without realising what he is doing, he becomes increasingly involved with his patient's personal problems; between the aloof rationalist and the passionate loyalist to causes there develops a romance which should bridge the gap and save them both. She has lost faith in her former goals, above all in her calling as a journalist, which she now finds irreconcilable with honor and decency. Infected by her instability, he also rejects his past with its absolute reliance on dehumanised science. Patient and doctor have exchanged places. The strange romance lacks a happy ending. Lucy offers her doctor a chance to justify himself through risk, by comitting himself to the defence of a political prisoner: but fearing to become himself entangled in the consequences, he draws back. The opportunity is lost, and does not return. Lucy is left with her dilemma; haunted by a tainted past, but sustained by a conscience that will not allow her to stand by and thereby collaborate with known wrong.

Total commitment to a common cause, with the consequent subordination of individual conscience to duty? or else the refusal to commit oneself, with its apparent preservation of moral integrity at the price of collaboration with evil? The dilemma posed was like an appeal for understanding from the older to the younger generation. To the accusations of the latter (the men of 'clean hands') was offered a questions: *What ought we, what could we, have done?* The ghost of Stalin, and the guilt of the 'fifties, was the hidden motivation force behind the human drama of the 'sixties. Putík unfolded his drama via introspection and the analysis of the psychiatric couch, probing mercilessly into the secret past of the sick girl. The analogy with his sick society could not be missed. The terrible shadow of Stalinism which lay heavily over Czech public life could only begin to be dispelled by an end to the gigantic cover-up still maintained by the Stalinists. Truth was still taboo to the public media – and this was the source of Lucy's aversion to her profession, which had failed in its primary duty. Only in creative art could some measure of reality be expressed, intuitively and symbolically.

Journalists were major figures in two other important novels of the time; in both books the self-deluding, self-defeating nature of their professional efforts is mercilessly revealed. The novels were Ludvík Vaculík's *The Axe*[34] and Milan Kundera's *The Joke*.[35] In the former a middle-aged and disillusioned journalist searches the past, not without sardonic humour, to illuminate the sorry mess of his present life.

His recollections centre upon the family circle of his childhood, dominated by the figure of his father. The latter is a character grown rare in serious literature of the sixties; a Communist positive hero. This serious, industrious and dedicated man was far away in Persia when the children were young; his regular letters, full of advice about running the household, brought a touch of the hardly imaginable, exotic outer world to that tiny village in Eastern Moravia. (The details are authentic to Vaculík's own life; some of the letters are free adaptations of the letters sent by Vaculík's father from Persia.) In the novel the father was a carpenter; the symbol of his craft was the axe; his house was built with his own hands; its construction reflects the integrity of his firm character. In his son's recollection he was an image of wisdom and strength. But there was something more – a reverence for the woods, the hills, the silence of the Moravian countryside. As if trying to recapture a lost experience, or perhaps to regain contact with something old and familiar, he would take his son into the hills before dawn, and pointing say: 'There is the place, my son. *Do you see?*'

In time the father had returned to his own land from the desert of his Persian exile, and lived through the wartime occupation. When his son saw him stealing timber, the father used a phrase to recur later: "*An exceptional situation demands exceptional methods.*" After the war he devoted himself to working for the Party, building a new future for the rural areas. Instead of a craftsman he had become an official: the innocence which his child had seen in him, gradually receded. In the face of mounting resentment by the villagers he energetically pushed forward the collectivisation measures. ('*An exceptional situation demands exceptional methods*'.) Subordinating personal considerations and loyalties to political planning he gradually lost touch with his own people, even with his own family. There is the shock of the remembered moment when mother cried to husband in anger and pain: 'I can see now, Dad, *you are no good.*' Ironically it was to impress his son and maintain his image of strength that the father obstinately held to his firm stand on collectivisation. On the day of the great family quarrel the boy saw his mother broken in tears; his father stormed out, and did not return that night. The irony was compounded when, after all, the father was charged by the Party committee with being too squeamish over collectivisation, and was thrown out of his position. Moving from blunder to blunder he helped to destroy his own community, and ultimately himself. The fallen idol of childhood, that tower of strength who held in himself the life-giving forces of renewal, had become the instrument of breakdown, and symbolised the collapsing structures of the rural culture he loved. At the same time his strength and independence was exposed as a sham when faced with the inexorable power of the political machine. The father left his native area to work for the Party elsewhere. Visiting him, the son, now a man, saw through the utter desolation of his existence, homeless, cut off by his official functions from his fellows, waging a hopeless and futile struggle, seeking a new 'future', with a new wife set to spy on him, leading what amounted to almost a posthumous existence. He had finally succeeded in creating in his native land the desert of his Persian exile.

Meanwhile the son (like Vaculík himself) a journalist in the city, is able to recognise in the microcosm of his family the disintegration of a whole social structure and its values. When he tries to use his position in the media to expose gross injustice, he comes himself into danger. In the cynical atmosphere of the newspaper office the degradation of standards is overtly accepted:

> In a feeble voice the editorial secretary remarked: 'And so we gradually turn ourselves into whores.' The boss wearily lifted his hands. He didn't like repeating the same words, but what could he do? 'If we let ourselves be thrown out, even bigger whores would take our place. How would that help anybody?' After this exchange it was Slávek's turn for a witticism. 'Right! In our hands lies the decision about what depths of whoredom this small nation can afford.' We laughed.

The Axe is a book which combines with great effect dialectical and stylistic variations. Its narrative structure is intricate, with sudden flashbacks, unexpected switches of time and viewpoint, and paradoxical juxtapositions:

> 'We've a lot to do,' he said and frowned, 'And we've a lot of enemies', he said, and mother died.

There are repeated motifs which strike a chord, and take on new associations in retrospect:

> Years and years ago a carpenter built a house. His wife died. He was left alone with the child. He sat in his workshop and sang. They took him away to the asylum and unless he died, there he is still.

The style is flat and anecdotal, apparently muddled in its time sequences. There are strange contrasts between the memories of the village, with its own dialect and rural culture, and the slick atmosphere of the city offices. The overwhelming impression is of collapse and alienation. A village community whose roots run deep into the earth, and which seemed as firm as the great trees which ringed it, disintegrates like quicksand. The replacement of old gods by new, results not in a new community but a vacuum, filled by futile opportunism and despair.

> It was incomprehensible, as if there were no nation left; only an adaptable population. Suddenly I asked: 'Do you think the people would rebel, if the alarm were sounded?'
> 'Don't worry.' he said; 'Why, Man, people have lost any real interest. You know the poor have never had it so good as to-day.' 'That's right' I said. 'Then why is it so depressing? Do you go to church?'
> 'No I don't,' he answered. 'The priest doesn't believe in it himself.'
> 'We've got no philosophy,' I said. And I really felt that we hadn't, although we've had the whole of Marx.
> 'Maybe you've got Marxism,' said Karel.
> 'Right.' I said. 'I keep forgetting.'

While *The Axe* gains impact from its apparently artless and naive presentation, Milan Kundera's novel *The Joke*, which is also concerned with Moravian rural culture, is ruthlessly intellectual. The central story of the book is that of its central character Ludvík. It was spite, resulting from humiliation, which turned him from the traditional Catholic faith of his village into a brash enthusiast for Communism. In 1948 he is a student, full of shallow certainty, and speaking author-itatively as if with a secret agreement with History and a license to make promises in her name. In a move which is to cause ripples for years to come, he converts his friend Jaroslav to the idea of using their native Moravian folk-lore as a platform for propagating the new living style, the collective life to be created by socialism. Jaroslav, who leads the local musical ensemble, is persuaded not only by the arguments but also by the handsome material incentives; and employs his energies in spreading appreciation of the old native folk-art and the new Songs of Stalin.

Ludvík's downfall begins with a foolish joke. Annoyed by his girl's absence at a Party school he sends her a telegram:

OPTIMISM IS THE OPIUM OF THE PEOPLE. THE HEALTHY ATMOSPHERE STINKS. LONG LIVE TROT-SKY.   LUDVÍK

The consequences of the joke are swift and drastic. He is publicly questioned, accused, humiliated before his fellows by the student Party leader Zemánek. As was normal on such occasions, hands are raised in unison to condemn him. He is expelled from the Party; from the university; and from the society of his friends; then called up for service in a punitive battalion. There, in the depersonalised life of the barracks, with its severe discipline, heavy work shifts, political indoctrination and primitive slogans of the radiant socialist tomorrow, his head regularly shaved to prevent the growth of any unseemly individualism, he realises that every thread to his former life is cut.

Fifteen years pass, and with the improvement in the political climate Ludvík ceases to be an outcast. Believing that he is totally disillusioned, he affects an ironic, sophisticated and sceptical manner: but an intense feeling of injustice leaves in him a neurotic desire for revenge. Suddenly an opportunity is presented when he is visited by a female journalist (a fraternity he particularly dislikes as shallow, loud-mouthed, and insolent). The journalist is Helen, wife of his old enemy Zemánek. The new joke he plans is to hit back at Zemánek by seducing his wife, a task which presents little difficulty. As one of the narrators of the book, Helen is allowed to reveal her character in depth. It is a shocking exhibition – incredibly shallow, intellectually limited, hypocritical, she has an apparently boundless capacity for self-deception which makes her unintentionally comic. She is of course an enthusiastic Party worker. The seduction of Helen is carried out with a deliberation so cold as to convert the experience for Ludvík into undiluted sexuality, and to maximise the humiliation of the woman. Amid the squalid details Ludvík is surprised by his own feeling of *lowness*, but even more by the feeling of pleasure which this degradation brings to him. The joke is apparently complete: but like the earlier joke, it badly misfires. To his intense anger and disappointment Ludvík discovers that Helen means nothing to Zemánek, who has the admiration of a much younger woman. In the intervening years Zemánek has changed his course, though not his character. Totally untroubled by the principles over which others agonise, he is now a reformer, idolised by his students as a rebel against the bad old Stalinist ways. Against his colossal opportunism Ludvík's attempt at revenge is powerless: Zemánek is magnanimous, even amused at the encounter with his old victim. Ludvík, who thought he was manipulating events, is revealed as a child compared to this man, who really understands the course of History!

The downfall of Ludvík coincides with that of his old friend Jaroslav, who has built a whole career on exploiting the folk-lore of the countryside. Like Ludvík and like Helen, he too is the victim of his own myths. Years of falsification and self-deception have cut him off from genuine understanding even of his own family. His human relationships have become as dead as the myths he propagates, which have become to him more real than the life around him. The symbol of old folklore is the annual celebration of the Ride of the Kings. To honour the father, his son is chosen to ride as the masked King in procession. Having deceived others, Jaroslav is deceived himself; and discovers that a trick has been played: his son had contemptuously rejected the role. A blinding quarrel with his wife ends in Jaroslav smashing up the home which had been the centre of his life. A moment of truth has come to all the chief participants, except for Zemánek, who is untouched by the common catastrophe. Ludvík has attained some sense of self-knowledge. He who once saw himself as a captain of destiny has been unable even to control the consequences of his jokes: once set in motion they live a life of their own, exposing him as not their master, but their victim. Which is more futile, to seek to shape the future? or to recapture a once precious past? The ensemble plays at the last concert, and Ludvík's thoughts keep pace with the music:

> I felt myself happy within these songs in which sorrow is not a joke, nor laughter mockery, love is not absurd, nor hatred restrained, where people love with body and soul... in hatred men reach for knife or sword, in despair throw themselves into the Danube: where love is still love, and pain still pain; where basic feelings have not been twisted, nor values despoiled. I felt at home among these songs; this is where I came from, my home, a home which I had betrayed, but which was all the more my home because of that – for the home we have wronged calls to us the more urgently.
>
> But then I realised that the home was not of this world: that what we were singing and playing were only memories, recollections, a pictorial record of something that no longer existed. I felt the firm ground of my home sinking below my feet: I felt myself falling, my clarinet in my mouth, down into the depths of years, the depths of centuries, those impenetrable depths where love is love and pain is pain. And I told myself with surprise that my only home was precisely this falling, this searching, yearning fall. And I abandoned myself to it, and felt its delightful vertigo.

Both *The Axe* and *The Joke* quite clearly belonged to the category of politically engaged books. Although some critics abroad interpreted them as anti-communist in intention, this was evidently not the view of the authorities, who authorised their publication. They were acceptable as reflecting, each in its own way, the official policy of the day, which was still *the exposure of past errors*. Both novels reached a wide audience, and this was no doubt influenced by the rather sensational interpretations put upon them. But basically they were subtle, philosophical works of high literature, appealing to an intellectual, or at least a thinking, audience. Their negative view of the tainted past was regarded as a positive contribution to its reform, and to the improvement of the Party's image. Their criticism of the contemporary scene was oblique.

This could hardly be said of another novel, not to be compared to the other two in literary quality, and overtly sensational in intention. It was *The Taste of Power*[36] by L. Mňačko, the *enfant terrible* of Slovak literary life. While the book belongs to Slovak literature, its publication in Czech translation in Prague at once lent to it an active role in Czech reformist movement. *The Taste of Power* is a pseudo-documentary, written in Mňačko's familiar, graceless style. The body of the country's leading political figure lies in state. Among the mourners is his personal photographer who followed the great man's career from youthful revolutionary to the highest office of state. The book is, like others, in the form of a retrospect. From the intimate pictures of the photographer is reconstructed in flash-back a sad sequence: energy, ideals, talent are slowly stifled by careerism, corruption, and gross abuse of power. (In one startling episode the statesman is pictured as ordering the arrest and frame-up of a family because they might testify to his own private excesses, including an attempted rape).

Mňačko used to boast that in an abnormal situation the only way to hold your own was by attack: the more you insulted people, the more they respected you, and that is why he went out of his way to cause political scandals.[37] The book first appeared in Vienna, but Mňačko insisted that authorisation had been obtained at home; that it had been read by the leading Party ideologists; and that its appearance in Vienna before the Slovak edition appeared was an accident due to bureaucratic muddle.[38] He was in Vietnam when the scandal broke, and the storm had somewhat abated before his return.

The publication of all three books reveals how wide were the guidelines over creative literature *for Party intellectuals*. The rationale behind cultural policy was that the Party had room for critics of the past, even as subtle and sceptical as Kundera, or as brashly sensational as Mňačko. Their criticism and rebelliousness was officially regarded as constructive. But there is little evidence that such tolerance was extended to criticism written from positions outside the Party; and when Mňačko's novel was being widely distributed, other work of much higher quality, and politically less objectionable, was still held back from publication. Party intellectuals (the category is elastic and includes writers like Kundera who were on the fringe of the Party) had a license to criticise; and the politically engaged works of de-Stalinisation are chiefly their creation. Many active writers were of course non-Party and Catholic; in their case rarely did anything which appeared as even obliquely critical of socialism or the present administration get past the censor. Their permitted area was non-political, and within this area the guidelines were wide and the rein loose; the mid-sixties were rich in creative literature in this neutral area. As much of Western literature tends to be non-political, new Czech literature now seemed closer in spirit to the rest of Europe than had been the case for decades. A consequence was the success of Czech prose in translated editions, and the success of Czech films, whose scenarios were written by Czech popular authors.

Hrabal's stories of the off-people, fringe dwellers to a socialist society, were politically neutral: but politically minded observers interpreted them as a gesture of escape from the socialist nightmare. The young novelist Vladimír Páral explored the sordid and boring world of sexual promiscuity in *Private Blizzard* (subtitled *A laboratory report on insect life*).[39] Four couples, two married and two unmarried, circle around each other in the ceremonial of unsatisfactory sexual relationships. The most stable relationship is that of a married middle aged man with a young girl: both carry on with the vague idea that eventually she will get married to someone her own age. When she does find a partner, he turns out to be the lover of her best friend. The satisfying climax of the book is a full-scale wedding in the bourgeois tradition. The ceremonial will continue in a new framework of deceit and hypocrisy. The authoress Alena Vostrá published in *Cool Change*[40] a study of human isolation in an overpopulated world. The book is an account of thirteen days in the life of a hairdresser in a small town. Stupid incidents, petty conflicts, the delusion of escape into homemade fantasies are all that mark the passage of this meaningless sequence: an absurd non-life, leading nowhere. Another aspect of this literary waste land was provided by the youth culture of Prague – the rock festivals and the student stage revues. At the Semafor theatre Jiří

Suchý had won such a reputation for his contemporary lyrics as to make him a poet in his own right. His verse was published in book form, and he was eagerly sought after as a writer by the film studios. The pair of artists, Suchý and Šlitr, became symbols of youth doing its own thing – a sub-culture whose appeal was enhanced by its apparent escape from the embracing structures of socialist culture.

Within this flourishing garden of politically neutral, strictly unofficial, art was a young authoress of unusual intellect and originality. It was Věra Linhartová, inconspicuous, secretive, diffident, as aloof from the young generation of writers to which she belonged as she was from the Top Brass of the Establishment writers. An art student who became an art historian, she worked first at the Aleš gallery in Southern Bohemia, then moved to Prague. Painting is a strong motif in her literary work, and her especial interests are in abstract and surrealist art: she began to publish only in the 'sixties when the door had been opened to intellectual and aesthetic unorthodoxy.

Her stories are usually more or less plotless; they deal more with the relationships of ideas than people; they are written in prose on the fringe of poetry, and their form tends towards the essay as much as the short story. It is a feature of her style to disclaim all effort at realism: her stories are the reverse of those in which the author appears as the narrator of a real incident, the epic-reportage type. She writes what are overtly intellectual constructions, shaped by the authoress, who does not hesitate to interrupt with discussions of issues raised by the account. She writes of events which (as she herself makes clear) never happened, except in her imagination: she is entirely the mistress of the construction and changes its direction at will:

> The strangest thing, which most strikes us at the beginning of every narration is the total void stretching before us. A moment earlier than we began to write, there was nothing... We can begin anywhere, everything is for us equally important... Before us there is no path, except that which we have just laid for our next step which we plan to make, firmly trusting that we shall not fall into the void. Incidents there have been, but we do not know of what kind: we do not even know whether what interests us was important, or whether any of it was important, or whether anything did happen.

Linhartová's work is literature based on literature and art: it is literature in which the central interest is the act of writing:

What am I, if I am not writing? Nothing: less than nothing. A shapeless cloud, at the mercy of every breeze. Like an unwritten musical score which no one plays.

Her books, *Space for Diversity, Discourse on an elevator, Examination of the Recent Past, A House in the Distance*[41] show a general movement away from the story form toward the essay; but even when she appears to be writing fiction, it is more like the framework for an aesthetic exercise, or an intellectual problem:

One evening Sophie dreamed – she was not really sleeping, it was just before she fell asleep – that the squares on the wall were moving. Her room had been let before, and in the place where her bed now stood there had been a child's cot, over which several large squares of different sizes had been painted on the grey wall at about a man's height. It looked as if someone had tossed a handful of toy blocks against the side of the room, where they stuck and merged into the wall. She knew right away that no one would believe it, but it never occurred to her that she ought to convince anyone about it. First because she was afraid the others would misunderstand her and so spoil her own pleasure, and also because she didn't like to communicate, she was not anxious to introduce others to what she considered her own personal sanctuary. Anyway, she was not sure if it wouldn't spoil everything.

The darkness now favoured the growing dimensions of the wall and the other things, now released from the cramped space between the door and window and between door and ceiling, which were part of it during the day. The darkness spread through the room and dissolved into an opaque grey. Sophie groped in it and lost her way: she could find no point she could recognise, which could help her by its familiarity. The squares turned into blocks and collided against each other in the fog. She could not decide whether they were all the same or of different sizes. She did know that against the surface of the wall some were small and some larger, but now she knew that they were spread about in space – it had been obvious before, but she had not noticed it – now by comparison there was the effect of the surrounding greyness which exaggerated still more the differences in distance. The blocks shifted slowly; when she watched one of them, the motion was

almost imperceptible, and she could not see it at all unless it
was approaching another block. Then they collided...

In the strange haunted world of Věra Linhartová one has moved
furthest away from the once mandatory style of socialist realism. The
abstract painters, the surrealists, and Franz Kafka are perhaps her
chief mentors. The intellectual aloofness of her work guaranteed its
political neutrality: in any case her world was a shrine at which only
the few initiated might be expected to worship. And yet in one sense
the disengagement of literature from politics could itself be construed
as an expression of political attitudes: and her aesthetic views carried
disturbing social implications:

> The image of the *passage*, which is apparently impassable,
> is so frequent in our time that we are forced to enquire
> whether it is not an expression of something germane to our
> time, perhaps something basic to it - the urgency of escape
> from an area which has become too closely limited.

With the work of Věra Linhartová we seem to have reached a
literary world which is self-sustaining and almost self-contained.
Like the world of dreams, it is free from the assumptions which
regulate our perception of the real, external world: the latter supplies
all the physical components; but their combinations and proportions
are strange – like spooky pictures, where a haunted house is depicted
with distorted proportions. Linhartová constantly reminds the reader
that the events do not correspond with any real happenings. And yet
they carry their own type of conviction, because they do correspond
with something which lies in a hidden area of our experience – like
something which we cannot for the life of us recall, yet feel that it has
happened to us – some experience we have known, and had forgotten,
until reminded by some thread of association.

Linhartová's surrealist style, though very individualistic, can be
linked with a movement away from realism in other artistic forms of
the time. The Czech New Wave films of the sixties combined the
'hidden camera' type of pseudo-reportage with a kind of stylised lyric
symbolism. Films not only assaulted the audience's senses via sight
and sound, but also provoked their feelings via the association of ideas
and memories. Kafkaesque symbolism is evident in the short film
Josef Kilian.[42] A cat is hired from a pet shop; but when the hero (J. K.)
wishes to return it, the shop has vanished. There are dire penalties for
misuse of borrowed cats and failure to return state-owned animals;

but a frantic search for the shop leads the unfortunate man only through a labyrinth of nonsensical bureaucracy; the elusive official who could supply the answer is always behind the next filing cabinet. The cat, greedily feeding on tinned mice, has become a symbol of nightmare. Two men in a pub doing a crossword puzzle ask 'What is the specifically human quality?' the answer: 'Obedience'. Like the spectre of Stalin, the shaggy cat goes everywhere with the bewildered Czech who seeks to return his embarrassing burden and be rid of the past. The past, however, has become the organising principle of the present. Not thus can the ghost be laid.

In the film *A Report on the Party and the Guests*,[43] seven guests are seen walking to a garden-party. Suddenly they are surrounded and threatened by a group who begin to interrogate them. This violent situation is interrupted by the arrival of the host who explains that the whole thing was a joke organised by the other guests. After this happy relief, all the guests take their place at the tables laid out for them, and dine amid great elegance and style. The host, who assures his guests that his only wish is to please them, gives vent to his own opinions on a variety of topics. The guests, out of politeness or a disinclination to disturb the pleasant atmosphere, gradually adapt their views to his, so that the *happiness* is unanimous. Except for one disturbing element; a dissenter who, like all trouble-makers, refuses to adapt to the majority feeling, and withdraws. The host is concerned at this jarring development, and permits his son to head a search party to find the missing guest and bring him back, so that he too can be *happy* like the rest. The guests leave *en bloc* to search for the victim. The party has become a hunt for the non-conformist. The screen darkens, and we hear the growling of fierce dogs as they track their prey. The fate of the dissenter from the ruling ideology is sealed.

Impact was gained by subtle resemblances recalling past situations and familiar public faces. Czech film directors were fond of using amateur actors whom they persuaded to improvise: for the cast of his film Němec assembled several well-known Prague intellectuals, and played a part himself. Scenes in the film unexpectedly recalled news reels from wartime Europe or Vietnam. (One hazardous slip was the casting of the writer Ivan Vyskočil as the host: it was only when the rushes were screened that his awful resemblance to Lenin was perceived[44] – a circumstance which indicates that subliminal associations affected the film-makers as well as the film.)

Ester Krumbachová, who wrote the script, regarded the main creative element as *distorted dialogue*. The microphone picked up only isolated fragments of conversations among the guests, who said nothing significant about themselves: the impression was of a sophisticated masquerade in which everyone pretended to a significance he did not possess: a confused pattern of apparently rational talk was going on, but not a single sentence made sense. The elegant game of make-believe formed a background to an increasingly ugly situation. In their polite apathy towards violence the guests typify the callous irresponsibility of the privileged, who, by their indifference, collaborate with persecution and infect each other with the gusto of the witch-hunt.[45]

Ester Krumbachová combined with Věra Chytilová to make another film, *Daisies*.[46] The opening shots show tanks and high explosive wrecking human habitations. The scene changes, revealing two girls sitting in swim suits near a pool. They move their limbs like puppets; have little to distinguish between them; and share the same name – Marie I and Marie II. They discuss the meaning of life. If everything else in the world is spoiled, why not they? They take their revenge on society by wrecking everything which offends them by transcending their own limited understanding. They fight and tear up each other's dresses: they tempt admirers, then walk out on them; cause havoc wherever they go; take a bath in soup; their vandalism ends in a glorious scene of gluttony, crockery smashing, and custard pie throwing. Then, in a send-up of socialist repentance for their very anti-social behaviour, they appear in a shroud of newsprint (the garment of official orthodoxy) and clear up the mess; shovelling spoiled food on to soiled table cloths, they 'put everything right'.

Daisies was like a poetic dream-fantasy pretending to be social satire, pretending to be light comedy. By her treatment of the material, moving jerkily between sequences and frames, and by imaginative use of colour the young director ensured that the film would not be regarded as a narrative sequence but rather as a hotch-potch of unrelated happenings illustrating the fascination of destruction. It is natural for people to want to create something, and those who lack this gift get their revenge by wrecking what they cannot understand. In the image of the oafish destroyers it was not difficult to discern the Czechoslovak cultural authorities, and this interpretation received unexpected confirmation. The spokesman for a group of angry deputies in Parliament denounced the film, although he admitted that he did not understand it.[47] The attack was printed, and at the theatre of satire, *Paravan*, read out from the stage. The audience, thinking it was part of the performance, was convulsed with laughter.

In the face of rebuffs, threats, disappointments, and repression, the New Wave films won world recognition for Czech modern culture. For past generations it was the poets who, as a matter of course, had been regarded as the avant-garde, and poetry as the heart and voice, of Czech culture, which thereby remained a closed mystery to the outside world. By their talent, and by the communicability of their art, the Czech film-makers at last succeeded in doing what had been denied to the poets. But in taking over their sceptre they acknowledged their inspiration. Not narrative prose but lyric poetry is the literary genre nearest to the spirit of the best Czech films of the New Wave. By the mid-sixties the film had won recognition in Prague as a central feature, perhaps *the* central feature, of new creative art; and in retrospect the progress seemed inevitable. From the darkest days of Stalinism to the high noon of 1968 one may document the great revival in a film sequence – from the unforgettable *Moon over the River* of 1953 to the peak of the New Wave in the late sixties. For long unacknowledged, the young film-makers of the Barrandov studios became recognised as the new poets of Prague.

It is easy to understand why films which won such golden reports abroad failed to awaken the enthusiasm of the authorities at home. Several of the films were held up after completion, and then released only for limited distribution. They include the film which so provoked the good deputies, *Daisies*. In the case of *The Party and the Guests* we have it on good authority that Novotný himself hit the roof when he saw it; and his favourite author, Jan Procházka, pleaded for it at the President's palace. The film-makers felt themselves constantly under suspicion and harrassment, though this could not be compared with the active persecution of writers in Stalinist days. It is in fact still unclear how far the harrassment was due to ideological intolerance, and how much to sheer philistinism and ignorance. For official purposes the film makers, like other creative artists, seem to have been regarded as a privileged group from whom a degree of non-conformity was allowed and even expected.

All through 1966 the cultural journals wore a refreshing appearance of lively controversy, and when publishing houses announced their 1967 programmes the lists included the latest works of the literary 'rebels'; a collection of work by the writers associated with the banned journal *Tvář*; reprints of some formerly taboo Ruralist authors; and at last, Jiří Mucha's diary from the punishment camps, *Cold Sunlight*. But behind this promising exterior lay an unpleasant situation of increasing tension between the authorities and the writers. The new

Press law was due to come into force from the beginning of the new year, and this could hardly avoid provoking the uneasiness of those who were to be its targets. In the journal *Kulturní tvorba* Miroslav Galuška published a plaintive article *Are We Well Enough Informed?*, in which he criticised the effects of restrictions on freedom of the Press: his article was summarised in *L N*[48]. In October 1966 a brief note in *L N* reported the minutes of a meeting of the Writers' Union Central Committee, which acknowledged receipt of a memorandum from the Communist Party C.C. concerning measures to ensure Party control over the Press: the Writers Union minuted its approval of measures to implement such control.[49] In December certain administrative changes were announced. The Ministry of Education and Culture was to be divided, as it had been in the early fifties: the new Minister of Culture and Information was a former official of the Ideological section, Karel Hoffman (recently in charge of radio). At the same time the head of the Ideological section, Pavel Aueršperg, was replaced by a hard-and-fast conservative, František Havlíček, an old agit-prop official. None of these moves boded well for non-conformists or reformers in the cultural sector.

Evidence suggests that during 1967 external pressures upon the Writers' Union and its weekly *L N* intensified. The editor-in-chief, Milan Jungmann, had, after three years of working in that capacity, still not been confirmed in his appointment by the Party Secretariat. Together with sub-editors Liehm and Vaculík he had become a common target of official criticism. Early in 1967 in response to this pressure Liehm and Vaculík 'took leave' (a graceful form of suspension), and Jungman resigned. In his place came a temporary replacement, the poet, Jiří Šotola. Šotola was one of the few senior members of the union acceptable to both Party authorities and to the writers themselves, a loyal Party man, he could also be trusted to stand by his fellow writers. Šotola fitted the current Party image of de-Stalinisation within the limits of permitted policy. Ten years before, as leader of the *Květen* group, he had been regarded as a rebel; now to the younger writer-dissidents, he seemed a pillar of the Establishment.

Šotola agreed to act as Editor only until the Writers' Congress was held; and after repeated delays and wrangling, a date was finally agreed – June 27-July 9, 1967. It was timed to follow the Soviet Writers Congress in May, and was itself to be preceded by a meeting of the Slovak writers in Bratislava. The fact that the authorities had finally assented to the Congress seemed to be a happy omen. The good profile maintained by Czech culture was accompanied by a repressive censorship (now fully in operation), and a running campaign of bluster, warnings, and threats to intellectuals from the Party hawks.[50] By its twin policy of overt relaxation and behind-the-scenes intimidation the Party was keeping its options open. In Spring 1967 there still seemed to be a chance that reform would continue, and that the liberals would win fresh concessions from the Novotný leadership. Whether the next move was more de-Stalinisation, or an about-turn to re-Stalinisation, depended on more things than the will of Novotný; the choice would be affected by the policies chosen in Moscow, which now was facing difficulties with its leadership of the Communist world. The evidence suggested that the Brezhnev line on dissidents near home was going to be harsh. A sign of leniency in Moscow would have been welcomed in Prague, and could have helped to prolong the atmosphere of reform, or at least postpone the confrontation which was shaping up. But news from Moscow gave no comfort for de-Stalinisers; the Soviet Writers Congress, from which some of Russia's best writers were barred, indicated a step backwards towards Stalinism.

In the interval which elapsed between setting a date for the Czechoslovak Writers' Congress and holding it, the delicate situation in Prague was complicated by grave developments abroad. Early in June the Near East erupted into war; the USSR reacted by drumming up support for the Arabs among the Satellite states in Europe; and Czechoslovakia responded by breaking off relations with Israel. The unseemly haste with which Prague led the race to oblige Moscow did nothing to improve Novotný's prestige at home, and destroyed overnight the myth that he represented a line independent of Moscow. The circumstances were particularly unfortunate for the public image of the Czech authorities. The situation whereby a small democratic state was threatened with extinction by powerful militarist neighbours invited comparison with Czechoslovakia's own position in 1938. It was easy for the Czech public to identify with Israel; and natural for them to rejoice in the triumph of David over a Goliath armed by the Russians. In any case there were powerful ties between Czech Jewry, including prominent intellectuals, and Israel: in the public media the official pro-Arab policy was put over in such a crude and one-sided fashion as could only alienate and disgust the more liberal sections of the Czech community. The anti-Jewish flavour was especially unfortunate, being so terribly reminiscent not only of Nazi wartime propaganda but also of the Stalinist line at the period of the Czech political trials.

At a time when the authorities and the Party intellectuals were feeling their way towards yet another delicate compromise, a hysterical campaign in the media and new pressure on writers to conform or be silent, could only make a bad situation worse. At a time when the Czech newspapers, following the Soviet line, were busily suppressing and falsifying information about Israel, the Czech writers themselves were fairly well informed of the realities. In fact a delegation of four writers had just returned from a fact-finding tour of Israel and the U.A.R. A symposium on their impressions was arranged and recorded by *Literární noviny*. The material was at once confiscated by the censors. The four writers included Procházka, the confidant of Novotný, and Lustig, the Jewish writer whose personal conscience had been sharpened by his own sufferings. It seemed that the authorities were reverting to the old repressive ways, contemptuously brushing aside considerations of truth and conscience. Optimists who had hoped to see in the coming Writers' Congress a sign of fresh détente in cultural life could only regard the latest developments with deep foreboding. The rift between writers and rulers was evidently widening, not narrowing:[51] and unless Party intellectuals and cultural reformists were prepared for ignominious surrender, a confrontation with authority could no longer be postponed or avoided.

IX

Trumpets at the Walls of Jericho

'We have been in the past a centre of advanced culture, craftsmanship, and honesty; and it should be a natural ambition of today to excel our yesterday. Without a living contact with our own past we cannot think of a worth-while future. But here too there is maybe an encouraging development. *Nobody now excludes from our national tradition T. G. Masaryk, his friends or his colleagues, nobody now says that Eduard Beneš was an agent of the imperialists.*'

Jan Procházka (*My* Oct. 1967)
(italicised words were cut out by the censor)

The operation of the new censorship arrangements did nothing to improve relations between the Party leadership and the Writers' Union, in 1967 still struggling to put out a weekly newspaper of literary character and some independence. From the onset of the new arrangements the number of interventions by the censors into *L N* had soared:[1] the Party leadership was still withholding its ratification of appointments made by the Union; and protests from the latter were answered by suggestions that the union should first put its own house in order. In consultations with officials from the Party's Ideological Department it emerged in no uncertain terms that Antonín Novotný was fed up with the writers and would put up with no more half measures: these prolonged and frustrating consultations have been amusingly described by an eye witness and participant.[2] The writers still had a choice. They could again make whatever minimal sacrifices were necessary, keep the paper going, and hang on in the hope of better times. Conversely they could take a stand on principle, allow the conflict to come into the open, and thus end the facade of voluntary participation in cultural policy. There was much to be said for the latter, more resolute, alternative. The relentless use of state censorship indicated that further concessions by the writers were pointless; ground saved by compromise was anyway being quickly eroded; and there was little to be gained by postponing a showdown. (Such a showdown, although unpleasant, and likely to involve the loss of jobs and privileges, was not at this stage regarded as involving the serious dangers inherent in such a situation in Stalinist days. It was assumed that neither Novotný nor the rest of the leadership was anxious to re-enter such dangerous waters.)

For the time being the caution traditional to Czech public life pre-vailed. The writers had no wish to start burning their bridges; maybe after all some independence could be preserved by delaying tactics: the communist members of the Union were aware of the personal divisions and chronic irresolution which lay behind the ostensibly inflexible menaces issuing from Party headquarters. But the issue could not be postponed much longer, and a showdown was expected at the Writers' Congress. It seemed quite possible that the situation would drift on like this for the rest of the year, and nothing had been decided.

In the case of all meetings which included non-communists it was standard practice for the communist participants to assemble be-forehand to agree on a common Party line towards the Agenda. Accordingly in addition to clearing with the Party Central Committee the *Draft Statement* which was to be presented to the Congress, there was convened on its eve (June 26) a meeting of the communist faction of the Union. In the chair was F. Havlíček, head of the Party Ideo-logical Department. He had eliminated any doubt about his attitude by publishing, a few days earlier, an article in which he maintained that the cultural front was presently exposed to enemy pressures and ideological diversionists: his thinly veiled, but clearly understood, message was that the future of the Union depended on the strictness of its adherence to a socialist (i.e. a Party dictated) programme.[3]

The opening speaker was Jiří Hendrych, Number 2 in the Party hierarchy; the aggressive tone of his address made it clear that the Party line was intended to be inflexible. He said bluntly that he was shocked by *L N*'s 'open attacks on the Party', and he congratulated the censors on their suppression of material. By an unfortunate error of judgement he chose to illustrate his point by reference to publicity on the Middle East war and the insolent opposition of *L N* to govern-ment policy. (He was referring in particular to a recent symposium by four writers who had visited the war area.)[4] He concluded by giving what amounted to an ultimatum to the writers to conform or to take the consequences. In accordance with the agreed agenda Hendrych's speech was followed by Šotola's report, which was quite factual, and had been written without knowledge of Hendrych's coming assault: the report detailed the disastrous effects of the censors' intrusions into journalism. Šotola's quiet and matter-of-fact approach made ap-parent the gap between himself, as representing Union opinion, and

Hendrych, representing Party authority; and writers present who had little to do with journalism, were shocked at some of the revelations. Without wishing or planning to do so, Šotola had contradicted Hendrych's thesis in full, and subsequent speeches made clear the hostility of the writers present towards the official Party line. Nothing annoyed the speakers more than Hendrych's gratuitous choice of the Middle East war policy, highly unpopular as it was, to reinforce his support for literary repression. Even Hendrych seems to have been taken aback by the expressions of anger, frustration and despair to which he had to listen. It was an ominous prelude to a Congress in which some hopeful writers had seen the possibility of reaching some understanding with the authorities. Such hopes died even before the Congress began, and it was perhaps the feeling that all was lost anyway that led certain speakers to express themselves later with unusual recklessness and with an apparent indifference to the consequences.

On the next day, the 27th of June, the Congress opened with an official speech of welcome by the veteran Závada, followed immediately by Milan Kundera, who introduced the previously prepared and approved *Draft Statement of the Writers Union*.[5] It was a tradition established in Stalinist times for an official viewpoint of a conference to be worked out in advance, discussed, amended, and finally submitted with official blessing so that participants could approve it with minimal changes: such a draft saved the proceedings from any danger of uncertainty, and enabled what should have been a discussion to become an orchestrated ceremonial. In this case the material in the *Draft*, while predictably uncontroversial, (being mainly concerned with the place of culture in the modern world) had already been subjected to fierce criticism at a full meeting of the Party Ideological Commission.[6] Having formally introduced the *Draft* Kundera proceeded to draw attention to one omission in it, namely any attempt to evaluate the literature of the immediate past. This omission he excused by the need to avoid the errors made by previous authoritarian assessments, and by the wish to allow work to go through a process of continuous free evaluation according to differing criteria.

Kundera's introduction of the document was presented in such a way as virtually to undermine it as an authoritative statement of Union policy: he made it clear that he understood it rather as a starting point for free discussion. From this Kundera proceeded to give his own contribution to such a discussion. His views amounted to a defence of open criticism and an attack on the repression of it. In connection with this he cited the recent crude attack in Parliament on the film *Daisies*, an attack which he characterised as an instance of ignorant and arrogant vandalism in high places – a vandalism far more pernicious than the hooligan type of vandalism which so incensed the current protagonists of law and order.

Kundera had prefaced his remarks with a contemptuous reference to the boring and authoritatively expressed speeches which normally accompanied such occasions. His words were amusingly illustrated by the boring and authoritative address of the next speaker, none other than Jiří Hendrych, who pompously conveyed the greetings of the central body of the Party. The juxtaposition of speakers was unlucky, and some suspicious souls later attributed it to malice. Oblivious of the painful impression he was creating, or else contemptuous of his audience's reactions, Hendrych harangued his restive listeners with a simplistic resumé of the intellectual situation. There were repeated references to American and Israeli aggression, to the sharpening of the ideological conflict, and to the need for harsh measures against those who would *open the door to enemy propaganda*: the only possible way to approach the problem of cultural advancement was that recently laid down by the Party. There was much more in the same vein, but the overall message was very simple. There must be an end to the present *chaos of criteria*; the Union must present a common front; *ideological pluralism* must stop. Hendrych's speech thus totally opposed the more liberal, pluralist views of Kundera, and slammed the door on any compromise or discussion.

The unpleasant confrontation of the previous day, the offensive and aggressive tone of Hendrych's present address, the general expectation of tension, allied to the overheated temperature of the June day, all combined to create an electric atmosphere which made the next speech perhaps seem more provocative than had been foreseen when it was prepared. Pavel Kohout began with an allegory. A small nation becomes an independent state, then is threatened by powerful and aggressive neighbours; for a moment he left open the identification – Czechoslovakia threatened by Nazi Germany in 1938? or Israel threatened by the Arabs in 1967? Kohout went out of his way to underline the parallel, which was an unspoken commonplace in Prague, and he asked by what right the Czech Press unanimously denounced Israel as the aggressor. He could prove that the unanimity was forced and false by recalling that the censors had confiscated all material which contradicted the official standpoint. Ironically the confiscation had been justified by the censors on the grounds that writers should concern themselves with literature not politics – an exact reversal of the pre-1956 concept that it was a writer's duty to make his work political. This led Kohout to discuss the working of the censorship, which he described as a disgrace, and whose idiocy and injustice he illustrated from his personal experience. He drew the conclusion that the repression of knowledge and free discussion encouraged ignorance and political apathy: these qualities, so evident in Czechoslovakia, he contrasted with the political awareness of young people in West Germany.

It had no doubt been expected that the menacing words of Hendrych would suffice to quell any thoughts of rebellion at the Congress. But the situation seemed now to be getting out of hand, and worse was to follow. Alexandr Kliment in his speech suggested that a formal motion be put to affirm the right of free speech, declare the existing censorship to be unconstitutional, and demand its repeal. He also asked for action to ensure that members had better access to information, pointing out the absurdity of the present position whereby they often depended on French or German journals to find out what was going on in the world:

Kliment: For instance I have in mind the letter of A. I. Solzhenitsyn to the IVth Congress of the Soviet Writers Union. I suggest that our Congress ought to be acquainted with that letter, and as I know the contents myself, I express my own solidarity with that writer. (*Applause*)

Kohout: I have a Czech translation of Solzhenitsyn's letter with me. Does the Congress want to hear it? (*Applause*)

Chairman: (K. Ptáčník): Comrades, though your applause is a sort of expression of your feelings, pardon me, but I must take a vote. (*All in favour; one against; two abstained*)[7]

Pavel Kohout then read out Solzhenitsyn's letter with its bitter attack on censorship.[8] As he began to read, Hendrych rose and walked out; he was joined by other high ranking officials of Party and state. As Hendrych passed the row of chairs where Kundera, Lustig, and Procházka were sitting, he said to them: 'You've lost the lot now. *The lot!*'

Thus on the first day of the Congress, even before the luncheon break had arrived, the rift between writers and authorities was wide open. During the afternoon L. Novomeský was due to speak, but he was too ill to attend, and his speech was read for him. This speech was demonstrably unaffected by the morning's events; it provided an independent witness from the Slovak side; but in its sad detailing of arbitrary censorship and cultural repression, the speech was as impressive as Solzhenitsyn's letter. During the afternoon there were various attempts to patch up the situation by compromise, and some conservative speakers attempted to defend the official standpoint; but their words lacked conviction.[9] There were also various attempts to collect petitions disassociating members from the "trouble-makers", and deploring efforts "to misuse the conference for dishonest political aims": but none collected enough signatures to make a petition worth presenting. The only compromise document which did attract substantial support was one criticising the conduct of the meeting but defending the principle of open discussion.[10]

The second day of the Congress opened without the presence of Hendrych and associates, but amid alarming rumours of the measures to be taken against the Union. The business of the Congress proceeded, led by a detailed review of Union affairs by Šotola. One of the succeeding speeches which particularly incensed the authorities was that by the film critic A. J. Liehm. His fault was not that he attacked official government views, but that he dealt with fundamental principles of cultural policy (which the Congress was in fact supposed to be discussing):

It is hard to believe, yet nonetheless true, that in spite of all historical experience the cultural policy of socialism involves the repetition of all the errors of which past regimes have been guilty. Slowly and painfully we are beginning to see that the basic fault lies not so much in any particular cultural policy as in the concept of cultural policy as such. The constant debacles which socialist cultural policy has suffered in the past and continues to undergo to this day, have finally convinced many people that socialism is incapable of solving cultural problems, and this in turn has resulted in an idealisation of the cultural life of the West. These debacles, I repeat, have their origins in a faulty concept of cultural policy. We are forever pointing the finger at this or that work, at this or that author, accusing him of misdeeds; only to reverse ourselves a few months or a few years later. There is a continual turnover of officials responsible for cultural policy. The reasons for dismissal are always the same: they were too liberal or too intolerant, too sensitive to pressure from below or too ready to invoke administrative machinery. Yet we all know these administrators are very similar in their attitudes and opinions, and the practical results of their regimes are almost indistinguishable. But still they come and go, and come back once again – not because they are good or bad, clever or stupid, hard-working or lazy, but simply because they are supposed to do a task which is by its very nature, impossible to carry out... All this naturally not only fails to help culture; it discredits socialism by revealing it to be a system incapable of solving a problem as old as humanity itself...[11]

A subsequent speaker, Ivan Klíma, returned to the question of censorship, and placed it in its historical setting. He quoted the Vienna edict of 1849 guaranteeing freedom of speech and publication unhampered by censorship; he mentioned the subsequent era of repressive absolutism in which these freedoms were denied; and finally recalled the restoration of freedom of the Press in 1867. Thus the Czechoslovak authorities who had recently chosen the date 1967 for the official *revival* of censorship, had proved by their acute sense of timing that they did not lack a gift for absurd humour.

The authority of the Party, which traditionally should have gone unquestioned, was now reeling under a series of blows – from the cool, contemptuous reasoning of Liehm to the outright ridicule of Klíma. but the culminating blow, which finally convinced the Ideological department that the Congress had been an orchestrated conspiracy against the Party, was delivered by the novelist Ludvík Vaculík. He began by remarking that what he had to say was anyway well known to all his audience. He spoke in a conversational, matter-of-fact way, and in essence his message was only that which he had conveyed in allegorical terms in his novel *The Axe*. His theme was the relationship between rulers and ruled. A democratic system makes the job of ruling harder, but it always carries the hope that the next government may be better than the last; the government falls, but the citizen is renewed. In contrast, a government which is based not on consent but on force leads its citizens into panic, apathy, resignation, and eventually into a new form of modern serfdom:

> In our country I don't think there are any citizens left. My reasons for saying this are based on years of work in newspapers and radio. For a fresh example I don't need to go far. This Congress did not take place at the time when the members of the organisation chose, but when the master gave his consent, after considering his own problems. In return he expects, on the basis of past millenia, that we should pay

homage to his dynasty. I suggest that we decline. I propose
that we have a good look at the text of the *Draft Statement*
and cross out everything that smells of serfdom...

Vaculík went on to discuss the character of power, and its effect on
those who serve it:

> Power prefers people of the same inner constitution as itself.
> But since these are in short supply, it has to make use of other
> people too, whom it adjusts to its requirements. Naturally the
> kind of people who are useful to serve power are those who
> long for power themselves; then people who are obedient by
> their nature: people with a bad conscience; and people whose
> appetite for comfort, advancement, and gain knows no moral
> limitations. Other people who have suffered humiliation and
> trustingly accept the offer of renewed self-respect; and again,
> people born stupid. For a certain time and in certain circum-
> stances and for certain purposes temporary use can be made
> of various moral absolutists, and altruistic but ill-informed
> enthusiasts like me. There are several long-standing techniques
> for adjusting people. Physical and intellectual temptation,
> the threat of suffering, involvement in compromising situ-
> ations, the use of informers, throwing groundless suspicion
> on a person so that he defends himself by a demonstration of
> loyalty, delivering people into the hands of evil characters
> and then hypocritically rescuing them. There is also the spread-
> ing of general mistrust. Trust is classified as trust Class A, B
> or C – and it is assumed that a lot of people lack it entirely.
> Information is similarly classified in quality – on pink paper,
> on green paper, on yellow paper, and on newspaper (*laughter*)
> ...

Vaculík proceeded to discuss the relationship between the rulers and
the artists; the latter bring credit on their country by their achievement (he mentioned by way of example the Czechoslovak pavilion at
the World Fair), and the government congratulates them, as though
it could claim credit for their work:

> We know that our best work is unwanted, that everything we
> do is at the mercy of God, deadlines are set and we do not even
> know the dates. Every cultural achievement, everything
> worthwhile that our people have done, every good piece of

manufacture, every good building and every good application
of thought in our laboratories, studies, or institutes, – all this
has been for years *in spite* of the efforts of our ruling circles.
It was accomplished in literal defiance of them...

Lastly Vaculík surveyed the disastrous effects which socialism had
brought to the country as a whole:

The continuity of aspiration towards state socialism was
transformed after the war into a direct programme for socialism. The particular conditions under which that programme
was approached... meant that distortions occurred in our
country in the process of implementation, and there were
events which cannot be explained in terms of the local environment, and are out of harmony with the character of our
nation and its history. Whenever anyone mentions this period
or asks for an explanation of why we squandered so much of
our moral and material strength, why our economy stagnated,
our ruling circles reply that it was necessary. From the point
of view of all of us here I do not think it was necessary at all.
Maybe it was necessary for the development of those organs
of power which more or less compelled every supporter of
socialism to go through that development with them. It must
be recognised that in the past twenty years not one human
problem in our country has been solved – from primary needs
like housing, schools, economic well-being to those more
subtle demands which the more undemocratic systems of this
world cannot solve – like the feeling of playing a full part in
society, the subordination of political decisions to ethical
criteria, belief in the significance of even humble work, the
need for trust between individuals, the raising of educational
standards of the people as a whole. I am afraid that we have
not improved our standing on the world stage; I feel that the
name of our republic has lost the good sound it once had...[12]

Vaculík had intended to speak frankly, as was theoretically his right
and duty as a Party member. But after all that had happened his words
were taken almost as a declaration of war from dissident writers to
the authorities. The second day of the Congress closed amid high
tension. Perhaps for the first time intervention by the security forces
seemed a possibility, and his friends discussed the likelihood of Vaculík's arrest.[13]

On the third and final day of the Congress the start was delayed for an hour to enable a meeting of the Party faction to precede it. The chairman was V. Bil'ak, Secretary for ideological affairs to the Slovak C.P.: he opened the proceedings by calling on Jiří Hendrych to speak. The latter's message was brief and to the point. He declared that the Congress had obviously been misused by a small group acting in concert; their attack on the Party and on the government had come to a head in the speech of Vaculík. Consequently the Party Central Committee instructed all Party members at the Congress to vote for a new list of candidates for the Writers' Union committee. If this failed to happen, the Party would wash its hands of Union affairs, and that would be the end of the Union.

Before the chairman could read out the list of 'recommended' candidates he was interrupted from the floor by an angry interjection in defence of the threatened writers: Vaculík himself then broke in, and repeatedly challenged Hendrych to substantiate his charges. As the two men shouted across the room at each other, the meeting began to slip out of control of the chairman. The slanging match ended only when Vaculík was pulled back into his seat by his friends. The chairman then read out the new list: of the 30 candidates whom the Party faction had earlier agreed to support, eleven had been deleted; they included the so-called *Literární noviny* group. The hour allotted to the meeting was now almost over, and the chairman was anxious to conclude the formality of election, but before he could put the motion to the vote, Goldstücker rose and asked that in view of what had passed, his own name should also be deleted. Other candidates then followed his example. This was open rebellion. For Hendrych it must have been a shock to see his authority still challenged in this unusual way: for it belonged to Stalinist tradition that once a group had been officially stigmatised, its members were isolated and abandoned. The fact that other communists of influence were siding with the victims against the leadership was not only a blow in the face for Hendrych, but proved that the victims were not, as alleged, a tiny group of conspirators but had wide backing among the writers.

Hendrych now backed down. Ignoring the chairman, he produced a new list which was a compromise on his first proposal: only four candidates were now to be deleted – Vaculík, Klíma, Kohout, and Havel: they were to be replaced by Skála, Hanzlík, Šuléř, and Frýd. The compromise was accepted by the meeting, which adjourned at 10.57 a.m., almost an hour late. By defying Hendrych, the communist faction of the Union had made explicit the gulf between *communist* writers and rulers.

After the fireworks of the first two days the proceedings of the third day were something of an anti-climax: Hendrych got through his compromise resolution on the candidates for election, but in the results of the ballot it was noticeable that the two candidates who attracted the lowest vote were Šuléř and Skála, both identified with Hendrych's rearguard action. Much of the day was spent in business sessions, which included the formal approval (with minor changes) of the *Draft Statement*, and of a letter to the Central Committee of the Party proclaiming the Union's intention to proceed in its efforts, side by side with the Party, towards the development of socialist Czechoslovakia, and stressing that the frank words expressed at the Congress should not be taken as a mark of opposition, but rather of trust in the democratic nature of Czechoslovak socialism. (The letter was approved *nem. con.*)[14]

An immediate problem was presented by the need to publish an account of what had transpired at the Congress. It had been expected that a detailed report, including the texts of the main speeches, would appear in the journals of the Union, *L N* and *K Ž*. Accordingly the documents and speeches were sent to the printers, and proofs were corrected by the individual speakers. But before *L N* could go to the press, the editors were informed that Party disciplinary proceedings were being taken against Klíma, Kohout, Liehm, and Vaculík, and that while the issue was *sub judice* their speeches could not be published Novomeský's speech must also not be printed until the Slovak CP had had a chance to discuss it. Various other speeches could appear only with certain omissions and emendations.

Responsibility for *L N* lay with the Union, but its leadership was now paralysed. The retiring chairman and secretary (Šotola and Špitzer) had laid down their office, but the incoming officials were prevented from taking up office, pending a Party enquiry. An attempt to set up an interim steering committee was vetoed on the grounds that this move required specific Party approval. The editorial committee of the paper was therefore left isolated. They declined to accept the censor's verdict, and sought a meeting with the head of the Ideological department to work out a compromise which would enable some sort of general coverage of the Congress to be printed. A compromise was finally agreed on, but it was immediately vetoed by the Party centre. In the event *L N* was able to publish only the formal speeches of Hendrych, Závada, Šotola; the text of the *Draft Statement;* and an exceedingly brief summary of proceedings.

Elsewhere in the Party press there was a coverage of the Congress which was predictably slanted, and of course included none of the 'opposition' speeches.[15] The appetite of the public must have been whetted by hints, contained in these reports, that certain writers had taken up unacceptable attitudes at the Congress. This could be concluded, for instance, from a cryptic comment in *Nová Mysl*[16]

It is not long since the IVth Congress of the Writers Union took place and it is necessary to say by way of comment upon it that some correct and valuable views about the further development of Czech literature were expressed; but there were also expressions of view which were criticised on the spot by the writers themselves, and especially by the party delegation, and, subsequent to the Congress, by First Secretary of the Party Antonín Novotný.

What it was that Novotný found it necessary to criticise was not specified; but clues were obligingly given in the printed text of Hendrych's second speech which had been delivered on the third day and after his stormy meeting with the Party faction:

Without regard to the viewpoint of the Party CC, as expressed by its delegation to this Congress, and with evident disinclination to heed it, several speeches have contained veiled or open attacks and insults levelled at our socialist organisation, government, and the internal and external policies of Czechoslovakia and the Communist Party.[17] The remark that *for 20 years not one human problem has been solved* is beyond the limit of even the most primitive anti-communist propaganda... The Party delegation is convinced that no Communist or decent citizen of a socialist state can permit that our people's socialist path should be *put on the same level as the era of the Dark Age and the Nazi occupation*, that the revolutionary role of our people should be belittled, and it resolutely rejects such opinions. With equal resolution it cannot permit that under the general slogan of freedom, humanism, and democracy, there should be smuggled into the Congress, and thence to the public, an attempt to demand the right of freedom on behalf of enemy opinions...

The publication of Hendrych's references to the insulting views of Vaculík and Kundera gave a tantalising publicity to them. In a tightly knit community like that of Prague it is virtually impossible to keep anything secret for long, and private copies of the speeches were soon in circulation. In its Autumn number (32/67) the emigré journal *Svědectví* published full texts,[18] whence reports filtered into the foreign press. The debate at the closed Congress had thus become elevated into a national and international scandal, only exacerbated by the clumsy attempts of the Czech censorship to stifle it. It is to be noted that the participants on both sides – the dissidents and the Party authorities with whom they negotiated – were anxious to keep the disagreement in perspective and avoid a scandal. Among the writers it was clearly understood, and Havlíček and Hendrych must have known, that the issue was one of literary freedom and censorship; there was no anti-Party, much less an anti-state, conspiracy. But the obstinate rejection of compromise by authority (presumably at the orders of Number One), the inflammatory accusations recklessly thrown about by Hendrych and repeated by Novotný, the absurd cloak-and-dagger atmosphere which accompanied the publication of the Proceedings, all aggravated the gravity of the situation. By implying the existence of an opposition movement[19] they encouraged its formation. By identifying with it the writers who were among the most popular representatives of Czechoslovakia abroad, they gave to the movement the stamp of international acclaim. By accusing the writers of organising a campaign in concert with emigré circles in Paris and other unspecified groups abroad,[20] they helped to transform what could have been shrugged off as a temporary incident into a crisis with international implications. The eyes of the West European press, especially the radical press, were now on Czechoslovakia.[21] At the same time the men around Novotný were not unaware of the effect this unwelcome publicity was having on the Kremlin, trying to mend its fences with the West, and watching how Novotný would cope with the crisis he had helped to bring about.

The Writers Congress had been over only three days when there began a political trial, the first to be staged in Prague since the early 'fifties. Three defendants were charged; the young writer Jan Beneš, who had already been held in custody for eight months; a young film scenario writer, Karel Zámeček, and *in absentia*, the editor of the Paris journal *Svědectví*, Pavel Tigrid. Beneš was charged with fraud and subversion, involving the illegal despatch of material abroad for publication; Zámeček with damaging the interests of the Republic while abroad; and Tigrid with subversion and espionage. The judge was Otakar Balas, well known for his conduct of the case against the Catholic writers in 1952 (the heavy sentences imposed on that occasion had only recently been rescinded). The timing of this trial immediately in the wake of the Congress, the nature of the charges against Beneš and Tigrid, and the rumour that exile groups had influenced the conduct of the Congress, all contributed to the popular impression that Beneš was the victim of an assault upon the writers, aimed to cow the dissidents and dissuade them from any thought of making common cause with political opposition outside the country.

The case attracted wide publicity: The London *Times*, *Le Monde*, the *Frankfurter Allgemeiner Zeitung*, and the *New York Times*, among other newspapers, closely followed proceedings. PEN International had already mobilised international sympathy for the plight of Beneš. Amnesty International sent an observer to report on the trial. (To compound its problems the Czech authorities, after granting facilities to the observer (Mr Paul Sieghart, a British barrister), then detained and deported him. A protest in London followed.) The results of the trial were acquittal for Záměček, five years for Beneš, and fourteen years (*in absentia*) for Tigrid. In Western papers speculation was voiced[22] that Beneš was being punished for having organised a protest against the Sinyavsky-Daniel trial in Russia: in Prague popular scandal connected him with the daughter of Hendrych himself, and the documents so faithfully reproduced in *Svědectví* were thought to have got there via this romantic route.

Those who suppress information cannot complain if they reap a whirlwind of rumour and speculation. The foreign press now pictured the muddled and irresolute Novotný as a new Stalin, awaited a new reign of police terror, and speculated on the possibility of an internal explosion. One crumb of comfort for the Czech authorities was that in all this ferment the Slovak problem had rather dropped out of sight: at the Writers Congress the Slovak writers had shown little initiative, and of those who did attend, a fair proportion had counselled caution and supported compromise. But in August even this comfort was shattered when the unpredictable Mňačko again hit the headlines:

> Prison, exile, or death? These seem to be the alternatives faced by writers in Iron Curtain countries if they deviate by a hair's breadth from the Party line. Death seems now to be out. Such a mitigation has been won by a small handful of brave writers who have faced the bitter anger of politicians, or near-politicians, in Moscow, Prague, and the other sombrely Red capitals. The latest victim is Mr Mňačko, who wrote a book exposing the demoralisation of a Communist leader, and has

protested against anti-semitism by going to Israel. He has
been deprived of his Czechoslovak citizenship... Last month
the Czech writer Jan Beneš was also imprisoned. We in the
West can only hope that freedom of thought and of the expression of thought, must in the end win through their un-
conquerable momentum. There have been martyrs in this
cause, and there will be others. Are we sufficiently grateful
to them?[23]

Mňačko had indeed defected on August 10 and he published the
reasons for his actions in typically flamboyant fashion in a statement
published on the following day in the *Frankfurter Allgemeiner Zeitung*,
headed MŇAČKO PROTESTS: I AM GOING TO ISRAEL:

> I am going to Israel. Thereby I wish to protest against the
> policy of the Czechoslovak government. In Czechoslovakia
> there is silence on the questions of the Near East; it is not al-
> lowed to express one's views on the matter. I am forced to this
> unusual step as I wish to express my views.
>
> It is impossible to support, by remaining silent, a policy
> whose aim is the destruction of a nation and the liquidation of
> an entire state...
>
> In our country the political trials of the Stalinist times had
> an unusually unpleasant taste; even today their effects linger
> on.
>
> In our press recently I have been reading about cosmo-
> politanism and Zionism described with a violence reminiscent
> of the Slánský era. The final cause of my departure to Israel
> was not a big event but a minor episode. I was reading about
> the trial of Pavel Tigrid. To the name of the accused they at-
> tached the Jewish name he had before he was converted to
> Catholicism; so they called him Tigrid-Schönfeld. It was no
> accident. At the time of the Slánský trials they used to stir up
> hatred against the accused in the same way. Today the process
> repeats itself. It is enough to read the title of an article: ZION-
> ISTS AND REVANCHISTS HAND IN HAND...
>
> If we want to have a socialist, humanist, healthy state, we
> must change the whole system. We must eliminate chaos, the
> bending of the law, the possibility of getting round the law
> when it suits the bosses, the possibility of applying it just when
> it suits them. We must get rid of arbitrary control. We have

gone a good way in this regard; but there is no guarantee that
there will not be new excesses...

Mňačko's gesture achieved its expected result of maximum world
publicity for himself, his books, and the cause he proclaimed. His
photograph appeared in a score of foreign journals; sales of his book
The Taste of Power soared: (it was reported that Richard Burton had
offered a huge sum for the film rights). Perhaps the most serious
aspect of Mňačko's behaviour was the general knowledge that he was
a member of the innermost ring of Slovak communists. The intemperate assault on the Prague leadership, slapped recklessly across the
European and world press, was taken as an indication of the true feelings of the Slovak communist leadership, expressed by the Slovak
CP's most embarrassing son.

The intense anger of Novotný was expressed in the immediate
expulsion of Mňačko from the Party, denunciations of his actions as
treason, and the deprivation of his civic rights. This perhaps unwise
decision prompted Mňačko to energetic retaliation by an appeal to the
International Court of the Hague whether the regime had the right to
take such action. At the same time, with a subtlety not entirely characteristic, Mňačko limited his attacks to the leadership, and avoided saying anything which could be properly interpreted as defamation of the
state. He also announced his intention of returning to Czechoslovakia
and defending himself in court against any charges laid against him.

At the time of the Writers Congress the silence of Mňačko and the
comparatively minor role played by the Slovaks had been puzzling:
their privately expressed sympathy with the dissident cause had found
little overt expression, save for the speech of Novomeský. It now appeared likely that this reticence was to be attributed to a cause which
would bring little comfort to the Novotný leadership. The Slovak
dissidents had avoided compromising themselves by taking sides in a
quarrel among Czechs, so that they could reserve their efforts for a
push with nationalist as well as reformist overtones, backed by powerful forces in the leadership of the Slovak Party. There was common
ground between dissident Slovak intellectuals like Novomeský, and
orthodox communists like Husák, in that both resolutely opposed
what they saw as a policy of Prague centralism, of which the arch
symbol was Novotný himself. Husák and Dubček could hardly approve of Mňačko's gross breach of Party discipline, but he was still a
Slovak Party intellectual, and his intemperate remarks about the
Prague regime, even if they had to be officially deplored, were received
not without a certain relish in Bratislava.

On the 15th August the Slovak Writers Union issued a statement[24] in which Mňačko's actions were condemned, in particular his decision to publicise his protest in the Western press and on television (in Vienna, from where programmes can be watched in Bratislava). He was accused of deserting the front, and of choosing the path of anarchy and political adventurism. Subsequently he was deprived of his seat on the committee of the Slovak Writers.

In Prague the Czechoslovak Writers Union now had a chance to improve its image with the Party leadership by a resolute condemnation of Mňačko. But its reactions were totally negative. As far as his membership of the Union was concerned, little could be done anyway, since the administration of the Union was still paralysed by the Party's refusal to recognise appointments. So Mňačko retained his membership. *Literární noviny* might have been expected dutifully to express indignation at the defection, but when the next issue appeared (on the 18th August) it carried neither the official announcement denouncing Mňačko, nor the statement of the Slovak Writers section. The way in which *L N* ignored the Mňačko affair was officially regarded as provocation, and the acting editor was privately assured that Novotný would never forgive it.[25]

At the time when Prague was in the grip of the Mňačko affair with its implications of anti-semitism, the Director of the American Jewish agency concerned with emigration to Israel, Mr Charles Jordan, happened to be spending a few days in Prague. On the evening of August 16 he left the Esplanade Hotel for a brief walk, and never returned. A fortnight later his body was taken out of the river: at the official inquiry a verdict of death by misadventure was returned. By special request a second autopsy was performed by a Swiss pathologist hired by the Jewish Agency, and this found that Mr Jordan had been drugged before he was drowned.[26] The unpleasant overtones of this unfortunate affair sent ripples of horrified speculation through foreign newspapers. There was nothing to connect the Czechoslovak authorities with Jordan's death, and no reason to suppose that it was anything but a sad co-incidence, but the inevitable suspicion could hardly have come at a worse time for the authorities. To add to the confusion, an incident on the Austrian-Czechoslovak frontier at the end of August resulted in the Czech guards opening fire, and in the death of an East German who was trying to escape to Austria. Sharp protests to Prague were without response, and the Austrian government decided to take the matter to the United Nations, a decision which was described in the Czech press as the culmination of a campaign against Czechoslovakia. The summer of 1967, which should have seen the country on the road to economic recovery, enjoying the extended freedoms which were expected to accompany the new economic model, and hosting a record tourist intake, found Prague in confusion, its leadership split and the country a target of appalling publicity abroad. This was the moment when a new scandal put Czechoslovakia once more in the international headlines.

On September 3rd the *Sunday Times* of London ran a feature article entitled MASS PLEA TO WEST BY CZECH WRITERS.

> Czechoslovakia seemed yesterday to be moving inevitably towards an explosive confrontation between intellectuals and the Communist party leadership of the kind which preceded the popular risings in Poland and Hungary in 1956. The already deeply embittered and open clash between the Czechoslovak writers and the party's cultural guardians has now taken a sensational new turn. The rebellious writers are now appealing *en masse* to world opinion for moral support in their struggle against censorship and victimisation.
>
> In an astonishingly outspoken and abusive 1,000 word 'Manifesto of Czechoslovak Writers to the World Public', smuggled out of the country last week, the party's leaders have been accused of carrying out a 'witch-hunt of pronounced fascist character' and of employing methods of 'state terror' against writers.
>
> The document, a copy of which came into the hands of the Sunday Times yesterday, has been signed by 183 writers, 69 artists, 21 film and television people, 56 scientists and publicists and other intellectuals. It was accompanied by an appeal for world publicity. The original is now in safe keeping in the West, but the list of its signatories is being witheld at present to reduce the risk of instant reprisals by the regime.

The newspaper then reproduced the text of the manifesto, which appealed to the world to rescue freedom and human rights threatened by the terror of state power in Czechoslovakia. The manifesto briefly recalled the circumstances of the Writers Congress and detailed the threats and persecution of dissidents which had followed: it stressed the *socialist* nature of the dissident opposition, and denounced the present regime for its violation of socialist as well as of humanist principles. The document cited the aspirations of Marx, Emerson, F. X. Šalda, Karel Čapek, and Dr Eduard Beneš, as evoking the principles for which the dissidents stood. It appealed for support in particular to ten Western intellectuals, a somewhat odd assortment ranging from Lord Bertrand Russell to John Steinbeck. The original of the manifesto remained in the hands of an emigré Press agency in London, which had shown it to the *Sunday Times* and released the text for world distribution.

Journals which printed the manifesto accepted it as authentic in the sense that it had originated in Prague (rather than in emigré circles abroad) and that it had indeed been signed by the people whose signatures were claimed for it. But doubts about the document's authenticity were expressed almost at once not only in Prague but also by Czechs in the West. It was really difficult to believe that such a high number of the writers could have been found to attach their names to a document so strangely and recklessly expressed, and appealing to the authority of such curious bedfellows as Marx and Emerson, President Beneš and J. F. Kennedy. At the time of the Press release Pavel Kohout happened to be in Hamburg rehearsing a play: he disclaimed all personal knowledge of the document which, as he said, must surely have come to his notice in Prague; he pointed out that writers had signed various lists to be attached to appeals (e.g. on the Vietnam war issue) and it would not be so difficult to get hold of such a list and attach it to a forgery. (Although Kohout's remarks were interpreted by some as a necessary gesture of discretion, they turned out subsequently to be correct. The author of the manifesto was later revealed as a Prague historian, Dr Ivan Pfaff; it had not originated from the Writers Union, nor from any considerable group of writers.[27])

In Prague the Party daily, *Rudé právo* (6/9/67), mentioned the affair of the manifesto; denounced it as a shameless provocation and a lie; and stated that the Writers' Union had denied all knowledge of it. This was correct in that the document had not emanated in the Union, and its leading members had heard about it for the first time from the newspapers. Unfortunately the Party Press faced the familiar problem of all who win themselves a reputation for lies, in that they are not likely to win belief even when they speak the truth. The Writers Union would have to denounce the manifesto itself; and although this too could be attributed to pressure put on them by the Party, at least it would carry more conviction than a release by the official Czech news agency or an editorial in *Rudé právo*. The editorial board of *Literární noviny* was given to understand that they could even print the text of the manifesto provided that they denounced it as a forgery. This time at least the writers could agree publicly with the Party line without any concession of principle. But to the incredulous anger of Party HQ the editors of *L N* declined the offer except on their own conditions, i.e. that they would also set the affair in its proper context and explain that such incidents are the logical result of suppressing genuine information. As *L N* was still not allowed to publish the actual viewpoints of writers, as formulated at the Congress, there was no reason for it to publish denials of alleged viewpoints either. The implication was that if they could tell the whole truth, in particular publish the material of their own Congress, they would be happy to deal with the manifesto as well.[28] At Party HQ the attitude of the writers, as expressed by its editorial spokesmen, appeared as equivalent to a suggestion that even if the manifesto had not originated in the Union, it still expressed a viewpoint with which the writers were in sympathy. Abroad the whole sensational business of the disputed document, the comments offered by the Western intellectuals to whom the appeal had been addressed, and the probing of special correspondents hastily despatched to Prague to get a hot story, bathed the regime in dreadful publicity.[29] President Novotný could hardly be unaware that his performance was being watched with critical eyes not only by his rivals in the Czechoslovak Politburo, but also by his patrons in the Kremlin. It was unbelievable that so much damage could be done by a small group of dissatisfied intellectuals, and that all the powers of the Party and state apparatus had not sufficed to bring them to heel. The situation had reached a stage where the Party leadership must either concede to the writers their basic demands, i.e. freedom to write and criticise as they thought fit (a concession which seemed likely to aggravate the threat to Novotný's now precarious position); or else it was necessary to take a really hard line.

On September 26-7 the Party Central Committee held a prolonged meeting to receive and discuss certain recommendations put before it by the Presidium in the matter of the Writers Congress. Introducing the business Jiří Hendrych reviewed the background to the Congress and the past activities of the Writers Union. He claimed that this had slipped out of the control of its communist majority into control by an opposition group who unscrupulously misused the Union, and especially its newspaper *Literární noviny*, as a platform for views hostile to socialism, this at a time when international tensions were high, and a hysterical anti-communist campaign was under way in Western Europe; ammunition for this campaign was freely offered by events such as the Writers Congress, Mňačko's actions, and the so-called manifesto of Czech writers.

In the ensuing discussion[30] there were various searing comments on the sins and shortcomings of the Union, and the conduct of the *L N* group, in particular Vaculík, Liehm, Klíma and Milan Kundera, and support was expressed for a hard line. On the other hand there were speakers (in particular the Slovak writer V. Mináč) who warned that administrative reprisals against offending writers would achieve nothing worthwhile, and could alienate the Party intellectuals, a result which could only harm the long-term interests of the Party itself. Although a full account of the debate has never been published (it was of course strictly an internal Party affair), and the extracts which were released in Prague are heavily selective, subsequent discussion, and the reports passed unofficially to exile sources, make it clear that the discussion was relatively uninhibited.[31] The decision to accept Hendrych's recommendations was not unanimous, and was received with grave reservations by some members. In the summary subsequently published in *L N* (after it had been taken over by the Ministry) it was emphasised that measures taken against certain writers were strictly an internal affair, and that the Committee was aware that its attitude would inevitably be branded in certain circles as repressive (Stalinist), and misused as grounds for attacks on Czechoslovakia's socialist regime.

The actual measures were summarised in a brief report in *Rudé právo* of 28. 9. 67:

> The Party Central Committee has approved certain steps intended to strengthen the close and comradely relationship between the Party and the writers; to create the necessary conditions for literary development and its realisation unhampered by narrow sectional or ideologically alien influences; establish the conditions for further dilineating the character of socialist literature and Czechoslovak culture.
>
> For attitudes irreconcilable with Party membership the CC has expelled from the Party I. Klíma, A. J. Liehm, and L. Vaculík. For political errors made in the course of his activities J. Procházka has been released by the CC from the position of Candidate of the C.C. Because *Literární noviny* in spite of the patient efforts of Party organs had completely passed out of the hands of the Central Committee of the Writers Union and become a platform for opposition political policies, the Party CC had recommended that it pass into the sphere of the Ministry of Culture and Information...

This was apparently as far as Novotný thought he could go at present in disciplining the dissidents, and to foreign observers the measures seemed remarkably unsensational. They were in fact too timid to be effective, and at the same time too provocative to be forgiven by the Czech reading public. The problem for Novotný was that there was no realistic alternative to reform, nor did the hard-liners in the Party seriously contemplate a return to the hopelessly discredited policies of the Stalinist era. To hit at writers who symbolised the cause of reform only made more difficult the task of rebuilding the Party and regaining public confidence. What was perhaps conceived by Novotný as a firm but limited operation, removing an irritant and teaching a lesson to potential challengers to authority, had the effect of pushing the reformers into the same camp as the dissenters, i.e. forcing into a common alliance those who genuinely supported the Party in their own way and those who genuinely opposed it. As far as public relations went, a halo of martyrdom was thrown around the 'opposition'; whereas those who stuck to the Party line, either out of loyalty or for temporary tactical reasons, were made to appear as collaborators with neo-Stalinism. The measures in fact cut the ground from under the feet of Novotný's supporters in the public media: ridicule and contempt followed men like Jiří Hájek and Ivan Skála; they were ostracised by the intelligentsia and their position rendered impossible. By identifying criticism with opposition the leadership alienated from the Party those who were anxious to save it. By outlawing open criticism, Novotný closed a safety valve and made more probable an internal explosion.

Three writers had been deprived of their Party status: Procházka's promotion in the Party organisation was blocked; Kohout, who had outraged Hendrych by reading out Solzhenytsin's letter, was admonished. Václav Havel, whom Hendrych affected to see as a sinister figure, the heart of anti-socialist opposition among the writers, was untouched by the reprisals, as he was not a member of the Party anyway. There were no arrests or prosecutions: the threat to dissolve the Writers Union did not eventuate (as it did five years later). The real sting of the measures was in the collective penalty against *Literární noviny*. As the newspaper was (like all the media) a public enterprise already, the recommendation to transfer it to the jurisdiction of the Ministry of Culture could mean anything or nothing. But its editorial board were not left in doubt for long. In accordance with the provisions of the new Press law of 1967 *L N* had lodged its routine application for registration.[32] The Union and *L N* were now informed that the newspaper was not in fact carrying out the objects which it had set out in the application, which was accordingly refused. Nobody had been forbidden anything; the paper had simply failed to be re-registered, and that week's issue (39/67 of 29/9/67) would be the last time it would appear as a Union publication. Wits in Prague pointed out the black humour of the situation; the *L N* writers had not been deprived of their jobs; they had only been deprived of their employer.

The Party centre had apparently decided in advance that the paper would go on appearing; but it would be published by another organisation and issued from another press. Control of the paper had been taken out of the hands of the writers, but the operation was to be carried through as unostentatiously as possible, so that it might almost escape notice. An editor-in-chief of the (now ministerial) paper was appointed at once. It was Jan Zelenka, a professional journalist from a Prague evening paper. He at once offered to the retiring editor, D. Hamšík, a job as his deputy under favourable conditions including the retention of some of the other senior staff. The offer was, however, declined, and Zelenka found himself surrounded by a general boycott, first by contributors, then by customers, as sales of the paper rapidly declined. At a later date Zelenka appealed for understanding of his actions. He claimed that his acceptance of the position was more or less forced on him as an act of Party discipline; that he accepted the job only as an interim measure; that he was assured that the writers would co-operate with him; that when he found that, after all, the opposition to the takeover of the paper was shared not by a single group, but was a question of principle for all writers, he was forced to carry out his melancholy task in total isolation and surrounded by universal hostility.[33]

The takeover of *L N* presented the foreign press with a new sensation, and mobilised radical intellectuals in the West concerned, as so often, with civic liberties, to the defence of the persecuted Czech writers. It must have been maddening for communist hard-liners who deplored the modern treatment of erring dissenters as kid glove pampering, to find that the feeble reprisals were portrayed as a neo-Stalinist inquisition. While it had at its disposal the whole orchestra of propaganda, the leadership discovered that its total volume counted for less than the silence of the writers. Across the bumbling and irresolute confusion of the 'sixties fell the terrible shadow of the 'fifties with the memory of its genuine inquisition. If the foreign observers who commented on the Czech crisis had actually studied the ministerial *L N* they might have discovered that apart from the missing names it was not really so very different from the old – heavily censored as it had been, and for much of the time far from sparkling. But the correspondents did not read *L N* (scarcely any of them knew Czech), nor did the general public. It was a dead duck, and all the efforts of Zelenka failed to break down the wall of silent hostility around it. The results of separating the journal from the Union were in fact to kill the journal as a possible means of Party influence, further to antagonise liberal views at home and abroad, and above all to close the ranks of the Czech writers against the Party leadership. The repressive measures taken against the dissidents were anyway too half-hearted to be effective; but their consequence was to identify the Union with the dissidents, and to destroy any remaining influence of the 'collaborators', i.e. those writers and publicists who stuck, with decreasing conviction and amid mounting odium, to the Party line.

From the point of view of the Party it was alarming that loyalties should be polarised by an overt rift between the power centre and the intelligentsia, which quite evidently was lining up with the persecuted writers. The rift came at a time when all the resources of goodwill and energy were needed for the success of the new economic measures. The latter were, it should be stressed, part of a reform programme intended to save not only the economy but the credit and the leading role of the Party. The programme implied certain fundamental principles which could crudely be summarised in the central principle that, if progress was to be achieved, social organisations must be free to promote their sectional interests by pressure on the central authority. Assuming that a one-party system was to continue, this meant that such organisations, after freely determining what were their vital interests, should press for them at the centre through their communist representatives: (this would reverse the tendency of Stalinist times whereby the centre so influenced the organisations as virtually to absorb them into the governmental apparatus.) Broadly speaking the reformist movement could hope to succeed only if counter pressures from below and above were able by competition to achieve an equilibrium which would shift in accordance with the changing needs, advantages, and values of the society. This could of course only happen if the centre would be willing to refrain from snapping its administrative jaws the moment it saw its own position threatened. If it could not refrain from this natural temptation, then the success of the reform programme was doomed, and the old bad ways of centralised bureaucracy would return, with all the dire consequences predicted by economists and sociologists alike. Conversely the reform programme might succeed, but not within the framework of a one-party system, *at least as the system was interpretated by the present leadership*. Those who wished to save the *system* by means of the reform, would be driven, in case of a clash, to jettison the *leadership*.

It could be expected that the real test of the reform programme would come when the expressed interests of labor organisations came into conflict with the interests of the power centre. But the test came in fact much earlier. Of all the social organisations with which the Party had to deal, the Writers Union was the freest, most vocal, temperamental, and influential, through its contact via the media with the general public. The writers had in common a very important sectional interest, namely their defence against the censorship, which hampered their efforts on every side. They were not allowed to press their case against the operation of the censorship by their writings in the press, as the censorship itself did not permit them. Therefore they had pressed their case via their own organisation, at their own Congress. Thus they provided for the reformers a test case of whether the Party leadership was prepared to let reform succeed. By treating criticism as rebellion, and invoking administrative measures against its critics, the leadership condemned itself. If reform was to succeed, *it must be under other leadership*. The fate of the writers had consequences far beyond the circle of their interests, and radically affected the development of the whole reform movement within the Party.

The confidence of writers that they enjoyed powerful support from within the ruling group was evident from the spirited defence which their bolder spokesmen offered to the authorities. On October 6th the Ideological Dept. of the Party summoned to a discussion the communist members of the Writers' Union. In earlier times such a 'discussion' was freely interpreted as an occasion for authority to transmit orders and hand out admonitions. On this occasion Hendrych addressed the gathering: his surprisingly mild tone implied that after all the aim of Party policy was reconciliation with the Party dissidents. He implied that penalties imposed had been intentionally of a token kind, intended as a warning: having shown that it could be firm, the Party would now show that it could also be generous, provided of course the writers should also show 'understanding'.

But his audience reacted with unwonted ingratitude. So far from expressing humble thanks and a promise of improvement, speakers rose, one after another, to protest at the repressive measures taken against their colleagues, and to emphasise their agreement with the rebellious sentiments whose formulation at the Congress had incurred the official displeasure of the authorities. Such speakers included older writers like F. Hrubín, reliving his 'voice of conscience' role of 1956, and, more surprisingly, younger men like A. Brousek who had hitherto tended to hold aloof from such polemics. It appeared that repression had acted to close the ranks of Party intellectuals, and convert would-be neutrals into active opponents. A hard note of defiance was sounded by a spokesman for the Slovak journal *K Ž*, when he openly offered the hospitality of his newspaper to Czech writers who were prevented from publishing in *L N*. If the exclusion of the Czech dissidents from their own paper was intended to ban them from publication, then the action of the Slovaks could be regarded as deliberate sabotage of the Czech authorities' policy, a sabotage which presumably was condoned, if not inspired, by men of power in the Slovak Communist Party.

This cool, almost contemptuous, gesture from the Slovaks was one of the shocks administered to Hendrych by the gathering. Another was the speech of Pavel Kohout, who pointed out that the so-called Writers' Manifesto had won credibility abroad only because the official suppression of news about the Writers' Congress had provoked misrepresentation. Secondly, one should consider the effects abroad of repression against Czech intellectuals. The international acclaim accorded to Czech writers and film-makers had done much to improve their country's image, and represented a serious contribution to European détente. It was difficult to estimate how much harm had been done to that image by the recent acts of repression. In any case the officially inspired view of the Writers' Congress as a forum for anti-socialist conspiracy was nonsensical, and an attempt to deceive the Party, the country, and the world. Yet this had been the expressed view of Party leaders such as Hendrych, Bil'ak, Havlíček, and Novotný himself:

> It is a crude falsification to declare that the attitude of Klíma, Vaculík, Liehm, Kundera, Kosík, me, and other comrades was directed against the Party. The truth is that the critical voices of these and many other communists have been for years raised... against certain comrades embodying certain tendencies which are, in the opinion of many of us, harmful to the Party. It was not the Party that was criticised at the Congress, but the methods by which cultural policy has been conducted, the letter and practice of the Press law, and other negative traits for which not the Party but some specific

individuals are responsible. Lots of us – including me – were in our younger days the troubadours of schematism (Stalinism), as comrades Novotný, Hendrych etc. are fond of reminding us... even so, in the life of most of us there is a sharp division, a computation of our own errors, a break which we have ourselves publically affirmed in writing. In the life of many of the comrades who never cease from sternly admonishing us there is, regrettably, no such break. That is a loss for our whole society; it is an illusion that authority is enhanced by a refusal to admit mistakes; in fact these mistakes continue to beget others.[34]

The clear implication of Kohout's speech was that the crisis which faced the Party was due not to criticism of the leadership's policies, but to the cover-up tactics of the leaders, who refused to admit their own Stalinist past, and, to protect their own position, were reverting to Stalinist methods. He had turned defence of the Party dissidents into open and personal attack upon the leadership. Translated from the language of Party protocol into direct speech, his words amounted to a call to Novotný and Hendrych to confess their guilt and resign. His challenge was the more grave in that he did not speak extempore or with passion; he read out a carefully composed address, copies of which he had already distributed to other organisations within the Party.

Pavel Kohout, in spite of his popularity as a writer, was obviously too small a figure in politics to head a movement designed to overthrow the leadership. His words represented a challenge made possible only by powerful backing within the ruling élite. The challenge to Novotný's position was from within the upper hierarchy of the Party; and the plight of the intellectuals was a ground on which, for the sake of public relations, the issue could be fought. Novotný now faced serious threats from at least three sides. The theoreticians of the New Economic Movement, and those Party influences which supported them, saw in the conservatism of the existing leadership a constant, and perhaps hopeless barrier to real progress. Secondly, those who wished to refurbish the public image of the Party found in Novotný a liability, because he was an embarrassing reminder of its Stalinist past, as well as a possible scapegoat for its present troubles. Thirdly, and most important, opposition to Novotný was coming to a head in Slovakia, where little hope of improvement in the area's difficult economic position could be seen until the rigid centralising policies of Prague were broken. Here nationalist, sentimental, and traditional attitudes combined with economic reasoning to demand a new deal, based on genuine Slovak autonomy, within which the area's resources might at last be developed along rational lines. In the Czech lands Novotný and his supporters could still hope to maintain control; for political opposition could not be mobilised, and only exceptionally could it be formulated, as long as the apparatus of censorship and social repression remained in loyal hands. A crisis in Prague might be expected only when the loyalists, i.e. Novotný's closest associates, should decide that they were backing the wrong horse, and it was time for a switch of loyalty. But in Slovakia it was a different matter. The Slovak Party represented a power base which was no longer under the control of Prague. On the day when the Prague loyalists recognised that the Slovak challenge was too serious to be ignored or crushed, their defection from the Novotný camp to that of the reformists would spell the end for the present leadership.

A meeting of the Central Committee of the Czechoslovak Communist Party (K. S. Č.) was scheduled for October 30th, on the eve of the celebrations for the Bolshevik revolution. A fortnight before the meeting, and in the framework of preparations for it, the Slovak Party leaders met the Slovak writers to discuss their attitude to events in Prague in the cultural field. The minutes of this meeting, which were published abroad,[35] show a significant closeness of view between writers and leaders which distinguishes the tone of the meeting sharply from that in Prague. From the start it was emphasised by a spokesman for the Party leadership that there was no intention of following the example set in Prague in their attitude to the Slovak writers: there would be no interference with *K Ž* and certainly no reprisals. In return the writers spoke with great frankness about their attitude to the repressive measures taken by the Czech authorities, measures which they regarded as scandalous. This firm line was taken not by a few rebels or hot-heads, but by the most respected and serious of the Slovak writers present. In particular Novomeský, who was regarded as closest to the Slovak Party leadership, spoke gravely of the warnings he had himself given to Henrych, warnings entirely ignored by him: the foolish reprisals were a terrible mistake which could only harm the Czech, and eventually the Slovak, Party. It was time for Czech and Slovak intellectuals to make common cause. The discussion was kept within the correct limits of the cultural theme – the conditions of writing and publication. But the implications were evidently political. In Bratislava an accord had been established, at least for the time being, between Slovak leaders and intellectuals to oppose policies made in Prague. In this they were expressing solidarity with Czech Party dissidents in the cultural arena. But since the latter was the arena in which the issues of the whole reform movement were being tested, the alignment of the Slovaks was in effect not merely with the harrassed Czech writers in their struggle against *literary* repression, but with the whole idea of the reform movement. When the Slovak delegation left for the October 30th meeting of the Party Central Committee in Prague it is uncertain whether it had a co-ordinated strategy to bring their opposition into the open and force the reformists to commit themselves. But the conditions were ripe for such a confrontation.

The meeting was to discuss and approve the draft of a thesis submitted by the Party Presidium on *The Status and Role of the Party at the present stage of development of Socialist Society*. In preparing the draft, members of the Presidium had had access to a mass of submissions from Party branches, as well as scientific papers prepared by the research teams whose work on the New Economic Plan had laid the theoretical basis for the reform movement. But the thesis which was tabled at the CC meeting showed little influence of these papers. It seems in fact that the tabled thesis had been substituted at the last minute for a more controversial draft which had been considered by the Presidium, and when A. Dubček rose to speak, he asked why the paper before the meeting differed from that previously approved by the higher body. Proceeding from this point Dubček made a series of pointed comments on Party work, in the course of which he criticised the quality of leadership and the dangerous incidence of conservatism and sectarianism which was still to be found there. He cited the views of Party centres which deplored certain attitudes, at present being maintained, as quite out of touch with changing conditions. Finally he asked the meeting to give consideration to any necessary changes in leadership and higher management in the Party: smoothly excusing his rather controversial address he said that it was only natural for conflict to arise even within the Party between new and progressive elements and those which remained traditional and conservative.

No one could miss the force of his abstractly framed attack on Novotný and his group, a member of which, Martin Vaculík, at once rose to criticise sharply Dubček's comments. After some hesitation other speakers joined the debate, and the weight of argument was running in favour of Dubček when the Chairman, Kolder, intervened to say that at the request of Comrade Novotný, he was asking the meeting to continue in closed session. He therefore asked all non-members to leave.

Novotný then spoke off the cuff and in considerable agitation. As far as talk of further democratisation was concerned, he said there had been too much of that already; he had already informed Dubček of his disagreement with his views, and in private had told him that he was acting irresponsibly, was too much influenced by local pressures, and had become the spokesman of narrow nationalism. Novotný's angry and unconsidered words were received in the meeting with embarrassment by Czechs and with hostility by Slovaks, who saw in them the vindication of charges that crude anti-Slovak prejudice existed in Prague. A significant and ominous contribution was that of Bil'ak, known as a conservative in political matters, but firm in his support of Slovak interests against Prague centralism. He left Novotný in no doubt that in this matter Dubček had the full support of the Slovak CP, and expressed open resentment at criticism of Dubček as a nationalist. It was after some hot debate that Novotný heard for the first time expressed to his face in public the phrase *the accumulation of functions*. Unbelievable as it might seem, he was being invited to resign. The meeting ended with the passing of the tabled draft thesis: but conflict was now in the open.[36]

By a coincidence Novotný's bad day at the meeting was further disfigured by a student demonstration on the streets of Prague that evening. Trouble with the students was of long standing; it revolved in particular around the issue of the Youth Movement, through which the Party dominated and absorbed all youth and student organisations. Student attempts to take over the running of their own affairs were repeatedly frustrated; the student newspaper was regarded with official suspicion as potentially subversive. In 1967 student opinion in Prague was simmering over the official treatment of two student leaders who had been thrown out of the university for their political activities, and subsequently called up for military service. In October there had occurred a series of power blackouts and a breakdown of services at the Strahov College. During a meeting to discuss conditions the lights failed; and the students, lighting candles, went out on the streets to demonstrate their plight. As the demonstration moved in the direction of the Castle, police blocked the way, and began to disperse the crowd by force. As the students fled, police pursued them into the college and beat up inmates in a fairly random fashion. The demonstration was ostensibly unpolitical; but the slogan of the students *WE WANT LIGHT* was interpreted by the police in an allegorical sense: in any case the known tension between students and the authorities was such that a demonstration of this character could not but assume political overtones.[37] This unpleasant incident, acted out under the eyes of the general public, advertised at an unfortunate time the repressive and anti-intellectual policies of the Party leadership. At the moment when Novotný needed above all to keep the quarrel within the closed doors of the Party where the ruling oligarchy might still settle issues among themselves, the demonstration added fuel to the whispering campaign of popular unrest, official mismanagement, and chaos in public life. What Novotný had to fear was not, in the first instance, the opposition of students, intellectuals, dissidents, or even his Slovak opponents. It was the impression abroad that he had lost control of the situation. This might well cost him the support of his own wavering adherents, and, much worse, the support of Moscow. It was there, in the final resort, that he must find his salvation. On occasions like the present anniversary of the Bolshevik revolution, it was the custom for the Kremlin to hand out expressions of its esteem to loyal servants. Nothing could have been more welcome for Novotný at this stage than some firm expression of Russian approval.[38]

After the meeting, and following the disturbing events of that evening, Novotný was due to leave for Moscow, where he was leading a Party delegation in honour of the Bolshevik anniversary celebrations. This was evidently his chance to restore his standing by obtaining the personal backing of Brezhnev. But Novotný's reception seems to have been less than cordial, and at no stage did he get the opportunity for that quiet man-to-man chat for which he had hoped. Later he complained[39] that he did not even get the chance to discuss the business with which he had been charged by the Presidium. The Moscow leadership, plagued by its own troubles, had understandably little desire to get mixed up in Czech-Slovak quarrels. Brezhnev did however agree to come to Prague on December 8th to look over the situation for himself. The whole Presidium was alerted that Brezhnev wished to see them: there was a two hour delay while he chatted with several of the Czechoslovak Party leaders, including Novotný and Dubček; then he met the Presidium briefly, and stated formally that he had no interest in interfering in what was Czechoslovak Party affair.[40] Thus any hopes Novotný might have entertained of a definitive endorsement from the Kremlin had failed: he might well look forward with foreboding to the adjourned CC meeting; this had to be postponed, as Novotný and Hendrych were both ill. It is possible to speculate that the task of the rebels was made less hazardous by the unexpected immobility of the two principals, and by the opportunity for what had emerged as the anti-Novotný group, to co-ordinate their tactics. Too much had been said at the earlier meeting for them to draw back now.

The Central Committee meeting opened on December 19th with a short agenda: only the economic situation and the relationship of the two highest functions (Party Secretary and President) were to be discussed. Novotný opened discussion of the second point, adopting a mild tone, and apologised for his ill-considered remarks at the previous meeting. He mentioned Brezhnev's visit to Prague, saying that mutual Party relations and Czechoslovak internal problems were discussed: he did not go into details.

After he sat down, a reformist, F. Vodsloň, rose, and delivered an impromptu speech in some agitation. He strongly objected to the way the committee had been misled by contradictory reports about who had invited Brezhnev. Although one report said that the invitation was issued by the committee of which he was a member, he had first read about it in the newspaper. Talk about the 'unanimous views' of the Presidium was also foolish when everyone knew that there was disagreement there. The foreign Press was able to write about it, but Party members were denied proper information. Vodsloň's angry words brought debate back to the problems discussed at the last meeting, on which no agreement had been reached at the Presidium. The veteran Fierlinger expressed alarm at the current state of the Party, and indicated that the present crisis would not be solved by Novotný's methods. Ota Šik, for the economists, made very clear the close relationship between the difficulties of implementing reform and the conservatism of the ruling group:

> We have condemned the personality cult and the glorification of Stalin, the mass violence, illegality, and violation of collective leadership. But we have failed to make clear the necessity for basic changes... such as would prevent such elevation of personal power over the rights of other communists from ever occurring again... We must eliminate the extreme accumulation of power in the hands of certain comrades, i.e. comrade Novotný, for in this I see the greatest obstacle to a rapid recovery by the Party. The Presidium has already decided in principle on the need... to separate the functions of President and First Secretary, but continues to delay action on this... Accordingly I move that in the first instance we request comrade Novotný to resign the position of First Secretary, and that we call on the Central Committee to release him from this position...

Šik continued with a complete set of proposals, including the setting up of a sub-committee to seek candidates for the job of First Secretary, and for additional members to the Presidium, which would change its character. In addition he suggested that a new set of guidelines be worked out in order to bring about a greater degree of democratisation in the decision-making process of the Party.

The meeting now had before it concrete proposals for reform of the Party by dropping Novotný, limiting the influence of his close supporters, and changing the form of the elections. The debate went on for three days, during which the strength of the anti-Novotný front became clearer. Apart from the economic reform group it included a number of influential and rehabilitated victims of the political trials, among whom Smrkovský was prominent, and, of course, the Slovaks. On the third day Dubček announced that Novotný had now put his position at the disposal of the Presidium. When Dubček proposed that a decision about filling the post be postponed, Smrkovský rose and demanded that a decision be taken at once, at that meeting. He said that he was particularly concerned at the suggestion that the Soviet comrades should be consulted about the decision: it was important that the USSR should not be dragged into an affair which was the responsibility of the Czechoslovak Party alone: and it was essential that the chance for renewal, and the momentum which had been engendered, should not be lost. He was right to stress the need for a rapid decision; but his move failed. A rearguard action was fought by the Novotný group. Both Chudík and Hendrych implied that Novotný was being sacrificed to a campaign run by a handful of dissatisfied intellectuals, whose misguided efforts stimulated the reaction of emigrés abroad, and other enemies of socialism. Surprisingly however, Hendrych revealed that he himself had voted against Novotný at the Presidium meeting. It was now evident that Novotný had lost. His closest henchman had deserted him, and the rearguard action was apparently aimed merely to protect the *system* from real change, while sacrificing Novotný himself. In the evening of the third day Dubček asked for an adjournment; he was exhausted and felt ill. The debate was concluded with a motion to adjourn until the New Year; to set up a subcommittee to draft proposals for a reform of working methods; and to propose a candidate for Novotný's job.

The Christmas vacation passed amid rumours that Novotný's supporters were preparing a military coup, and that plans were ready to be put into operation for the arrest of leading Party members of the 'opposition'. It is not impossible that various contingency plans were prepared at Security headquarters, and the subsequent suicide of General Janko, and the flight of General Šejna, later shed a sinister light on the rumoured preparations. But it is hard to believe that Novotný would have put his fate in the hands of the generals, or sanctioned the arrest of the Slovak First Secretary without the explicit authority of Moscow; nor is such resolute action consistent with Novotný's record. In fact none of these sensational moves eventuated: The Czechoslovak army command was true to its record: it did nothing.

The adjourned meeting opened on January 3rd. It soon became clear from Novotný's report that the Presidium and the sub-committee had not reached agreement; their main submission was to continue discussions on the basis of the draft resolution. The matter was thus thrown back to the Central Committee. Novotný admitted that there was a general feeling in favour of separating the functions of Party First Secretary and President, but when or how it should be done would require careful consideration. It seemed that the whole question was likely to be postponed indefinitely. But the firmness of the anti-Novotný front became clear during the debate and influenced the Presidium members present. On the second day O. Černík reported that the sub-committee had decided that the problem submitted to it should be solved at this meeting of the CC. Novotný had been asked to meet the sub-committee and prepare proposals which could go before the Presidium that evening.

On the 5th the Secretary of the Central Committee, Kolder, informed the meeting that unanimous agreement had been reached, and that the recommendation would be conveyed by comrade Novotný. The latter then rose, and in a gracious speech asked that he be relieved of his position as First Secretary of the Party; in the name of the sub-committee he then put forward as his successor the name of the Slovak Secretary Alexander Dubček, a 'fine and happy choice'. The motion was put to the vote in the afternoon, and was carried unanimously.

Thus, after a decade of rule during which his power had seemed dictatorial and unchallengable, Antonín Novotný laid down his position in a smooth – almost a humdrum – transfer of office. He retained his high position as Head of state, with all the powers and privileges that went with it. No sensational publicity accompanied his fall. The transfer of office was reported by *Rudé právo* in the course of a flat summary of Proceedings of the CC meeting. The news item concluded with a brief tribute to Novotný for all the successes attained during his years of service. In *Kulturní tvorba* of 11/1/68 the appointment of Dubček was noted in a few lines under a photograph of him shaking hands with a Soviet cosmonaut. Sceptics, instructed by long experience of the devious tactics of the ruling élite, might be excused for doubting that anything was changed except the facade of the power apparatus: Novotný had become an embarrassment to the Party, so he had been made a scapegoat; Party policy would be continued in the same old way, only under other names. In this, however, they were wrong. A door had been opened, and this time it would not easily be slammed shut.

X

The Summer of Dangerous Hope

This Spring, as in 1945, we were given a great opportunity. Once more we had the chance to take into our own hands our common cause, which is termed socialism, and to mould it into a form more suited to the good reputation we once enjoyed, and to the good opinion we once had about ourselves.

That Spring is now over, and it will never return. When winter comes, we shall know everything.

from '2,000 Words, to Workers, Farmers,
Scientists, Artists, and Everyone.'
L.L. 27. 6. 68.

At this moment shooting can be heard from Vinohradská St. People are fleeing from machine-gun and automatic rifle fire towards our building, shouting, 'Dubček, Dubček, Dubček...'

(broadcast from Radio Prague at
7.07 AM, 21. 8. 68)

The ousting of Novotný from the Party leadership had been brought about by a temporary alliance of men who shared limited, short-term aims. To progressive technocrats like Šik and Mlynář the fall meant the removal of an obstacle to economic rationalisation, whereas to conservative Slovaks like Bil'ak the fall represented a defeat for the cause of Prague centralism. To the opportunists and careerists with whom Novotný had surrounded himself – men who had seen with increasing concern the deteriorating position of their patron, and consequently of themselves – his fall meant the sacrifice of a scapegoat to safeguard the continuance of the present system. Among these varied elements of opposition more or less the only point of general agreement was the need to get rid of Novotný, who had become an embarrassment to them all.

Ten years of his stewardship had accustomed the Party to a situation in which all difficult questions were referred upwards for decision to a clique of Novotný's henchmen, conditioned to seek the initiative from Number One. A result of the system had been an avalanche of problems so complex and manifold as to baffle the comprehension of the power centre to cope with them in any better way than by aimless procrastination and muddle. With the removal of Novotný the prospects for an eventual improvement of the system brightened: but for the moment the entire ramshackle apparatus of decision-making and control lost its central directing force. As head of state and member of the Party Presidium Novotný was still a powerful element; but his opponents had a common interest in preventing any attempt at the re-assertion of his central influence. Likewise there was no question of replacing the authoritarian rule of Novotný by that of the new First Secretary, Alexander Dubček, who had been a compromise candidate, little known in Prague, and without real authority over the Presidium.

Only a minority of those who helped to bring down Novotný had any formulated programme to be put into action once he was removed, as we know from subsequent admissions.[1] Their aims were essentially negative: while they were not sure what positive goals they sought, they knew what they did *not* want, and that was the leadership of No-votný. Only the economic reformers had a definite line of action worked out in advance, and for the time being this became the main platform of the post-Novotný administration. The principles of the re-form programme could arouse little enthusiasm in conservatives like Hendrych, Bil'ak, or Kolder; but they were prepared to go along with it as a way of alleviating the country's severe economic situation; provided that the liberal principles proclaimed by the reformers were not implemented so seriously as actually to weaken the power system, and their position in it. Theoretically, this is just what the reforms would do, if indeed the principle of economic liberalisation were to be carried into the political field, as the reforms required. The mechanism of political control had to adapt to some extent to the working of the economic mechanism: economic reform implied some measure of democratisation in social and political life.[2] For the new plan to operate properly, at least conditions had to be established to enable the undistorted expression of consumer choices and the venti-lation of preferences and grievances in industrial life. Increased free-dom in the social sphere implied a relaxation of control over the public media, and it was at this point that the aims of the economic reformers had touched the demands of writers and journalists. An increased freedom of speech and publication was a necessary implication of the reform plan.

If freedom of utterance were taken seriously, so that decisions arose out of confrontation of alternative policies, there were serious im-plications for the selection of personnel – not only of enterprise managers but, eventually of political leaders as well. The Communist

Party was, and expected to remain, the dominating political force in the community: political democratisation meant in the first instance the democratisation of the Party. By the fall of Novotný the power of arbitrary decision had been transferred from Number One to the Presidium; the next step was to return it from the Presidium to the Central Committee, where it properly belonged, and where the reformers and liberals had their power base. Real democratisation of the Party meant that eventually the Presidium should return to its proper function as a standing committee of the CC, freely elected and supervised by it: the standing committee should act in response to the wishes of the wider body, which represented the wishes of the Party rank and file, and, theoretically, the wishes of the community at large.[3] Insofar as the Presidium in January 1968 was largely composed of Novotný's nominees and included Novotný himself, it might seem that an acceptance of the reform plan amounted to a death wish by the majority of Presidium members: in free competition for office, and in any contest of credibility, the ex-Novotnyites would be the first casualties. But logical implications are very different from political realities. Once they had dumped Novotný, his old associates could quite blandly claim a change of heart, or a shocked comprehension of previously concealed misdeeds, and proclaim themselves as long-frustrated reformers themselves. This is in fact what many of them did. But in any case few could have expected that democratisation would in practice mean more than a cautious continuation of a liberalisation trend which had operated until recently under the control of Novotný himself. In January democratisation was accepted as official policy even by conservatives, who had good reason to suppose that it would never go so far as actually to threaten their own control of the system. In the long run however, the aims of reformers and the interests of conservatives might well collide; and the moment of truth would be when democratisation threatened to transform the power structure. Past experience suggested that if that moment ever arrived, that would be the end of the reforms.

For the time being the main problem was the absence of an acceptable policy-making system at the top. So much of the day-to-day control had been kept in the hands of Novotný, and so arbitrary had been the decision-making process, that his absence caused a temporary paralysis of decision. The system had long cured officials of any inclination to show initiative. At the centre of power there was an uneasy coalition of forces. For nearly two months the new First Secretary, A. Dubček, gave no firm lead; and during that period the position of the conservatives was steadily eroded.

The reformers attracted support from the intelligentsia, as the programme with which they were identified was both hopeful and liberal. They also gained heavy backing from a formidable group of old communists whose past had rarely been identified with liberalism. These were rehabilitated victims of Stalinism, of whom two men stand out, Gustav Husák and Josef Smrkovský. Separated as they were from the young reformers by a generation of time and an ocean of experience, the communist victims had a deep common bond with them in their implacable opposition to the Novotnyites. Having helped to get rid of Novotný, in whom they saw the surviving embodiment of the Stalinism which had so wronged them, they had no intention of allowing his henchmen to carry on in positions of power, with an authority even enhanced by their desertion of their leader. It was not merely personal vindictiveness which influenced the victims of Stalinism. Since 1954 Novotný and his men had sporadically proclaimed their own rejection of Stalinist methods, while at the same time they had done everything to maintain the great cover-up of the past, which implicated them all. What the victims wanted was an end to the cover-up. They sought to justify not only themselves and their dead comrades who could not be restored to life, but the honour of the Party itself, and, in the case of Husák, the honour of Slovakia. The full exposure of the past – an exposure which must destroy many who still held authority in the Party – this was the minimum aim of the returned victims. Thus they threw all their weight behind a move for free utterance, the open investigation of past crimes, and the democratisation of public life. So they found common cause with the reformers, the genuine liberals, and the writers. In January, when the press was still timidly releasing only bare details of what had transpired at the CC meeting, Smrkovský and Husák were already publishing articles demanding a degree of democratisation which should include the people's right both to elect and to depose its leaders whenever it saw fit.[4]

At the highest level of the Party serious tensions were developing almost from the day of Novotný's fall; and the struggle for power was influenced not only by the personal pressures of cabinet politics behind closed doors, but also by pressures from outside, which were reflected, maintained, and stoked up, by the public media. Partly it was due to the practical paralysis of the press censorship. Although this was, since 1967, able to operate under legal statute and known guidelines, in fact the latter were much less important than the day-to-day directives from above. When Novotný fell, the directives more or less ceased. In the lull which followed, the censors gladly avoided any initiative which might one day disadvantage them (if, e.g., they suppressed the 'wrong' material). The lull was like a pleasant holiday, during which the censors were spared those tense confrontations with angry editors, and the more enterprising editors found that the limits of permissiveness had become quite nebulous. The unmuzzling of press, radio, and T.V. was not a sudden act, much less the result of a Party directive. Neither Dubček nor anybody else *ordered* the press to be free, but his non-committal attitude, and the general paralysis of decision, enabled an atmosphere of freedom to develop. For the time being free criticism helped the reformist leadership of the Party by throwing a critical light on the past of Novotný's former supporters. By their continuing influence they posed a constant threat to reformist policies, and consequently the loosening of controls on criticism was welcome to the reformers. Once the writers scented real freedom, they did not allow the pace to slacken, until it became a self-sustaining process. When it became clear how serious a political factor press freedom had become, it had also become apparent that to revoke that freedom would be a grave political decision with unforeseeable consequences. For by March the new freedom of utterance had become the pledge, the proof, the most obvious tangible gain, of that whole movement of revival which was associated with the Prague Spring of 1968.

Soon after Novotný's fall, action was taken to close the rift between the Party leadership and the Writers' Union. On January 12 B. Laštovička, President of the National Assembly, wrote officially to the Union expressing his personal regret that certain 'innocent remarks' which he had made about the conduct of the Writers' Congress had been misunderstood. He assured the Union of his esteem, and indicated the high value which was placed on the continuance of good relations between the writers and other elements of public life.[5] The election of Union officials had been hitherto blocked when the choice of Jan Procházka as Union Chairman had been declared as unacceptable to the Party. On January 24 the Union central committee met, and elected Procházka to the office of Vice-Chairman; the new Chairman was to be Dr Goldstücker, who had sided with the dissidents at the Congress, but was considered as a loyal Party man. At the committee meeting it was resolved to ask the Party to reconsider the expulsions of Vaculík, Klíma, and Kundera, and to petition President Novotný for the release from prison of Jan Beneš. The meeting was given to understand that it could expect its newspaper *Literární noviny* to be restored to its control. In effect the meeting foreshadowed the annulment of all the repressive measures taken against the writers in the previous year, and declared peace between the Party and the Union. As a mark of its benevolence the Party also allowed Jiří Hájek, who had supported Hendrych's hard line at the Congress, to be sacked from his editorship of the journal *Plamen*.

To some observers it seemed as if a miracle had happened. The writers, who had dared to confront the centre of political power had emerged victorious. In the eyes of the public their prestige soared. The writers might well see themselves now as the conscience of the nation, and the voice of political renewal; and what is more, they had an excellent chance of being taken seriously in their claims. Political realists at the centre of power recognised their influence and the moral authority they had acquired in the eyes of the public. To the reform group the writers had become important people, whose support might soon be crucial. Other members of the political establishment showed less enthusiasm for them. The President was in no hurry to accede to the request for Beneš's release, and left him in jail until March. When the Union officially requested a licence to resume publication of their journal *L N*, the request was turned down on the grounds that a journal of that name was already in existence. There were also problems of circulation, distribution, and the provision of newsprint. The real problem was what to do with the existing *L N* and its staff, who had done the Party's behest in taking over the paper when it was removed from the control of the Union. The final result of the negotiations was that the present Ministry newspaper *L N* would continue with its existing staff; and a licence would be given for a new Union paper, to begin on March 1st. The two newspapers would run in competition; and, to make justice perfect, they would divide the name (*Literární noviny*). The ministerial journal would change its name to *Kulturní noviny*; the new Union paper would be called *Literární listy*. But the Union got back its old editorial offices, and the staff of *K N* had the humiliation of being moved out to make way for them. On January 27 the Ministerial journal ran an editorial explaining the situation. It claimed that in the spirit of recent Party resolutions, it favoured a modern conception of socialist culture, and a confrontation of even radically divergent views; it also claimed that it was *not* going to be the official voice of the Ministry, nor a pillar of conservative forces.[6] It welcomed the revival of the Union paper, and implied that the writers and liberals, so dedicated to the free exchange of views, should be actually glad of the competition. Observers might well note the irony of the situation. The dissident writers were, through their Union, once more in alliance with the rulers; their rivals had been vanquished. The dissidents now had the opportunity of defending the rights of those with whom they disagreed: but in this case the opportunity had little appeal for them.

The Ministerial journal, appearing on February 3rd under the name of *Literární noviny* for the last time, put out a thinly veiled attack on Novotný himself in an article *Not Only a Decumulation*, stressing the dangers of a power concentration in the hands of one who puts himself above the law. The drift of the article was that the ousting of Novotný from his Party leadership was not the end of a process, but the beginning; its aim was the complete democratisation of the state and Party apparatus. In this connection the term 'pluralist democracy' was now put forward. The same issue of *L N* examined the delicate question of how parliamentary democracy could be combined with the 'leading role' of any party.[7] On February 13 *Rudé právo*, the Party daily, printed an article by Z. Mlynář setting out in popular terms the aims and methods suggested by the reform group. 'The movement away from power concentration in the hands of an individual implied radical changes in the whole system: direction from above must give way to participation from below. Reform involved changing the internal relationships of the social components: *every institutional component of the political system must be an independent political agent*; and the real independence of groups, interests, and individuals *must be protected by the legal order*. The protection of civic rights, especially the right of free utterance and minority viewpoints, was absolutely basic to the reform plan'.[8]

By mid-February the Press was getting into its stride; and waves of criticism were washing around elements of the power system hitherto regarded as taboo. Since January Prague had been buzzing with rumours of a planned coup to rescue the collapsing position of Novotný; the guilty men were said to be in the Party's department concerned with Military Security (Mamula), and in the Party organisation at the Ministry of Defence (Šejna). On January 25 Šejna's adjutant was arrested: under interrogation he is said to have implicated Šejna himself. A month passed with no overt action against Šejna: then on February 25th came the stunning news that he had defected. It was suspected that he was heading for Jugoslavia, but he turned up in the USA, where he published his own side of the story; gave a Press interview; and passed damning comments on various of his former colleagues high in the Party.[9]

The position of the conservatives in the Presidium had been weakening fast; the defection of Šejna (to America of all places) provided the Czech Press with a first class scandal which they exploited with gusto. It was a mortal blow to the Novotný faction, and to Novotný himself. Among the first casualties was General Mamula, who was replaced by General Prchlík; on March 14th the Second-in-Command of the Ministry of Defence, General Janko, shot himself. The old power group was falling to pieces; and the writers could rub their hands at the thought that it was Mamula, as Novotný's right-hand man, who had personally arranged the 1967 reprisals against them.

In the popular Press what had begun cautiously as a dutiful expression of approval for liberalisation, and a few daring forays into contemporary comment, was developing into a free exchange of views, with few holds barred. *K N*, as if to justify its continuing existence by advertising its 'independence of Ministerial control' was something of a pace-setter in the cultural field until the appearance, on March 1st, of the new Union Journal *Literární listy*. The latter, running under its old editorial staff, at once raised the stakes of independent utterance, as if determined to outdo *K N* and reveal it as a tame cat of the old ruling group. On February 10 *K N* printed a leader discussing the general failure of confidence towards and within the Party; the alienation of the younger generation from politics; the tensions between Party and the intelligentsia; and the existence of deep divisions within the Party leadership itself.[10] On February 17 *L N* actually printed an attack on an article in the Party theoretical journal *Nová mysl*.[11] On February 24th *K N* summed up the developments of the past two months as an attempt to revive the influence of public opinion over the political system, an attempt which, it admitted, was still regarded with scepticism, as if the changes so far represented nothing more than the changing of the guard, while the system went on as before.[12]

This was a shrewd comment. After years of lies and broken promises, all ending in disillusion, it was natural that news of change should be received with deep scepticism. But among the sceptics was a core of people determined to use every opportunity to prevent a recession to another era of neo-Stalinism. The freeing of public expression was a real gain, which might be revoked at any time. While it lasted, it was vital to bring into the open not only the misdeeds of the past, but also the real issues of political democracy. While Husák and Smrkovský welcomed free speech as a means of exposing the errors of the past, others saw in it a chance at last to awaken public opinion, and galvanise public activity to an extent that, when the 'new guard' had consolidated their positions, it would be difficult for them to tighten the screws again. It was, above all, the non-Party intellectuals, who saw that they had a chance to expose not only the guilty men, or the 'deformations of Socialism', but the *system*; and that this chance would last only as long as the interval of freedom. The changes of personnel which had taken place so far gave absolutely no guarantee that the system would change; after all, they had seen liberalisation before, and what had happened in Poland once Gomulka had become secure in his power. The only chance for real improvement lay in pushing the limits of permitted freedom as far as they safely could be pushed, and creating a climate of action in which the *political structure* could be changed. While the reformist leaders aimed at the democratisation of the Party, and defended its 'leading role' in society, the freeing of the press gave a platform to those who were determined to end the Party's 'leading role', if that meant (as it did) its monopoly of power.

In its first two issues the new Writers Union journal *Literární listy* printed the answers to a questionnaire addressed to a number of intellectuals, both Party and non-Party, *Where from? With whom? and Where to?* The answer of Ivan Sviták was as follows:

> From totalitarian dictatorship towards an open society; towards the liquidation of a power monopoly; and towards the effective control of the power elite by a free Press and public opinion. From the bureaucratic management of society and culture by the 'hard-line thugs' (Wright Mills) towards the observance of basic human and civic rights, at least to the extent that applied in the bourgeois democracy of Czechoslovakia. With the labour movement, but without its professional officials; with the middle classes without their groups of voluntary collaborators; and with the intelligentsia in the lead. The intellectuals of this country must assert their claim to lead an open socialist society towards democracy and humanism if the restitution of the editorial board of a literary journal is not going to turn out to be just another act in a senseless farce, based on the interaction of the unscrupulous and the power-hungry.[13]

It was the clearest expresion to date of what many sceptics had thought, but left unsaid: that the political reformers in the Party, and their supporters among the intelligentsia, were playing out a comedy, intended to delude the public into thinking that changes at the top were taking place in accordance with pressure from below. But once the new leadership was safe, the comedy would end, and so would the interval of freedom. Sviták was spelling out the views of those who rejected the comedy, and were determined to use their freedom to participate actively themselves in the reform process. And the reforms they had in mind were structural, not mere matters of personnel.

By March the tone of the public media revealed that democratisation was getting out of hand; i.e. it could no longer be regarded as a phase of *controlled* liberalism. Certain members of the Party leadership who had so far co-operated with reform, now seem to have decided that democratisation had gone far enough. In reply to a questionnaire *What do you take as positive in social development since the January meeting of the Party CC; and to what have you reservations?* Kolder, the Secretary of the committee, wrote:

> I take as positive: a move to democratise public life, and, combined with it, a renewal of initiative, communist frankness and addiction to principle, civic consciousness and comittal. I have reservations towards: those gestures which conceal conservatism behind the interests of the working class; and likewise towards those which, in an extravagant desire for intellectual exclusiveness, lead away from the goal of unity of progressive forces...[14]

In a chorus whose unanimity matched that of the Novotný days, every person praised the progress of democratisation; but Kolder's reservations were shared by others: Dr J. Kozel deplored those elements which 'stood in the way of the healthy current, those whose efforts slowed down the cementing of all creative forces...'.[15] This was a thinly veiled reference to intellectual wreckers like Sviták, who refused to play the game of 'progressive unanimity', and were blatantly using their freedom to alert the public about the real issues, as they saw them.

Free criticism in the Press was shaking the position of the Kolder group in the Party leadership. But it went further, in subjecting to close scrutiny the attitudes of publicists who now advertised with enthusiasm the new Party line. The Writers Union itself had always been a Party-run institution; and in spite of its clashes with authority and its sporadic forays into political unorthodoxy, it had never been anything but communist in principle. The reformist line of the Party was in accordance with the liberal Party line taken by the Union leadership; from its start then, the restored Union journal *L L* might well be taken as a

faithful expression of Party leaders' current views. Its competitor
K N found it perhaps amusing that the proponents of unorthodoxy
should now be orthodoxy's voice, and suggested that a new *monologue*
had begun.[16] When *K N* implied that *L L* was really the platform of a
literary monopoly – that the 'dissidents' had been less interested in
breaking down monopolies and more in asserting their own – it was
easy for the Union to dismiss it as the spiteful comment of defeated
conservatives. The editors of *L L* were anxious to show their independence even of the reformist Party leadership, and the Party
liaison officer was requested by Dr Goldstücker not to appear at any
further Union meetings. The Union itself declared that it did not need
Party tutelage, and refused to negotiate either with Hendrych or with
the Minister of Culture, Karel Hoffman, on the grounds that it had
lost confidence in them.

But suspicion of the Union came not only from conservatives, but
also from radicals. When Sviták talked of the restoration of the Union
journal as possibly becoming yet another episode in an irrational
farce, he was using *L L* to air his own deep distrust of the Writers
Union itself as an organ of the Party Establishment. In fact the Union
was coming under fire from both sides of the reform movement. Old-
guard communists saw the leadership of the Union as rather reckless
in its demands for total freedom: if the pace were pushed too fast and
too far, it might undermine the position of the Party itself. On the
other hand non-Party intellectuals, who were determined to push the
pace as hard as possible while the chance existed, suspected the Union,
and its bevy of Party intellectuals, of a desire to orchestrate the
progress of free criticism; and certainly to avoid any real threat to
Party authority.

To no section of the population was the voice of the radicals more
welcome than to the students. Their relationship with the Party apparatus had long been difficult. The Party had always authoritatively
claimed to speak in the name of the young, but twenty years of disillusion had widened the gap between the two. By 1968 it was apparent
that Czech youth was quite alienated from the ideology of the Party
and perhaps from any ideology; the proportion of Party members
among students had fallen to five per cent. The Party reform movement, in its desire to attract support and participation throughout the
community, naturally sought student support in 1968. Just as the
Party had made up its quarrel with the writers, so it promoted better
relations with students. Attempts were made to breathe new life into
the Youth Union (Č.S.M.), and in March a mass meeting was addres-

sed by communists prominent in the reform wave, including Smrkovský, Procházka, and Kohout. The meeting coincided with a period of
violent student unrest in Poland, and the apprehension was evident
in the tone of several of the speakers: Czechoslovakia, as Procházka
said, could not afford *a new Budapest*. It was a grim hint of what could
happen if democratisation got out of hand.

At this point a change was made in the official arrangements for
the organisation of young people. The old Youth Union was allowed
to lapse, and a loose federalisation of groups took its place. This
suited the university students, who set up their own organisation The
Union of University Students (S.U.S.), with their own newspaper,
Student. The Union became one of the most radical pressure groups
in the community, and the journal one of the most uninhibited and un-
controllable. The combination of non-Party intellectual dissidents
and student groups was a potential threat to Party control in the whole
country. In the structure of power the students had no share or responsibility; but when the pace of reform began to be set by free debate
in the media, *Student* itself became a new pace-setter. The student
community and their journal became a natural platform for the radical
intellectuals. On March 20th in a public lecture at the Charles University (later printed in *Student*) Ivan Sviták proposed a whole programme of action:

> We support the 'young guard' who want to displace the old
> bureaucrats in the Party; but it must be clearly understood
> that we support the programme of the new team, not their
> personalities; and that their maximum programme is our
> minimum one.
>
> Collaboration between social critics, intellectuals, and high
> Party officials of the state bureaucracy is a temporary ex-
> pression of an identity of interests between these two groups.
> This identity of interests will vanish at the point when, after
> consolidating their power, Party officials will come to
> consider democratisation as a closed subject. At that point
> democratisation will have ended and democracy never begun.
>
> Therefore intellectuals who can see what is happening be-
> hind the scenes of the power struggle, and who understand
> the historical processes at work, must speak to the nation
> about something more than democratisation. Their political
> programme must run roughly along these lines: *We want
> democracy, not democratisation. Democratisation is our
> minimum programme on the road to democracy.* [17]

With cruel accuracy Sviták analysed the nature and record of the communist dictatorship in Czechoslovakia and found it totalitarian in the extent of chaos it had created, thoroughly conservative and inefficient, periodically installing phases of democratisation and then withdrawing them, but never bringing about any basic changes in the system as a whole; the entire structure buttressed by a spontaneously spouting geyser of official stupidity, gushing forth in the official Press and the tolerated cultural publications. It was only the threat of economic collapse which had shaken the grave-like quiet of this dictatorship and its truncheon-assured stability. So a change in the ruling groups had begun; but the possibility of real structural change was still far away: in the structure of power *nothing* had changed. The illusion of change was being maintained, and the point of the game was to turn illusion into reality. So far the one new factor in the situation was the lapse of censorship and the consequent genuine expression of public opinion:

> It will be towards this very area that the counter-attacks of conservative forces will be directed in the near future. They will call for moderation, and will offer new economic programmes and fresh personalities instead of fundamental political changes. We, on the other hand, must endeavour fully to exploit the tolerated limits of freedom, in order to press for democratic elections as the next step towards establishing a European socialist state. This progress is possible only if the fundamental conflict of the contemporary Czechoslovak state is resolved. This conflict does not arise from the relationship between the Czech and Slovak nations, but from the mechanisms of the totalitarian dictatorship... *We must liquidate this dictatorship, or it will liquidate us.*

Whereas the Action Programme of Party reformers involved the exposure of past misdeeds, the programme put forward by Sviták for students and intellectuals involved the exposure of present illusions. Whereas their programme called for the reform of the totalitarian system, his programme called for its liquidation. The programme of the students rested ultimately on the defence of civic and human rights. It rejected collaboration with all politicians who had been involved with the operation of the power system, and also collaboration with writers and intellectuals who had compromised themselves by their manoeuvres with the authorities.

To an observer of the political scene in March, it might well seem that the chances for success of the students' programme were slim; for it was hardly reasonable to expect those who controlled the power machine to assist in its destruction. The only chance for democracy, as opposed to democratisation, was for policy to be taken right out of the hands of the rulers, and for policy making to become the province of the media – an incredible idea, but one which at one time seemed to be happening. In the period of change between the fall of Novotný and the establishment of a new ruling oligarchy, the media were establishing themselves as an independent political force. This was because they were able freely to propose and debate public issues; were in daily contact with, and readily responded to, public opinion; and above all because, by their very freedom, they represented the heart of political revival. While the Party Presidium and the CC were still working out their Action Programme, it had already been left behind by public opinion, led on by the media. While sections of the press became more radical in their demands, the more conservative journals weakened in their conservatism. As a matter of fact professional journalists, being state employees, had never been in a strong position to protest; and in 1967 their Union had feebly accepted the hard-line Party view by condemning the Writers' Congress. In 1968 the journalists felt able to demonstrate a more independent line. In March the Journalists' Union deposed its Chairman, Hradecký, and elected a new committee by secret ballot. Of particular significance was the appointment of a new editor to their own journal, *Reporter*; it was Stanislav Budín, who had long ago been expelled from the Party; had spent the Second World War in New York; had been a victim of Stalinist persecution; and combined liberal views with close personal ties with the reformers. Under his guidance *Reporter* took its place among the most liberal and sophisticated of the current political journals.

Among the hard crust of conservatism was the journal *Kulturní tvorba* published by the Central Committee of the Party and controlled by its Ideological Section. Through January and February *K T* stuck closely to an orthodox line. Then in early March Hendrych resigned as Head of the Ideological Department; and on 21. 3. 68 *K T* printed a brief announcement that the editor, J. Kolár, had been relieved of his duties. His departure was the signal for a change in the orientation of the paper, which now took up a liberal line on a variety of subjects, including the rights of student dissidents, the cover-up of the past, and the freedom of the press. The Party daily, *Rudé právo*, echoed, with some vacillation, the current Party line of reformism, but the hard-liner Švestka continued as its editor. By the end of March the Czech press showed a fair spread of viewpoints, from the cautious orthodoxy of *R P* to the selfconscious radicalism of *L L* and the tear-away tactics of *Student*. The radicals were setting the pace; and the absence of control was already awakening grave disquiet in certain quarters so far identified with liberalism. In March Laco Novomeský resigned from the editorship of the Slovak journal *Kulturný život*: he objected to the inclusion of certain material, including the transcript of a talk by Mňačko, who was still in exile. Novomeský was over-ruled by his own editorial Board, which accused him of refusing to publish material critical of his more conservative Party colleagues. Novomeský then transferred to the journal *Predvoj*, formerly edited by Husák, and was followed by several of his colleagues from *K Ž*. The division in the Party leadership was no longer merely between Novotnyites and reformers, but between those who sided with the official reform programme and those who tolerated much more radical ideas including ideas critical of the Communist system itself. Influential members of the Slovak C.P. who had hitherto supported the Prague reformers, now began to waver in their support. In their aims democratisation seems to have taken second place to federalisation; to them the main gain resulting from the decentralisation of control was the chance of an autonomy which would enable them to put their own ideas into operation in Slovakia. This main objective seemed now likely to be attained, and at this point their enthusiasm for further democratisation cooled. The gradual withdrawal of Slovak support seriously weakened the position of the reformist leadership in Prague, and left Dubček himself rather isolated from his own power base in Bratislava. In this delicate situation he was understandably reluctant to antagonise any more pressure groups, and accepted with relief the support of even such turbulent and unpredictable allies as the radical intelligentsia, including its non-communist section.

Although Press censorship was inoperative, the institution remained, and the possibility existed that it could be reactivated at any time. In mid-March members of the Censorship Board issued a statement deploring the institution; pointing out the illegality of its origin; blaming Hendrych for misleading the Board over the case of the writers in 1967, and expressing no confidence in the responsible Minister, J. Kudrna. On March 15 President Novotný dismissed Kudrna; at about the same time the Chief Prosecutor Bartuška was also dismissed. On March 20 a delegation from the National Assembly asked Dubček to consider the position of Novotný. Two days later

Novotný resigned as President. His resignation was hailed as the end of an era, and the beginning of a new age of freedom. Among his last official acts as President, Novotný signed the papers for the release of the imprisoned writer Jan Beneš. Amid the euphoria proper to such symbolic occasions romantics could rejoice that the sword at last had yielded to the pen.

With the elimination of Novotný and his closest associates from public life it was possible to argue that the period of retribution was closed, and the Party leadership could now concentrate its energies on the tasks of reconstruction. That was the view of many reformers: others however regarded the influence and danger of neo-Stalinism as far from ended, and were prepared to view any proposal to end the investigation of the past as a new attempt at covering up the Party record. The sceptics among communist, and especially among non-communist, intellectuals, were watching with suspicion every move of the Dubček leadership for signs that, as in the past, the sacrifice of selected scapegoats was being offered as the price of maintaining the system intact. The radical journals, rejoicing in their uncensored free-com, did not allow the fall of Novotný to deter them from the relent-less pressure for total exposure of past, and of present, errors. It must have been clear to the radicals that by their pressure upon the reform leadership they risked turning its benevolent tolerance into enmity, and, worse still, that by pressing too hard and too fast, they might dis-credit and destroy the very policy of liberalism which allowed for the possibility of change. But the radicals who wished to alter the system, had no real choice: to maintain the pressure during the present interval of freedom was their only hope.

By early April it was clear that the radical intelligentsia were not going to be satisfied with the changes in personnel which had hap-pened so far. Pressure for thorough-going changes in the system was kept up via the media (especially in *L L*, *Student*, and *Reporter*) and encountered a response of extraordinary public support, as measured in circulation figures, opinion polls, and public speeches. On the other hand an increasingly firm opposition to futher 'concessions', i.e. further democratisation, was expressed by influential Party members who saw with alarm a real danger that the entire structure of authority might collapse about them.

Twenty years of communist rule in Czechoslovakia had produced an army of officials, both governmental and Party, on whom the ad-ministration of the country depended. Within the whole intricate ap-paratus of control, the centre of authority lay in the Security network, which supervised the apparatus, and ensured the continuity of absolute control. In the long run the real test of reform was whether it would change this, the heart of the system. Political leaders could be dismissed, changed, reshuffled, without radically affecting the system itself; as long as Security continued to act above and beyond the law, the structure of power was safe from interference by reformers. The secret workings of Security must be, in the end, the ultimate target for those who sought political change: the radicals could best probe the intentions of the reform Party leadership by challenging them to end the cover-up over the activities of the Security services – - not only their activities in the past, but at the present juncture as well.

Even in democratically organised communities Security services tend to be insulated from political changes going on around them, and from serious public investigation into their activities. In the case of an authoritarian state, the curbing of the power of Security involves the possibility that the state will cease to be authoritarian. In Czechoslovakia in 1968 there were men in the apparatus of power who believed that to threaten the authority of Security by exposure meant a threat that the communist system might be brought down; and that this was in fact the aim of those who sought to reform the system by attacking the heart of its power. And yet it was logical that any genuine exposure of the past must touch at a thousand points on the role that Security had played in the 'distortions of socialism'. It was a dilemma for Dubček. After so many commissions of enquiry into the past had ended in vague, or whitewash, documents; or, where they had probed more deeply, the reports themselves had been suppressed, Dubček could not afford to discredit the reform movement by yet another cover-up action. On the other hand he certainly could not afford an exposure which might threaten the position of the Party itself. An additional complication – perhaps the most dangerous element in the whole situation – was that a real exposure threatened to bring disgrace not only on the Czechoslovak communists, but also upon the leaders of other Fraternal Parties – in the first instance upon the Communist Party of the USSR itself. Everyone knew, though there had long been an accepted taboo on utterance, that the activities of the Czechoslovak Security services had been guided and watched by the Soviet secret police. The worst excesses of political persecution – as instanced in the rigged trials of the fifties – had been directly inspired by orders, and supervised by agents, of the USSR. The dangers of free utterance sprang into horrid prominence when Bacílek was interviewed by journalists, bombarded with questions, and incautiously admitted that the Soviet Presidium member Mikoyan himself had been directly implicated in the rigging of the Slánský show trials.[18]

On April 2nd the journal *Student* published a copy of a letter addressed by Ivan Sviták to the Public Prosecutor, in which Sviták demanded an official enquiry into the circumstances surrounding the death of Jan Masaryk in 1948. Sviták suggested that a *prima facie* case of murder had been made out against Czech Security, and he recalled the reconstruction of the affair by the German journal *Spiegel* (7.4.1965), which had implicated Major F. Schramm, a Czech liaison officer between the Czechoslovak and the Russian secret police (Schramm had himself been murdered later in 1948). Sviták could not have been unaware of the grave implications of his action; publication of the letter was a test of the limits of free utterance. The implication, that the Russians were responsible for the death of Masaryk, must have appeared in Moscow as a gesture of deliberate provocation. Either the Dubček leadership had sanctioned the gesture, and was prepared for a confrontation with Moscow; or else Dubček had lost control. In either case his position, in the eyes of Moscow, was serious. It appeared that the influence of the free media was pushing Dubček towards an upleasant choice. Either he would have to curb that freedom which was so far the one positive gain of the reform process; or else he must face the enmity of those who stood at the centre of the power structure in Czechoslovakia, Security and their allies in the Party apparatus, backed by pressure from Moscow.

It was known that developments in Czechoslovakia were arousing disquiet among the ruling groups in other European communist countries. In the light of previous experience it might have been expected that a gesture of displeasure from Moscow, relayed obliquely through a satellite country, would be sufficient to warn Dubček that it was time to put the democratisation trend into reverse. A suitable opportunity for a reproof to the Czechs appeared when their Party leaders attended a routine conference of Warsaw Pact allies at Dresden in March (Rumania was not invited to attend). In the communiqué[19] released after the meeting there was nothing to suggest that Dubček had lost the confidence of Moscow. But a few days later some carefully chosen words of criticism were made at a philosophy conference in Berlin by ideological spokesman for the Communist Party of East Germany, Kurt Hager, member of the E. G. Politburo. He claimed that reactionaries in West Germany were taking comfort, and their propaganda machine was gaining encouragement, from the published statements of certain people in Czechoslovakia, in particular from the words of Smrkovský, and from writers' and journalists' open attacks upon the leading role of the Communist Party, its leaders, and its officials.[20]

Hager's words were obviously an expression of an official attitude from Berlin, an attitude probably cleared and approved by Moscow. They were a warning to the Dubček leadership that things had gone too far: it was time to drop the wild radicals (as Smrkovský was assumed to be), and to return the Czechoslovak C.P. to a more orthodox line. A year earlier, the hint would perhaps have sufficed. But in March 1968 Hager's tactless and insulting remarks were like petrol thrown on a forest fire. The uncensored Czech Press commented on his words with scorn and anger: even the Party ideological journal *Kulturní tvorba* rejected his attitude as an unwarranted interference in Czechoslovakia's internal affairs.[21] Writers and radical journalists whom he had especially singled out for rebuke, (correctly) assumed that his gesture was an official attempt from abroad to halt the democratisation movement, and the Czechoslovak government openly agreed with the radicals: the Minister of Foreign Affairs, David, sent for the East German Ambassador, and officially protested against the action of Hager.[22] The Czech rebuke to their German allies was most popular in Prague: the policy of reform was already taking on an aura of nationalism, as the new communist leadership appeared as defending Czechoslovak interests against outside pressure from its own 'fraternal allies'. If the Hager gesture was intended to split the Czech communist movement and discredit the radicals, it was an utter failure: the radicals were shown as the opponents of Stalinism both at home and abroad.

Writers were using their freedom to awaken the public conscience. In the new Union journal *L L* the editor Dušan Hamšík published a careful analysis of the situation in an article *Trials that made History*.[23] Why dig up the past? it was all so long ago; the dead could not be brought back to life; recriminations would further poison the atmosphere; revenge could begin a further round of vicious persecution. Regretfully he suggested that it *was* necessary to disinter the past - not so much to punish the guilty as to discover what had really gone wrong, and to learn from it in the future. What had been done in the 'fifties was unprecedented in Czechoslovak history; the judicial murders had been accomplished by rigged trials followed by the execution of entirely innocent people. The trials had been planned by the Party, instrumented by the secret police, and supervised by Beria's agents from Moscow. The victims of the Slánský trial were not punished for what they had done, but for what they represented.

The trials in fact were a way by which the Stalinist (Soviet) model of socialism was imposed on a country which had tried to find its own way. Slánský and the other communist leaders were condemned *as representatives of a specific Czechoslovak road to socialism.*

It was significant that Hamšík, in stressing the need for investigation of the truth, was concerned throughout with the cause of socialism, rather than with the good of the *Party*. The move to disengage the two things must have come like a blow in the face to those who had for so long automatically equated the socialist cause with the Czechoslovak Communist Party; and equated the good of the Party with their own control of its structure of power. The reform movement within the Party had been designed to improve efficiency, and to mend fences. Within three months it had been swallowed up in a much wider movement aimed at a wholesale reformation of social and political life in the spirit of humanist and democratic socialism. It was in the serious and radical journals that this movement found expression. The pages of *L L* were opened to humanist spokesmen even outside the socialist field.[24] The editors welcomed a new development, the formation of a *Club of Committed non-Communists* (K.A.N.) in which members of the intelligentsia grouped themselves with the intention of putting forward a viewpoint not necessarily in harmony with any Party line. It was a disquieting move in the eyes of those who saw in the new club a possible platform for anti-communist feeling. Even more alarming was the news[25] that an organisation of ex-political prisoners had been formed. It was named K231, following the nomenclature of the law 'for the protection of the republic', under which its members had become the victims of official illegality. The club grouped together judicial victims of the Stalinist system, both communist and non-communist; it came into being without official encouragement, but without official hindrance either; and once inaugurated, it spread through the country. Its meetings were conducted always according to a given style: on the platform there was an empty chair for the dead, and a bible lay on the table. Attracting together the lost, the broken, the angry, and the forgiving, it made a great impression, both by the dignity of its proceedings, and the terrible revelations to which it gave a voice. To those who feared for the future of the Party and the adverse effects of publicity, K231 seemed to be the most threatening development to date. It was like an accusing finger pointing to the monstrous record of the past: by existing, it provided a potential forum for those elements in society which had most reason to hate the Party, and to challenge its continuing monopoly of political power.

It was now three months since Dubček had been elected First Secretary, and the reform programme had become the top priority of the Party. Since then the Secretariat had been working on a detailed programme of action, to be presented to a full meeting of the Central Committee in early April. In the meantime the freeing of the media, and the energetic use made of that freedom by journalists and writers, had quite transformed the atmosphere in Prague. What would have appeared in December 1967 as liberal and daring proposals, were in April 1968 taken for granted. During the public debate which had been taking place there had emerged a number of vital questions; and those who looked with hope or anxiety on the development of the political situation sought in the Action Programme answers to these questions. They were: Was the present freedom of the Press, radio, and TV going to be institutionalised by the official abolition of censorship? Would the Party and the government at last permit a full and unrestrained enquiry into the political trials? Did the Party intend to resume its search for a national road to socialism, rejecting the Soviet model which had been imposed in the fifties? What did the present leadership mean by the term 'the leading role of the Party'? and, combined with this, were there going to be free elections at which the voters could choose the party of their choice, i.e. was Czechoslovakia to continue as virtually a one-party state, or was there going to be a genuine democracy, in which rival parties would compete for power?[26]

The long and rather tedious report[27] in which the Central Committee published its Action Programme touched on all these questions. The principles of free speech, assembly, and association, were affirmed: a new Press law was foreshadowed which would define the circumstances in which information could be restrained by a state body: generally speaking, the practice of pre-publication censorship should be eliminated. The Czechoslovak way to socialism (as evidenced in the 1945-8 period) was the way chosen by the present leadership. It was admitted that the inclusion of Czechoslovakia in a system of socialist states had brought changes to the character of the state which were alien and harmful (the imposition of the Stalinist model). The report contained assurances that the Party was taking active steps to rectify past injustices and a Commission of Enquiry had been set up to this effect.[28] To avoid the possibility of future violations of legality and justice, certain changes would be made in the administration of law enforcement. The powers of the ordinary police would be strictly defined by the legal system in the interests of crime prevention: the duties of the Security Service would be limited to counter-espionage; in no circumstances would it have power to coerce Czechoslovak dissidents or to settle political controversies. The report also had much to say on the economic reforms; and on the question of Slovak autonomy.

The Action Programme of April 1968 was the political platform of the Czechoslovak communist reform movement, the expression of 'socialism with a human face', as it was termed. Much of what it said was vague, and could have meant much, or little: a great deal depended on interpretation. The actual report was so long and tedious that probably not many people read it. The enthusiasm of those who took its liberal statements literally was not entirely matched by the techno-crats of the economic reform movement, who recognised in it a com-promise between political centralism and genuine reform. The Pro-gramme made it clear that the 'leading role of the Party' was going to be maintained, though it was not going to monopolise political power. The Party would co-ordinate the efforts of people so as to turn the Party line into reality. Sectional, organisational, and social interests would be channelled through the National Front.

Did the Action Programme promise democratisation (e.g. a relax-ation of the one-party system), or democracy? Obviously, the most it promised was a step towards the former. As far as the National Front was concerned, it had long since ceased to exist as a genuine coalition of parties, and for twenty years it had been used as a facade for one-party rule. In spite of the charges of *revisionism* which were to become a feature of the attacks upon Dubček, it is hard to see his policies as anything but orthodox in intention.

A number of personnel changes were made in the Party and govern-ment leadership. Only Dubček, Černík and Kolder retained their positions on the Presidium. Novotný, Hendrych, and Chudík lost their seats, and reformists Kriegel and Smrkovský moved in. But so did Slovak Chief Secretary Bil'ak, and Švestka, editor of *R P*, both con-sidered with good reason to be old-guard conservatives. The new President was a political nonentity, General Svoboda, who had col-laborated with the communist take-over in 1948, and was regarded as *persona grata* to the Russians. Reformers Císař and Mlynář became members of the CC secretariat; but so did Alois Indra, a conservative, of whom more would be heard later in the year. A new cabinet was formed, led by Černík as Premier, replacing Lenart. The new Minister for Culture and Information was a former editor of *Kulturní tvorba* and ambassador in London, M. Galuška. He was a good choice be-cause of his attractive public image, and his easy relations with the writers. The vital portfolio of Minister of the Interior fell to a former political prisoner, Spanish Civil War veteran, General Pavel. An old and trusted member of the Party, he was regarded as a reformed ex-Stalinist of the Smrkovský type. In the new government the influence of the communists was no less than in Novotný's time; portfolios were monopolised by Party members, together with a few fellow-travellers. The new leadership of both Party and state was a balance between progressive communists of the Dubček type, and conservative communists who had not been closely identified with Novotný, or, as in the case of Kolder, had actively opposed him. The Action Programme reflected the aims and ideas of the reform movement in the Party. Democratisation did not mean any surrender of authority by it, except to the extent that this authority would be expressed by wise leadership and co-ordination, rather than by an integrated command plan in which directives were issued from a central authority and relayed downwards via levels of control. The Party, as the avant-garde of society; would provide the programme and the leadership, under the aegis of which the choices and conflicts of sectional interests would be settled. This was apparently the way Dubček envisaged the 'leading role' of the Party; it was an extension, into the whole societal area, of the reform movement's plan for economic change. The Action Programme had liberal and democratic aspects; what it proposed was merely a democratised version of the existing socialist system; it did not imply democracy, in the sense that the will of the electorate should prevail, via the competition of programmes and parties. The three months which had elapsed since the media were unmuzzled had accustomed the reading public to the expression of political ideas far in advance of the Party programme as revealed in April, and of the structure of power from which the programme emanated. In fact a comparison of ideas expressed in the Party Press in January with the ideas put forward in the Action Programme of April reveals how little they had changed. Dubček's democratisation programme remained within the broad limits of the reform programme put forward in Novotný's day: the programmes and ideas now familiar in the media knew no such limits.

At the end of March the Czech members of the Writers Union had held a full session, the first since the now famous June Congress of the previous year. Goldstücker, in the chair, reported to the meeting on the negotiations which had meanwhile taken place between his committee and the Party HQ. The main points covered in his report were arrangements for the resumption of the Union journal *L L*, and a request for the inauguration of a rehabilitation commission to deal with the case of writers who had been wrongfully penalised in the past era. Within the framework of the Union an enquiry was set up, headed by the poet Seifert; it was hoped that measures would be taken as soon as possible to compensate the victims of injustice, including those who had suffered in 1959 and later. The Union insisted on the posthumous rehabilitation of the writer Záviš Kalandra, who had been executed in 1950. The committee had approached the non-communist dissident critic Professor Václav Černý, and offered him membership of the Union. After Goldstücker Jan Procházka spoke briefly, commenting on certain complications involving the Ministry of Culture, in connection with the publication of *L L.* A surprise announcement was that a decision had been taken for the Writers Union to publish a daily newspaper. It was noticeable that the focus of interest was not so much creative literature as the involvement of the Union in public affairs: the project of launching a daily newspaper was obviously of the first importance in this regard, and would certainly add, perhaps dramatically, to the political influence of the Union.

The political content of the speeches by Goldstücker and Procházka, speaking for the committee, was echoed by the speeches from the floor. The first was in the form of a public announcement, signed so far by twenty writers, that within the framework of the Union they were founding a Circle of Independent Writers (K.N.S.)[29] to represent the views and look after the interests of non-communist members of the Union. (This was perhaps the first open 'opposition party' set up within any official body). Several speakers[30] now rose to point out that a number of Union members, now running a reform line, had in fact actively collaborated with Stalinist repression themselves and assisted in the persecution of non-communists and dissidents; that the Union had allowed itself to be used as an agency for Stalinism; and that in spite of this the communists still assumed it as their natural right to guide the Union on its new course. Perhaps the Ministry of the Interior should be asked to supply a list of Union members who had, over the last 23 years, collaborated with the Ministry, and with the Gestapo?[31] It was suggested further that a special Writers Congress be held, to which the exile writers should be invited.

The lively debate, in which several of the members accused of Stalinism tried to defend themselves, revealed quite dramatically the deep distrust and division within the Union. Everyone knew that it had been constituted by the Party, organised after its own model, led by Party nominees, and made to carry out Party policies, including the crude anti-cultural policies of Stalinist days. As communist dissidents, men like Kohout, Vaculík, and Procházka could with justice claim that they had resisted pressure from above, and had helped to change Party policy, so that their own views on cultural freedom had eventually become official policy. Thus their present collaboration with the Party leadership in the reform course was not to be compared with collaboration with Stalinism. But now the past came up to confound them. They had in fact themselves collaborated with Stalinism in the 'fifties, and been among the most fervied in their loyalty. So their present collaboration and loyalty was not above suspicion. Now that the time for free-speaking had come, some non-Party men revealed their repugnance at the idea that the Union leadership and Party men like Procházka, the personal friend of Novotný, should still presume to speak in the name of the *writers*, some of whom had never been allowed to join the Union, and some of whom still regarded it with contempt as the voice of the ruling group.

To outside observers the writers often appeared as a united group, pushing hard for freedom of publication for themselves, and for democratic conditions for society. By the conservatives they were often portrayed as verging on anarchy in their rejection of political authority. But among the writers themselves the divisions were both deep and wide: they represented a repertoire of attitudes, from old-guard cultural apparatchiks, like J. Pilař and Ivan Skála, to communist reformers, now the official leaders of the Union. Much more radical in their ideas were those like Milan Kundera, of the Party men, and V. Havel, of the non-Party group, whose support for the socialist cause in general did not include any particular love for the Czechoslovak Communist Party or its leaders. A further group of incalculable importance in the situation were those members of the intelligentsia who did not belong to the official organisations at all, and had no responsibility for their appalling record in past days. Writers like Václav Černý, theoreticians like Ivan Sviták, and critics like Jindřich Chalupecký, who had been excluded from influence and denied recognition, returned to the scene with an authority enhanced by the fact that they had suffered by discrimination, and had no part in the collaboration in which so many of their colleagues were implicated. Those who had suffered, and had been proved right, were now listened to with respect. Moderate reformers like Goldstücker, eager for change but anxious for the future of the Party, found themselves pushed further in radicalism than they might have chosen, for even he, a communist ex-prisoner, could hardly compete in authority with those whose opposition to

Party tyranny had been consistent, and had formed the organising
principle of their career. In any case, the lifting of concealment on the
crimes of the regime now turned up so many horrors as to render
difficult the position of any who spoke from a Party position.

The public media were opened to letters and articles which documented at first hand and in horrific detail the record of how police
provocation, wire tapping, spies, and informers had been exploited by
Security; illegality had been systematically practised by legal organs
of the state; and elementary human rights had been contemptuously
trampled under foot by officials who for the most part were still in
positions of authority: it detailed the treatment of political prisoners
at the hands of the secret police and in the 'reformatory camps',
including beatings, torture, and public executions.[32] (A mass of carefully documented material was compiled by a Commission of Enquiry
set up by the organisation of ex-prisoners K231, and eventually
published abroad.)[33] The Writers Union was active in following up
complaints of this nature published in their column: In addition *L L*
serialised the memoirs of Madame Slánský (the widow of the executed
Party Secretary Slánský), and Evžen Loebl.[34] In these accounts the
evil role played by the Soviet Secret Police and their supervision of
Stalinist methods in Czechoslovakia was made quite clear. All this
material, politically so explosive, was naturally more of historical than
of literary importance; and it was a fair criticism of *L L* that it was becoming a political rather than a literary journal. But in May *L L* fulfilled both political and literary tasks by publishing extracts from Jiří
Mucha's long awaited, long banned, book *Cold Sunlight*,[35] a record of
the camps, which became the book of the year; of which more here-
after.

Party reformers who would later be described as conservative, had
welcomed an end to the cover-up over the misdeeds which had been
committed in the name of socialism. The revelation of the truth of
Stalinism was regarded as essential in the interest of saving the Party
and vindicating its communist victims. But the revelations which the
media unfolded in the Prague Spring were so grave in their implications,
so terrible in their accusations, as to call into question the Party's claim
to rule at all. And while the record of vicious illegality was being
documented by survivors, as if risen from the dead to confront their
torturers, public confidence in the Party's capacity was being undermined in less spectacular ways. Through the Spring, in the Press, radio,
and TV, a series of papers, talks, discussions brought out in con-
scientious detail the story of official mismanagement which had led

Czechoslovakia in 1948 from a path of promising economic growth, based on a sound industrial potential, to its present unenviable position as a backward, sick member of the East European community, plagued by chronic shortages, industrial imbalance, low productivity, and economic decline. The fallen leaders had already been damned by the sensational, but selective, material released about them. But the public reeled before this stunning record of official incompetence, arrogance, tyranny, sadism, and corruption. It hit directly at the whole system and at those who ran it – not only the leaders but the whole bureaucratic apparatus of control, and, at its heart, the corps of secret police which had been guided by the agents of Moscow, had violated the rights of its own people, *and still controlled the organs of power.*

The mass of incriminating data was like an avalanche rolling down upon the authorities; and neither the personnel changes which had taken place in Party and government, nor the promises of the Action Programme were sufficient to stop the mounting pressure for a new deal, and absolute assurance that such events could never occur again. In Prague was quoted the current watchword of the Israelis, recalling the Nazi gas-chambers, *Never again like sheep: Never again like sheep.*[36]

The one-party system of government still operated; the communists still controlled all the organs of power and administration; only the public media were uncontrolled. But political pressure made itself felt, not only in words, accusations, exhortations, confessions, but through the social organisations, including the Party branches, through the Club of Committed Non-communists (K.A.N.), the League of ex-prisoners (K231), The Society for Human Rights (S.L.P.)[37] and the Circle of non-communist writers within the Writers Union, which itself was drawn into a loose affiliation with other groups of the intelligentsia. In spite of the system, designed to channel all political activity through organisations of the Party, or controlled by it, an opposition front was being formed, and because the media were open to it, was effectively operating, in the sense that the rulers could no longer afford to ignore its pressure. Instead of public opinion being moulded by propaganda from above, pressure from below, generated to some extent by non-communists, was relentlessly pressing on the policy makers above. The reform movement which had begun from within the Party had already spread out of the hands, and partly out of the control, of the communist leadership.

As the 'Opposition' never became a legal entity, to be measured by votes and the institutional participation in affairs, its composition is a matter of conjecture. It comprised a very wide front of opinion which might be styled 'progressive', stretching from democratic socialists (both Party and non-Party) to non-socialist democrats. After 1969 it was frequently claimed that it was heavily influenced by anti-communist reactionaries whose aim was the restoration of capitalism and the rejection of the entire socialist programme of social welfare.[38] One may assume that anti-communist elements did indeed support the opposition front; but it is hard to find a trace of such reactionary sentiments in views publicly expressed during the Prague Spring. The most commonly cited ideal of the day was rather the democratic humanism of the Masaryk period, and a synthesis of pre-war Czecho-slovak democracy with the social welfare of the post-war period. But if the views of the opposition were not anti-socialist, it is true to say that they were anti-Soviet. From the mass of statements and opinions publicly proclaimed by the progressives certain demands constantly recurred. They were: to end a situation where Czechoslovakia's vital interests, and the administration of her policies, were subjugated to the USSR; to restrain the power of the police over public life, so as to protect civic rights and end the possibility of a return to the police state; to eliminate from positions of power at least those officials felt to be a menace to a free society because of their record of criminal violations of legality and common humanity; to examine carefully the status of the Party's private army, the so-called People's Militia, which had no proper place in the institutional arrangements of the country; and to end the era of absolute one-party rule, so that the 'leading role of the Party' could be reconciled with the existence of a legally operating Opposition.[39]

Such radical demands were bound to awaken intense disquiet in those conservative elements who still formed a majority in the ap-paratus of control. One would have expected them to mount a vigor-ous rear-guard action in the media, especially in the Party Press: in fact their overt reaction was surprisingly feeble. Even *R P* under Švestka followed with docility a reformist line as faithfully as it had previously followed that of Stalinism. The conservative point of view, as such, rarely appeared in the Press, which seemed to be completely won for the radicals. When they were questioned by journalists, the Stalinists defended themselves by the simple expedient of blaming others. On his role in the rigged political trials, Dr Urválek, the Chief Prosecutor, blandly claimed that he had no idea that the confessions were false; and that anyway the whole thing had been set up by Gott-wald and Bacílek. When the latter was questioned, he said he had only acted under the orders of Gottwald, who himself was carrying out the bidding of Stalin, relayed by Mikoyan.[40]

Freedom of publication had revealed such things from the past of the Party as to damn it, as well as its former Stalinist leaders, in the eyes of the public. Now that the communists were on the defensive, they were subjected to more than subtle intellectual criticism, such as emanated from writers in *L L*, or university critics in *Student*. Some ugly threats of reprisals for communist crimes were heard at factory meetings, and a wave of anonymous letters directed against Communist Party members was an unpleasant feature of the developing situation. In April there were meetings of the Party district branches, and in May meetings of Regional Secretaries. Reports from these meetings indicated that among many of the members, and especially among the officials, there were grave feelings of disquiet at the way things were moving. Many felt seriously threatened, and complained that instead of reviving, the Party was wilting under the pressure of an anti-communist offensive which its liberal policies were encouraging. The drumfire of attacks on Stalinism was in fact, they alleged, a general assault on the role of the Party itself, and upon its allies in the Warsaw Pact countries. Branch Secretaries reported a collapse of morale in the Security services, which had become the target of violent public criticism; in such an atmosphere these services were shunned, and the Security apparatus which was the guarantee of the socialist system, was being steadily eroded. Security chiefs who had recently attended a seminar with General Pavel, had openly expressed their disquiet and dissatisfaction at the progress of events.

The report of the Branch Secretaries' meeting was debated in the Presidium, where Dubček himself conceded his belief that a constant stream of one sided criticism in the press was directed at discrediting the Party; at a time when the latter was temporarily disorientated and in a state of crisis, the non-communist, and often anti-communist groups were functioning in a very systematic way. Nevertheless he re-affirmed his belief that the proper policy for the Party was to redeem itself by its actions, and prove that the goal of true democracy lay through socialism. Other liberal speakers stressed that the bad press which the Party was getting was due to its undoubtedly bad record in past years; the solution was not to return to repression to stop the criticism, but to prove by example that the Party had indeed made a fresh start; the regeneration of the Party would be brought about by resolutely turning away from its old Stalinist ways, not returning to them. Nevertheless even the reformers admitted that things were not going well; the Party was under heavy pressure from the public, encouraged by the media, and was in a state of crisis. J. Piller claimed that the fault lay in the slowness of the present leadership to give a firm lead. After the changes in January there had been a period of irresolution, when the press had seized the initiative by presenting its own programmes: instead of the communists leading the pace of reform, they had often found themselves reacting to the leadership of others, not always well intentioned towards them.[41]

When one reads today the account of the Branch Secretaries' meeting in May, 68, it is difficult to avoid the impression that the reform of the Security Service and of the Party apparatus, envisaged in the Action Programme, did not make great headway; and that the democratisation process was held back, or sabotaged, at its most sensitive point. While the personnel of the Security Service successfully resisted change, they did not fail to stress to the leadership their belief in the danger of 'counter-revolution'. We know from Kolder that in May a detailed report was submitted to Dubček, which claimed that a subversive organisation was at work, led by Professor Václav Černý and sponsored by the French Intelligence Service.[42] Pressure against General Pavel from his officers was strong; and only three weeks after his appointment the direct command of the secret police was transferred to his deputy, Šalgovič. It was a decision with momentous consequences, and it is notable that it was the democratic process itself which made possible the resistance to Pavel's reformist efforts. General Pavel was in fact the first Minister of the Interior since 1948 who was subject to open criticism by his subordinates.

The strength of the conservative faction in the bureaucracy and in the apparatus of repression assured their continuing ability to protect themselves against serious change. But their trump card lay in the support they drew from the USSR and its satellite regimes. In Czechoslovakia's neighbours, Poland and East Germany, the authorities felt their own position threatened by the open propagation of political heresies across the frontiers, in particular by the fact that the leading role of the Party was being questioned, the possibility of an official Opposition was being aired, and that public discussion had become so free as to elude the control of the Czech authorities and become a basis for organised action. Such developments, being an internal affair of the Czechoslovak Republic, were theoretically the concern of that country alone. But the outrageous ideas there being propagated were felt to be infectious, especially in view of the camaraderie which existed among the intellectuals of the satellite countries. This was exemplified when Professor Kolakowski, on the black list in his native Poland for his radical ideas and consequently excluded from his own university campus, was invited to lecture at the University of Prague. Futhermore writers like Ivan Sviták pointed out the defects of the socialist system as it operated in other countries as well as their own; nor did they hesitate to comment specifically on the repressive and totalitarian aspects of their communist neighbours.[43]

Anarchy in the Czech press, ideological neutralism or even anti-communism in politics: this was the impression that Czechoslovakia made on its communist neighbours, and it appeared to them as an indirect threat to themselves. No less unwelcome to them was the tone of nationalism which the Czech reform movement seemed to be assuming. When Czech journalists wrote frankly about the realities of international relations (as they increasingly did), their remarks were regarded as insulting towards their fraternal allies, and designed to weaken the solidarity of the socialist bloc. When Czech students took to the streets to demonstrate about the treatment of Jews and student dissidents in Poland, the Polish government, not surprisingly, blamed the Czech authorities for tolerating such a demonstration, and pro-tested officially. The need for a specifically Czechoslovak road to socialism was a plank of the Action Programme which could mean anything or nothing. But it acquired sinister overtones when inter-preted by the Czech media as a license to criticise their own allies, to diverge from the Soviet line on such fundamental questions as the attitude towards Israel, and to suggest that the Czech authorities might well dispense with the services of their Russian advisers.

In Russia, Poland, and East Germany the tone of the controlled Press towards Czechoslovakia grew sharper during May. There were vague references to the attempts of imperialists to stir up counter-revolution in the socialist states; and references to the joy and sinister hopes expressed by reactionary circles in the West about the Czecho-slovak new course. Czech liberal intellectuals and writers associated with the reform movement came in for personal attack. In Poland J. Barecki commented on the anti-Polish attitude of 'Zionist and anti-socialist elements' in Prague, citing the novelist A. Lustig by name.[44] In Berlin Dr. Herbell fired broadsides at Ivan Sviták, 'a so-called philosopher who advocates counter-revolution in the fashion of the Kronstadt mutineers'.[45] In Moscow an article in the *Literary Gazette* charged V. Havel with running around America repeating slogans coined by the enemies of communism, and with advocating the over-throw of communist leaders, in the first instance in the Writers Union.[46]

The same journal accused Jan Procházka of ignorant generalisations about socialist agriculture, of spurning the working class, and of currying favour with the shattered remnants of reaction.[47]

A stream of Russian polemics attacked a wide spectrum of Czech intellectuals, from T. G. Masaryk to L. Vaculík. Then during May, the Soviet press widened its scope from attacks on errant individuals to attacks on the Czechoslovak reform movement itself. On May 11th an authoritative article in Izvestia practically identified the current of Czech liberalisation with the influence of Western reaction, aiming to stir up counter-revolution and overthrow the socialist system. The concept of a legalised Opposition was dismissed as an obvious manoeuvre in this direction. Given the existing position of a power stuggle between two competing systems representing communism and capitalism, the existence of a 'counter-revolutionary' movement in one socialist country was regarded as a threat to the whole socialist community. 'Certain confused elements within the system' (i.e. the Czechoslovak reform group) 'had unwittingly become the peddlers of bourgeois ideology, and were becoming the catspaw of Western reactionaries whose aim was the destruction of socialism'.[48]

This was a clear warning that unless the Czech leadership reversed the democratisation process, it could be in serious trouble with its allies. If the consequences of reform in Prague were felt to be a threat to the interests of Moscow, then the latter would feel free to take the necessary steps to halt the process. On May 4th Dubček, Černík, Bil'ak, and Smrkovský were summoned to Moscow, where they were treated to a tirade of criticism from Brezhnev on the trend of events in Czechoslovakia. To the surprise of his guests Brezhnev produced a whole dossier of quotations from Czech newspapers, journals, radio commentaries, and public speeches, to which he took a strong exception. Evidently he was being carefully briefed by press-watchers in Prague. The Czech leaders were thrown into consternation by this cascade of material, much of which they had never heard of, as it was derived in some cases from local newspapers with limited circulations. They tried to explain to Brezhnev that the upsurge of political excitement and critical comment, some of it rather reckless, was a passing phase: angry remarks passed at a meeting of perhaps fifty people or less at KAN or K231 were of little consequence politically: far more significant was e.g. the enormous acclaim which had greeted the Communist leaders at the recent May Day celebrations. Brezhnev listened with impatience and disbelief; he demanded firm measures against all expression of political opinion in disagreement with Party policy.[49] The

Czechs emphasised the importance of maintaining democratic procedures; they promised, however, that if these failed to control the situation, administrative action would be taken to control any form of extremism.

Brezhnev's blunt warnings were backed up by action. On May 8th an informal gathering of Warsaw Pact leaders was held in Moscow without the participation of either the Czechs or the Rumanians. On May 9th came reports of Soviet troop movements southwards through Poland towards the Czechoslovak frontier. At the same time the idea that the Czechs were already in the toils of Western reaction was spread by a bizarre story that American soldiers and tanks were already deployed on Czech territory under the pretence of assisting in filming a scenario about the last war.[50] The ground was being laid for possible military intervention to 'save Czechoslovakia for socialism'; a French news flash claimed that the Soviet general Yepishov had already reported that the Red army was ready to move at any time in answer to any appeal from the Czechoslovak authorities.[51] On May 17th a high ranking Soviet military delegation including Yepishov landed at Prague airport on an official visit: an enterprising Czech TV reporter asked the General to comment on the report.[52] On the same day in the evening came a surprise news flash that Kosygin himself had landed in Prague to take a health cure at a Czech spa. A week later it was officially confirmed that Warsaw Pact manoeuvres would be held on Czechoslovak territory.

The Party Presidium met on May 7th, and the full Central Committee at the end of May. Published reports made it fairly clear that reform policies were meeting tough criticism within the leadership. Complaints made at the Presidium of anti-socialist forces at work in the country were echoed at the meeting of the Slovak Party CC on May 22nd. In Prague the Ministry of the Interior clarified the political situation by noting that any attempt to organise a new political party would be officially regarded as illegal. On the day the CC met, *Rudé právo* published a serious analysis of the current situation from the pen of Kolder, who called for Party unity, and an uncompromising attitude towards the efforts of 'rightist forces.' On the following day *R P* published a speech by Císař, generally regarded as a radical reformist, sternly taking to task journalists for their irresponsible involvement in matters outside their understanding. *R P* also published a translation of Bil'ak's speech to the Slovak CC, in which he sharply attacked the information media, especially in Prague.

Sympathy with conservative views was revealed by Dubček himself

in his report to the CC, in which he claimed that the regenerative political process was now endangered not merely by conservative (Stalinist) elements, but also by what he described as anti-communist tendencies; by the work of organisations without legal basis; by 'unobjective
criticism' in the media, by the reactivisation of discredited elements of
the old bourgeoisie; by false information circulated by foreign news
agencies; and by elements like K231 which included (in Dubček's
words) people who had been rightly sentenced for anti-state activities.
He reaffirmed the 'leading role' of the Party; dismissed the idea of
disbanding the People's Militia, and rejected the possibility of allowing any new political parties to enter public life. Thus he advertised to
the world, and especially to his critics at home and in Moscow, that
the regenerative process was going to remain firmly in the hands of the
Party.

On the other hand a decision was reached by the CC to hold a
special Congress of the Party in September. This was a response to
demands from regional conferences, and was regarded as a test of
support for the reform wing: in the words of Dubček, without a
special congress to elect a new CC 'definite guarantees could not be
given for a thorough realisation of the new policy'. Novotný and those
leaders who were closely identified with his policies had their membership suspended.[53] At the special Congress it was expected that a new
Committee would be elected in which the conservatives would be
swept away. On the agenda was also to be a review and determination
of political policy, including the method of holding elections: this was
to 'prevent any further instances of people being able to abuse their
personal positions to persecute their opponents by undemocratic
methods' (Ota Šik). Dubček's attitude at the May meeting seems to
have been a cautious compromise. On the one hand he was ready to re-
assure his Warsaw Pact allies, alarmed at the pace of liberalisation,
that democratisation did not mean democracy in the Western sense.
On the other hand he reassured his supporters within the Party, and
outside it, that there would be no return to Novotný days. A new deal
would have to be made, combining the new freedoms with political
stability based on the existing political order:

> No democracy, including our socialist democracy, can carry
> on for very long if it tolerates... unfettered criticism. This is
> all very well when it helps to remove old obstacles which stand
> in the way of social progress. But once these obstacles are
> gone, in order to govern this society democratically you need

a properly worked out, and smoothly functioning, system of
institutions, organs, and organisations, working in a new way
and with new efficiency along policy lines, while still remaining under constant control by the citizens of the country.

On the sensitive question of who should control the media, Dubček's
policy was vague. The implication of his words and his actions throughout, is that the media should not be controlled by the police or the
Interior Ministry: the media were social organs, and as such presumably should eventually come under the restraint of the social institutions, in particular, Parliament. But the Party press would properly
remain under the control of its social organisation, the Party.

Military manoeuvres by the Warsaw Pact forces began on Czechoslovak soil, thus providing for even the dullest observer a warning of
how very precarious was Czech independence and how restricted were
the options open to her government. In this tense situation Dubček
might well feel that neither the media nor the intelligentsia nor the
pressure groups which had formed outside the Party were likely to go
on using their right of dissent and criticism to the extent of threatening the future of the reform movement and of Czechoslovakia itself.

Unfortunately for Dubček, the realities of power politics, so apparent to himself and the ruling group, were not so obvious to a
public fed for twenty years on official deception and illusion. The
radicals had been expecting warnings, and some dramatic gesture, to
pull them back into line and make them tone down their inconvenient
demands for greater freedom. Once they relinquished the pressure, the
chances were that the trend towards liberalisation would be reversed
in the best Gomulka style, and a new era of repression would begin.
The victims of past political persecution realised that if they missed
their chance to assert their rights now, the chance might not return.
On May 18th two representatives of the former Social Democrat
Party, Bechyně and Janýr, had informed Smrkovský that the Social
Democrat Party was being re-formed, and intended to re-enter
politics. Smrkovský played for time, asking the two representatives to do nothing precipitate. At a later conference the communists
made it absolutely clear that, while they would welcome the activity of individual social democrats within the Communist Party,
they would not permit the public activity of any rival party. On May
22nd *Student* published an open letter, revealing the situation and
defending the rights of the Soc. Democrats to independent political
activity. Other journals joined in the argument. The reactivisation

of the Social Democrat Party, with its strong traditions of Czech working class support, was regarded as a grave threat to the continuance of the CP's 'leading role'; the fact that representatives of the Soc. Dems. were trying to assert their rights to independent political activity was also regarded in Moscow as a sign that the Dubček administration did not have the situation under control. To allow the Soc. Dems. to re-enter politics might well be fatal for Dubček's position. But overtly to prevent it would advertise the failure, or at least the drastic limitations, of the democratisation process. During June the Soc. Dem. representatives proclaimed their right to re-enter political life as a party; but they did not force the issue by calling the party back into existence. Their leaders continued to negotiate with Smrkovský and Kriegel, and they agreed to do nothing which would complicate an already tense situation. In a gentlemen's agreement the two sides promised to take no further step without prior consultation, and to call off the campaign of arguments and accusations in the press.[54] The agreement was well meant, but ineffective. Not all writers were prepared to exercise restraint on important public issues in order to spare the communists embarrassment; and there was strong suspicion of all efforts to talk editors into voluntary restraint. Unfortunately for Dubček the sins of the Party's past, and the example of Gomulka's Poland, were still pursuing him.

It is tempting to speculate why, when a plea for voluntary restraint did not succeed, the authorities did not fall back on administrative action. In mid-June Parliament passed an amendment to the Press law suspending preliminary censorship by state bodies.[55] But the personnel which had operated censorship remained more or less intact in their offices, and the whole system could have been unofficially reactivated at any time. A simplistic reading of the situation might suggest that by the single act of quiet censorship the Dubček leadership could have saved itself from attack by the conservatives, and the mounting wrath of its external allies, and thus eventually have saved the country from military occupation.

Free-ranging criticism by the press was certainly regarded not only by the Kremlin, but also by many Czech communists as dangerously anarchic, and a thing that sooner or later would have to be curbed. Discreet appeals to editors to withhold stories were made, but in some cases rebounded on the authorities, when journalists got hold of the story, and exposed the attempts to muffle it.[56] Again, the past of the Party was pursuing it: many vigilant people were watching for moves to suppress information. To be effective, action against the media would have to be fairly drastic. Within the Presidium plans were put forward, including the introduction of reliable personnel into controlling positions in the press, radio, and TV. At one stage the Premier foreshadowed a plan to set up a Board to supervise broadcasting, and to guide the media.[57] But none of these ideas eventuated. By June it was perhaps too late; in the sense that to regain control of the media such tough measures were required that the authorities balked at them. The spectre of 1967, and the debacle which had followed the suspension of *L N*, returned to haunt the proponents of resolute action. Given the cultural traditions of Czechoslovakia, and the political context of 1968, the idea of remuzzling the press might seem simple, but its implications were thoroughly unpleasant. Realising the danger, writers kept the limelight on the question of press freedom, and ensured that any move to limit it would run into maximum trouble. An alarming development, from the conservatives' point of view, was the willingness of some of the newly formed Workers' Councils to take up the issue. By June the Trades Union movement had become very interested in the question of press freedom; the possibility now existed that any overt attempt to restrain it might be answered by strike action in industry.[58]

It was a dilemma for the Party leadership. The risks of seeming to defy the directives of their Soviet ally were daunting, and reinforced by the fact that Czechoslovakia was now temporarily occupied by allied soldiers. But the political risks of overtly returning to the bankrupt policies of Novotný, which they had themselves repeatedly denounced, were also appalling. The basic justification for the reformist leadership was in its determination to reverse Novotný policies of internal repression, and freedom of publication was the great proof that they were doing so. To move against their own liberal allies in the media was extremely distasteful to the Dubček group, and the temptation was rather to defer decision in the hope that time would bring a solution: the Russians would see that events in Czechoslovakia in no way threatened their position, and would withdraw their troops: offending editors would see the folly of sensationalism in such an explosive situation; if the leadership kept its patience, the intelligentsia would continue to show its support for the reform programme by behaving moderately, and persuading the hot-heads to curb their excesses. On June 22nd the responsible Minister, Galuška, appealed to the media to show understanding of what the government was doing, and restraint in their reaction to it. On June 26th Dubček himself met the press, and emerged from a long and heated session with the hopeful claim that in his opinion the two sides now understood the other's point of view. By an unfortunate coincidence on the very next day *L L* and three other newspapers simultaneously released the text of a statement, which because of the interest and hostility it aroused, was to become a key document in the history of the Prague summer of 1968. It was the so-called Manifesto of 2,000 words, drafted by the communist novelist L. Vaculík, and signed by a cross-section of the intelligentsia.[59]

It opened with some downright statements about the bad record of the Czechoslovak CP: poor leadership had transformed it from a political party into a power system, attractive to power-hungry egotists, calculating cowards, and guilty men. The worst deception practised by these people was that they falsely represented their own arbitrary rule as the will of the workers, who were in fact excluded from decision making. Although everybody knew this, the censorship had prevented it from ever being admitted. Since January the Party had been trying to undo some of the harm it had done: the progress it had made so far was only the first instalment in paying a debt which the Party owed to those whom it had long excluded from equal civic rights. The present revival had brought forward no new ideas, it was in fact reviving ideas older than the errors of socialism; and even this step had been taken not in response to the pressure of truth, but because of the grave economic situation, and the weakness of the old leadership:

> In this moment of hope we appeal to you; our hopes are still threatened; it was months before many of us believed that we could speak out; even now many still do not accept it. Nevertheless we *have* spoken out, and so much has been revealed that we must somehow complete our aim of humanising this regime. Otherwise the revenge which the old guard will take will be terrible. Above all we turn to those who have so far hesitated. This is a time which will decide the situation for years to come... Decisions can be reached only on the basis of discussion, and this requires freedom of utterance, which is in fact the only positive democratic achievement of this year.

The manifesto went on to caution listeners that it was useless to toy with the idea that democratic revival could take place without, or in defiance of, the communists; improvement could come only through the Party, which must be given time to work. Suspicion had arisen that the process of democratisation had stopped (hence radical pressure was necessary); it would be truer to say that it had become less evident; economic pressure upon the government, e.g. increased wage demands, would do nothing but compound the difficulties under which it was working. What the workers should demand was rather increased honesty and efficiency in the running of enterprises; and the cutting out of dead wood. People who had misused their positions of authority must be got rid of:

> We must find ways to induce them to resign, e.g. by public criticism, draft resolutions, demonstrations, work-ins, drives to collect money for presents for their retirement, strikes, boy-cotts. But we must reject all methods which are illegitimate, wrong, or crude: for such methods may be ammunition for them to use to influence Alexander Dubček.

The manifesto asked for solidarity in defence of a free press, which should become the platform for all positive political forces. Fears had been expressed that Czechoslovakia's internal development could become the object of interference by foreign forces. In this situation the government should know that it would be supported – with arms if necessary – so long as it carried out its mandate; and Czechoslovakia's allies must know that its alliances, friendship, and trade agreements would be respected. It was a time not for excited reproaches and mutual suspicions, but for co-operation. The coming summer would be decisive for the future of socialism in Czechoslovakia. To the manifesto was appended an impressive list of signatories from the arts, sciences, industry, sport, education, film and literature. After its publication scores of letters poured in to the journals from others who wished their support for the declaration to be added.

During the Spring of 1968 *L L* and other journals had lent space for the publication of numerous joint letters, declarations, resolutions, and programmes framed by various groups. The manifesto was thus far from being unique, and it said little which had not appeared in print before. In content it kept within the accepted limits of the Party Action Programme; it stressed the need for loyalty to the Warsaw Pact allies, and for general support to the Communist Party in the solving of the country's difficult problems. Nevertheless the response to the manifesto was dramatic. Smrkovský was on his way to a parliamentary sitting when he ran into Švestka, editor of *R P*, and Zimyanin, editor of *Pravda*, and former Soviet ambassador in Prague. Zimyanin was in an excited condition, and demanded to know what

Smrkovský thought of the manifesto, which he described (in a phrase to become familiar by repeated quotation) as an 'incitement to counter-revolution.' It was the first time Smrkovský had heard of the offending manifesto, but during the parliamentary session he managed to get a copy of the text, and raised the question in parliament, finally persuading the members to reconvene next day to take up a position upon it.[60] Dubček himself was rung up by Brezhnev, who angrily asked for an explanation. Dubček had also not seen the text, and could give no satisfactory answer. Later he considered replying to it in a speech to go out over the TV network that evening. But the speech had already been taped, and the Director, Pelikán, assured Dubček that it would be technically very difficult to make an insertion in it at this juncture. Dubček agreed, and arranged for the matter to be considered at a meeting of the Presidium that night.[61] The Presidium issued a statement condemning the clause mentioning strikes etc. as incitement to attack Party officials and disrupt the system. While conceding that the signatories meant well, the official statement declared that the manifesto could open the way for anti-communist tendencies, and would tend to damage the success of the Action Programme.[62] That night the cabinet also met to consider its attitude to the manifesto. Smrkovský had advised the Premier, Černík, that it was essential to take a firm line in condemning it; at 1 a.m. he rang Černík to ask for the result, and to his surprise learned that the cabinet had not agreed to take any action. Smrkovský then took action himself by driving to the cabinet meeting and warning the government that unless they did as they were told, they would be out of office within a week. Faced by such resolute action the cabinet agreed to recommend to parliament that it condemn the manifesto. This it did *nem. con.*, after a stormy session in which some conservative members used violent language, including the claim that the manifesto was a call to counter-revolution.[63] Smrkovský himself described the manifesto as a tragedy with far-reaching implications. It was rumoured, and the rumour was echoed by *L L*, that communist parliamentary Deputies had met, and discussed the possibility of mobilising the People's Militia, forcing the dismissal of Interior Minister Pavel, and occupying the offices of newspapers, radio, and TV.[64]

The publication of the manifesto had already become an important factor in the developing political situation, and, as Smrkovský foresaw, a link in a tragic train of international consequences. The hysterical reception in official quarters to its publication must have been a surprise to its authors. In less tense circumstances the manifesto might have passed, together with a dozen other resolutions and declarations, into journalistic limbo. But the official over-reaction, made to placate an irascible ally, blew the affair up into an international scandal. Once foreign journalists scented a story, they splashed translated extracts from the document across the world Press, selecting out of context the most sensational bits. The wild talk of reprisals by Novotnyites, once printed and discussed, put them into an appalling light and sharpened the internal tension between radicals and centrists. By their attitude to the manifesto a group of men who had originally supported the reform wing, now won an unpleasant reputation as neo-Stalinists and servants of Moscow; the group included Indra, Kolder, Bil'ak, and Švestka. It is indicative of the quality of debate that both sides used the same arguments, namely that reactionaries were using the situation to mask their intention of springing a coup. The terminology was the same; the interpretation different. *Reactionaries* meant to one group the ex-Novotnyites who were trying to turn back the clock of reform; to the other group it meant radicals who were bent on undermining the system of one-party government. Men noted, as a legacy of Stalinism, the reversal of criteria, and the survival of double-think.

By far the most serious element in the situation was the attitude of Moscow. It was expressed in a leading article in *Pravda* of July 11th which characterised the manifesto as a blatant attempt to discredit the Czechoslovak CP; to destroy its leading role in society; to undermine the Warsaw Pact; and to pave the way for counter-revolution. It welcomed the fact that the CC of the Czech and the Slovak Parties had condemned the declaration; and it expressed pleasure at the receipt of a letter from a committee of the Czech People's Militia expressing determination *to defend the people's achievements against any threats.* Nevertheless 'certain *reactionary Czech publicists* were still defending the document; these were the people who had repeatedly called for the end of the CP's leading role and for the *restoration of capitalism.*' The most ominous section of the *Pravda* article was slipped in unobtrusively among its criticism. It drew attention to the similarity between the tactics of the Czechoslovak *counter-revolutionaries* and those of their Hungarian counterparts in 1956. The implied threat did not need to be stated overtly.[65]

Early in July Dubček received letters from his Warsaw Pact allies proposing a meeting of the five fraternal party leaders in Warsaw. On July 8th a reply was sent declining the invitation at this juncture. It did not suit the Czechs to have their affairs discussed in front of a group of leaders come to criticise them, and Dubček proposed that bilateral discussions would be more fruitful. The invitation to Warsaw was repeated, and again declined. But the meeting was already convening. The representatives of the USSR, East Germany, Poland, Hungary, and Bulgaria met on July 14th, without the presence of Rumania or Czechoslovakia. As a result of that meeting an official letter was sent from the five communist allies to Prague. As if to advertise to the world their displeasure with their Czechoslovak ally, and the latter's overt humiliation, the letter was published on July 15th in *Pravda*.[66] This time the niceties of diplomatic protocol were cast aside, and the letter did not disguise its function as an ultimatum to the Czechs. 'The countries of the Warsaw Pact had no intention of standing by and seeing Czechoslovakia break away from the socialist commonwealth: likewise the threat to subvert the Party's leading role and liquidate the socialist system threatened the foundations of the Warsaw alliance itself. The Czechoslovak leaders had received from their allies repeated warnings, and had given assurances that any danger to socialism would be repelled. Yet things had turned out otherwise. Taking advantage of weakness in the leadership of the Czechoslovak CP, reactionary forces had unleashed a campaign with the obvious aim of destroying the socialist system and putting Czechoslovakia against the other socialist countries. The Czech political associations which had formed outside the framework of the National Front had shown themselves as centres of hostile reaction. Anti-socialist and revisionist forces had taken over the Press, radio, and TV, and turned them into platforms for attacking the CP and disorientating the working class. It was because this outrageous campaign had met no serious rebuff from the Party leadership that the reactionaries had now appeared openly before the nation with their political platform, the *Manifesto of 2,000 words*, which contained an open appeal for strikes, disorders, and action against the CP and against constitutional rule. In essence this manifesto was an organisational-political platform of counter-revolution. A situation had therefore arisen which endangered the vital common interests of the socialist countries: the people would never forgive them if they looked on with indifference in the face of this danger.'

The letter laid down certain demands upon the Czechoslovak authorities:

a. 'resolute action against the rightist forces, including the mobilisation of all means of defence at the disposal of the state.

b. a cessation of activities on the part of all political organisations that opposed socialism.

   c. an assumption of control by the Party over the mass news media,
including Press, radio, and TV, and the utilisation of these
media in the interests of the working class and socialism.'

Thus by the so-called Warsaw letter the Russians advertised to the
world that their minimal demands on the Czechs were the restoration
of Party control over all political organisation and publication. The
situation was obviously critical, and the reaction from Prague was
swift. Dubček went before TV in a nation-wide hook-up to ask for the
support of the Czech and Slovak nations in continuing the post-
January course, and implementing the Action Programme of the
Party. He promised that no principles of that programme would be
sacrificed, and that the leading role of the Party would be exercised,
not by ruling over society but by serving it. There would be no return
to the repressive measures of the past; on the other hand, democracy
meant civic discipline; and there must be no dramatisation of existing
tensions, nor inflaming of political passions.

The text of the Czechoslovak CP's official reply to the Warsaw letter
was released at almost the same time. The heart of the reply lay in its
introductory paragraphs:

> We can see no realistic reason for calling the present situation
> (in Czechoslovakia) counter-revolutionary, for implying a
> direct threat to the basis of the socialist system, or for claim-
> ing that Czechoslovakia is preparing to change the orientation
> of our socialist foreign policy, or that there is any danger of
> our country breaking away from the Socialist community.

Point by point the reply rebutted the charges of the Warsaw letter,
explained the aims and methods of the Czechoslovak democratisation
process; and pointed out that doubts in the minds of the Czech people
(about Soviet intentions) arose from the repeated changes in the time
of departure of the allies' armies from the country, now that the
manoeuvres were over. On the other hand the reply assured the Russians of continuing loyalty, and reminded them that the manifesto had
been rejected by the Party leadership and by the National Front. As
far as the new political organisations were concerned, new laws on
assembly and association would be prepared after the September
Congress. But Czechoslovak public opinion would not countenance a
revival of censorship; the Party did not intend to return to the discredited methods of bureaucratic-police rule; nor did it approve of
the idea of conferences at which one fraternal party was judged by the

others without the presence of its representatives.[67] In rejecting the terms of the ultimatum, Dubček and his colleagues set themselves officially on the side of liberal democratic principles against the principles of the police state; and together with his fellow countrymen, including the non-communists, against the imperial Centre. The fact that Moscow had chosen to conduct the quarrel and the humiliation in public, made more outrageous the defiance of the Czech leaders, and the consequent reversal of the humiliation upon the head of the Kremlin leadership.

The Czechoslovak leaders were well aware of the need for caution, and had no intention of provoking Moscow further than was necessary to maintain their position. But in the over-heated atmosphere engendered by the quarrel some rash, perhaps unwise, statements were bound to be made, and to attract publicity. It was during the same week as the quarrel that General Prchlík gave a Press conference in Prague, in which he commented on changes desirable to improve the system of political management in the sectors of Defence and Security. During his remarks he implied that in future the Party should stop trying to run these sectors; he also commented on the unfavourable conditions under which Czechoslovakia operated in the Warsaw Pact, e.g. that the so-called Joint Command really meant command by the Red Army Marshals, with the allied commanders operating merely as liaison officers. (He revealed that other allied representatives as well as the Czechs had asked for a reform of the system, so that they could have a hand in the decision making, but nothing had been achieved.) Answering questions, Prchlík said that it was deplorable that the Warsaw conference had convened without Czechoslovakia, and without considering her views; lastly, he suggested that Czechoslovakia should insist that there should be no interference in her internal affairs by outsiders.[68]

On July 23rd Prchlík was attacked in the Soviet army journal *Krasnaya Zvezda* for his remarks. Two days later the Presidium of the Czechoslovak CP resolved to dissolve the Eighth Department of the Central Committee, which had special responsibility for Defence matters. As Director of that Department General Prchlík then lost his position, and his *ex officio* status on the Party Central Committee. On July 28th the Czechoslovak news agency ČTK announced that it was empowered to report that General Prchlík's views did not correspond with the official standpoint. It was an encouraging sign for Moscow that Dubček was willing to yield to pressure: by the same token the fall of Prchlík sent a wave of apprehension and distrust through Dubček's supporters among the radicals and students. The gravity of the situation, and the obvious danger of Soviet reprisals, had sobered down the tone of the media, and an informal liaison committee of editors had now been formed to maintain close contact with the Secretariat of the Party Central Committee. In this way it was hoped that further provocation of the USSR could be avoided without the need of any form of censorship. Under the shadow of military intervention the Party leadership and its radical critics were closing ranks.

While in Prague the news media and the non-Party organisations co-operated to avoid weakening the position of the Dubček administration, and the latter continued its conciliatory attitude towards Moscow, the response from the latter remained alarmingly threatening. On July 22nd *Pravda* published what amounted to an official rejection of the point of view taken up by the Czechoslovak Presidium. Contemptuously brushing aside the Czechs' version of the situation in their own country, in a key paragraph *Pravda* insisted on its own sensational interpretation.

> The right-wing, anti-socialist forces in Czechoslovakia, encouraged and supported by imperialist reactionaries, are moving towards a position where the Communist Party's leading role will be eliminated, the socialist system undermined, and the capitalist order restored. They have taken over the mass media – Press, radio, and TV –, are exploiting them for anti-socialist propaganda, and are trying to inflame hostility towards the USSR and other socialist countries.

The article noted that the Czech leadership had ignored proposals put forward by the fraternal parties for an offensive against anti-socialist forces; mobilisation of all means of defence; an end to the activities of all organisations 'opposing socialism'; Party assumption of control over the media, and their use in the interests of socialism; solidarity in the Party itself; and a return to the principle of democratic centralism.[69]

This could only be interpreted in Prague as a recipe for neo-Stalinism; its terms were fairly explicit. As a minimum was demanded the re-imposition of censorship, the banning of all 'suspect' organisations, and the revival of the old system of control from the top, operating through the bureaucratic Party apparatus. The article contained some thinly veiled threats that time was running out; unless the Czech leadership took action against the 'counter-revolutionary forces' the fraternal parties would 'fulfill their obligations to the world communist movement.'

On the same day that *Pravda* printed what was in effect a new ultimatum, the TASS newsagency in Moscow released a report that the Czechs had agreed to hold bilateral talks between the Presidium of the Czechoslovak CP and the Soviet Politburo: the venue was to be at Čierná-nad-Tisou, on the Slovak side of the frontier with the USSR. While the tone of the Czech media remained restrained, and polemics with the Warsaw Pact allies were avoided, the tone of the Soviet and satellite press remained threatening. The barrage of vituperation from East Germany, the knowledge that Czechoslovakia was virtually isolated, and the fear that her leaders were being driven inexorably towards a policy of capitulation, all these features were unpleasantly reminiscent of that summer thirty years before when the fate of the country had been sealed at Munich. At this moment of danger the political barriers which had divided the nation so long were melting away: never before had the communist leaders carried with them so many hopes and such goodwill of their people. On the eve of the conference at Čierná *L L* published a letter written by Pavel Kohout, but expressing the hopes and deep anxiety of many. Addressing the Presidium the letter asked them to stand firm:

> ... it is your mission to convince the leaders of the USSR Communist Party that the process of revival in our country must continue... All we seek can be expressed in four words; socialism, alliance, sovereignty, and freedom... We ask you to explain; but also to defend the road on which we have embarked. Only dead shall we be diverted from this path...[70].

Copies of the letter were posted up in centres all over the country; tables were provided at which people who wished could sign their names to the appeal. It was later claimed that over a million signatures were collected. It was a striking communal gesture, and Smrkovský later recalled the great impression it made upon the delegates.[71] They reached Čierná on July 28th, the day before the talks were scheduled to begin. They were not expected to last much more than one day. (On July 31st Tito was due to visit Prague, and Ceaucescu of Rumania was due on August 2nd).

Meetings between the leaders of socialist states are generally festive occasions, boosted by ostentatious expressions of friendship and mutual esteem. On this occasion the bands, flowers, and toasts were absent. A bullet-proof train pulled the sleeping cars which were the

Russian quarters, across a heavily guarded frontier. Not far away on the Soviet side a whole combat division was deployed ready for action. The Czechoslovak delegation also used sleeping cars as its headquarters. During the day the two trains stood side by side, the Czech on the standard gauge, the Russian on the broad gauge. Each night the Soviet train backed slowly across the frontier: the Russians did not fancy the hospitality of their ally. Local well-wishers plied the Czechoslovak delegates with helpful but unnecessary advice not to enter the Russian train in case it carried them on an unscheduled visit across the border.

The fact that the whole Presidium of the Czechoslovak CP was participating in the talks was expected to turn to the advantage of the Russians. Brezhnev could play on the Czech weak link, the conservative members, Kolder, Bil'ak, and Švestka, who were known to favour the Brezhnev line against Dubček. But the first day's talks ended in complete deadlock; in spite of the Russian pressure, and the help it received from within the Czechoslovak delegation, the Dubček leadership stood firm. Negotiations continued on the following day without progress, and in increasing acrimony. The climax came when Shelest, from the Soviet side, accused the Czechs of fomenting rebellion on Soviet territory by a propaganda campaign to detach Ruthenia from the USSR. At this Dubček rose, declared that it was pointless to continue, and walked out of the talks at the head of the delegation. The Czechs now prepared to return to Prague.

Later that day the four Russian principals, Brezhnev, Kosygin, Podgorny, and Suslov, called upon Dubček in the Czech train. In a gesture of reconciliation they apologised for Shelest's behaviour, and asked for the talks to continue the next day with a view to reaching a speedy agreement. They repeated their minimum demands – the restoration of official control over the media, certain personnel changes, and a tightening of Security. The Czechs agreed to continue the talks, and Premier Černík telephoned Prague to arrange for Tito's visit to be postponed for a few days. Next morning Brezhnev pleaded illness, and Dubček visited him in the Soviet train, where they talked in private. It was apparent that the Russians had abandoned the idea of driving a wedge into the Czechoslovak delegation; Brezhnev now ignored the Czech conservatives, and suggested that negotiations be continued between the principals on each side.

That afternoon some sort of agreement was reached. We know from several sources the demands posed by the Russians, but Dubček's exact commitments are a matter of dispute. This is the more unfortunate as the Russians later were to claim as a cardinal sin of the Dubček leadership that it had failed to carry out the terms of the Čierná agreement.

The Russian demands could be summed up under four heads. Dr. F. Kriegel must be dropped from his post as Chairman of the National Front; C. Císař must be dropped from his post as Secretary of the Central Committee. There must be no legalised revival of the Social Democrat Party. The organisations KAN and K231 must be banned. The authorities must resume effective control over all the information media.

In return the Russians promised a cessation of attacks on Czechoslovakia in their own controlled press; and the immediate withdrawal of all military forces from Czechoslovak territory.

The Russian demands obviously constituted a gross interference by the USSR in Czechoslovak affairs, but Dubček found it politic to agree to them. The first three demands were at least in the power of the authorities, however loath they might be to carry them out. But the reassertion of control over the media was more difficult. It was a step which would be bound to awaken a storm of anger and distrust in Prague, and would do much to undermine Dubček's position with his own people, however much it might increase his standing with the Russians. To revive the censorship law which had just been annulled would be tantamount to abandoning the revival programme on which his authority with the people rested. On the other hand it was doubtful if sufficient control to satisfy the Russians could be imposed without censorship. Dubček's assurances to Brezhnev seem to have been vague: control would be reasserted, but without violating democratic norms. By this assurance Dubček put his own future, and the future of the reform movement, into the hands of the media, and made the test of his good faith the Kremlin's judgement of Czechoslovak publishing. A brief and non-committal communique was issued.[72]

As part of the package deal Brezhnev proposed that the leaders of the Warsaw Pact countries should meet in two days' time at Bratislava. The conference met, without preparation, agenda, or even knowledge of what exactly was the point of the meeting. In fact there was no negotiation; the only task of the conference was to draft a communiqué in general terms about socialist co-operation in international affairs, to condemn American imperialism in Vietnam, etc. It was purely a public relations gesture to present to a sceptical world a show of unity; the Czechoslovak problem was not mentioned. The meaningless platitudes which filled the communiqués after the Čierná and Bratislava meetings awakened grave suspicions in Prague that the true substance of the agreements was being concealed, and that Dubček had secretly conceded to the Russians all the gains of the reform period.[73]

For almost a fortnight the Soviet press refrained from hostile criticism of events in Czechoslovakia: in the Czech press also restraint ruled. The Presidium urgently sought the co-operation of the journalists, and official briefings stressed the need at this time to consider the effect on Czechoslovak vital interests of whatever was published. Perhaps it seemed to the Czech leadership that the aim of satisfactory restraint was being achieved without drastic action or repression. But the situation did not satisfy Brezhnev, who telephoned Dubček daily with complaints that the agreement was not being kept. Dubček asked for time, explaining the delicacy of the position, and promising that satisfactory measures would be taken shortly; the September Congress of the Party would put things right in a way that Dubček could not do by merely administrative means.[74]

During this fortnight of uneasy peace Tito and Ceaucescu carried out their official visits to Prague: their official welcome was warm and demonstrative; their reception by the Czech public was wildly enthusiastic. The symbols of Jugoslav and Rumanian defiance towards Soviet imperial control were the idols of the hour in Prague, and none could miss the significance of their tremendous popular welcome. While pessimists anxiously scanned the Czech daily press for signs of renewed censorship, and radicals closely watched for signs of regression from reform policies, stands were set up in central Prague to collect signatures for a mass petition calling for the disbandment of the Party's private army, the People's Militia: among those who signed were members of the Militia itself.

On August 14th the interval of peace abruptly ended when the Russian literary journal *Literaturnaya Gazeta* opened a new attack on the Czechoslovak Writers Union and their journal *L L*. It was the signal for a renewal of the polemics, and of claims in Russian journals that the Czechoslovak leadership had shown itself incapable of carrying out its obligations. The response from the Czech press was generally cautious.

A conference of editors and media directors was held in Prague in an atmosphere of deep foreboding. Speaking for the Party leadership Kriegel reminded his listeners that a sword of Damocles hung over all their heads. Dubček himself was to receive the visitors; but a surprise message informed them that he had been unexpectedly called away. He had in fact left for Slovakia for confidential discussions with the Hungarian leader Kadar. Whether the latter's visit had been suggested by the Russians, or was an act of goodwill on his part, is unknown. But his message to Dubček was an urgent warning that unless something were done quickly to satisfy Russian demands, extreme measures might be expected. On Monday 19th Dubček received a second warning in a private letter from Brezhnev.

On Tuesday afternoon, August 20th, the Party Presidium began a meeting at 2 p.m. On the agenda were only two items, a draft report of the Central Committee, to be presented to the September Party Congress, and an item which had been deferred from the last meeting. This item was a study of the internal political situation in Czechoslovakia following the Čierná and Bratislava meetings. The paper stressed the weakness of certain reformist policies. Kolder and Indra (of the CC secretariat) supported the conclusions put forward in the paper. Kolder then brought forward a new fifteen page report containing material strongly critical of current policy. Bil'ak and Rigo spoke in support. Kriegel attacked the papers as nothing but a rehash of the Warsaw letter, and Černík charged Indra and Kolder with actions tantamount to treason. In retrospect it seemed that the debate had been brought on to force a split in the Presidium on the basic question of continuing with a line of policy in defiance of Moscow, and to bring on a vote of no-confidence in the Dubček administration.

During the debate Černík was seen to retire repeatedly to the telephone, where news was coming in about unusual movement on the frontiers. In the early evening several unscheduled flights had also arrived from the USSR, and the Russian planes were standing at Prague airport. At 11.40 p.m. Černík was again summoned to the phone. When he returned to the chamber, he asked for suspension of the debate, so that he could make an announcement. Military units of the five Warsaw Pact allies had crossed the frontiers and had begun occupying the country.

Smrkovský put through a call to the Presidential Castle to inform Svoboda, but could not contact him. Madame Svoboda told Smrkovský that the Soviet Ambassador Chervenenko was at that moment with the President; when the audience was over, Svoboda would come to the Presidium building. There confusion reigned: Černík and Dubček seemed on the point of collapse. Dubček now offered to resign. If the conservative group was acting in accordance with a plan agreed with the Russians, this was the moment when a new leadership could have been expected to take over, and declare its willingness to cooperate with the Russians. Prague could have awakened on Wednesday to an accomplished fact. The entry of the Warsaw Pact troops could have been represented as a gesture of support for a new Czechoslovak leadership which had approved their entry.

If this was the plan, it failed. The moment of panic passed. Dubček's offer to resign was rejected. The Presidium agreed that it had to take up an official attitude to the invasion, and a message was sent to Broadcasting House that a communiqué would be released soon. For an hour debate was indecisive. It continued until after midnight and the conservatives kept the discussion going, evidently hoping that events would soon force the issue in the way they expected. The radio was due to go off the air at 2 p.m. and time was running out when Smrkovský rose to guillotine the debate, and propose that a form of words for the communiqué be put to the vote. The text was that of the communiqué shortly to be released:

> Yesterday, August 20th, 1968, at about 11 p.m. the armies of the USSR, the Polish People's Republic, the German Democratic Republic, the Hungarian People's Republic, and the Bulgarian People's Republic crossed the state frontiers of the Czechoslovak Socialist Republic. This took place without the knowledge of the President of the Republic, the President of the National Assembly, the Prime Minister, and the First Secretary of the Communist Party Central Committee. The Presidium of the CC was then in session, preoccupied with the preparations for the Fourteenth Party Congress. The Presidium calls on all citizens of the Republic to keep the peace and not to resist the advancing armies, because the defence of our state borders is now impossible.
>
> For this reason our army, Security Forces, and People's Militia have not received orders to defend the country. The Presidium considers this action (the entry of the troops) to be contrary to the basic principles of relations between socialist states and a denial of the fundamental norms of international law.
>
> All leading officials of the Party and of the National Front remain at their posts to which they were elected as representatives of the people and the members of their organisations, according to the regulations of the Republic. The appropriate constitutional bodies have called into session the National Assembly and government, and the Central Committee Presidium is convening the Party CC in order to deal with the situation which has arisen.[75]

This communiqué, though framed in the mildest terms compatible with the situation, struck a blow at any plans for the takeover of power, by putting on record, before the Russians could disable or control the radio stations, that the invasion had no official sanction from Party or government; that it was in fact not a demonstration in support of a new, already elected, leadership, but a crude violation of national rights.[76]

Voting on the communiqué was open. Smrkovský went round the table asking each member separately for his vote – Yes or No. He began with Kolder and Bil'ak, who voted against. The motion was carried, seven votes to four. President Svoboda, who had meanwhile arrived from the Castle, was present at the vote, sitting next to Dubček.[77]

The communiqué was at once released to the media, which had been waiting for it. From Radio Prague the announcer began to read it, but before he had completed the first sentence, the sound went dead. About a quarter of an hour later a call came in from the radio station at Strahov to say that Karel Hoffman, Director of Broadcasting, had forbidden the broadcast to go out. He had in fact switched off the medium-wave transmitter. From Strahov the technician checked with Smrkovský if the communiqué was genuine. Smrkovský assured him that it was, and that Hoffman was evidently sabotaging the broadcast in the interests of the invaders. After this the technicians took action to restore transmission, and the communiqué went out. By chance it was picked up almost at once by the Vienna monitoring service, which then communicated it on a world-wide hook-up. The Soviet plan to stage a *fait accompli* had now completely broken down. It had failed in the committee room when the Presidium, by their vote, had denied retrospective legalisation to the occupation. It failed again with the media, where neither Hoffman, at Radio Prague, nor Švestka, at *Rudé právo*, could control their infuriated staff.

Meanwhile at Prague International Airport things had gone smoothly for the invaders. The operation began with the landing at 2 a.m. of Russian troops to seize the buildings and supervise the landing of equipment and soldiers. The Russians were assisted in the operation by the Czech officers in charge of airport security and passport control, who were obviously involved in the plot. As they landed, the Russian troops left at once for Prague to secure arranged objectives.[78]

At Central Committee headquarters the Presidium meeting was over, and members dispersed; Černík had left at once for the cabinet room. Dubček, Smrkovský, and Kriegel, chief targets of the invasion, stayed in the building and awaited their fate. Švestka had left for the offices of *Rudé právo*, where he stopped the printing presses. But after a delegation from the Party group in the paper had contacted the Presidium and been informed of events, technicians re-started the presses. In spite of Švestka's efforts *R P* went out next morning carrying the communiqué, and news of the invasion.

At about 3 a.m. Russian soldiers burst into government headquarters, arrested Černík, and led him away at bayonet point. They then destroyed the central switchboard. An hour later Russian armoured cars arrived at the Central Committee building. A cordon was thrown round it, and a tank took up position before the main entrance with its gun trained on the building. Russian paratroops entered, sealed off all exits, and rounded up all the inmates. After some delay several civilian cars arrived, carrying an officer of the Russian KGB, accompanied by an interpreter and a group of Czech Security men, who identified the wanted men. One of the Czech Security officers then arrested Dubček, Smrkovský, and Kriegel with the words, 'In the name of the revolutionary government, led by Comrade Indra, you are taken into custody'. The Russian KGB man had given him the formula before making the arrest.[79] Smrkovský and Kriegel were frisked for guns. The fourth man who was wanted was the Minister of the Interior, General Pavel, but he was not in the building, and escaped arrest. The detained men were kept in the office, but for the time being nothing more was done to them. As they stood by the window looking down into the street, a demonstration of young people began to form up before the Russian cordon. The demonstrators were singing the Czech national anthem. An order was given to the troops, and they opened fire over the heads of the young people. But one shot hit a boy in the front row: he died on the pavement almost immediately.

Meantime Czech Security officers were raiding the homes of prominent reformist politicians. Císař was arrested at his flat, and driven to police headquarters under guard.

In the Central Committee building at about 9 a.m. the Russian KGB officer in charge ordered Dubček, Smrkovský, Špaček and Kriegel to follow him into an office nearby; there he informed them that in two hours time they would face a revolutionary tribunal headed by Comrade Indra. The morning passed without further developments: evidently the Russians were still awaiting instructions what to do with the prisoners. At 2 p.m. the latter were ordered to move, and were taken down the back stairs: Smrkovský later recalled the dreadful feeling that they were being taken down to the cellars for execution.

They were in fact taken out into the back street; loaded into two armoured cars; and driven to the airport, from where they were flown eastwards into Russia.

From 4.30 a.m. on Wednesday 21st, Radio Prague had been on the air, repeating the proclamation of the Presidium, and giving a commentary on events in Prague. Its broadcasts were unequivocally in the spirit of the Dubček leadership. When the Russian troops soon took over the main TV studios in Prague, the service was continued from an outer suburb. During the morning troops entered Broadcasting House in central Prague; and transmission ceased, only to be restored shortly afterwards. There was some shooting in the streets nearby, during the course of which one or two Russian tanks were set on fire. The studios were badly damaged, and went off the air. But radio stations in the provinces then took over the service, and broadcasting remained in hands loyal to the legal authorities during the whole period of the resistance. The newspapers likewise using clandestine, improvised offices, managed to put out editions unregulated by the occupation troops. The latter had in their power communications and buildings; they had kidnapped the government Party leaders, and they held the cities at their mercy. But their apparent authority was illusory, because they lacked the control over the media which was necessary to put their case, and to transmit their basic orders.

The Russians had not come totally unprepared for a media war, and as the occupation began, the East German station, renamed Radio Vltava, began to pump out propaganda for the invaders. But the material and the announcers were so obviously of foreign origin, the presentation so crudely slanted, that it proved counter-productive. Even worse was the Russian pamphlet campaign. The invading troops had brought with them copies of a *Proclamation to save Socialism in Czechoslovakia*:[80] it claimed that right-wing anti-socialist forces had been trying to discredit the Party, attack the alliance with the USSR, and generally to destroy socialism in Czechoslovakia. The authors of the pamphlet, who claimed to be Czechoslovak state and party officials, then stated that they had appealed to the USSR and other fraternal allies for help, and asked the populace to support the allied troops. The pamphlet echoed the line being put out by the TASS newsagency and broadcast by the Vltava station, namely that allied military assistance had been requested by Czechoslovak Party and government leaders.[81] The line would have been consistent, although implausible, had the Czechoslovak Quislings succeeded in taking over the Party and government leadership during the night of Tuesday, August 20th, and thus retrospectively confirming the claim. But their failure, and the fact that the legal Czechoslovak authorities went on functioning even after their leaders had been kidnapped, made the Soviet propaganda embarrassingly out of date. By the afternoon of Wednesday the troops had ceased distributing the leaflets, and were observed burning them in the streets. Earlier, the official Czech News Agency had been given a copy of the text by its ex-Director-General, Sulek; but it declined to transmit it.

During the first days of the occupation the prime targets were government and Party headquarters, the Central News Agency, newspaper offices, radio and TV studios, the buildings of the Writers' and the Journalists' Unions, the Faculties of Arts and Law of the Caroline University, banks, telecommunications centres, and prisons. But the massive military operation, which did such irreparable harm to the international standing of the USSR, continued to fail in its primary aims. Brezhnev had repeatedly demanded that Dubček bring the media under control; but a quarter of a million soldiers were unable to do so. While the radio continued to broadcast through a network of clandestine transmitters, special editions of newspapers, leaflets, and mimeographed proclamations kept appearing on the streets during the whole week of resistance. The campaign of opposition to the invaders became a great communal experience, reflected and inspired through the media. Rarely can mass popular involvement have been so clearly expressed as in the organisation of the token strike which stopped all work and traffic in Prague at a given signal. For an hour on Friday 23rd the occupation troops found themselves in the empty streets of a dead city.

The Czech newspapers carried the latest bulletins from the legal authorities, news of the occupation, and a stream of protests from social bodies and individuals. Among the organisations which published denunciations of the invasion were the Trades Union Council, the Prague City Council, the Academy of Sciences, the Union of Journalists, and the Writers Union:

> The long uncertainty about whether the USSR is to play the role of apostle or policeman in the socialist camp has finally been resolved. The great socialist power is returning to the tried and tested traditions of Cossack diplomacy. By this retrograde and fascist-like action, the Soviet Union has deprived itself of the right to take any leading role in the international Communist movement. Armies of tanks cannot sup-

press the longing of nations for freedom; ideas cannot be shot
dead. There are not enough jails in Czechoslovakia to accommodate all those who today raise and hold high the
banner of freedom. We assume that all those who have dealt
this deadly blow to the prestige of the Soviet Union and of
socialism will one day be called to answer for their actions:
L. Brezhnev; N. Podgorny; A. Kosygin; W. Ulbricht; W. Gomulka; J. Kadar; T. Zivkov.

On behalf of the Czechoslovak Writers Union, whose
buildings in Prague have been seized by the occupation troops
and are being guarded by their tanks, we turn to the intellectual community of the whole world. Raise your opposition
to this unjustified aggression! Boycott all activities of the
occupying power anywhere in the world!... Freedom is indi-
visible; it is not only we who are at stake, but you too...[82]

Besides this collective gesture of anger, individual writers put their
private protests on record. Jarmila Glazarová and Jan Drda, who
had long carried the stigma of collaboration with Stalinism in the early
fifties, now came forward to express, in the depths of disillusion and
despair, their grief and abhorrence at the actions of a Russia which
they had idealised for most of their lives.[83]

It was thought in Prague that one aim of the invasion had been to
forestall the holding of the Party Congress in September, which had
been expected to strengthen the position of the reformist leadership,
and oust the remaining conservatives. If that was the aim, it was sadly
frustrated. On the second day of the occupation the Congress was
summoned as an emergency measure ahead of the scheduled time. In
spite of all the unusual difficulties two thirds of the elected delegates
managed to assemble at a large factory plant in an outer suburb of
Prague. Delegates included Government Ministers who had escaped
arrest, and who brought to the Congress the latest news of developments in Parliament, which was also in session. Among the delegates
was the Minister of the Interior, General Pavel, for whom Šalgovič's
men were searching. Only the Slovak delegates were poorly represented; they had reportedly been turned back by the occupation
troops.

In spite of the extraordinary circumstances – the building was
guarded by the People's Militia, and escape routes were constantly
kept open – the Congress proceeded in a businesslike, almost routine,
fashion.[84] It elected a new Central Committee, which included all the

Dubček leadership, and from which were excluded all those who were believed to be collaborating with the occupation forces. It agreed to send an expression of support to Dubček, and to protest at his arrest. It drafted an appeal to communist parties abroad for their support; and in a final resolution, it solemnly proclaimed that it rejected the occupation of Czechoslovak territory by foreign troops, and demanded their immediate withdrawal. The successful convening of the Congress and its solidarity in face of the occupation killed any claim that Dubček had lost the confidence of the Party rank and file, or that the mass of communists welcomed their 'liberation' at the hands of their 'fraternal allies.'

The situation of the known collaborators had now become highly unpleasant and dangerous; the clandestine radio was broadcasting the numbers of their cars, and their fellow-countrymen were looking for them. When members of the government were questioned whether they had indeed joined in any appeal to the Russians to intervene, no-one admitted having done so. Neither did any high Party official ever admit the charge. Those who had given themselves away by their actions as acting on behalf of the Russians, kept discreetly out of the way, and felt safe only under the shadow of the Soviet Forces. The Russian promises that their troops would be withdrawn as soon as the crisis was over must have sent a chill down the backs of those Czechs already being denounced as traitors, and whose names were to be seen painted on walls over drawings of gibbets. The atmosphere was enough to persuade waverers not to commit themselves to the Russians, and there were several apparent changes of mind among prominent people; ex-Premier Lenart, who was at first reported to have joined the group led by Indra in forming a new post-Dubček administration with Russian help, now lined up with the patriotic resistance. On the first day of the occupation Šalgovič detained at Security Headquarters those officers suspected of loyalty to the Dubček administration. Within a few days the officers had been released; Šalgovič himself was sacked; and General Pavel had taken over personal command of the Security Police.[85]

By Saturday August 24th the Kremlin leaders had tacitly acknowledged the failure of their plans, and abandoned the idea of forming a new government and Party leadership to carry out their orders. The so-called revolutionary government of Comrade Indra was thus relegated to limbo, and the Kremlin resumed negotiations with the Czechoslovak leaders. The kidnapped men were brought to Moscow for face-to-face discussions, and agreement was reached within two days.

The Czechs agreed to declare invalid the Fourteenth Congress which had just met in Prague, and whose published resolutions had been so very damaging to the Russians. A meeting of the old Central Committee was to be called within a fortnight: it would take steps to strengthen Party control; to replace certain individuals who had incurred the displeasure of Moscow; and to resume control over the information media. Reliable men (i.e. acceptable to the Russians) would be put in charge of press, radio, and TV. No revival of the Social Democratic Party would be tolerated. There would be no reprisals on those who had collaborated with the Russians in Czechoslovakia. A treaty legalising the stationing of Russian forces on Czechoslovak territory would be prepared. The troops would not interfere in Czechoslovak internal affairs, and they would be withdrawn as soon as the situation permitted. (This clause, which did not appear in the Russian draft first submitted to the Czechs, was inserted at their request). Concessions on the Soviet side were their withdrawal of an original demand for the Czechs to acknowledge that the Soviet troops had entered the country to save it from a counter-revolution, and the Russian promise to withdraw the troops.

Once the agreement had been signed, the Czechs were free to return home and resume their offices. There were a few hours to wait before their aircraft was ready, and while they were still in the Kremlin, Lenart was sent to ask Smrkovský and Dubček if they would join their Warsaw Pact allies in the next room where Ulbricht, Gomulka, Kadar and Zivkov were waiting to celebrate the occasion by a toast in cognac. It is pleasant to know that the Czechs refused this grotesque invitation, whose level of hypocrisy must have few parallels in the history of modern diplomacy.[86]

During the negotiations which had concluded their long ordeal, Dubček had suffered a heart attack, and most of the Czechs had been in a state of nervous collapse. They reached Prague unannounced, in the morning darkness of Tuesday, August 27th, six days after the invasion had begun. They were driven at once to the Presidential Castle, where they spent the next few days in a state of physical and mental exhaustion.

The crisis was over.

The Coming of Winter

The pushing and coughing died away as the procession halted before the Jan Hus monument... Then the bells stopped: hats were removed: faces and bodies were damp with rain and tears. One could hear only the beating wings of the pigeons, terrified by the sudden, deep silence...

(at the funeral of Jan Palach 25. 1. 69)
Listy 6. 2. 69.

The newspapers which appeared on the streets of Prague on August 27th 1968 continued to show a vigorous opposition towards the occupation. The Party daily *R P* that day printed agonised letters from veteran communist writers Jan Drda and Jarmila Glazarová denouncing the occupation.[1] On the same day the evening paper *Večerní Praha* gave a round-up of international reactions towards the invasion, ranging from protests from politicians of all parties in England, to demonstrations by left-wing workers in European cities denouncing the Russian action.[2]

Meanwhile the returned Czechoslovak leaders were already at work. At 8.15 a.m. Radio Prague broadcast a short tape-recorded message from Smrkovský, obtained soon after the delegation had arrived from Moscow. Its essence lay in one short sentence: '*We have all come back including Kriegel*': a full report was promised soon. Later in the morning Smrkovský attended a brief session of Parliament, and reported on the negotiations in Moscow: as soon as he completed his address, he dashed off to attend a meeting of the Party Central Committee. At Prague Castle a Cabinet meeting was held which went on until midnight and was attended by the President.

In the afternoon Radio Prague broadcast the text of the communiqué agreed upon in Moscow. It expressed Soviet support for the existing Czechoslovak Party leadership and its efforts to implement the 1968 programme: referred to an agreement to normalise the situation in Czechoslovakia by immediate measures; claimed that troops which had entered Czechoslovakia would not interfere with its internal affairs, and that they would be withdrawn 'when the normalisation of the situation permitted': and announced that the Czechoslovak government had demanded the removal of the '*so-called quest-*

ion of the Czechoslovak situation' from the agenda of the United Nations Security Council. The communiqué concluded by emphasising the unswerving determination of Czechoslovakia and the USSR to resist the militaristic, neo-Nazi forces that threatened to encroach upon the inviolability of existing borders; and explained that the Moscow talks had been held in an atmosphere of *frankness, comradeship*, and *friendship*. The ending was worthy of Kafka himself: the hypocrisy and deep unreality which pervaded the whole document could only arouse deep disquiet and foreboding in those who heard it.

By agreement the four principals, Svoboda, Dubček, Černík and Smrkovský spoke to the nation in that order. All stressed the need, in face of an extraordinary situation, for calm, prudence, discipline, and a return to normalcy. They promised a continuation of the post-January policies, and confirmed that Soviet troops would leave the country.[3] Years later Smrkovský, whose speech was the frankest, and aroused resentment in Moscow,[4] reflected upon his own words. In retrospect he could justify his faith only in terms of the enormous moral authority which the Party had achieved in the wake of the occupation. ' Catastrophe had brought the nation together, and the moving force had been the Communists, who had co-ordinated resistence, maintained free communication, and run the administration in face of intense difficulties and without pressure from above. Denounced for years as a monolithic organisation manipulated by an authoritarian hierarchy, the Czechoslovak Communist Party in time of crisis had operated without leaders, and had carried with it the hopes and trust of the nation. In August 1968 the Party stood at the peak of its authority; if the unity of will, revealed in such dramatic and touching circumstances, could be preserved, even now there was hope.'[5]

The leaders' assurances and requests for co-operation in implementing the agreement met with a mixed reception in Prague. From Party groups at the university and the Academy of Sciences, from industrial plants, and from the mass media came resolutions condemning the Moscow communiqué as a humiliating capitulation accepted under unbearable pressure in unacceptable circumstances. They demanded the immediate and unconditional withdrawal of foreign soldiers and Security men, together with financial compensation for the havoc they had created; the firm maintenance of all the democratic freedoms attained since January; official recognition of the elections held and the motions passed at the Fourteenth Party Congress held in face of the occupation; and the publication and free discussion of all secret undertakings given in Moscow by the leaders in the name of Party and government. Particularly harsh was the reaction of *Student*, which appealed for continuing resistance, and termed the acceptance of the Russian terms as treason. (Four days later the editors published an official apology for their intemperate language; and at the same time announced that in view of the changed circumstances *Student* would cease to appear.[6]

The protests drew attention to a factor whose implications the leaders themselves did not care to stress. By returning to their posts and appealing for unity in implementing the agreements reached at Moscow, they were calling to an end to all resistance to the occupation, at the same time as they were spreading the soothing but, in the event, the misleading impression, that the Russians would soon be leaving. If resistance to the occupation continued, it would now appear as resistance to the Dubček leadership. Only optimists could avoid the conclusion that the reformists had accepted a position in which they would first help the Russians by ending the resistance, and then would begin the liquidation of their own reforms. Sceptics noted that the new course was a reversion to traditional Czech *realism*. Through co-operation with overwhelming force perhaps a way might be found to salvage some of the reform programme; in any case the alternative was too awful to contemplate; passive resistance would soon have developed into violent confrontation, the crushing of opposition, and the imposition of military rule, or a native Stalinist administration thirsting for vengeance. The alternative to capitulation seemed reckless and suicidal. Like President Hácha in 1939, President Svoboda in 1968 settled down to make the best of an impossible situation. Both accepted the inevitability of *co-operation* with the powerful neighbour who had occupied their country: both rejected the term *collaboration* to describe the policy they proposed. The usage of words was already being adjusted to the new situation.

The extent of the Czech capitulation was not made clear either by the communiqué or by the speeches of the leaders who presented it to the public. It was generally suspected that behind the Moscow communiqué lay another document, or at least, another understanding, too harsh to be communicated openly at this point of time. In fact a comprehensive document, referred to as the Moscow Protocol, had been signed by the Soviet Politburo and by the Czechoslovak representatives in Moscow on August 26.[7] The document was never published in Czechoslovakia – in fact a clause stipulated that in the interests of friendship between the two countries the terms remain confidential – nevertheless it was soon leaked from a member of the Czech side; the document was published in Paris and circulated in Prague. Confirmation of its authenticity was provided by the fulfilment of its terms in the 'normalisation' programme which put them into effect. Terms of the Moscow Protocol which did not appear in the communiqué were as follows: the Fourteenth Party Congress would be declared invalid, and all its resolutions would be reconsidered; the Central Committee of the Czechoslovak Party would carry out certain personnel changes, dismissing individuals whose activities did not conduce to establishing 'the leading role' of the Party; measures would be taken to control the communications media, and to end the activities of social organisations of an anti-socialist nature; the Social-Democratic Party would be banned; changes would be made in top jobs in the press, radio, and TV; the activities of the Ministry of the Interior would be reconsidered, and measures would be taken to strengthen its role in society.[8]

When Cabinet met on August 27th, approval was given for some immediate and extraordinary action to control the public media. A few days later the government set up an *Office for press, radio, and TV*: on 3. 9. 68 the first directive was issued from that office, and others followed. Organs of publication were furnished with a list of topics to be avoided: they included criticism of the Warsaw Pact countries, of the Czechoslovak CP, the National Front, the Army, Security, and of the occupation troops; the term *occupation* was not to be used; the term *neutrality* was to be avoided in the context of international affairs; personal details were to be carefully checked before publication; certain specific details, separately listed, were to be regarded as state secrets, not for publication. Later directives banned the publication of improvised remarks or personal comments on, or by, men prominent in public life, with a view to preventing their use for misleading or sensational interpretation.[9]

Examination of journals which appeared subsequent to the issue of the Directives shows that they were interpreted liberally. There was no dramatic change of tone, and certainly no reversal of the view that the entry of the Russian troops had not been authorised by any responsible body; it is notable that the illegality of the Russian presence was still being stressed in Czech official publications addressed to overseas (e.g. in the October issue of the English-language journal *Czechoslovak Life*). Editors simply substituted for the term *occupation* the word *intervention*: the euphemism *fraternal assistance* had not yet appeared in the Czech press.

Undertakings made in Moscow about personnel changes were carried out, though not exactly in a way expected by the Russians. The offending Ministers, Pavel (Interior) and Hájek (Foreign Affairs), and Šik (Vice Premier), handed in their resignations: Kriegel was dropped from the Party Presidium, and later from chairmanship of the National Front. Hejzlar and Pelikán lost their positions as chiefs of radio and TV respectively: Císař was dropped from the Secretariat of the Central Committee. But in almost all cases comfortable jobs were offered to these people, some of them in official positions abroad. On the other hand certain individuals who had identified themselves as actively pro-Russian during the occupation also lost their positions; they included Kolder and Švestka, dropped from the Presidium (Švestka was also sacked from the editorship of the Party daily *R P*), and Indra was demoted in the Secretariat. At the same time both the Presidium and the CC were enlarged by the co-option of new members, some of whom had been elected at the Fourteenth Congress and were known to be firm reformists; they included Z. Mlynář, K. Kosík, and M. Hübl. The general effect of the personnel changes was to fulfill undertakings made under pressure in Moscow, without however altering the complexion of the committees, or undermining the influence of the reformist bloc: in some cases the changes were obviously used as an occasion to get rid of those regarded as tools of Moscow.

Three weeks after the invasion it seemed that the Russians had in fact gained very little as a result of all the efforts they had made, and in return for all the abuse and humiliation they were encountering abroad. The eyes of the world were now on Prague, and the whole future of international détente was in question, amid violent anti-Soviet demonstrations abroad (the Soviet Exhibition at London's Earls' Court was set on fire by student radicals), and, in the Western press, dark warnings of bloodthirsty Stalinist reprisals in Prague. The situation was delicate, and the Russians wisely confined themselves to discreet pressure. On September 11th private talks were held in Prague between a Soviet delegation led by Kuznetsov and a Czech group headed by Smrkovský, in which the Russians voiced sharp dissatisfaction with the progress made so far towards 'normalisation'. They objected to the way Smrkovský himself had presented the agreement to the Czech public; to the way the Presidium and CC had co-opted certain people without any consultation with the Russians; and to the continuing defiant tone of the media, which were harping on the damage done by foreign soldiers and the need to get rid of them quickly (the offending papers included the official voice of the Party,

Rudé právo). 'Russian troops were meeting with open hostility wherever they went. At the official level there had been virtually no progress made towards the re-establishment of normal and friendly relations.'

The response of Smrkovský was not very promising. He assured Kuznetsov that the government was doing its best in the extraordinarily difficult circumstances, but there was no chance of a rapid return to friendly relations; the Czech public was in no mood to accept any sudden change of face. 'As far as concerned the friends of Moscow who had been demoted, these people were totally discredited in the eyes of the public, and no one would work with them; they would be only a liability in implementing the agreements; anyway Kolder was a notorious alcoholic, and his own constituents were fed up with him.' Smrkovský gave little ground to the Russians and at one stage took the initiative by complaining that elements of the press in the Russian bloc were still publishing absurd allegations about counter-revolutionaries in Czechoslovakia. The Czech position, as voiced by Smrkovský, was that all specific agreements concluded with the Russians in Moscow would be carried out; but the Czechs would do it their own way, and the Party was still committed to a continuation, as far as possible, of its reformist policies.[10]

The firm tone of Smrkovský in these confidential discussions does not seem to be at variance with the public address delivered by Dubček on September 14th. He stressed the need to carry out both the terms of the Moscow protocol and the post-January policies, and claimed that it was possible to combine these two things:

> The basic question today is the normalisation and consolidation of conditions, and the departure of foreign troops from our republic. That is what the Moscow protocol says. How are we to understand the term 'normalisation'? All sorts of speculations are being spread by various quarters on this question. Normalisation certainly includes fully restoring the political, economic, and cultural life of the country. It includes developing the activities of the legally and democratically elected organs of our working people, the further socialist development in the land, and increasing the leading role of the Party and the working class... In future we must avoid all extreme standpoints that could complicate our future development. We must work in such a way that will not allow scope for forces that would like to misuse the present complex period in the direction of anti-socialist tendencies and ideas...

> It is imperative to prevent even more thoroughly the vestiges
> of anti-socialist forces from taking an active part in politics...
> Swift administrative measures have to be taken, and in this
> connection the government has taken certain well-known
> measures concerning the right of association, the press, po-
> litical organisations, the National Front, etc.; the measures
> we have taken in Party organs will be expressed in legal form.
> In no case shall we allow anyone to carry out anti-socialist
> activities, which would be at variance with our post-January
> policy...

Dubček made it clear that the political clubs would be suppressed,
and so would any attempt to renew the Social Democratic Party. At
the same time he attacked certain unnamed elements who had done
much to discredit the Party before January, who had still learned
nothing, and were trying to turn the clock back to pre-January conditions (to neo-Stalinism); Dubček warned that there could be no return to such conditions. He cited the pledge in the Moscow protocol,
and assurances from the Soviet comrades, that the military and
(Security) organs of the five powers would not interfere in internal Czechoslovak affairs: there would be no reprisals.[11]

The assurances given to Moscow, and mentioned in Dubček's
speech, regarding the political clubs, were carried out at once. On
the 5th September the Preparatory Committees of KAN and K231
were informed that the Ministry of the Interior had declined permission for their registration; the clubs then asked their branches to stop
all activities.[12] The Social Democrats had never come back into official existence, and from now on they ceased all organised activity.

Action to suppress the non-Party organisations was one of the first
fruits of the Moscow agreements; no difficulty was involved for the
authorities, and it appears from Dubček's own comments that it
caused them little concern. Far more delicate was the problem of how
to handle the communications media: any action to limit free utterance
involved the future relationship of the authorities to the cultural
associations and to the intelligentsia generally.

The journals had been a key force in the resistance to the occupation;
when resistance ceased, several journals as a mark of protest voluntarily went out of existence; these included *Student, Kulturní tvorba,
Literární listy,* and *Kulturný život.* The building which housed the
Writers Union had been one of the first to be occupied by Russian
soldiers during the occupation; on September 11th it was handed back

to the writers. On the 17th the Committee of the Czech section of the Union met, and issued a formal statement of its position. The document recapitulated its history, its close association with the socialist movement, and its struggle since 1956 against bureaucratic and repressive action in the Novotný era. The Union had supported from the beginning the reform led by the Party; it strongly rejected what it termed the 'crudely distorted and unsubstantiated attacks from abroad on the ranks of the writers'. It welcomed the clearly formulated assurances of the authorities on the freedom and security of the individual, the absolute need for freedom in scientific research and artistic creation, and for lively contact with the outside world.[13] The committee also decided to publish a new weekly as a successor to *Literární listy*, and to request permission for its registration. At a later meeting (October 4th) it was resolved to grant unpaid leave to the President of the Union, Goldstücker, who was in England,[14] and to appoint J. Seifert to act in his place. Goldstücker had been the target of some particularly venomous attacks in the Russian press, in which he was charged with being a counter-revolutionary, a Zionist agitator, and a member of the CIA. At the time Goldstücker was not only President of the Writers Union, but also Professor of German and Vice Rector of the Prague University: as a former victim of Stalinist persecution, he was a symbol of victimisation in the cultural sphere. On his behalf a proclamation was issued by the Arts Faculty of the University, the Students Council, the Writers Union, and the Academy, joined by Trades Union and Communist Party branches; it totally rejected the attacks upon him by the Russians as unsubstantiated invective, and denounced publication of the attacks as a violation of the Moscow agreement.[15]

In the earliest days of the occupation the foe against whom the Red Army had 'come to give assistance' had been generally termed by them as counter-revolutionaries. During September there was an apparent shift in the Russian attitude. Instead of claiming that the invasion had forestalled a violent counter-revolution by pro-Western forces, it was now alleged that the leading role of the Czechoslovak CP had been threatened by the growth of anti-socialist forces in society: the object of the military intervention had thus been to help the Czechoslovak Communists to reassert their leading role, and put firm constraint on anti-socialist elements. In his public statements Dubček went along with this thesis. Since the term 'anti-socialist' was evidently being used in a very loose way, it could be a method of dividing the resistance to occupation: in the first instance it was taken to refer to the non-Party political clubs, then to non-Party reformers like the writer Václav Havel; by a further stretch it was used to attack Party members like Goldstücker; in the not too distant future it would be used as a term to brand the leaders of the Party itself, including Dubček. The Czechs were not slow to see the implications of this manoeuvre, against which their best defence was to stand together, regarding an attack on one as an attack on all. Hence the unusual unanimity of the intelligentsia in rebutting the attacks on Goldstücker, who was regarded as something of a test case.[16]

The four Czech leaders, Svoboda, Dubček, Černík and Smrkovský must have been aware of the eventual threat to their own positions; to survive it was necessary that they should present a solid front. But by the middle of September Smrkovský realised that he was being eased out of the inner circle. When Černík returned from a trip to Moscow, the other three met without him to discuss the news that Černík had brought; from that time Smrkovský was sure that the united front was cracking, and that he would be the first member of the leadership to be eliminated at the wishes of the Russians.[17] At the beginning of October crucial negotiations were carried on in Moscow with regard to the process of normalisation, and the status of the occupation troops. The principals on each side were Brezhnev, Kosygin, Podgorny for the USSR, and Dubček, Černík, Husák (now Secretary of the Slovak CC) for Czechoslovakia. The ensuing communiqué noted that the Czechoslovaks would 'intensify the struggle against anti-socialist forces, and would sign a treaty on the 'temporary stationing of allied troops in Czechoslovakia'. On October 16th in Prague was signed the Soviet-Czechoslovak Treaty, which ratified and regulated the 'temporary stationing' of Soviet troops on Czechoslovak territory.[18] The Russians had thus secured a major objective, the legalisation of the occupation: it was ironical that the legalisation should be carried out by the very leaders whom the occupying troops had come in to oust and arrest.

The Treaty was a government rather than a Party matter, and required the assent of Parliament. The vigorous debate showed that freedom was still alive in Czech public life. Černík presented the bill as 'one which settled not the causes but the consequences of the new situation, one filled with pain, bitterness, tension and misunderstanding: the treaty defined the purpose, location, and status of the Soviet troops, and the temporary nature of their stay; it simply took note of an existing situation'. Speakers vainly queried the vagueness of the terms, and asked for a time-limit to be put on the stay of the troops. When it came to a vote, only four members voted against ratification, and ten abstained.[19]

Meanwhile an ominous development had been the emergence of a new political group of 'old communists' known as the Gottwald party: their meeting, in Prague on October 9th, received favourable publicity in Moscow. According to a report from Radio Moscow on October 11th the meeting approved a number of resolutions, which included approval of the Soviet intervention, criticism of current Czechoslovak Party leadership, and demands for a harder line on the information media. The group was regarded as ultra-conservative (neo-Stalinist) by the Czech public and Party leadership alike. The Russians took up no official attitude towards it, but the significance of this alternative centre of influence for Moscow was obvious: if the Dubček administration proved troublesome to the occupiers, they had a pliant weapon near to hand. Dubček could comfort himself that almost any concessions by him to the Russians would be justified, if the alternative were to hand over power to the Stalinist extremists.

Two months after the invasion freedom was still very much alive in Prague: the lively, at times reckless, tone of the journals revealed that there was little official restraint on publication; and the frontiers were wide open for travel. There had indeed been no reprisals. In that brief period it seemed that the improbable had happened: 'socialism with a human face' could go forward, even under the shadow of Soviet tanks. It was a hopeful, but, in the event, a premature impression.

October 28th was the fiftieth anniversary of the foundation of the Czechoslovak Republic, a day inevitably associated with the memory of the President Liberator T. G. Masaryk. The systematic denigration of his name by the communists until the sixties had done little to dim his reputation as the great symbol of Czech nationalism. Since 1948 the significance of the anniversary had been played down; but this year preparations were made to celebrate the occasion as a great patriotic occasion. On the eve of the anniversary the national leaders laid flowers on the graves of all the past Presidents; the ceremony included a helicopter pilgrimage to Lány, where both T. G. M. and his son Jan are buried. On the 28th Prague was a mass of Czechoslovak flags: the palace guard had to be called out to control the crowds outside the Presidential palace, where a special session of Parliament was being held. (Ironically, the session approved the bill ending the existence of the Republic as constituted in 1918, and bringing into existence from January 1st 1969, a new Federal Republic of Czechs and Slovaks.) During the day, which had been declared a public holiday, large demonstrations moved through Prague carrying patriotic and anti-Soviet slogans. In the evening at the National Theatre, in the presence of Svoboda and Dubček, a performance was held of the opera *Libuše*,

the great fanfares of which had inaugurated the life of the Republic
fifty years before. Now, in 1968, it stood out as a memorable day on
which the feelings of the Czech people, after weeks of fear and tension,
were expressed in a great communal gesture of faith and hope. Saluting
their past they honoured their present leaders. Never had the Party
stood so high in popular esteem; and rarely had the nation shown
such demonstrative unity.

On October 31st the Czech section of the Writers Union approved a
document which made clear its attitude to the present situation. A
key passage in the preamble declared:

> As far as concerns us, writers, we are determined to do every-
> thing to support policies which may lead not to an apparent,
> but to a genuine solution to the present situation; and thereby
> to a further development of what we have become accustomed
> to term 'socialism with a human face'. But we are not, and
> never will be, prepared to admit to crimes which we did not
> commit, nor to give thanks for 'help' which is nothing but a
> mockery. We are not, and never will be, prepared to call a lie
> 'truth', and injustice 'a practical necessity'. People can be
> eliminated by force; but not their ideas. In this century alone
> we in Bohemia have three times witnessed how monolithic
> systems have crashed, that the voice of truth might be heard
> again. The 'fifties remain for us a warning that conscience is
> no empty concept. We love life; but more precious to us is the
> heritage that we desire to leave to our children. The judge-
> ment of people is passing: the judgement of History lasts for-
> ever.[20]

There were other signs of stiffening resistance to the policy of submission. The voice of the occupation forces was the Czech language
journal *Zprávy* which the Russians printed and distributed outside
the control of the Czechoslovak administration; it had in fact no legal
right to distribution according to Czech statutes. There were endless
resolutions tabled protesting at the existence of this journal, and
eventually the Union of Czechoslovak Journalists requested that a ban
be put upon it. In Parliament F. Kriegel complained that he had been
the victim of slanderous defamation on the pages of *Zprávy*, and
Cabinet was forced to take up an attitude to it: they issued a statement that the methods used by the journal were in fact having a harmful effect upon the normalisation programme, and upon Soviet-

Czechoslovak relations. From the office of the Prosecutor General came a ruling that *Zprávy* had, by its content – including attacks on the Czechoslovak government and the Party – indeed violated the law of the land, as well as the agreement on the stationing of foreign troops in Czechoslovakia. The new Censorship department (the Office for Press and Information) announced that the question of a ban would depend upon the government.

The central symbol of Russian propaganda was the notorious *White Book*,[21] a crude collection of documents and statements put together by Soviet journalists to denigrate the Czech reform movement and to argue the existence of a counter-revolution. At the end of October this publication was the subject of a searing analysis in the journal *Reporter* and on national TV. Thus the censorship, which the Russians had done so much to bring about, was seen to be permitting open attacks upon Russian policies at the same time as it was threatening to close down their own propaganda journal. During the same week as *Reporter* was pursuing its uninhibited criticisms of the Soviet guests, *Politika*, the ideological organ of the Czechoslovak Communist Party, warned its leadership of the danger of retreat before pressure: 'It would be tragic if the leadership of our Party and government were to win the confidence of allies by doing things that would destroy the trust of their own people.'

In September a group of scholars at the Institute of History of the Czechoslovak Academy of Sciences had published in a limited edition, not to be distributed through commercial channels, a volume in answer to the Russian *White Book*. The Czech publication, entitled *Seven Prague Days*, but more often referred to as *The Black Book*,[22] comprised a series of documents drawn from press and radio material published during the first week of the occupation. Meticulously detailing the timetable of Russian action and Czech response, the book provides a stunning indictment of Soviet actions; it was obviously intended as a counter to charges in the *White Book*, and to ensure that however much the record might be falsified in days to come, there would remain a permanent record of primary source material for future historians. The book ends with an Epilogue containing a series of resolutions from factories, Trades Unions, scientific and Party groups protesting at the results of the Moscow negotiations. It is worth quoting from the resolution adopted by the Institute of History which prepared the collection:

Our attitude to the aggression of the five countries against Czechoslovakia has been expressed again and again since the first day of the occupation. Yesterday, after the release of the communiqué on the Moscow negotiations, and after the speeches of the President and the First Secretary we also expressed our attitude in a statement handed to the legal Czechoslovak Radio.

We continue to reject the terms of the *Diktat* accepted under conditions of unheard-of pressure; in particular we reject the cynical phrases of the communiqué. We stand without reservation behind the policy adopted in January 1968, and especially behind all the decisions of the Fourteenth Party Congress... There is no reconciliation possible with the occupiers. A free people cannot live on its knees...'[23]

The firm note of defiance was typical of many publications in the cultural sector. Writers made the most of their freedom, as long as it lasted, and continually stressed the danger of any compromise or acceptance of a 'realistic' attitude towards the occupation. Once the front of resistance cracked, the way would be open to force the Czech leaders to co-operate in their own destruction.

November 7th is the anniversary date of the Bolshevik revolution; as such it is the day when representatives of the USSR invite friends and diplomats to join in their celebrations. This year the invitations went out as usual. But in Europe, outside the Soviet bloc, the reception halls were largely empty. The boycott was general and included the Soviet Embassy in Prague. On the streets of Prague there were some ugly demonstrations: Soviet flags were burned; water cannon and tear gas were needed to disperse the angry crowds. Amid signs of open defiance rumours ran through the capital that Russian tanks were preparing to roll once more. Events had reached a point where the Czech authorities' room for manoeuvre was small: it seemed that they were being forced towards a choice between standing beside their own people in defiance of the Russians, or of ranging themselves with the occupiers against their own dissidents.

The tone of the East European press had now hardened towards Czechoslovakia, and the tone began to resemble that of the weeks preceding the invasion. There were bitter complaints that false, mischievous, and anti-socialist statements were being permitted to appear in the Czech press. The implication was that if the present Party leadership could not, or would not, control the situation, it was time for them to hand over to other Czech leaders who could.

On November 7th Dubček attended a ceremony to honour the Russian war dead. It was an opportunity for the neo-Stalinists to show their strength, and they turned up in force. When he left, a threatening crowd gathered around his car; fists were shaken; and for the first time he was booed. On the following day a suspension order was put on the journal *Reporter*, and two days later on *Politika*. A meeting of the Party Central Committee was scheduled for November 14th: it was anticipated that it would see a final show-down between the reformers and the conservatives. On the eve of the meeting Gustav Husák spoke in Slovakia to a gathering of the People's Militia. In a fiery speech he denounced current 'deformations of Marxism', 'anti-socialist liberalism', and 'anarchist forces'.[24]

The Central Committee meeting which began on November 14th saw an open confrontation between defenders and opponents of the reform movement; and among the most eloquent defenders were communists prominent in cultural life. The meeting was informed by the Rector of the Prague University, O. Starý, of numerous resolutions demanding a continuation of post-January policies; from his own point of view he deplored the activities of dogmatic (Stalinist) pressure groups, who used language reminiscent of crude anti-semitism and fascism. Ivan Málek, of the Academy of Sciences, complained that parts of the reform programme were already being discarded: the communications media were under pressure; certain journals had been banned; and at the same time nothing was done to stop 'the illegal distribution of other publications full of lies, that made people's blood boil' (an obvious reference to the Soviet publication *Zprávy*). On the other hand a bevy of Party politicians, including Bil'ak, Nový, Kolder, and Jakeš, criticised the leadership for weakness, improvisation, the under-estimation of rightist opposition, and for permitting signs of anarchy and disorientation in Party work. The former Minister of Culture, Karel Hoffman, claimed that the present leadership was incapable of dealing with the situation; right-wing forces had exploited the position, and proved that whoever ruled the country, it was not the Party Presidium.

The strength of the opposition apparently convinced the leadership that there was a real likelihood of their being swept aside in favour of the Stalinists. They therefore adopted the unorthodox plan of out-manoeuvring their opponents by a direct appeal to Brezhnev, who happened to be in Warsaw that day. On the evening of the 15th Dubček, Černík, and Husák slipped away to Warsaw, taking with them the draft of a compromise resolution they were prepared to put before the

CC meeting. The manoeuvre was entirely successful: Brezhnev received them affably; assured them of his continuing confidence in them; and approved the draft, which he hardly bothered to read. At four a.m. on the sixteenth the trio returned in triumph to Prague, and the same day they presented their motion before the meeting, where news of the secret deal was already circulating. The draft was adopted: the threat to change the leadership had been averted. But the price was a set of compromises which undercut the position of those supporting the continued implementation of the reform programme, and which eventually was to lead to the fall of the Dubček leadership itself.

The actual document[25] was vague and rambling in the traditional Party style; subject to varied interpretation, it could have meant much, or little. The main objectives of policy which it indicated were fairly predictable – the strengthening of Party unity; closer co-operation with the Soviet bloc; and firm implementation of the Party's leading role. Perhaps of greater significance was the preamble, which gave a retrospective survey of events since January. In this section a good deal of attention was devoted to the activities and influence of the mass media. It was alleged in the document that they had been infiltrated by right-wing, opportunist elements who had misused their position to confuse public opinion, blacken the image of the state and Party apparatus, and turn attention away from positive features of post-January policy. It claimed, in a palpable hit at the Stalinists, that 'their sectarian-dogmatic attitudes had played into the hands of anti-socialist elements, who had misused the democratisation process to work against the Party, via such organisations as K231, KAN, and the organisation of Social Democrats. In these manoeuvres the anti-socialist elements had been aided by the media, which had given them disproportionate publicity, e.g. the journal *Student*, which took up a more or less openly anti-communist line. Great attention would be paid henceforth to the behaviour of the media, whose proper role was to organise the citizens into implementing official policy, and to take a firm stand against all signs of bourgeois ideology:'

> The publishers bear the main responsibility for the correct orientation of the contents of what they publish, in accordance with the needs of the development of socialism. In cases where the workers in the information media do not respect the interests of the state, and of socialism, and the policy of their institutions, the appropriate organisational cadre conclusions must be drawn. The Czechoslovak Communist Party CC is

aware of the exceptional importance of the information
media in supporting policy, and it will pay close attention to
the trend they follow. It will establish political and cadre
conditions which favour this aim...

On his return to Slovakia Gustáv Husák also made a lengthy public
statement in which he gave his interpretation of the CC resolution:
because of his record he was already considered to be Dubček's likely
successor; and his interpretation accordingly carried significant
weight with the public. He claimed that post-January policies would
continue; there would be no return to the discredited policies of the
'fifties. On the other hand the altered situation since August had
compelled certain changes. There was now a law on censorship;
certain restrictions had been placed on publication and on the right
of assembly. Socialist legality would be protected; but it also would be
enforced: the Czechoslovak and the Slovak Communist Parties were
not going to submit to ultimatums and pressures applied by student
or any other associations:

> I should also like to mention the question of the mass media...
> The resolution of the Party CC states clearly that in this field,
> which is of extreme importance for forming public opinion
> and orientating the public on basic issues, the Party cannot
> renounce its decisive influence and the implementation of its
> leading role. This theoretical principle must now be applied
> to the practical sphere. Of course we do not intend to do this
> insensitively: we don't want to make journalists and such
> people into robots or executors of some illiterate orders. We
> want to reach an agreement with this wide front of mature
> workers on how to apply this line laid down by the Party com-
> mittees to every aspect of their work. We want to seek methods
> of co-operation, creativity, agreement; this is how we want
> to implement the Party's leading role. However, where we do
> not meet with goodwill; where there is no willingness to sup-
> port this line, we shall have to take cadre measures, and use
> other means to ensure the maintenance of the Party's leading
> role...[26]

In spite of the claim that the post-January course would continue,
and although the leadership remained in the hands of Dubček,[27]
suspicion was widespread that the era of reform was drawing to a
close. Freedom of the press was seen as the test of open politics, and

the threatening references to the communication media were received with deep disquiet. On November 16th students began a sit-in at the Faculty of Journalism at the Prague University: the student strike spread to other tertiary institutions throughout the Czech lands, and some Secondary Schools joined in.[28] Expressions of sympathy for the students came from many quarters – collective farms, factories, associations of intellectuals, and from the Minister of Education himself. The student action gained symbolic significance from its timing, the anniversary of the closing of Czech universities by the Nazis in 1939. Student demands included support for the April 68 Party Action Programme, and a speedy abolition of the censorship introduced since August. The fear that freedom of expression was to be further curtailed expressed itself in other manifestations. The Co-ordinating Committee for Creative Unions issued a public statement expressing grave disquiet at the trend of events. At factories signatures were collected for mass petitions in defence of press freedom.

Eyes were upon the Party chiefs to discover their real intentions. Would they supply the leadership to resist further Russian demands? or were they covering their submission by soothing but meaningless gestures? The crisis which might have been expected to produce an answer, passed without any certain indication. The leaders still seemed to be playing it both ways: to the protestors they showed understanding, and asked them for patience and understanding in return. To the Russians they showed just enough co-operation to allay their exasperation at the slow process of 'normalisation'. To those who remembered the similar tactics of the Czech Protectorate government thirty years before, this seemed a policy of hopeless drift: by concessions they were simply delaying a final capitulation to the threat of force, and buying time, when time was in fact working against them.[29] At the CC meeting certain personnel changes had been approved, which appeared to strengthen the position of the hard-liners. The big Four of the reform movement (Dubček, Svoboda, Černík, and Smrkovský), still held the initiative in their hands. But the foursome seemed to be falling apart under pressure: recent public statements by Svoboda and Černík rendered their position increasingly ambiguous. It was suspected that Smrkovský was Dubček's only reliable ally left in the inner Presidium, therefore rumours of Smrkovský's impending fall were received with grave concern. On December 11th a delegation left for Kiev at the invitation of the Soviet Politburo: Smrkovský was neither invited nor informed. On their return Smrkovský sought to know the reasons for his omission; and whether the question of his future had been discussed at Kiev with the Russians. He obtained only evasive replies, and drew appropriate conclusions.[30] His official authority rested mainly on his Presidency of the National Assembly; but with the forthcoming federalisation of the country's institutions a new Federal House of Assembly would come into being. A ready opportunity to ease Smrkovský out of his position thus appeared; he would simply not be appointed to the Presidency of the new House: this could be justified on the grounds that, with a Czech as Federal Premier, it would be reasonable to expect the appointment of a Slovak as Parliamentary President. The matter was regarded as delicate; and Smrkovský was expected to co-operate in putting through the changes, which meant in effect his own demotion. But Smrkovský declined to co-operate. In a bold gesture he issued a press statement that a recent medical check-up had happily confirmed that he was entirely fit to carry on his duties, and *did not intend to abandon them.*[31]

The Smrkovský question was now a matter of public knowledge and concern; his future was rightly interpreted as indicative of what was in store for the entire reform programme. Amid rising tension resolutions began pouring into Party HQ expressing support for him, and demanding that he continue in his position. On December 21st Dubček addressed the CC of the Slovak Party in an attempt to calm the situation. His speech, although intended to be conciliatory, contained ominous warnings that untold damage was being done by obstruction to the implementation of the November policy. The Party was facing a crisis, and impossible demands upon the leadership were forcing them towards the adoption of undesirable measures.[32] The crisis was made worse by a radio speech by Husák in which he violently attacked irresponsible agitators and anti-socialist elements, and named Smrkovský as the centre of a right-wing pressure group. In Slovakia a new and frightening element entered the situation when Smrkovský's name disappeared from the press; evidently he was the subject of a total ban in the media, and the first prominent figure since the time of Novotný to become a non-person. In Slovakia at least the Party seemed to have got the press under control.

Tension in Prague was high during the Christmas holidays, and the threat of a general strike hung over the country. A high Soviet delegation visited Prague for secret talks: on New Year's Day 1969 Dubček was in conference with the leader of the Soviet delegation until after midnight, and a special meeting of the full Presidium was called for the next day: it issued a general statement deploring threats of direct action, and condemned extremist pressures in the news media.

Smrkovský was now under intense pressure to end the crisis by a voluntary statement of submission. Dubček himself indicated that the situation was critical, and that a general strike would involve Soviet military action. Smrkovský finally submitted to pressure; in a public statement he announced that he was giving his support for a Slovak President of the Federal Assembly. He appealed for calm, and assured his supporters that the decision was his own, and asked the Unions not to take strike action. Thus the crisis was averted, and Smrkovský began his descent from the centre of power. The lesson was not lost on the public: the solidarity of the Big Four had been broken, and effectively Dubček was now isolated. His turn would not be long delayed.

A year had now passed since the advent of the reform team and the beginning of such high hopes, which had since faded into deep disillusion. The Smrkovský crisis had hardly died away when the public was convulsed by a totally unexpected and tragic development.

On January 16th 1969 a student, Jan Palach, as a mark of protest set himself on fire in the centre of Prague, on the Wenceslas Square. He died in hospital three days later. The act was undertaken without the knowledge or consent of the student organisations. Nevertheless they accepted the sacrifice as a true expression of their own feelings, and they identified themselves with his gesture. It was recognised on all sides as an act of the gravest consequences, a symbolic protest of youth against political compromise and betrayal: by its appeal to an absolute standard of ethics it renewed contact with the national tradition of the Hussites and their leader who had gone to the fire as a witness to conscience and truth.

Representatives of the Students Union met the Czech Premier and presented requests for publication of Palach's final note; for public recognition of his sacrifice; and for the granting of his demands, which were; the abolition of censorship and the banning of the Soviet journal *Zprávy*. The first two requests were granted; the third was refused. A tribute to the dead student was read over the radio by the veteran poet Závada:

> Jan Palach is dead. His death shocks us, as did his act. Let us bow our head before him with deep emotion and respect. He sacrificed his life because he knew no other way to express his feelings, and those of his friends. His was an act of desperation, but, at the same time an expression of the high heroism of the young. Yet by tragic self-sacrifice we achieve nothing.

Our entire history has been tragic, and if we have held our place on the stairway of history as a civilised nation, it is because we have always found a way out of hard situations by intelligence and determination. Not by passivity or evasion, not by sudden catastrophic solutions. I believe that our two peoples will find their way out of our present situation; and I believe that the young of this nation will light this way by their unsullied devotion to truth; by their fire and eagerness. But if we are to hold on to the end, we must not expend our energy fruitlessly. Perhaps our way will be harder and duller; but it is the only path that leads to our final goal.

Jan Palach is dead: and we shall never forget him. His act is unique in our history, and in its uniqueness it cannot be repeated. It is a tragic sacrifice at a time of tragedy.

When the funeral cortege of Jan Palach moved slowly through Prague, past throngs of silent mourners, the crowds and the mass emotion recalled the funeral of the President Liberator, T. G. Masaryk, thirty two years before. But in January 1969 men knew they were burying the hopes of the Prague Spring.

During the months which had elapsed since August the atmosphere in Czech public life had changed insensibly; the high note of national pride, discipline, and sacrifice had given way to calculation, scepticism, and resignation. Palach's symbolic gesture, with its agonising appeal to the nation's conscience shocked and shamed his elders. But in general its effect was not to inspire a new wave of resistance, but rather to illuminate the angry despair in which he had died, and in which others mourned him. His death was followed by discussion, protests, demonstrations: but the Czech sense of realism asserted itself, recognising that the cause of resistance was lost; and the price of continuing defiance was too high. The conservatives were quietly moving into positions of power; and men who had identified themselves with reform were adapting their views. Dubček remained: but his fall seemed to be only a matter of time.

It came in bizarre circumstances. At the end of March the Czecho-slovak ice-hockey team twice defeated their Soviet opponents in championship events. The triumph of David over Goliath was hailed in the Czech media with a joy tinged with open malice. In the centre of Prague, and in other towns, huge crowds vented glee and hatred in wild scenes in which Soviet soldiers and installations were attacked. Within forty-eight hours the incident sparked a crisis. Amid rumours

of a second Soviet intervention Marshal Grechko flew into Czechoslovakia after an emergency session of the Soviet Politburo. Grechko
presented himself not to the Czechoslovak government in Prague, but
to military HQ at Milovice, where he conferred at length with Czechoslovak officers. Prague was full of rumours that a military coup was
about to take place: Czech officers loyal to the Russians would seize
power and call for assistance from the Russians to put down the
'counter-revolution'. But Grechko travelled to Prague, and presented
to the government what was in effect an ultimatum: either they would
put their own house in order, or else the Russians would do it for them.
Submitting to pressure the Czechoslovak Presidium issued a statement in which they completely identified themselves with the Soviet
view of the situation, condemned 'anti-socialist and rightist forces'
as responsible for the crisis, and blamed Czech journals, including
Rudé právo, for their attitude. On the same day the government announced new stringent measures to control public order, foreshadowed a more drastic form of press censorship, and promised to bring
anti-socialist elements of society to justice. It seemed that crisis had
been averted once more at the price of these new acts of submission.
But it was only then that the real price became apparent. Suddenly,
fierce and hardly veiled personal attacks on Dubček were made, first
by Husák, then by President Svoboda himself. On April 14th new
Soviet air manoeuvres began over Czechoslovakia. Two days later
there took place a number of police raids, in which over a thousand
people were detained. A special meeting of the Party Central Committee was called for April 17th: at the meeting of the Central Executive
which preceded it, Dubček offered his resignation. A few hours sufficed to complete his fall. The CC meeting which appointed Gustáv
Husák in his place carried through further personnel changes which
ensured that the reform movement would no longer be a serious threat
to 'normalisation'. Among the new moves was the appointment of a
new editor to *Rudé právo*; the liquidation of the Party journal *Politika*;
the creation of a new Committee for Press and Information (censorship); and the banning of certain journals: they included *Listy* and
Reporter, the official voice of the Writers' and of the Journalists'
Union respectively. The authorities would henceforth have to worry less
about awkward questions or criticism. The popular dissident F. Kriegel was expelled from the Central Committee, then from the Party:
other well-known reformers soon followed, including eventually those
who, like Černík, had deserted Dubček to save themselves. A great
purge of Party membership was launched which was finally to reach a

fitting climax in the expulsion of Dubček himself from the party on which he had sought to set a more humanist image.

* * *

In surveying the literary output of the years 1967-69, in spite of the violent political convulsions, it is convenient to regard it as a single period with common features. The Russian invasion did not end the period of free expression and publication: the restrictions which appered in 1969 at first were aimed mainly at the mass information media, and it was not until nearly the end of 1969 that the heavy hand of political censorship fell on Czech creative literature.

After the turbulent events of 1967 the following two years were the freest in cultural affairs since 1948, and one might expect that this would have proved to be a golden age in Czech literature; but it would be a bold critic who would venture such a judgement. In fact the year 1968 was quite disappointing in its literary harvest. Various factors contributed to this result. The great changes at the centre of power in the early months meant that for a while there was a certain paralysis and disorganisation in cultural life at the official level. When it was clear that a wide measure of freedom was available, some writers actually delayed releasing manuscripts, or asked for them back from publishers in order to revise them. The Union of Czechoslovak Writers was struggling to regain the ground it had lost in the tussle with the authorities in 1967; and even after it won back control over its own publishing house and resumed publication of its own journals, endless energy was exhausted in cultural politics during the reform period. It seems ironic that after struggling for so many years to free literature from political pressure and for the right of artists to devote themselves entirely to creative work, when these conditions were at least fulfilled, so many writers found it necessary to divert their energies and use their influence within the political arena.

The pattern of publishing was also affected by another factor. During 1968 and 69 a number of books were published which had been written years before, but whose release had been delayed by censorship or by political considerations. Writers who had been on the black list, and whose work was little known to the reading public, now reappeared on publishers' lists: they included V. Renč, J. Zahradníček, and J. Palivec, who had been in serious trouble in the 'fifties; the critics V. Černý, and Z. Kalista; novelists J. Durych and F. Křelina; E. Hostovský and J. Čep, who had been living abroad for twenty years and had previously been denigrated as renegades.[33] In the 'fifties and early 'sixties publication programmes had been manipulated to victimize dissidents: now priority was given to those writers whom cultural politics had once helped to destroy. Early in 1970 the Institute of Czech Literature in Prague actually put on an exhibition of Czech books written abroad during the preceding two decades. It was a symbolic gesture, honouring the return of authors to a public from whom they had been forcibly separated in the recent past: by an irony of timing the exhibition coincided with the beginning of a new political campaign which would again drive the same writers from their native literature. At the same time as the reading public was resuming contact with formerly black-listed native authors, it was also making new contact with modern West European writers whose work had been hitherto taboo, and with dissident writers in the Soviet bloc, whose work now was able to appear freely in Prague. Thus the literary harvest of the 1968-9 period did not directly reflect current literary development: published material of the period shows a strange mixture of styles, fashions, and eras, so that it does not fit easily into any simple literary sequence. This feeling of incoherence is increased by the fact that so much of the writing of this period was of the nature of protest against a variety of prescriptions, imposed forms, and social taboos. A protest loses its force and much of its interest once the object of its attack is outdated: in the present case some of the objects had long been discredited, but the full force of the protest had been delayed by the mechanism of political control and censorship.

During the era of Novotný creative literature had dealt with sensitive social issues obliquely and via allegory. In the Dubček era the issues could be dealt with directly, so that a feature of the literature of the reform period was reportage and social documentation. In the field of politics the most striking example was the *Czech Black Book*. In the field of literary politics two works appeared, both of interest primarily to the literary historian. They were the official record of the *Proceedings of the IVth Writers Congress* of 1967,[34] and a book, *Writers and Power*, by the former editor of *Literární noviny*, Dušan Hamšík.[35] The *Proceedings* were published in a limited edition and in rather poor format: it was obviously a rush job by the Writers Union publishing house. The more sensational speeches had been known, and had been circulating in Prague for some time, but this was the first time the complete record was available to Czech readers. Excerpts from the proceedings had appeared in Paris in the exile journal *Svědectví*: one effect of the official publication of the *Proceedings* was to confirm in impressive fashion the accuracy of *Svědectví*'s sources of information and to confirm the credibility of its other documentation. *Writers and Power* was a readable account of the struggle between the writers' organisation and the authorities, culminating in the official takeover of the Union newspaper in 1967. The book thus supplied the background to the *Proceedings* of the Congress, and should be read in conjunction with them. Hamšík prefaced his book with a brief account of its origin and publication. It was finished in July 1968, was scheduled for printing in August, and for release in December. The last issue of *Literární listy* to appear (in August 68) announced that the next issue would begin the serialisation of the book. When Hamšík returned from his summer holidays, the typescript was still in the publishing house, but the building was occupied by Soviet troops and the editors were debarred from it. The book was finally published in 1969.

During the reform period the rehabilitation tribunals were sitting in Prague, former political prisoners were claiming their rights, and journals were publishing frightening revelations of brutality in the Stalinist camps of the 'fifties. At the same time a crop of creative literature appeared which centred on the theme of prison or camp life; most of the books had been written in the preceding decade or in the early 'sixties. They included a book of poems by Jan Zahradníček, entitled *Four Years*.[36] In 1956, after five years imprisonment, the poet was released to sit by the death-bed of his two daughters: after their funeral he was returned to prison to serve out the remaining four years of his sentence: he died soon after his final release. It is the four years of his resumed captivity which are the subject of this posthumous collection. It was edited by Bedřich Fučík, formerly an editor of the Melantrich publishing house, an author of the dialogue between Catholics and Marxists, and himself a fellow-prisoner. In 1969 Bedřich Fučík published his own interpretation of Zahradníček's post-war poetry in a collection of essays, *Collection of Twenty five*,[37] edited by Václav Černý.

Much less famous, but hardly less striking, was a slim collection of poems by an almost unknown writer, *Madian Day*[38] by F. D. Merth. The book was beautifully illustrated by a photographic assemblage of symbolic objects, and was edited by Zdeněk Kalista, who had shared Zahradníček's captivity. The poems reflect the lonely introspection, the strange dreams, and the hallucinations of a poet totally withdrawn from the society of men into an inner exile of the spirit. The book was privately printed outside Prague, distributed to a select circle of readers, and remains a scarce and touching memorial to this strange period of literary intermission.

Among the many prose works on the theme of political imprisonment a few may be singled out as of special interest: the genre brings together writing of varying literary quality but of shared importance in the record of social and intellectual history. *The Escape*[39] by J. Hejda, on life in the notorious Leopoldov prison, can be compared to *Colour of Sun and Night,*[4] by L. Reinerová; this pre-war communist had been arrested in 1950, and released after Stalin's death: her account is set in the framework of the police interrogation during which (as in the case of the legendary drowning man) she relives a lifetime of experience. *Prisoner of the President*[41] by V. Škutina, a popular TV scenario writer, was the account of his arrest and imprisonment in 1962. At a time when political tensions were relaxing and the 'Novotný liberalisation' era was getting under way, Škutina was charged with defaming the President by saying publicly that he was an ass. (Škutina was released after serving ten months, on the grounds that his words did not constitute a legal offence.) During the reform period Škutina was a prominent television personality; and in April 1969 he received an award from the Ministry of Culture for his work in the field of TV drama. In July 1969 his book was published by a local press in Northern Bohemia: in a short preface Škutina explained that he had at last decided to publish the work, to document the dangers of a police regime at a time when political dangers were again on the increase. During the same month, while Škutina was vacationing abroad in Jugoslavia with his family, he was prosecuted, and on his return arrested. Together with the journalist J. Lederer he became one of the first victims of renewed repression in the literary field.[42]

A writer who specialised in the literature of the camps is Karel Pecka, who was himself arrested in 1949 for contributing to an illegal newspaper, and sentenced to eleven years imprisonment: he was released in 1959, and his stories of camp life circulated on the underground distribution network in Prague. In the years 1967-8 three books of his appeared, *Fever, What Men Die of*, and *The Great Solstice.*[43] Pecka prefaced the book *Fever* with a quotation from Shakespeare's *Romeo and Juliet*:

> For naught so vile that on the earth doth live
> But to the earth some special good doth give,
> Nor aught so good but strained from that fair use
> Revolts from true birth, stumbling on abuse:
> Virtue itself turns vice, being misapplied,
> And vice sometime's by action dignified.

The novel traces in parallel the progress of two different, but related ordeals. A prisoner, serving a life sentence for attempting to cross the frontier illegally and killing a guard, escapes: his desperate situation leads him on into further violence which costs the life of three more people before he is finally gunned down by police. His terrible ordeal outside the camp is matched by that of his fellow-prisoners within, who suffer the consequences arising from his escape. Prisoners and guards alike are caught in a web of tragic experience from which there is no escape. The author added an explanatory comment to his novel: '*Fever* is an essay upon man's situation at a time of great tension... Questions of humanity and inhumanity, fate and ethics, truth and lies, the interchangeability of roles and aims, of the meaning of life and death...'

The camp literature published in the reform period included at least one work which is likely to become a classic of modern Czech prose. It was *Cold Sunlight*[44] by the author Jiří Mucha, a diary of prison life based on scraps written in the mines six hundred metres below ground and carefully concealed during his confinement in the fifties. 'It is difficult to write about the twentieth century without having been behind bars,' reflected Mucha. The life of the modern political prisoner found its aptest recorder in this sensitive and gifted artist whose childhood had been spent among the masters of Czech Art Nouveau, and whose adult activity had put him near the centre of European creative writing. *Cold Sunlight* is without sequential plot; the thread is the mental world of the imprisoned intellectual, moving between the impact of prison routine, memories of childhood experience, and recollections of literature. The physical environment which frames his life is harsh, but not lacking in moments of memorable experience:

> On the floor above us were the condemned cells. The inmates wore clogs; they could never sleep, and all night long you could hear them pacing to and fro; the clogs went 'clap-clap; clap-clap'. From dusk until dawn. Then the clogs stumped along the corridor, down the stairs, to execution. We knelt down and prayed. The whole prison. Yes; it was very beautiful.

Mucha was held for a time in solitary confinement: during these endless days he sought to escape into dreams, to persuade himself that the daylight was unreal, and that only in dreams was he living a true life. There were strange fantasies:

One day I was condemned to leave my grave. That is probably the way it is in an organisation which is concerned with re-embodying the spirit. A committee – three figures in black gowns sitting in permanent session since creation – re-members: We still have x here. What to do with him? How long has he been lying in that grave? – A year – Has anyone got his sin record? – I might be able to find it, but it will take some time. – No need to hold things up. Can one assume that he pulled the wings off flies? – One can assume that any mortal has pulled off a fly's wings at some time. – Good enough. Six years purgatory!

Released from solitary, Mucha was faced with tasks that exceeded the limits of his physical endurance. But at least he was restored to human society. The prison was richly variegated in its selection of human types: lawyers rubbed shoulders with pickpockets; ministerial private secretaries swung a pick next to violent criminals; ordinary factory workers toiled beside drug-pushers and burglars. The active life of prison work was in some way a liberation compared to the life of those who still awaited their fate, sometimes for months or years:

Pankrác prison is made up of cubicles where people await their trial as if in a sterile solution, in small polished test-tubes, neatly numbered and arranged side by side in a huge experimental rack... There they wait: nothing is done with them; they are fed on minimal rations to keep the body functioning; and everything around them is continually cleaned, as in a laboratory. But they are not people. Only embryos in glass jars. Tens, hundreds, thousands of embryos, labelled with number and date. But those in detention prison pending investigation, those in grey cells with cold stone walls, they are practically dead – dead except for the heart. There is silence, utter silence everywhere; except that three times a day the lock rattles and the door opens wide enough for the corpse to reach out for a plate of food. It is deposited on the floor by invisible hands, like an offering at the entrance to a tomb. In their grey, denim uniforms, their eyes blind-folded, the dead are walked silently down the corridors, there and back, like blind men. No one brought here is allowed to see more than his four walls and himself. Everything else for him is darkness and groping.

Mucha's book resembles other examples of Czech camp literature in that it is less an exercise in horror or anger as the documentation of an episode in the nation's past, in the hope that a new generation will not have to re-enact it. It is natural to compare *Cold Sunlight* with Solzhenitsyn's classic *A Day In The Life of Ivan Denisovich.* The physical conditions described are similar; but the comparison reveals how different is the background and orientation of the two writers. Unlike his Russian counterpart Mucha is the complete West European intellectual. In thoughts he retraces his steps across France and England. The world of Penguin New Writing is like home to him; Lehman and Lawrence Durrell are his fellow spirits. He reads postcards from friends on the Riviera reproaching him for neglecting them, reviews of his work in the *New Statesman* and the *Times Literary Supplement.* In mood he is philosophical, sceptical, almost nonchalant; he makes few moral judgements; he is never resigned to martyrdom: in the prison he finds unplumbed depths of broad humour in the Schweik-like characters about him, and macabre fun in the paradoxical situations. Like Solzhenitsyn he shows how men confined behind wire can draw together into some kind of human fellowship; so that the wire comes to signify a defence, protecting a haven of hope and security from the great, destructive storm which rages outside:

> Sourek is due for release, and this morning, as so often happens, he suddenly got depressed. All at once life outside appears in its full nakedness, insecurity and cruelty. Prison is a full stop after weeks, months, or years of pitiless chase. Those who come inside have escaped a world which, incomprehensibly to them, had been trying to destroy them with all the means at its disposal. A sense of injustice had alternated with a sense of helplessness; all attempts to escape the crushing pressures had been in vain; and in the end everything had collapsed. Their homes had been swept away; their property confiscated down to the last overcoat; their families flung into misery; until at last the prison gate closed on the consummated tragedy.
>
> Then comes despair. And after despair, the acceptance of the inevitable. And finally the harassed human being finds himself in a haven of peace and oblivion, in the barbed wire cage of the camp. Here is the end of struggle and responsibility: everything that happens is happening outside; and nothing but indistinct echoes reach across the wire; here ceases all fear of tomorrow, the next hour, the next moment.

It is not easy to assign *Cold Sunlight* to any literary genre; it shares the qualities of reportage and creative literature: both in theme and style it is at home in the Czech writing of the 'sixties, for the fantastic mental world of the prisoner does not detract from its essential realism. In this, and in its strange interaction of human types and values, Mucha is close to Hrabal. In a book *Atrocities and Legends,*[45] Hrabal claims that the final piece in the collection, 'Atrocity on a public execution', is a collage, formed of extracts from anonymous letters interlarded with his own thoughts, which often agree with the insults and exceed them. He finds it natural, indeed inspiring, that his work should make readers' blood boil. He muses on the fate of a criminal, Mr. Alois Polach, sentenced to death in 1966 for brutal child murder and the rape of old women; if he, Bohumil Hrabal, were publicly executed instead, it would be a revolutionary moment for the nation from which to date its trend to genuine socialism. It would also be an exciting new experience for him, satisfying his insatiable thirst for new encounters amid the rich tapestry of life:

> What a terrible shame I didn't ride from Poříčany that day
> on the track car into the mist. They sent a shunting engine
> after it with a goods van, and the van ran into the car from
> behind, and the two workmen on the treadle flew into the air
> in a loop and landed on the bank and rolled into the ditch.
> But the goods van made mincemeat of the car, and the fore-
> man hung over the condensor like a towel over an oven. So the
> engine rode out of the mist, and a carter waved his whip to
> draw the engine driver's attention to his peculiar passenger.
> Pity it wasn't me hanging there over the condensor instead of
> the foreman. What a shame! It would have been the experi-
> ence of a lifetime!

In his strange situations and paradoxical combinations of elements Hrabal shows a leaning towards surrealist art, together with a rich propensity for macabre humour. In Hrabal we find not merely the genuine language of the Prague streets but the folk literature of the 'sixties. The writers of his generation generally rejected bombastic rhetoric; Hrabal goes further, and shows scepticism of 'literary' literature, including his own. A leitmotif of Czech writing of the 'sixties is scepticism of the values proclimed both in official aesthetics and in the social area. Writers spent a great deal of energy in analysing and exposing pseudo-value systems, and false trails, the destructive effects of ideological systems, and the disintegration of human relationships in an alienated environment.

Scepticism expressed via the medium of absurd literature was re-presented by Ivan Vyskočil, whose *Little Plays*[46] are in fact stories in which the audience is invited to participate in working out the action. A situation is outlined, then analysed; characters and behaviour form the subject of free speculation and exercises for the reader. Alienation to the extent of loss of identity is a favourite subject with which Vy-skočil plays. A person suffers from schizophrenia resulting in the separation of his human self from his official functioning; the latter acquires authority, and the human self adapts to its image. The shadow wins independence, and breaks away from its owner; the behaviour pattern of the shadow diverges sharply from the owner's, and the latter seeks to imitate it lest the discrepancy awake unwelcome attention. In the *Secret, secret agent* a man ceases to recognise his own self, and sees no anomaly in shadowing him. A serious devotion to observing the expectations of social convention leads a person in-to the loss of his original self, so that only the official image remains. Writer, actor, and psychologist, Ivan Vyskočil was one of the founders of the Prague literary cabarets, through which Prague theatre began to live again in the late 'fifties. In his later work theatre became anti-theatre, and the gay satire of earlier days became an intellectual challenge in a guise of loose improvisation.

Scepticism towards the value system of his own society is revealed in merciless detail in the works of Vladimír Páral: a Czech critic once said of him[47] that in his books he threw more light on the development of his society than can be gleaned from all the work of statisticians, historians, and economists. Páral set out to write a series of five novels based on the reality of industrial life in Czechoslovakia in the sixties: the early volumes, *Trade Fair of fulfilled Wishes* (1963) and *Private Whirlwind* (1965), were followed by *Catapult* (1967) and *Lovers and Murderers* (1969).[48] The environment in which Páral set his novels was thus similar to that of the hero-of-labour construction novels of the Stalinist period; the forced optimism of the latter was matched by the alienated horror of Páral's fictional world. His characters, usually technicians, are as uniform, colourless and uninteresting as the goods which they help to mass produce. In fact their efforts in this regard are minimal; intense rationalisation of production has left them with little gainful work, and the typical technician is a parasite who fills in his time with pseudo-activity. In his books Páral seeks to portray *homo statisticus*, the compilation of consumer research, a person who maximises undifferentiality so as to bring his level of dis-cordant human individuality into the category of zero. The stunning boredom of his contribution to the industrial ant-heap is matched by the utter triviality of his private life as a unit of consumption. In the third volume of the series Páral's hero becomes self-conscious of his frustrating position and seeks means to correct it. He tries to jump off the moving belt of his existence and to find an emotional satisfaction in sex. This modern Don Juan succeeds in siting a repertoire of lovers along the path of his commercial journeys. Regrettably he soon discovers a horrible resemblance between the mistresses themselves and the wife at home. In any case he knows no other technique of communication save that of his own environment, from which he was seeking to escape. If sex can offer no way out of frustration, perhaps worldly success may do so. But here too his intensified pseudo-activity serves only to illuminate its frustrating futility. There is no escape from the life assigned to a producer-consumer unit, whose mentality is formed by commercial ads and whose outlook is the product of abbreviated slogans. He retains some individuality via his dissatisfaction, and graduates into the status of a cardboard rebel: but he lacks the initiative ever actually to do anything. He plays with the idea of total destruction; but the initiative would have to come from outside, and he prays for a miracle; when heaven grants him the catapult of his dreams, the end of our depressing hero is worthy of his mismanaged life. The literature of industrial alienation reached a peak in the novels of Páral: after his work it was difficult to believe that the socialist-realist construction novels of the 'fifties could ever be revived except as a caricature of themselves.

If Páral summed up current disillusion with industrial life and the human relationships it engenders, it was Ivan Klíma who, in a novella published in 1969, dealt finally with the theme of judicial murder and the corruption of justice. His book *A Ship named Hope*[49] included in addition to the story which gave the book its name, a shorter piece entitled *The Jury*. For three days the jurors hear a crushing indictment of the accused; the weight of evidence against him makes his condemnation seem a mere formality. But the jury includes an archivist (the narrator) whose profession has made him sensitive to legal injustices of the past, to witch-burnings, forced confessions, and political murders. When the prosecutor calls for the death penalty, the archivist realises that he has reached a crisis of conscience. On the last day of the hearing the accused fails to appear, and one member of the jury is missing. The irregularity of the proceedings together with mounting doubts lends courage to the jury to demand to see the accused; and eventually the President of the court bows to their wishes, and conducts them to his cell. He is already dead; 'shot while trying to escape'. A member of the jury whips off the blanket and finds the head severed from the shoulders ('Guillotined while trying the escape'). The jury are now invited to reach a verdict. As the sentence has already been carried out anyway, the question has become purely a moral problem. The verdict of the jury could make no possible difference to the fate of the victim; their verdict was needed simply to put the seal on a formal process of murder; the law courts now appeared in their true function, as an exhibition of power by the rulers. A verdict of Not guilty would be regarded as an assault on the fabric of authority. One by one the jurors are pressured into submission; the archivist is the last to vote, knowing that his obstinate resistance cannot save the victim, but only ruin himself. With a supreme effort the conquers his fear, and pronounces his verdict; Not guilty. The trial is over; the jury depart. In the street the archivist is confronted by the President of the court. It was an awkward moment:

> He smiled faintly... 'I suppose you feel good now. I imagine you feel sublime.'
> I thought I detected a sneer in his words.
> 'I am glad I did not contribute to the confirmation of the sentence', I said painfully, 'and so approve that premature execution.'
> He said: 'I am surprised you use the words *execution* and *sentence*'. He looked round in case there was anybody listening; then with a smile, as if imparting a secret, almost sweetly, he said: 'It happened, after all, before you jurors came to a verdict. So from the legal angle...' He smiled again. 'But you know how it is. One should call things by their correct names. At least, speaking in confidence, and before one's conscience. Yes,' he said in his quiet unruffled voice,... 'but I understand you. Each of us has a different role to play over the dead. The combined effect is what we jurists call *justice*. All, that is, except for that young man, of course. He got it into his head that, if he's innocent, someone else must have... But you know anyway.' He smiled quietly, and moved away with short steps.

It was the smile of the President which brought the archivist to a realisation of the situation. His struggle with conscience, his preoccupation with honour, with truth, and justice: it was all properly a part of the process of "*justice*"; the man was dead; nothing was changed; the gesture which had seemed so great and had been purchased at so high a risk, was as futile as it was socially unimportant. All he had done was to prove his right to *eccentricity* in Kafka's Prague.

During the reform period situations which had been familiar in literature in parable form, now appeared direct; and this demystification of theme can be compared to Hrabal's realism in language. When everything could be openly said and printed, the use of the symbol and the parable become unnecessary. But the habit of use was so ingrained that the audience did not cease to search for allegory even when none was intended by the writer: readers were also aware that among the books now appearing were many which had been written long ago and which had been suppressed for their daring qualities. The advent of demystified literature did not prevent the public from seeking to decipher what they still saw as parables. As an example may be cited Václav Kaplický's novel *The Witch Hunt*. [50] This story of eighteenth century Moravia fell within the framework of Kaplický's cycle of historical novels, and had actually been published as long ago as 1963. But when a decision was taken in 1968 to film the story, the thematic material of the Inquisition, faked trials with forced confessions, and the hideous effects of dogmatic ideology enforced by terror, inspired a general belief that the *Witch Hunt* was concerned with other trials and other dogma.

In 1968 one of the successes of the stage in Prague was a play by the Czech lyric poet F. Hrubín; the play was entitled *Oldřich and Božena* or *Bloody plot in the Czech lands*. [51] According to the legend Prince Oldřich puts away his noble wife Jutta for her failure to give him a son, and takes a peasant girl Božena, who conceives a child by him. To avenge the insult to Jutta, and to prevent the growth of a native Czech dynasty the German Emperor sends to Bohemia a disguised agent. The theme is set in the opening words of the play: 'I came to this country to prevent the birth of a child.' The old sentimental story was presented by Hrubín to his modern audience as the relentless pressure of external power upon Czech leaders, the deliberate attempt by outsiders to sow division among Czechs, the use of threats and violence to prevent the birth of a new hopeful element, linking old Czech traditions with the native stock. At the end of the play the Prince sets on fire the woods around the palace; the flames destroy the would-be murderers; and the Bohemian kingdom, liberated from enemy threats, can move forward towards a more hopeful future. In 1968 the temptation for Hrubín's audience to take his play allegorically was apparently irresistible. [52]

In 1969 another Czech poet, Jiří Šotola, published a novel, *The Society of Jesus*,[53] which few readers could interpret as anything but a parable, whose impact was enhanced by its mature restraint and poetic artistry. The book was set in the eighteenth century when, according to the traditional view, the defeated Czech nation was forced to submit to an imposed religious ideology, and entered its darkest age of national humiliation.

In a cold cell an aged Jesuit stands whispering his penitence before the cross, in the uttermost depths of shame and despair for his life's work: What could have gone so terribly wrong, so that the road he once chose out of self-denial and idealism had led him into a labyrinth where he had lost his way forever?

Thirty years before, the young Father had come to the house of the wealthy widow Countess Maria Maximiliana to be her confessor: it was the mission laid upon him by the Order. It was some time before he realised the true nature of this mission. Although she was still young, it was his task to prepare her not for life, but for death – a pious death with the blessing of the powerful Brotherhood, which demanded from her, penitence, self-abasement, obedience, her spirit, her mind and will, all she was, and all she had. A strange bond develops between the two lonely people – the watcher and the watched, the priest and his victim, as years pass, and they grow old together, each repressing and concealing the timid urge to rebellion which occurs to them with decreasing frequency. Tortured by doubts, misgivings, and guilt, but bound by his oath, of total obedience to the Brotherhood, the Father carries out his mission, driving the Countess inexorably, into surrendering more and more of her possessions and her will.

There was a time when the Father had believed that a way could be found out of his dilemma. When men of goodwill gained high office in the Order, then the mistakes of the past could be corrected. His hopes centred on the young and talented Father Tanner, who became Provincial of the Order in the Czech lands. But in the ascent to power Tanner himself had changed. When the Father, in a final hopeless bid to save himself, came to beg for understanding and help, Tanner, whose mind was on more important things, could hardly bother to listen:

> Father Provincial, our work at Košumberk is senseless, a snake eating its own tail. It does nothing for the people. They are afraid. They are silent, indifferent; they want to survive. That is the sum total of our achievement. We no longer take

soldiers with us; we have become soldiers. We win victories. We have power, authority, property. And we have nothing... We have ruined the Countess's life. She gave us everything we asked for. And in return we have destroyed her... I shall never forgive myself. We have to start again from the beginning. Stop while there is still time. Return to the days before we had power, but when we still had truth...

The answer of the Provincial was brutally forthright: Father Had was already a marked man; his doubts were known within the Brotherhood: Tanner himself could be compromised by his visit. From Father Had the Order demanded obedience, zeal, his life, conscience, spirit and freedom:

If we order you to kill, you will kill. The Order alone knows what is, and what is not, a sin. We have been indulgent with you long enough. Now we shall be firm; we shall crush your bones. Those are the demands of the Order. Will you resist?... Stop this futile worrying about the folk at Košumberk: Whether they are silent, or not silent. If they want to live, or die. What does it matter? Everything is futile, in the end is death anyway. There is no sense, only the Last Judgement. And the glory of God. And the victory of the Church. Even if its victory were to be over a world in flames, and mankind annihilated...

Father Had is aware that the more successfully he carries out the behest of the Brotherhood, the more harm he inflicts on those to whom he ministers. But he is bound to absolute obedience, and can contemplate no existence outside the rigid regime of his Order. To its glory he builds a chapel; then a Residence, so that more Jesuits can join him, and help to smell out heresy. The authority of the Jesuits now extends all over the region. A feeble attempt at defiance is ruthlessly punished by the headsman and the gibbet. The victory of the counter-reformation is complete in the area; heresy is rooted out; the Czech people conform to an authority derived from Rome.

Father Had's crowning achievement is the construction of a splendid new church which will dominate the countryside. While the serfs labour upon it, a great fire destroys their homes. But although they now have nowhere to lay their heads, they continue to work on the church. Terrified by the warnings of God's vengeance for heresy, they spend their last energies on the monumental structure which is the symbol of their oppression. Seeing his fellow-countrymen so totally cowed and humiliated Father Had reflects that perhaps it was their survival from the flames which had undone them. It was the relentless, the irresistible will to *survive* on any terms, which had broken their spirit, and rewarded their conformity with tears and abasement.

Years of utter obedience to incomprehensible orders and senseless discipline reduced Father Had to a pliant tool of the Order; but unfortunately for him, he neither lost his doubts, nor attained to cynicism. Retaining his humanity, he destroyed himself. When he at last fell under the open displeasure of the Brotherhood, he was supplanted and put under the command of the dutiful Brother who had been planted upon him as a spy. At last the Father had become a victim of the pitiless mechanism of which he had been a component, and whose face had become his nightmare.

Above the quiet Czech village rose the powerful, vaulted structure which attested to a life's work in the service of the Brotherhood and of Rome. Above the Czech peasants, above their fallen aristocracy, towered the splendidly adorned church, like a vast heap of futility, dwarfing the crushed folk who lay in the shadow of its terrible magnificence.

It was natural that Šotola's readers should see in his novel a parable of their present situation. Once more a great ideological movement had taken the wrong path; a church which in the search for power had lost its faith, would demand from its cowed subjects an outward show of assent to its tired rituals and empty litanies. The old mantle of eighteenth century Catholicism had fallen upon the communists, who once had been followed as the hope of the future. The relentless cycle of Czech history seemed to be repeating itself in a further instance. In 1968, as in 1938, the Czech nation had been abandoned by world opinion and betrayed by its allies: ironically in 1968 it was the new liberators who had become the new oppressors.

Amid the bitterness of disillusion it seemed hardly to be noticed how long was the interval of freedom which reigned between the Soviet invasion and onset of darkness. It was 1970 before the great purge in public life began. It was a purge which swept away over half a million ordinary Party members, and removed from positions of influence all those suspected of liberalist leanings and all who refused to pay lip service to the new imposed orthodoxy, which included a denunciation of the reform leadership as 'right-wing opportunists', and expressions of gratitude to the USSR for its 'fraternal intervention'. The purge involved a massive reshuffle of personnel, as new men moved into influential positions. There was naturally a great lack of suitable people, as an overwhelming majority of Party leaders were compromised with the reform movement, and the new ruling group was forced to fall back on elements they might have preferred not to use, in particular men long discredited by their Stalinist past. Nevertheless the machinery of administration ran on, without interruption, as the new appointees took over the sensitive areas of Security, Police, Armed Services, Justice, etc. Only in the cultural sector did continuity break down. There almost all the leading figures had identified themselves positively with reform, and in most cases they refused to recant, even under cajolement and pressure. The Writers Union declined to purge itself, to disclaim its opposition to the occupation, or to reject its elected leaders. In the end the Union was expelled from the National Front; its premises were taken over; and as an organisation it was officially disbanded. Books were banned; libraries purged; the literary journals liquidated; university departments were closed down. Writers, artists, scientists, and intellectuals of all kinds who failed the loyalty tests were fired, and prevented from further employment in any cultural capacity; a few were arrested; some left the country; most relapsed into silence. In due course a brand new Union was created of willing collaborators; but few writers of stature cared to be associated with them. The administration of the cultural sector passed back into the care of men of the 'fifties: discredited in the 'sixties as Stalinists, they returned in the 'seventies as agents of re-Stalinisation.

The return of the old guard could inspire little public confidence in the wisdom or sincerity of the new Party leadership; those who saw themselves as a manipulated mass, subjected and deprived, found in the 1968 leadership and its champions both martyrs, and symbols of freedom. Nevertheless disillusion suggested that the high hopes of 1968 had been unreal and romantic. So, as cultural repession hardened and voices of criticism were silenced one by one, the impetus to defiance died away, and the feeling of hopelessness and apathy increased. But too much had been said to be easily forgotten. The Czech writers had claimed for themselves the hard role of conscience of the nation, and had sought to justify the claim by their efforts. After 1970 they lost their public, but in its eyes they retained their role: so compelling was the silence which fell upon Czech literature that all the beating drums of orchestrated propaganda did not suffice to drown its impact.

It was winter in Prague; and this time it seemed as if the spring would never return.

XII

Politics and Literature

A history of European literature based on the developing role and status of the writer in his society would show great vicissitudes. The earliest Classical tradition reveals the artist as a hired entertainer, who sings to his hosts marvellous tales which link their past to the immortals and reflect back to his noble audience their view of themselves. He is completely dependent upon their pleasure and hospitality; respected for his age and talent, he nevertheless occupies a place at table not far removed from that of the wandering beggar. But within two centuries art has become an accomplishment of the Ionian aristocracy: needing no patron, Sappho sings to please her salon of cultivated friends, and to express herself. In Athens Solon addresses his audience with authority, accepting without question the role of spiritual guide and political leader: at Delphi the anonymous priestess of Apollo recites in His name oracles in verse which her noble supplicants receive with reverence, as words of holy inspiration. Later, in Rome, imported Greek slaves transmit to their haughty masters the literature of what is already a decaying society across the sea. Soon Roman aristocrats are amusing themselves by penning accomplished verses addressed to their friends: it was a consummate stylist and a connoisseur of poetry who led his troopers across the Rubicon. But with the advent of the Augustan Principate the status of the writer begins to decline: soon he is the servant – the honoured servant – of a powerful and ferocious Establishment. Later there is book-burning and the silencing of inconvenient voices: soon the Emperor Domitian is to preside over a cultural desolation.

Czech writers of the twentieth century inherited a tradition which accorded enormous prestige to their profession. The revival of the Czech nation in the preceding century had been based upon the revival of a national Czech culture, for it was the Czech language which was the determinent of the nation. Paradoxically, as European culture became more cosmopolitan and international, and as the idea of *national* culture became ideologically less meaningful, so to the Czech nation-builders their own national culture became ideologically vital. History gave to the Czech writers a great opportunity, and they accepted with gratitude and enthusiasm the role of standard bearers of their nation and keepers of her conscience. Once the idea of the nation-state had been realised in practice by the proclamation of the Czechoslovak Republic in 1918, the political importance of the writers declined: but they were disinclined to relinquish a status which they had become accustomed to regard as their natural right. What had now become the older generation of writers still saw themselves as nation builders; while the youngest generation of writers saw themselves rather as leaders of rebellion against attempts to reassert the discredited values of the pre-war world. Reacting against petty Czech nationalism they sang the Internationale, and wrote upon their banners the slogans of the Third International. But older and younger, conservatives and revolutionaries, accepted the idea of the poet as social leader, and this illusion was assisted by the special conditions of Czech public life. Seeing themselves for so long as a small threatened community amid an alien sea, the Czechs have evolved a close and inward looking national consciousness: the language barrier limits the range of distribution of their literature: the national capital Prague has preserved a somewhat parochial quality, in which there is an intricate and apparently all-embracing network of personal inter-relationships which make it impossible to keep a secret or to avoid becoming involved in the affairs of other people. Prague has some affinities with the closed society of the classical *polis*, in which the artist and his public are in constant and intimate confrontation. This may serve at times to diminish the respect of the public for the writer, but it does not allow it to forget him.

It is possible to argue that Czech tradition and circumstances have in recent times tended to exaggerate the social importance of the creative writer; this was especially so in conditions of stress. During the Nazi occupation resistance to Germanisation was regarded as a national duty, and the preservation of the national culture was its symbol. After the liberation, and during the transitional years between 1945 and 48, when the country balanced between East and West, the cultural traditions and orientation of the Czech people became an important public issue. At that time the Communist Party leaders were playing an astute game for power, and the allegiance of the intelligentsia was of vital consequence both to them and to their opponents. The latter were at a disadvantage in that they were neither united among themselves, nor did they have any plan or wish, to *mobilise* the intelligentsia in their cause. The Communists on the other hand had no such inhibitions, and used great efforts to win the allegiance of artists and intellectuals. While some Party leaders held a liberal, co-operative attitude towards the intellectuals, others persisted in regarding them as a privileged minority willing to lend themselves as a tool of either the bourgeoisie or the proletariat. Consequently they could not be trusted, and as soon as conditions permitted, it would be necessary to bring them firmly into line via administrative sanctions and organisation.

The immediate post war period saw a rapid deterioration of international relations and a sharp polarisation of influence between East and West in Europe. By 1948 Czechoslovakia was the only remaining member of the Soviet bloc which was not directly under the control of the Communist Party. After February, when the Czechoslovak Communists had at last taken over, the defection of the Jugoslavs from the Cominform and the apparent drift towards war faced the Czech leaders with a series of crisis, and accelerated the pace of their ruthless internal measures of control. Every aspect of public life was politicised: the conscious realisation that government derived from public acceptance as well as from the organisation of resources, alliances, police and Security organs, pushed the authorities into taking a hard line with the intelligentsia, whose efforts in the sphere of public relations were of such importance to the struggling regime. The duties of the writers in the social process were clearly mapped out for them by Party pundits like Gustav Bareš. It was the duty of the writers to *interpret* their age by clarifying the vital issues and chanelling thought in a progressive direction; to *educate* the public by clearing away the remnants surviving from the past era of Fascism and bourgeois conservatism, and by assisting in social change and ethical revaluation; to assist in *creating* the new age of socialism by building the new socialist culture. Thus began the imposition of the disastrous *command plan* for culture. The *mobilisation* of writers and intellectuals was a well-chosen term; for the whole process preserved an atmosphere of wartime pressure. The fears of neo-Nazi counter-attack, of international capitalist intervention, and of deviationist treachery from within, were deliberately fostered by a deafening public relations campaign, as if the aim were to re-create the Russian post-revolutionary era of the wars of intervention. In such an atmosphere any attempt at liberal utterance was not only useless, but dangerous, and among the early victims of this hysterical campaign were those who had helped to inspire it.

The passage of time showed a widening discrepancy between the stated socialist ideals for culture, and the reality of the command plan.

The ideals included the democratisation of culture by returning it to its natural owner and audience (the proletariat), and by establishing a closer relationship between the creative artist and his audience. This was regarded officially as an important part of the building of socialism, and the social commitment of the writer to this goal was expected. But practice soon revealed that the commitment of the writer was demanded for narrower and much more controversial aims. After the exposure of the Titoist heresy, and the imposition of the Soviet model on all the satellite states, the idea of a specific Czechoslovak road to socialism itself became a heresy, and the cultural sector was mobilised to proclaim it as such. The idea of a Czech national culture had become a dubious and dangerous concept: but it was this idea that the writers had traditionally done so much to foster, and it was their role as its champions to which they owed so much of their prestige and influence. At the same time the lowering of the iron curtain and the deliberate curtailing of Czechoslovakia's links with the West tended towards the provincialisation of her culture; the artist was liable to find himself suspected not only of 'petty nationalism', but also of 'cosmopolitanism'. After living for so long under alien domination, the Czech writers had a tradition of championing their nation against its oppressive rulers. An unforeseen result of the cultural plan was that instead of culture being brought nearer to the masses, it became further alienated from their tastes; and the writers, whose co-operation in the cultural plan had been demanded and expected, found themselves taking up a more traditional role of siding with their people against the imposition of an alien ideology. The communists had been at pains to represent past cultural history as a conflict between the demands of a ruthless Establishment, surrounded by its hired lackeys and collaborators, enforcing alien doctrines upon an unwilling people in whom the fire of independence was stoked up and kept alive by dedicated native intellectuals. After the political victory of the socialist cause the new rulers now found themselves cast in the role they had themselves attributed to the old, and the writers began to slip into the recalcitrant, if not openly rebellious, role which was traditionally theirs.

During the period characterised by the cult of the plan, culture took its place, together with economics, defence, health, etc., as a public sector of administration subject to overall control via a hierarchy of authority. The cultural sector itself comprised several branches, including radio, journalism, education, etc., of which creative writing was only one part: its activities were co-ordinated with those of other branches of public life. Within the cultural sphere the activities of the writers, via books, manifestos, congresses, etc., attracted some limelight: but time diminished their influence and authority, which progressively shrank in relation to that of the administrative and supervisory staff, until the creative writers came to find themselves regarded as poor relations, if not as parasites, or nuisances. As literature became increasingly exploited for propaganda and misused for the propagation of lies, and as collaborating writers found themselves manipulated by authority and corrupted by privilege, it was the administration of the cultural sector, including the distribution of literary patronage, which became the central issue; and literary values slipped into the background. The diversion of literary energy into planning, conferences, lobbying for position, and polemics, resulted in the eclipse of literature in favour of bookmanship; that is, literature became increasingly a vehicle for disputation. The issues which were debated in committees or discussed in pressure groups appeared, elaborately camouflaged and via an intricate system of codes and allegories, in published work. Socialist literature, which the planners intended to approximate to mass taste and to influence it, became in fact increasingly scholastic, unreadable, and worthless as an instrument of propaganda, where it was not actively counter-productive. Within the literary sector the writers had themselves become less important than the new breed of literary theoreticians whose province was the *politics of culture*, and the garb they wore was that of the critic. During the 'fifties two key issues became dominant: *who was to dominate the literary sector?*: and *how far could the autonomy of the sector be re-established?*

The struggle over these issues was not between the communists and their opponents, for the latter had been eliminated from all positions of influence. From 1948 onwards publication, and the control of the literary sector, was more or less monopolised by the communists. The struggle was between the Party intellectuals and the Party watch-dogs – specifically the Ideological Department of the Party Central Committee. Writers did not like being manipulated by officials and hatchet men; nor did they enjoy the whispered derision and hardly veiled contempt which soon replaaced their former popularity. The writer who had so recently seen himself as a guide and leader, now knew himself to be the servant of a central authority over which he had practically no influence. This terrible slump in the writer's position was sufficient in itself to encourage him in an attempt to reassert the influence of the profession over its own affairs. The need to do so became increasingly apparent as the disastrous effects of central planning in culture were revealed. By 1953 serious tension had developed between the authorities and the Party intellectuals. Among the officially supported writers a rift had appeared between those who stuck to the Party line at all costs, and those who questioned it. Thus began the long tussle between the so-called dogmatists and revisionists. Both sides operated from Party positions, but their tactics differed. Both could claim that they supported the theory of proletarian culture against that of the bourgeois. But the revisionists sought the right of the profession to serve the Party in their own way, and not be manipulated by the ideological bureaucrats. In 1948 it seemed that the Party leadership had solved the problem of potential opposition in the sensitive field of culture by incorporating it into the sphere of state administration under the supervision of Party officials; by monopolising the media of publication; by closing down all opposing or inconvenient associations and journals; by sacking, silencing, or arresting possible dissidents; and by organising collaborating intellectuals into subservient Unions, designed as levers of control from above. But by the mid-fifties the authorities had the mortification of finding unmistakable signs of opposition within the Unions themselves. In the case of other cultural areas, e.g. education or journalism, control by the authorities remained more or less firm, because teachers and journalists were public servants and could easily be disciplined. But the writers were harder to manipulate; not only because of their proverbial temperament, their irritating propensity to disorder and to tantrums, but because they were not normally employed on a regular basis. They could be prevented from publishing what was unacceptable to authority; but they could hardly be regimented into writing what they did not want to write. In the literary sector there was more field for manoeuvre, and in any case some of the toughest hard-liners in the Party leadership at times betrayed an ideologically unworthy weakness in matters of literature. Zápotocký wrote sentimental stories (for which he received the humiliating ridicule of Stalin); Kopecký never freed himself from his nostalgic attachment to the novelist Šrámek, and weakly connived at a heresy in permitting the filming of the nostalgic *Moon over the River* at a time when it contradicted the official line which he was himself enforcing. Because of the greater laxity and disorder in the control of the literary sector, the writers were able to get away with a great deal more rebelliousness than intellectual workers in other sectors. Consequently the writers' brushes with authority were watched carefully by the rest of the intelligentsia as marking the limits of permitted recalcitrance. As tension between the authorities and the intelligentsia increased during the 'fifties, it fell naturally to the writers to lead the way in rebellious protest.

Such tensions were an irritant, but hardly a danger to the authorities. In the event of serious conflict they disposed of ample means to bring the intelligentsia to heel. Whether the writers liked it or not, they would continue to proclaim the Party line as the truth; for the Party by now had established a monopoly of truth. But when Moscow changed course and proclaimed Stalinism as a heresy, the Czech leadership was caught napping. It became the duty of the Party to confess and redeem errors committed in its name, without, of course, conceding any doubt about the Party's continuing right to lead, and to lay down the *new truth*. The blame had to be kept away from the place where it belonged, i.e. with the Party leadership, and was to be shifted on to its instruments. It was up to the writers, who had proclaimed the now discredited truths of the past, to accept the blame for previously misleading the public. But in the first place the writers and intelligentsia generally showed an understandable reluctance to shoulder the blame for errors which had been forced upon them against their will, and they defended themselves by pointing out their own impotence in matters of policy. Secondly, when de-Stalinisation became official Party policy, it destroyed the influence of the dogmatists, and vindicated the position of the revisionists. At the 1956 Writers congress the revisionists, allying themselves with non-Party elements, boldly denounced the cultural repression of the past years; demanded the release of imprisoned writers; and renewed the claim of the poet to be the conscience of his nation. Listeners were reminded of a very old and precious part of Czech tradition - the Hussite claim of the individual to assert his right to choose the truth as he sees it, even in the face of overwhelming pressure upon him to deny it. In May 1956 there was a mood of elation in the Writers Club in Prague. The dogmatists were routed; the revisionists were taking over the Writers Union; and literature had openly assumed the perilous role of defending the cause of cultural freedom.

Although the claims of the literary rebels were not conceded by the authorities, and indeed provoked a brief period of attempted re-Stalinism, the position of the dogmatists within the Union was permanently weakened. Writers closely identified with the dogmatic faction, lost their moral standing among the writers, and were at best merely tolerated in the Union as representatives of external authority. After a short but unpleasant period during which revisionism itself was fiercely denounced as a heresy by the Party ideologists, the leadership resigned itself to the fact that Stalinism was no longer a viable policy, and that the intelligentsia was irretrievably revisionist in its views. From 1956 to 1967 there was more or less constant tension between the Writers Union and the Party Ideological Department over the question of cultural freedom and the autonomy of the literary sector, with both sides gaining or yielding ground according to the political climate: the Moscow line of international détente at this time was not conducive to severe repression in Prague. Looser control, and more daring forays by the writers into literary freedom drove the Czech authorities to fall back increasingly upon the weapon of censorship – an *illegal* weapon – thus weakening their moral position still further, and compounding their troubles with both writers and public.

It may seem strange that in conditions of more or less totalitarian government the political importance of dissident intellectuals should exceed the influence of their opposite numbers in free and democratic societies. During the 'sixties at an international conference a Czech intellectual was complaining of harassment from his government. In reply a West German philosopher (J. Habermass) pointed out that in the Bundesrepublik the situation of sociologists was much worse, because they were totally ignored by both government and public, and so played no public or social role whatever. The social importance of the intelligentsia in Czechoslovakia was not only due to the traditionally high role conceded by public opinion to the artist and thinker. At a time when no opposition politics were permitted – when no official Opposition was deemed to exist – then its place was taken, in the eyes of the public, by the officially tolerated opposition of artists and intellectuals. The work of creative writers like Klíma, Kohout, and Vaculík was interpreted politically: abroad almost the only Czech literature which received serious attention was that which could be conceived as political documentation. It seemed to many that Czech literature had become an interesting political surrogate.

Probably the writers always over-estimated the impact of their efforts on politics, and the authorities, sensitive to any signs of challenge, seemed to take them at their own valuation. Socially committed literature supported the abstract goal of anti-dogmatism and the right of conscience. The specific aim to which it dedicated itself was that of freedom of publication; and the authorities' increasing use of censorship ensured that this aim was kept fresh. In this game of literary politics the rebels treated literature as their opponents had done, namely as a weapon in a social cause: just as the dogmatists had misused literature for propaganda and indoctrination, so the rebels used it to rebut lies and expose injustice. The communist writers, who continued to dominate publication, had changed the slogans on the banners they bore. But they still carried banners, and claimed the right to lead. At times it appeared that the fight for the control of the cultural sector had left little time for questions of literary value, or the tastes of the literary consumers.

While the literary stalwarts of the Party debated the fate of socialist realism and de-Stalinisation, a new generation was knocking at the door of public life and literature. Excluded from all influence on policy, they kept aloof from the unending controversies of their elders. In politics they identified one common enemy, namely the bureaucracy. In literature they derided the changing slogans, and, boldly reviving the heresy of *art for art's sake*, they sought a new literature divorced from service to any political campaign. It was the younger writers who produced the new literary forms, the New Wave in films, the new satire, and the new Schweik-like realism. All this was a reaction against the florid, rhetorical style of socialist realism, and represented an escape into paradox and irony. But their work also revealed a search for escape from collectivism, a return to the private world of dreams, amusement, idleness, and fantasy. The failure of community effort, the discrediting of official guidelines, had turned younger artists away from any desire for public responsibility. Their aim was not to use poetry as a prophet does, appealing for faith in a social cause, but to end the didactic role of literature, and to restore to it traditional criteria of aesthetic value. In spite of their talent and literary successes the younger writers had very little influence on cultural politics. The older generation of committed writers kept control of the Union in their own hands, and continued their intermittent struggle with their cultural supervisors. The younger generation found themselves used from time to time as allies in the struggle; but if they became inconveniently assertive of their own ideas, they found themselves dropped; the sad fate of the journal *Tvář* is a melancholy reminder of such conditions.

In spite of the tensions the 'sixties proved to be a good era for Czech literature. The Party intellectuals who ran the Union were far more tolerant towards their non-socialist colleagues than dogmatists had been, and tended to accept them as allies in the cause of cultural freedom. The men to whom Novotný entrusted the job of supervising culture and ensuring its ideological correctness, found themselves confronting an obstinate mood of opposition from the intelligentsia which stretched from the Marxist Left to the politically uncommitted philosophers, social scientists, artists, and writers. The centres of organisation of the Arts and Sciences continued to be the Unions, which, in spite of the tensions with authority, still worked closely with the Party. But to an increasing extent it was the independent, non-committed writers, because on the whole it was they who published the best books, who were coming to dominate *literature*, although they had little say in the running of the *literary sector*. The Writers Union was becoming a Party facade: theoretically it organised the production of creative literature in the interests of the Party: actually it stood between the authorities and the independent writers, and to a varying extent protected their interests. When the going was rough, it was an advantage to the independents that their cause should be re-presented by writers like Šotola and Klíma, whose standing in the Party was considerable. But it was a false position that the stars of Czech literature had little direct say in the organisation of the profession. The poets Holan and Seifert, the novelists Mucha, Hrabal, and Linhartová; the critics Černý, B. Fučík, and Chalupecký; the dramatists Havel and Topol, these are examples of the best in current Czech literary life, whose careers nevertheless depended on the inter-play of political forces over which they had no control.

When the conflict between the authorities and the Union reached its climax in 1967, and the Party leadership used its power to crush the rebels, it was the Party intellectuals who were publicly identified as the rebel leaders, and it was they who earned the reprisals. Consequently it was they who were vindicated on the fall of Novotný. It seemed that they had deserved the right to go on running the literary sector even when the new Party leadership conceded autonomy to it, and no longer attempted to interfere with freedom of publication. The Union was no longer needed as a barrier protecting writers from rulers: in the prevailing climate of decentralisation, and the relaxation of the whole system of control from above, one might have expected the Union to dissolve itself, or become a social club, after the fashion of PEN Club branches abroad. According to Czech writers now living abroad a Writers congress was in fact planned for Autumn 1968 to consider dissolving the Union's existing structure and reorganising it as a loose association of autonomous clubs, linked together only by mutual consent and common interests. Its links with the pyramidal structure of state authority were to be broken. As a sign of the separation the chateau at Dobříš which had been presented to the Union and remained as a symbol of official patronage, was to be returned to state ownership.

These hopes and intentions were never fulfilled: all plans were changed by the events of August. But in any case the view that the free conditions of the Prague Spring would result in the Union losing its political flavour proved to be quite false. The prestige which it had gained by its resistance to the Novotný leadership gave to the Union considerable moral authority in cultural affairs. In the Spring it took the initiative in forming a Committee of Arts groups, uniting the associations into a kind of cultural front, to exert political pressure. The new conditions under Dubček permitted the competition of political viewpoints, but not of political parties: the authorities insisted that politics still had to be conducted within the framework of the Communist-run National Front. There was much political activity in a vacuum of political relationships; and into this vacuum the Writers Union moved. By its leadership of the Cultural Unions and its deep influence on the public media the Union was able to operate more or less as *if it were* a political party. Within the Union the communist members collaborated closely with non-Party democrats and the independents who had been welcomed to full membership. By practical example they gave an impetus to, and provided a forum for the idea of a pluralist democracy. In the writers' weekly *L L* social and political discussion swamped literary news. The Union which had been set up to control the writers, was now working to influence the authorities, both by direct lobbying and via its effect on public opinion. The common policy of the writers and the cultural associations was basically that of cultural freedom: to achieve that aim communists and non-communists alike lent support to the policies of reform, as summed up in the somewhat strange slogan of 'socialism with a human face'. That part of the intelligentsia which had most influence on policy were the social scientists, who directly influenced events by their co-operation in the reform plans. They welcomed the help of the writers as allies in a common cause: and the writers' work in the media made them seem to be the inspiration of the whole movement. In the early summer of 1968 there was a time when, instead of the media following the guidance of the political authorities, it seemed to be the media who were guiding them. There were examples of writers like Jan Procházka who moved directly into the political arena; others temporarily abandoned the role of creative writer for that of political commentator and lobbyist. Official statements, resolutions, and petitions were issued from the Union from time to time. There were several occasions when the intelligentsia presented, through the cultural associations, a common front in the media. The most spectacular of these efforts was the so-called Manifesto of 2,000 words, whose political impact was felt as far away as Moscow.

During the reform period literature was at last rescued from political guidance and official pressure. In the new atmosphere of open discussion and the confrontation of ideas, literature was no longer needed as a substitute for politics. When everything could be said openly, the assertion of values by means of literary allegory had become redundant. In Novotný's time a book could attain literary distinction by its unveiling of hidden truths or suppressed scandals. In 1968 the popular press was flooded with such a plethora of appalling scandals as to make the subtle creations of the literati pale by comparison. As a result of their victory communist literary rebels like Klíma, Kohout, and Vaculík lost much of their importance as writers: their work was already becoming dated, as the documentation of what had been a sick society. While the Writers Union became even more political as an organisation, the literary arena became once more dominated by creative writers rather than by literary politicians. The results are difficult to document in terms of literary history, because the interval of freedom was so short, and publication policy was influenced by such factors as the moral duty of righting past injustices by printing books which had been previously suppressed: thus when political pressure no longer operated from the side of the authorities, political factors remained as a residue of the past. But certain trends may be identified in the totality of published work, including books, journals, radio, TV, lectures, and public discussion.

Perhaps the most striking trend might be described as 'cultural resumption'. This appeared in various ways. Among the intelligentsia it appeared as the urge to catch up lost ground in the cultural development of Western Europe, with which Czech national traditions were felt to be so deeply involved, and from which political pressures had sought to keep them apart. In theoretical discussions it appeared as an expression of the conflict between the idea of Man as an economic unit of production and consumption, manipulated and manipulating via power, and the concept of Man as an existentialist being, a creature of individual moral responsibility, in constant search for his own salvation or damnation, to whom all systems of economics and power were at best a mere background to real living, and at worst a necessary evil he had taken upon himself. Theoreticians reflected that just as mediaeval philosophy had developed within the unyielding framework of theology, so had 20th century thought developed within the no less unyielding framework of ideology: in both eras the theoreticians had been faced with the need to emancipate their thinking from its conceptual framework. Marxist literateurs resumed the broken threads of the pre-war avant-garde, including those aspects of it which had been glossed over or suppressed – the work of Karel Teige and Záviš Kalandra, the dissent of Hora and Neumann from the Party line in 1929, and long ignored classics of Marxist thought, Trotsky, Bukharin, Gramsci. There was a general tendency to look back to the period between the two world wars, and to recapture the atmosphere, ideas, and ideals of the Czechoslovak First Republic. The escape from the bonds of imposed ideology, the resumption of protestant and humanist traditions, the revival of Czech nationalism, the return to the best in pre-war thought, all these trends came together and were symbolised in a renewed reverence for the President Liberator T. G. Masaryk, who became almost a cult figure of the Prague Spring, whose photograph was displayed in so many windows, and whose grave was never without offerings of fresh flowers.

The view has been expressed that the overall effect of the role played by writers and journalists in the Czech reform movement was ultimately disastrous, for it was, in the end, the lack of restraint in the public media which frightened the East German and Russian leaders, and so set the tanks rolling, to destroy all the hopes of the Prague Spring. Conversely it can be argued that there was always an irreconcilable conflict between the idea of genuine democratisation of the socialist system, and the continuation of the socialist model as interpreted by Moscow. According to this view, either the reformist ideals would have been quietly buried by the Dubček group after it had consolidated its leadership and made its peace with Moscow; or else reformist ideas unacceptable to Moscow would have prevailed in Prague, and external intervention would sooner or later have been inevitable. It was because they were aware that the interval of freedom might be short that the writers kept up the pressure for reform in the media: they realised that once the momentum for cultural and political liberalisation was lost, that would be the end of the reform movement. The dangers of political recession or external intervention were inherent in the situation, and the writers responded to them. If by their actions they precipitated the invasion, it was only because they clarified the issues to the public, and made it practically impossible for the Dubček leadership to appease Moscow by abandoning the reform programme.

Nevertheless there is a natural temptation in retrospect for observers to blame the writers for the tragic consequences of their campaign. It is tempting to see them in the role of Don Quixote, blind to the warnings of reality, living out their foolish dreams, and by their art persuading others to share them, until the harsh world of political realism turned them into a nightmare. Abstract ideas and ethical principles are the province of intellectuals: the claim of Czech poets to speak for the nation in terms of *conscience* likewise reveals an ethical basis to their viewpoint. It is a sad truism that the worlds of ethics and of politics are far apart, and to confuse them is disastrous. The writers have been blamed for misreading the situation in 1968, and for refusing to acknowledge its unescapable realities. According to this interpretation the writers used the prestige and leadership they had won in opposition to Novotný, to take part actively in a political game whose hard rules they either did not understand, or else declined to acknowledge. Losing contact with reality, they destroyed their cause, and themselves.

But if one examines the social role of the Czech writers over a longer period, charges against them that they were unworldly, and lost contact with reality, seem rather paradoxical. It is necessary only to recall their disturbing influence during the 'fifties. In the Stalinist period the system had been set to ensure that orders were passed from the pinnacle of authority downwards through the transmission belts to the base of the pyramid to be unquestioningly obeyed. At the same time the transmission belts operated in the reverse direction to pass upwards messages of cheerful compliance. The leaders set in motion the command plan; the functionaries organised its transmission; and then informed their superiors that it had been carried out successfully. The flow of orders downwards and reassuring information upwards formed a closed and self-justifying system, which no hint of failure was allowed to disturb. The more things went wrong, the more energetic were the efforts to conceal the increasing gap between the enclosed and self-deluding world of the pyramid, and the reality outside. It became necessary to close down all channels for the transmission of information outside those organised by authority as part of the system: foreign newspapers were banned as a matter of course, and foreign broadcasts jammed, in case they disturbed the picture which authority presented. It was a pseudo-reality, whose falsity became more and more obvious, so that in the end everything that was officially stated to be true, became instantly suspected of being the reverse of truth. *Information* came to be interpreted as *misinformation*: men confessed to crimes which they could not possibly have committed, and the processes of trial and execution were set in motion to confirm the legality of illegality. Justice and crime, truth and lies, changed places; and all the force of state authority was mobilised to prevent the exposure of what was manifestly a gigantic deception. When the emperor donned his new 'clothes', the admiration of the populace and their assent in the deception was assured by unspoken threats and the manipulation of public emotion.

It is the fate of intellectuals to be condemned as unworldly, and of writers to be written off as dreamers. But in the years which preceded the Prague Spring and constituted the moral preparation for it, it was the so-called real world of politics which depicted a pseudo-reality, and the writers who unveiled the realities of the situation. It was their efforts in this regard which brought upon them reprisals, and the repression which they encountered from the authorities that drew their constant attention to the need for cultural freedom. It was the dedication of the writers to this single aim that made them seem the heart and soul of the reform movement: for without freedom there could be no lasting reform.

Politics and literature intersect at many points in the life of a society: the aims of politicians and writers tend constantly towards collision. In the long term they appear as potential allies; for the dreams of poets may mature into the social blue-prints of intellectuals, and eventually into the platforms of professional politicians. A group image presented by a writer may so endear itself to a class or nation that the latter comes to adopt it as its own, and to live by it, without ever acknowledging its origin in the mind of an artist. The writer not only observes society, he helps to mould it by his observations; and those who would lead the society must pay heed to the national image and living style which it has made its own. The poet may claim the elevated social role of the guide and prophet, whose delicate antennae reach further into the future than others, and whose song, like that of the miner's canary, gives encouragement or warning to those who follow him. In that situation the responsibility of the canary is great, but its future problematical. Its gift of song gives it power; but its life is at the mercy of the miner who feeds it.

In the earliest civilised European societies of which we have exact knowledge, the land, and goods, and the services of the community belonged to a small ruling group who redistributed them in accordance with their own system of rewards and incentives, social utility and the requirements of the power system. The place of the artist was secure, provided that his services were rendered in accordance with the social needs recognised by the rulers. The artist was the servant of his royal patron, and, if he wished to survive as an artist, rendered to him the due expected. In modern times the relationship of artist and patron is rarely so simple. In a free society the writer is connected indirectly to his audience by publisher, book seller, book club, and library. The writer's financial return is decided ultimately by the market mechanism of demand and supply; and in the first instance by the publisher's reader, who tries to forecast it. The future of the writer is very insecure; and a conflict may well arise between his own taste and that of his audience: he may have to choose between commercialising his work, or not selling it.

In a society where culture is a sector of public administration, the dilemma of the writer is rather more complex. He is torn between the desire to please his audience, to please himself, and to please the official whose approval is needed for the publication of the work. The official bases his judgement not necessarily on his own taste, but *ex officio*: in discharging his office he must anticipate the wishes of his political masters. These may happen to coincide with the taste of the writer's readers, and of the writer himself. In that case there is no problem, and the official would become redundant. In general all three tastes are likely to differ, and it is the verdict of the official that will prevail. The narrower is the oligarchy to whom the official is responsible, the smaller the chance that its taste will be a popular one: when the pinnacle of authority is a dictator, the chances of the ruler's wishes coinciding with that of the populace is minimal (which did not prevent either Roman Emperors or Stalinist dictators from issuing judgements *in the name of the people*).

In an authoritarian state, official patronage assures the supply of officially approved literature. Writers generally have the choice of contributing to its production by offering their talents and incorporating their services into the official mechanism. The Czech experience seems to show that in a regrettable number of cases this results in the writer forfeiting his own self-respect as well as his readership: adjusting himself to the imposed needs of the system, the writer loses his creative ability, and fades into honoured ignominy, despised by his fellow writers, forgotten by readers, praised only by those critics whose favour is the kiss of death. Some writers are ruled out of publication for their known convictions or past behaviour; others do not care to publish in such conditions, and decline to co-operate with the authorities. So, like the banned artists, their names disappear from publishers' lists, and have a good chance of being forgotten. A few writers choose the dangerous path of illegal publication, on the underground circulation or abroad: in which case they run the risk of becoming the centre of a literary, and eventually of a political, scandal.

In many cases the writer attempts a compromise between the requirements of the system and his own creative ideas and standards. He pays
his dues to Caesar by outward conformity, by assent to official social
myths, and by overt support for the social rituals in which he is required
to participate. The conflict remains between his own views and those
he proclaims, and we know from the agonised confessions of Czech
artists that this conflict can give rise to traumatic feelings of guilt
which influence his writing. A common pattern is for the writer to
salvage his self-respect by concealed defiance of the imposed norms.
The defiance must be concealed from the watchdogs of the regime, but
to be effective must be apparent to the initiated among his audience.
Thus his work becomes a kind of puzzle, meaning different things to
different people. Following the semantic trend of the times, words
are used to mean the opposite of what they say; the most innocent
statement becomes pregnant with unexpressed meaning. Eventually
the excitement of decipherment becomes the major interest in creative
literature. In this Kafkaesque situation literary criticism is a part of
cultural politics. The relationship between the writer and his audience
is subordinated to the relationship between the writer and authority,
while the audience stands on the sidelines as a witness of their intricate
manoeuvres.

Even in a very authoritarian society expressions of literary dissent
are hard to eradicate; in many cases the unpleasant publicity which
follows excessive repression makes it scarcely worthwhile, except in
an emergency. It is less trouble for the authorities to tolerate a known,
limited, and closely watched element of cultural dissidence within the
ruling group. As it is likely to be the only form of dissidence permitted,
this element becomes the symbol and the advance guard of reformist
ideas. Thus, upon the impractical dreamer, the reluctant artist much
more at home with abstractions than with the hard facts of political
life, there falls the ill fitting mantle of the potential revolutionary. It is
not surprising that Plato, who understood both literature and politics,
regretfully decided that poets would have to be banned from his ideal
Republic.

The classic stereotype of the artist is Don Quixote, whose dreams are
so compelling, whose faith is so incorruptible, that he will acknowledge no practical obstacles as valid. Knowing that dreams crumple
before the reality of force, we regard the knight with affectionate incredulity. We love to share his dreams; but we do not believe in them.
But when a society reverses its criteria by proclaiming as truth what
is manifest falsity, the unshakable, if illogical, faith of Don Quixote

persuades men not only to share his dreams, but also to will them to come true. For the dreams are more real then the windmills of official deception.

The role of Don Quixote is not one favoured by writers. Committed to lost social causes, he presents an absurd figure, symbolising the practical futility of the poet. And yet, in face of certain defeat and general mockery, he asserts a system of values in which he believes. Even more tragic, if less absurd is the fate of the artist who avoids conflict by betraying his ideas, and himself. There remains an honourable escape route in the avoidance of social commitment, and withdrawal from the heat and dust of the arena into the monastic cloisters of pure art and intellectual abstraction. But the conditions of the twentieth century, with its realisation of Man's precarious situation as a helpless cog in a gigantic industrial and political machine, has made withdrawal a difficult choice. Even against his wishes the intellectual is condemned to be free. If his spirit will not permit him to eat from the trough of imposed beliefs and activities, he is bound to accept the dangers of dissent, which is the mark of his freedom, and of his humanity.

Notes

Chapter I

1. *Osudy dobrého vojáka Švejka za světové války* vols. 1–4, J. Hašek, 1921–23.
2. *R.U.R.*, K. Čapek, 1920.
3. *Hovory s T. G. Masarykem*, K. Čapek, 1935.
4. *Továrna na absolutno*, 1922; *Krakatit*, 1924 both by K. Čapek.
5. For a history of the Czech Surrealist movement see *Surrealistické východisko*, S. Dvorský, V. Effenberger, P. Král, eds., 1969.
6. *Kritický měsíčník* 1938–42 and 1945–48 (the journal was banned from 1942–45 by order of the Protectorate authorities).

Chapter II

1. *Doom and Resurrection* J. L. Hromádka, Macmillan, N.Y., 1945.
2. "Soviet-German friendship represents the cornerstone of the international situation against which the imperialist and anti-Soviet plans of the Anglo-French bloc have already been shattered." (From a resolution of the Central Committee of the Czechoslovak Communist Party, Dec. 1940).
3. *Kritický měsíčník* 1945, p. 9–15.
4. *K. M.* 1945 p. 123–9; 153–163.
5. The Proceedings of the Writers Congress of 1946 were published in full in the volume *Účtování a výhledy* (Retrospect and prospects) ed. J. Kopecký, 1948. For comments on Beneš's speech in the light of later developments see F. Buriánek, *Impuls* 1966 p. 408–11.
6. A. A. Zhdanov speaking at the First Congress of Soviet Writers in 1934. His speech, together with other material, was published in Prague under the title of *O umění* (On Art) in 1950.
7. *Za Heydrichem stín* J. Andrejs 1947; *Aby národ žil* R. Rédr (Brno) 1948; *Muži jdou v tmě* J. Marek 1946.
8. *Němá barikáda* J. Drda 1946.
9. *Městečko na dlani* J. Drda 1940.
10. *Básně z koncentračního tábora* J. Čapek 1946.
11. *Poesie za mřížemi* 1946.
12. *V německém zajetí* Jiří Beneš (Havlíčkův Brod) 1945.
13. *Poslední dopisy* 1946.
14. *Továrna na smrt* Ota Kraus and Erich Schön, 1946.
15. *Oni přijdou*, M. Jariš, 1948.
16. *Reportáž psaná na oprátce*, J. Fučík, 1945 (English translation by S. Jolly *Report from the Gallows*, London 1951).

17. The authenticity of the book is still a matter of controversy. Stylistically it is characteristic of J. Fučík: doubts about its authenticity have been fed by the loss, or unavailability, of the original manuscript, and by the secretiveness of the authorities; e.g. in his novel *The Joke* M. Kundera referred to the problem, but was persuaded to delete the passage.

18. *Dík Sovětskému svazu*, 1945, *Panychida*, 1946, both by V. Holan.

19. *Jobova noc* (Night of Job), F. Hrubín, 1945; *Povstání z mrtvých* (Resurrection) V. Závada 1946.

20. *Mrtvá ves* (The Dead Village), V. Fischl, 1945, (tr. L. Lee).

21. *Černé světlo*, V. Řezáč, 1940.

22. *Rozhraní*, 1944 (English translation by F. Long, *If the Mirror break*, N.Y., 1959).

23. *Nástup* (Line-up), V. Řezáč, 1951. See Chap. III, p. 00

24. *Lidé na křižovatce*, M. Pujmanová, 1937.

25. *Hra s ohněm*, 1948.

26. *Život proti smrti*, 1952. See Chap. III, p.

27. *Limb a jiné básně*, 1945, *Ódy a variace*, 1946, by Jiří Kolář; *Osudy*, J. Kainar, 1947; *Tento večer*, Ivan Blatný, 1945; *Cizí pokoj*, Jiřina Hauková, 1946; *Podle plotu*, Oldřich Mikulášek, 1946.

28. *The House*, by Ivan Blatný (tr. K. Offer).

29. *Říká se jaro*, J. Hauková; the poems are included in the volume *Letorosty*, 1970.

30. *Problémy nadporučíka Knapa*, J. Mucha, 1946. The book was first published in English in 1945 (tr. by E. Osers).

31. *Spálená setba*, J. Mucha, 1948 (*Scorched Earth*, tr. E. Osers, 1952)

32. *Žíznivé léto,* 1935; *Pozdravení slunci*, 1937.

33. *Stará země* and *Svatý Václav*, 1946.

34. *Oheň proti ohni*, J. Mucha, 1947.

Chapter III

1. *O umění*, A. A. Zdanov (with an Introduction by F. Nečásek), Orbis, Prague, 1950.

2. Z. Kalandra was put on trial on 31. 5. 1949 together with Mme. M. Horáková: he was condemned to death for 'treason and espionage'. The case against him was blackened by reference to his political attitude in 1936, and to a pamphlet, *"The Dark Background to the Moscow Trials"* in which he had comments on 'Stalin's attempts to terrorise Leninist revolutionaries'.

3. *Malé povídky pro Mr Trumana*, 1951.

4. *Veliké století*, F. Kubka: in its final form it was reduced to five volumes.

5. Chap. II, p. 38.

6. Among the better-known examples is *Dům na zeleném svahu* (The house on the Green Slope) by A. Sedlmayerová.

7. *Nástup*, V. Řezáč, 1951.

8. The completed trilogy consisted of *Lidé na křižovatce*, (1937), *Hra s ohněm*, (1948), and *Život proti smrti*, (1952).

9. *Luisiana se probouzí*, K. F. Sedláček, 1952.

10. *Plným krokem*, J. Otčenášek, 1952.

11. *Dvě jara*, B. Říha, 1952.

12. *Veliký orloj*, V. Nezval, 1949.

13. Though intended as a harmless send-up, the parody was officially regarded as a gesture of protest against an *official* poet. The Security Police opened an enquiry into the incident; it was established that the 'subversive pamphlet' (as it had become) was the work of an underground organisation among the students. A 'Trotskyist' conspiracy was uncovered, and arrests followed. The writer A. J. Liehm recalls his bewilderment at the time. A close friend of the culprits, he knew that they could not possibly be guilty of the charges. On the other hand he could not bring himself to believe that the Party would countenance such gross injustice. The conflict between the official version and the evidence of his own senses posed a terrible dilemma. If he could not believe that the Party was guilty of injustice, the fault must somehow be within himself. Although the 'pamphlet' was intended harmlessly, the fact that its authors had been blind to the harm it could do, revealed their lack of vigilance, their political immaturity, and lack of conviction. Perhaps, after all, an insensitivity to class issue was the first step in subversion. Such a crisis of doubt tests the real believer and exposes the weakling. A true communist would accept the verdict of the Party *even if it seemed to conflict with the evidence of one's own senses* (*Lit. nov.*, 23. 5. 1964).

14. *Stalin*, 1949.

15. *Zpěv míru*, 1950.

16. Translation by J. Lindsay and S. Jolly (*The Song of Peace*, Fore Publications, London 1951).

17. In his speech at the Writers' Congress in Prague 1956. Nezval's speech was later published as a monograph *O některých problémech současné poesie* (Some problems of contemporary poetry), 1956.

18. *Bez obav*, 1951.

19. *Z mého života*, by V. Nezval, p. 307, (2nd ed. 1961).

20. *Píseň o Viktorce*, 1950.

21. Ivan Skála's article was published in *Tvorba* 12/1950, pps. 285-6.

22. L. Štoll's speech was published in full under the title of *Skutečnosti tvář í v tvář*, (Orbis, 1949); for the quote see pps. 7-8.

23. *Třicet let bojů za českou socialistickou poesii*, L. Štoll, (Orbis, 1950).

24. At a time when ideological exhortation was regarded as a substitute for economic incentives, a ground for condemnation of literary work was its expected effect on productivity in the factories. The following illuminating minute gives an example of the Party line zealously applied in the field of library policy:

> Our view is that the book is a powerful instrument of instruction, and we wish to bring into the education of the working man the *hero*

of labour type, from Soviet and native literature... This means that, for our purposes a significant number of books remains useless or even harmful. It will be necessary to remove such books from libraries, and replace them with new educational books, capable of influencing the reader so as to improve his attitude to work, and so raise his productivity...

(from the archives of the Institute for the
History of the Czechoslovak Communist Party,
F 11, O-5-14, p. 9).

25. Gustáv Husák and Laco Novomeský were rehabilitated in the 'sixties. Husák became First Secretary of the Czechoslovak Communist Party in 1969 after the removal of A. Dubček, and President of the Republic in 1974.

26. A revealing comment on the tension between Party and government is revealed in a document circulated by Gottwald after the fall of Slánský:

'The apparatus of the Central Committee and its workers gradually became accustomed to intervening in the business of the various offices and Ministries, over the heads and without the knowledge of the responsible comrades. This method of work, where the Central Committee apparatus, the secretariat and its co-workers intervened often with various authorities, offices, Ministries and institutions, this state of affairs was not only correct but necessary before February, when... important sectors of the state and economic administration were held by our class opponents and enemies. At that time it was not only logical, but absolutely necessary to interfere in such places by means of our apparatus over the heads of our enemies... But after February, when our Party became the governing, the only responsible, party, when it occupied all important positions, our central apparatus continued its old, pre-February practices... The practices of our central apparatus made many people ask... who governs in this Republic?... Is the Government at the Powder Tower, or is it in Straka-Palace and in the Castle? The comrade Ministers will testify from their own experience in their departments that some of their subordinates did not know whom to obey, whether the Minister, or the official of the secretariat of the Central Committee.'

27. For the transcript of the trial see *Trial of the leadership of the Anti-state Conspiracy Centre* published by the Czechoslovak Ministry of Justice, Prague, 1953.

28. *The Invisible Writing*, A. Koestler, p. 493, London, 1954.

29. By the Czechoslovak Supreme Court, after a full enquiry in 1963. For full details of the enquiry and subsequent investigations see *The Czech political trials 1950–54*, ed. J. Pelikán, Stanford, 1971.

Chapter IV

1. *Studené slunce*, by J. Mucha was first published in 1968. See Chap. XI, n. 44.

2. Jan Drda in *Literární noviny*, 11. 7. 1953.

3. *Rudé právo*, 13. 12. 1953.

4. *Karel Čapek*, by S.V. Nikolsky (tr. K. Jiroudková), Brno, 1952.

5. *Sloky lásky* by Shchipachev (tr. L. Fikar), 1952.

6. *Básnický Almanach*, 1953.

7. *Literární noviny*, no. 19 of 1952.

8. J. Palivec had lived in France, and had translated the work of Paul Valéry into Czech: he also translated Coleridge's *Ancient Mariner*. Palivec spent the war in Prague; and was a member of an anti-Fascist resistance group. He was arrested in 1952.

9. V. Renč was a foremost poet in the pre-war period. A member of the ruralist school of writers, he was uncompromising in his attitude to what he regarded as unprincipled liberalism. He had indeed (like the communists) attacked Karel Čapek.

10. Zdeněk Kalista had been among the first wave of communist poets in the early 'twenties, and had been a close friend of Wolker, on whom he published a sympathetic study. Kalista wrote Poetist verses, but later turned from creative literature to History, and became one of the most eminent historians of the baroque period. Arrested in 1952, released in 1961, he was restored to his university Chair in 1968, shortly before the Soviet invasion.

11. Ehrenburg's essay 'On the work of an Author' was printed in the Soviet journal *Znamya* in October 1953. It was reprinted in Prague in *Literární noviny* in November 1953.

12. *Zasmějte se včerejšku* (Laugh at yesterday), J. Marek, 1953.

13. *Rudé právo*, 13. 6. 1954.

14. *Člověk zahrada širá*, M. Kundera, 1953.

15. The poem 'Odcházím' dated by Milan Kundera to 1953, was included by him in the collection *Monology*, 1957.

16. *Literární noviny*, 3. 4. 1954.

17. *Stalin je život budoucích*, 1955.

18. *Z domoviny*, V. Nezval, 1951.

19. *Šel malíř chudě do světa*, J. Seifert, 1949.

20. *Maminka*, J. Seifert, 1954.

21. *Český sen*, J. Kainar, 1953.

22. *Zlatovláska*, J. Kainar, (premiere 1952).

23. *Chrpy a města*, V. Nezval, 1955.

24. *Poslanie do przyjaciela*, A. Wazyk, 1955, (tr. G. Gomori).

25. *Poemat dla dorostlych i inne wierze*, 1955.

Chapter V

1. *Literární noviny*, 24. 12. 55.

2. For examples of the comments see *Aby žádný talent nechyběl* (So that no talent is left out), *L N*, 31. 3. 56: *Ne fronty ale literatura* (Not fronts but literature), *L N*, 14. 7. 56: *Co chceme* (What we want), *L N*, 21. 4. 56.

3. *Rudé právo, 23. 4. 56.*

4. *Literární noviny* published shortened texts of the main speeches: Hrubín's speech was printed in full (*L N* no. 18, 1956, p. 10). Extracts from the speeches of the younger writers were printed in *Květen*, 1956-7, pps. 291-8.

5. It was later revealed privately by one of the imprisoned writers that Seifert's well-meant intervention actually harmed their plight. Preparations had been made for their early release, but these were cancelled, and the writers compelled to serve out their sentences. Five years elapsed before all were free.

6. For an explanation of the programme see the paper by M. Holub in *Květen*, II/1, 1956, p. 1-2.

7. *Pathologie*, from Holub's first collection of poems *Denní služba*, (The daily round), 1958, (trans. by G. Theiner).

8. *Okamžiky* by E. Petiška, 1957.

9. *Svět náš vezdejší* by J. Šotola, 1957.

10. *Monology* by M. Kundera, 1957.

11. *Mistr Sun o básnickém umění* (Master Sun on the poetic art) by J. Kolář, 1957: *Oheň ve sněhu* (Fire in snow) by J. Hauková, 1958: *Můj zpěv* (My song) by F. Hrubín, 1956: *Chlapec a hvězdy* (Boy and stars) by J. Seifert, 1958: *Krajem táhne prašivec* (Wanderings of a skunk) by O. Mikulášek, 1957.

12. *Květen*, 1955, p. 289, (B. Březovský).

13. *Občan Brych* by J. Otčenášek, 1955.

14. See above p. 61.

15. *Jdi za zeleným světlem* by E. Valenta, 1956.

16. *Ibid.*, p. 182.

17. *Ibid.*, p. 186.

18. *Noc a naděje*, 1957; *Démanty noci*, 1958, both by A. Lustig.

19. *Romeo, Julie a tma* by Otčenášek, 1958: (English translation *Romeo, Juliet and the Dark*, Artia, 1959).

20. *Zbabělci* by J. Škvorecký, 1959.

21. The students' programme, which was drawn up on the basis of consultation between the representatives of several universities, was circulated illegally in pamphlet form. It was summarised in a despatch from Prague by the correspondent of the New York Times (NYT, 27. 5. 56), and some of the details were confirmed by the attacks launched upon them in the Party press. The exile journal *Československý přehled* published a summary of the students' programme (*ČP* June 1956, p. 8-10).

22. *RP*, 20. 6. 56: see also V. V. Kusin, *The Intellectual Origins of the Prague Spring*, Cambridge, 1971. Dr. Kusin, a distinguished Marxist theoretician, was himself a participant in the reform movement in higher education.

23. In the USSR, Stalin's own aides and executioners blandly (and briefly) assumed the role of righteous reformers in 1956, and were actually accepted as such by Western politicians and public opinion.

24. *RP*, 12. 6. 56.

25. *Mladá fronta*, 17. 4. 56. See also *Svědectví*, no. 11, 1960, pp. 208–49.

26. *RP*, 7. 11. 56. Attacks on national Communism, and 'unwavering support' for the USSR were themes stressed at a joint conference of Czechoslovak and East German Party leaders in Prague (*RP*, 21. 12. 56).

27. K. J. Beneš in *LN*, 22. 12. 56.

28. *RP*, 19. 6. 57.

29. Details of the Party intervention in the Škvorecký case were divulged ten years later (*Literární listy*, 16. 5. 68).

30. *LN*, 10. 3. 59, printed the text of Štoll's speech.

31. *On Socialist Culture* – Documents relating to the Congress of Social Culture, published by Orbis, 1959.

Chapter VI

1. Jan Pilař, writing in the bi-monthly brochure published by the Writers Press, July, 1959.

2. B. Březovský, writing in the same brochure.

3. *Úroda*, Pavel Bojar (together with Olga Bojarová), 1961; *Veliká samota*, Ivan Kříž, 1960; *Zelené obzory*, Jan Procházka, 1960.

4. *Jarní vody* (Spring waters), 1952; *Horké dny* (Hot Days), 1953.

5. F. Benhart, writing in *Plamen*, 12/1961.

6. *Veliká samota*, I. Kříž, 1960.

7. The series was entitled *Život kolem nás* (Life around us).

8. Some contemporary critics hailed the book as a great advance. It is interesting to note that years later the conservative critic V. Černý agreed with them; he regarded *Green Horizons* as one of the few successful socialist realist novels (*Svědectví*, XIII, 49, 1975, p. 93).

9. *Časová tíseň*, Jiří Fried, 1961.

10. *Nylonový měsíc*, Jaroslava Blažková, 1961.

11. From *Rozpleť si vlasy* (Ruffle your hair) by Ivan Diviš, 1961.

12. *Na střeše je Mendlessohn* (Mendlessohn on the roof) by Jiří Weil, 1960; *Ulice ztracených bratrů* (Street of lost brothers) by Arnošt Lustig, 1961, were among the better examples.

13. 'Lidice' from *Heinovské noci* (Heine Nights) by K. Šiktanc, 1960.

14. *Lazar a píseň*, Josef Kainar, 1960.

15. *RP*, 11. 12. 1960.

16. From *Venuše z Méla* (Venus de Milo), Jiří Šotola, 1959.

17. From *Lijáky* (Showers), Miroslav Červenka, 1960.

18. *Noc s Hamletem*, Vladimír Holan, 1964.

19. *Ortely a milosti*, Oldřich Mikulášek, 1959.

20. *Hrací mlýn*, František Gottlieb, 1959.

21. *Lampa*, Josef Hanzlík, 1961, (tr. Ian Milner).

22. The theme of man's creation of light by labour and sacrifice had been treated by Wolker in 'The Eyes of the Stoker', and by Nezval in 'Edison'.

23. *Mladé víno*, 1961.

24. *Patnáct Májů*, 1960.

25. 'Polonius' from *Slabikář* (Spelling book) by M. Holub, 1961.

26. *Achilles a želva*, 1960.

27. *Divadlo*, no. 1, 1960.

28. *Antigona a ti druzí*, P. Karvaš, 1962.

29. *Majitelé klíčů*, Milan Kundera, 1962.

30. *Umění románu*, M. Kundera, 1960.

31. *Bedřich Václavek a vývoj marxistické estetiky*, K. Chvatík, 1962.

32. *Patnáct let české literatury,* Jan Petrmichl, 1961.

33. *LN*, 19. 1. 63.

34. The most dramatic gesture of de-Stalinisation in Prague was the destruction by dynamite of the gigantic Stalin statue in 1962.

Chapter VII

1. The uncertainty of the thaw and the feeling of continuity with the Stalinist past was underlined by a rather farcical incident at Moscow in December 1962, when Khrushchev visited an exhibition of modern art at the Old Riding School. His horrified reaction to the 'advanced' paintings, and his angry identification of experimental art with Western decadence and capitalist deviation convinced many observers that the thaw was over already (see *Khrushchev on Culture* Encounter pamphlet 9, London, 1965).

2. *One Day in the Life of Ivan Denisovich* appeared in the journal *Novy Mir* in November 1962. It was serialised in the Czech journal *Plamen* in 1963.

3. J. Čutka, writing in the Party theoretical journal *Nová mysl*, 1963, p. 209.

4. 'The XII Congress showed it has no illusions about any simple solutions for the tasks which lie before us... Whoever has studied the main speeches and the final conclusions must be aware that the time is irrevocably over when it was possible to side-step serious issues of social development or merely gloss over them with salvationist dogmatic formulae...', J. Hájek writing in *Plamen*, 1/63.

5. Dubček had played no significant part in the purges of the early 'fifties. His position in the Party had been that of a minor provincial official until summoned to Prague in 1960 by Novotný as a Secretary to the Central Committee in place of O. Černík.

6. 'The cult of the plan brought about a situation in which the measure of people's merit ceased to be their socially useful work; it was replaced by another, purely administrative one - the fulfilment of planned indexes. The

pursuit of indexes became the leading idea of society. The pre-eminence of the plan was not always decided by the fact that its goals were in harmony with the needs and capability of society... the plan was elevated to the status of a moral code. What should have been the instrument had become the goal.' R. Selucký, *Kulturní tvorba*, 7. 2. 63.

7. *O mystice, rozumu a účelnosti pravdy*, J. Rozner, *LN*, 23. 12. 63.

8. M. Hysko in Pravda (Bratislava), 28. 2. 63. Dr. Hysko, formerly an active journalist, was then teaching at the University of Bratislava.

9. The campign included demands for the recognition by Prague of the patriotic role played by the Slovak National Council during the war, and retraction of the false charges laid against it in the Party Press. There was also a spirited defence of the pre-war Slovak intellectuals (the *Dav* group) previously labelled as decadent, bourgeois, social-fascist etc.

10. *Dobrý den* by L. Novomeský, *Plamen*, 5. 63.

11. The *Proceedings*, including Novomeský's speech, were printed in *KŽ* of 27. 4. 63 and 4. 5. 63.

12. See p. 35.

13. Michal Chorvath's poem was published in *KŽ*, 13. 4. 63.

14. L. Mňačko, *Pravda v literatuře, LN*, 25. 5. 63.

15. The speeches were printed in *LN*, 24. 5. 63 and 1. 6. 63.

16. In the Party journal *Nová mysl* (pps. 868–72 of 1963) Šotola summed up the proceedings of the congress as sound criticism without rhetoric. He mentioned among points of discussion the need to revaluate avant-garde literature of the thirties, and a return to sounder literary criteria. He also drew attention to criticism of the Writers' Union itself and of *LN*'s editorial policy, hinting that changes would have to be made if much improvement was to be expected.

17. Ivan Skála resigned in the summer of 1964.

18. J. Brabec's article *Třicet let po třiceti letech* (*Thirty Years after Thirty Years*) was published in *LN*, 15. 6. 63. As an academic employee of the Institute Brabec was a member of the team led by Štoll.

19. *LN*, 13. 7. 63. The rumours of tension between the Writers Union and the Academy seemed to be confirmed when the Union publishing house (Československý spisovatel) published the *Dictionary of Czech Writers* (Slovník českých spisovatelů) in 1964. The book was a team project of the Institute, but its publication had been held up, apparently because the *Dictionary* contained favourable references to writers who had been imprisoned or were abroad.

20. *Pravda* (Bratislava), 3. 6. 63.

21. *RP*, 13. 6. 63. A mysterious touch was added to the affair by the failure of Radio Bratislava to televise Novotný's speech.

22. *The Times*, 12. 6. 63. The article was headed *President Novotný denies differences with Russia on de-Stalinisation.*

23. Replies to Hysko's charges appeared in *RP*, 15. 6. 63 and in *Pravda*, 23. 6. 63. On 26. 6. 63 Dubček himself criticised Hysko in a speech to Party officials in Slovakia. Jiří Hendrych's speech appeared in *RP*, 29. 6. 63.

24. Sartre's speech was printed in *Plamen* 1/63.

25. *Plamen*, 6/63.

26. The Proceedings of the Liblice conference were published in Prague in 1964 under the title of *Franz Kafka*.

27. Garaudy's article appeared in *Les Lettres Françaises* 6. 6. 63; Kurella's reply was in *Sonntag*, 4. 8. 63.

28. Z. Pešat in *LN*, 25. 4. 64.

29. Solzhenitsyn's book was serialised in *Plamen*, 1/63 – 4/63; Šotola's poem appeared in *KT*, 17. 1. 63; Mňačko's article appeared in *KŽ*, 6. 12. 62.

30. 'The almost imperceptible testing of what it is possible to state publicly and get away with, has been a great pastime among Czech and Slovak intellectuals ever since 1956... We have all developed a very refined sense in this respect. We can almost smell such an exploration in the page of print: we know exactly where to place it, and how to hedge it in the preceding and following paragraphs. We are guided by what at any given moment it is permissible to write and what it is not; what separates the provocative from the treasonable (in the eyes of District Party Secretaries); the suggested from the stated; the implicit from the explicit.' The passage is taken from an unsigned article by an unknown Czech writer, published in *Survey*, no. 51 of 1963.

31. *Zámek* by Ivan Klíma, staged in Brno, 1965, text published 1965.

32. The interpretation was subsequently denied by Klíma (*The Politics of Culture*, ed. A. J. Liehm, p. 359).

33. *Konec masopustu*, by Josef Topol (presented at the National Theatre in Prague in 1965).

34. *Zahradní slavnost* by Václav Havel, (premiere in Prague, Dec. 1963).

35. An example would be L. Bublík's *Páteř* (The Spine).

36. *Vyrozumění* by V. Havel; written in 1959, it was first performed publicly in 1965. An English translation by Vera Blackwell, entitled, *The Memorandum*, was published by Penguin in 1970 (*Three East European Plays*).

37. An echo of a much-quoted remark by President Novotný.

38. See his interview with A. J. Liehm (*op.cit.*).

39. *Král Vávra* by Milan Uhde.

40. The part of one of the tourists was played by V. Havel.

41. *Oneskorené reportáže* by L. Mňačko, Bratislava, 1963.

42. *Smrt se jmenuje Engelchen*, Czech translation from the Slovak, Prague, 1959.

43. For more details of the cases, and of Mňačko's investigations of them, see *The Seventh Night* by L. Mňačko, (p. 101-5), London, 1969. (Mňačko left Czechoslovakia in 1968.)

44. The book was published by the State Press for Political Literature, in effect by the Party itself, as Mňačko claimed (*KŽ*, 25. 7. 64), and was honoured with a State Prize.

45. Hochhuth's letter, dated 23. 9. 64, appeared in *Die Zeit*, n. 42 of October, 1964. For a study of the Mňačko case in English see *Survey*, April, 1965, p. 5 ff.

46. *KŽ*, 12. 2. 64 and 19. 3. 63.

47. *Studené slunce* by Jiří Mucha was finally published in 1968. For the complications which attended the publication of Mucha's book in Czechoslovakia see J. Pilař, in *LL*, no. 13, p. 8.

48. *Zeď* by Jaroslav Putík, 1962.

49. 'I cannot say that the revelation of Stalinist deformations shook my whole world to its foundations; there were many things I had guessed long before. Nevertheless this was the final and decisive blow... This is when my novella *The Wall*, based on the theme of the occupation, came into being... Somehow I felt the need to purge myself of this subject, to shake it off, though of course it was the story of the occupation as seen through the backward glance of a person who had lived through the 1950's.' (*The Politics of Culture*, p. 240.)

50. *Hodina ticha* by Ivan Klíma, 1963. Klíma had previously published a book of journalist sketches on the same area of Slovakia (*Mezi třemi hranicemi*, 1960).

51. *Pan Theodor Mundstock*, by Ladislav Fuks, 1963.

52. *Černý kolotoč* from the collection of the same name by Josef Hanzlík, 1963.

53. *Potlesk pro Herodesa* by J. Hanzlík was included by him in the collection published under the same name in 1967.

54. *Až přijde kocour*, directed by Vojtěch Jasný, was released in 1963.

55. *Reportáž z novostavby ubytovny* from *Anamneza* by M. Holub, 1964 (tr. by G. Theiner).

56. *Směšné lásky* by Milan Kundera, 1963.

57. *Druhý sešit směšných lásek*, 1965.

58. *Nejsem si jist* by Ivan Vyskočil from *Malé hry*.

59. *Vždyť přece létat je tak snadné* (Flying is actually so easy) by Ivan Vyskočil, 1963.

60. *Démon souhlasu* by Dominik Tatarka, 1963: the story first appeared in *Kulturný život* in 1956.

61. *Hovory lidí* (People Talking) with illustrations by Kamil Lhoták, 1954.

62. *Skřivánek na niti* (*A Lark on a thread*) the book was printed, but not released.

63. *Perlička na dně*, 1963.

64. *Pábitelé*, 1964.

65. *Taneční hodiny pro starší a pokročilé*, 1964.

66. *Ostře sledované vlaky*, 1964; the film, directed by Jiří Menzel, was released in 1966.

67. The extract is from *Dancing Lessons*.

68. See e.g. the comments of F. Benhart in *Plamen*, 12/64, p. 155.

69. Aragon's speech was printed in *Pro a proti*, 1963, p. 17-24.

Chapter VIII

1. The official statistics for the relevant years (*Statistické ročenky ČSSR*) set out the situation in terms of output, productivity, and consumption. The U.N. Economic Bulletin for Europe, vol. 18, no. 1 of Nov. 1966, in which the capital output ratios of countries in the Soviet bloc are set out, reveals the alarming situation of Czechoslovakia.

2. The New Economic Model of Czechoslovakia aroused wide interest in Western Europe, and there is a considerable literature available on the subject: see e.g. *Main reports and Documents concerning the new system of management,* Prague 1965; *Plan and Market under Socialism,* Prague 1967; R. Selucký *The Plan that Failed,* Nelson, London 1970: *The Czechoslovak Reform Movement* ed. V. V. Kusin, London, 1973, pp. 179–235.

3. The wide implications of the New Model on political and social life generally were apparent to the reformers from the start, and at the Academy of Sciences a group research project was launched on the human and social circumstances of the technical-scientific revolution; see R. Richta *Civilisation at the Crossroads* Prague, 1968. For a popular discussion of the documents see the English language journal *Universum* (Prague), 2/66, p. 84–6.

4. *Dědictví humanismu a naše doba* by J. Prusek, *L N*, 1/65; *Homines enim sumus* by M. Jodl, L.N. 46–65; *Budoucnost humanismu*, M. Jodl, 39/65; *Humanismus, sociologie a politika* by Z. Mlynář, 48/65.

5. The first steps had already been taken to evaluate the ethical ideals of T. G. Masaryk; L. Nový *Filosofie T. G. Masaryka*, Brno, 1962.

6. 'The Czechoslovak Writers Union was created on the Soviet model, and in this case the implications are far from being entirely positive. The Union meant subordination and co-ordination, and given certain conditions, that can be dangerous.' J. F. Franěk, *Impuls* 1/66, p. 62. Such comments were fairly common in the journals in 1966.

7. See e.g. M. Grygar *Pálení mostů?* (The Burning of bridges?), *LN,* 18/65.

8. Pasolini led a group of Italian writers to Prague, where they discussed, among other topics, the theme of Politics and Literature. The discussions were reported in the Italian journal *Rinascita*, 23/1/65.

9. During 1965 foreign material carried by *LN* included contributions from Garaudy, Sartre, Togliatti, G. Grass, and Peter Weiss. In the same year A. J. Liehm published a collection of interviews with foreign Marxists, *Rozhovor*, Prague, 1965.

10. The finest example of this work is probably the collection *Poetismus*, ed. K. Chvatík and Z. Pešat, Prague, 1967.

11. Karel Teige, *Jarmark umění*, 1964; *Svět stavby a básně*, 1966. This latter work was intended to be the first volume in a series of his collected works.

12. Writing in *Plamen*, 3/65, V. Neff recalled the brilliance of the literary talent of Prague before the second world war, citing authors like Křelina and Hostovský who had been taboo. 'The twenty five years which followed, did

terrible things to that great generation! How many of them died in the camps! How many left for abroad! How many were forcibly silenced!'

13. *Slovník českých spisovatelů*, 1964.

14. V. Černý, *Středověkž drama*, Bratislava, 1965; V. Černý also resumed publication in certain of the cultural journals.

15. J. Kolář, *Náhodný svědek*; K. Bednář, *O propast opřeno*; A. G. Nor *Vichřice*; J. Hauková, *Mezi lidmi a havrany*, all appeared in 1965. Books by the exiles J. Voskovec (*Klobouk ve křoví*), and Egon Hostovský (*Cizinec hledá byt*) also appeared then.

16. *Komedie o umučení a slavném vzkříšení pána a spasitele našeho Ježíše Krista*, text published 1967.

17. *Hlavní správa tiskového dohledu* (Central Agency for Press Supervision). Some detailed evidence of how the censorship worked is supplied by Dušan Hamšík in his book *Spisovatelé a moc*, 1969 (the English edition is entitled *Writers against Rulers*, London, 1971. References below are to the English edition.) A detailed breakdown of the censors' interventions are given by Hamšík, p. 141; for a discussion of the censors' work see Hamšík, p. 97–102.

18. *Poslání a stav kulturních časopisů* (The role and condition of the cultural journals – the Viewpoint of the Central Committee of the Czechoslovak C.P.) *Nová Mysl*, 4/64, p. 385–406. For a discussion of this document see *Svědectví*, 24, p. 373–382.

19. The document contains several references to the operation of censorship, references which would presumably not normally have been passed by the censors. The document itself was prepared as a sub-committee report, intended for internal circulation only. After Mr Švestka, a member of the committee, had published a summary in his newspaper *Rudé právo*, the whole draft was released for publication in the Party journal, and having been passed by the Presidium, the document was not itself censored.

20. The reference is apparently to the article *Především myslet* (Think first) by K. Minarik in *KŽ*, 5/64.

21. *Plamen*, 1/64, had published an exchange of views between J. P. Sartre, Ernst Fischer and others on the question of peaceful co-existence and ideology.

22. 'Of course the cultural journals should express themselves even on the very serious and controversial problems of our society. But the vital thing is that the viewpoint they adopt should be uniformly in harmony with the spirit of Party policy, with the line set by Party bodies, and with the Party's efforts to solve these problems; that they should help the Party to unite the workers and strengthen confidence in the Party.' *Nová Mysl*, 4/64, p. 386.

23. Hamšík, p. 97 ff.

24. Dr Hübl was reinstated at the Party Academy as Rector in 1968. He was arrested in 1972.

25. Extracts or summaries of the contributions were printed in *LN*, 23/65, p. 1 and 3.

26. Havlíček's remarks were printed in *Nová mysl*, 10/65.

27. Šotola's comments on *Tvář* were printed in *LN*, 36-65 p. 4.

28. *RP*, 5th and 6th Oct. 1965 (Ivan Skála).

29. *LN*, 42/65.

30. *LN*, 1/66.

31. *Věční milenci* by Bohuslav Březovský, 1966.

32. *Svědomí* by Jaroslav Putík, 1958.

33. *Smrtelná neděle* by J. Putík, 1967.

34. Sekyra by Ludvík Vaculík, 1966.

35. *Žert* by Milan Kundera, 1966 (English translation *The Joke*, London, 1969.)

36. *Jak chutná moc* by L. Mňačko, 1967 (English translation *The Taste of Power*, London 1967).

37. *The Seventh Night* by L. Mňačko, London, 1969.

38. Mňačko, *ibid.*, p. 151-3.

39. *Soukromá vichřice* by Vladimír Páral, 1966.

40. *Vlažná vlna* by Alena Vostrá, 1966.

41. *Prostor k rozlišení*, 1964; *Rozprava o zdviži*, 1964; *Meziprůzkum nejblíž uplynulého*, 1965; *Dům daleko*, 1968, by Věra Linhartová.

42. Pavel Juráček wrote the scenario for *Josef Kilián*, and helped to direct it; the film won the Grand Prize at Oberhausen, and was widely distributed abroad. The initials of the hero (J.K.) are the most obvious of Kafka references in the film.

43. *O slavnosti a hostech*, directed by Jan Němec, 1966.

44. For an account of the troubles caused by the film, see *All the Bright Young Men and Women* by J. Škvorecký, Toronto, 1971, p. 126 ff.

45. Ester Krumbachová's comments were published in an interview with A. J. Liehm, *LN*, 50/66 (the interview was republished by A. J. Liehm in *The Politics of Culture*, p. 125-6).

46. *Sedmikrásky*, directed by Věra Chytilová, 1966.

47. The attack on the film became a byword for official vandalism and ignorance; it was referred to, e.g. by Milan Kundera in his speech at the Fourth Congress of the Writers Union; see also Jan Procházka, *Politika pro každého*, 1968, p. 39.

48. *KT*, 48/66. The article was featured in *LN*, 50/66.

49. *LN*, 44/66, p. 2. The Committee of the Union met on 21/10/66.

50. Hamšík, p. 18-21.

51. Hamšík, p. 33.

Chapter IX

1. For the statistics of censors' interventions see Hamšík. *op. cit.*, p. 141.

2. 'In private conversations these men (from the Ideological Dept.) would suggest that Number One, as he was called... was angry and impatient, and would not put up with any more half-measures. Heads would anyway have to roll. "So why don't we meet him half-way and sacrifice a few heads of our own choosing? We can make sure in this way that nothing too unpleasant happens to them. They can just leave the paper and do something else; no one will bother them and they won't lose by it. Otherwise..." At this point the Ideological Department officials would shake their heads as if they could already hear Number One's thunderbolts descending...' Hamšík, p. 21.

3. *KT*, 22/6/67.

4. The symposium, by Daněk, Procházka, Lustig, and Klíma was mainly concerned with the historical background to the M.E. war. The article was promptly confiscated by the censors, who then circulated it as a confidential document among the inner ring of Party officials, whence it somehow reached West Germany and was published there. Procházka later published one of his articles from the Egyptian journey, with the comment that the article, submitted to *LN*, had been stopped by the censor on 23/6/67, (J. Procházka, *Politika pro každého*, (1968), p. 157–9).

5. The Proceedings of the Congress were published in full in 1968 from the stenographic record, *IV Sjezd československých spisovatelů/Protokol*. The Draft Statement appears on p. 7–13.

6. Milan Kundera mentioned the criticism in his introduction of the Draft (p. 22). Among the criticisms offered were: vagueness on questions of freedom, democracy, big-power conflict etc.; half-hearted support for progressive movements abroad (e.g. in Vietnam); failure to identify clearly culture with socialist revolution; false ideas about the First Czechoslovak Republic; and a general disinclination to take up a positive attitude towards literary production. These overt criticisms are echoed in other confidential papers circulated by the Central Committee; see *Svědectví*, 34–6 of 1969, p. 336–42.

7. This is how the voting appears on the minutes (*Protocol*, p. 46).

8. Solzhenitsyn's letter included bitter criticism of the censorship and of the Soviet Writers' Union for its cowardly attitude. The letter was denounced and banned from publication in the USSR, but Czech writers who attended the Moscow conference brought back copies to Prague.

9. Hamšík, p. 54–6. Two Czech writers who delivered speeches of this kind were J. Hájek (editor of *Plamen*), and the poet Ivan Skála, well known for his Party activities in the 'fifties.

10. The document was introduced by the Slovak M. Válek on the evening of the second day (*Protokol*, p. 157–8.).

11. *Protokol*, p. 102. An English translation of Liehm's speech is reproduced in his book *The Politics of Culture*, p. 65–6.

12. Vaculík's speech appears on p. 141–151 of *Protocol*. For an English translation see e.g. Hamšík, p. 181–198. It appears in abbreviated form in the collection of documents entitled *Winter in Prague*, ed. R. A. Remington, M.I.T. Press 1969, p. 5–7.

13. For the writers' reaction to the speech see Hamšík, p. 62–4.

14. *Protokol*, p. 198–9.

15. The journal *Czechoslovak Life*, printed in Prague for foreign readers, contains a characteristic passage condemning contributions to the Writers Congress for their 'demagogical character and their attempt to create a political opposition platform'. (*Czech. Life*, 6/12/67, p. 11).

16. *Nová mysl*, 15/67, p. 3–10.

17. *Nová mysl* printed a shortened version of Hendrych's speech. It omitted the sentence 'In the aristocratic performance of writer (*sic*) Vaculík were contained direct insults at our people and the representatives to whom it has entrusted the direction and organisation of our society and state.' (The use of the term *writer*, instead of the normal term *comrade*, as referring to a Party member, was intended as a rebuke.) The full text of Hendrych's speech is to be found in *Svědectví*, (34–6 of 1969, p. 342–3), which includes the missing (censored?) sentence. When the record was published in Prague (*Protokol*, p. 169) it of course printed the full text, from which the missing sentence is quoted above. However the text of *Svědectví* reads, instead of *aristocratic*, the word *anarchistic*, which is perhaps a truer record of what Hendrych actually said (*LN*, 40/67, p. 3). (A number of confidential Party papers are reprinted in the same issue of *Svědectví*, which had obtained them from unknown sources. A comparison of such documents with the texts of those subsequently released in 1968 confirms the accuracy of *Svědectví*'s documentation.)

18. *Svěd.*, 32/67, p. 487–531.

19. *Svěd.*, 34–6 of 1969, p. 339–42 (taken from a letter from the Party CC to the Party group in the Writers' Union.)

20. *Svěd.*, 34–6 of 1969, p. 343–4 an exchange of letters between B. Laštovička (President of the National Assembly) and the Presidium of the Writers' Union.

21. See e.g. *The Economist*, 15/7/67; *The New Statesman*, 21/7/67 recalled that J. Beneš had provoked the Czechoslovak authorities in 1965 by suing the Ministry of the Interior for infringing his civil rights by denying him a passport.

22. At the time of the Tigrid indictment a rumour was circulated in Prague (reportedly by the Security Police) that Tigrid was really an agent of the Communists, and that it was he who had betrayed Beneš; consequently that the trial of Tigrid (which obviously could do him no harm) was merely a device on the part of the Czech authorities to protect their secret agent. This choice story (if indeed it was inspired by the Security Police) evidently was intended to frighten people from having contact with Tigrid, in which case it was certainly a flop. But rumours in Prague are a common phenomenon, and vie with

each other in their incredible permutations of sardonic humour and cynical duplicity.)

23. *The Daily Telegraph*, 17/8/67.

24. The statement was read over Bratislava radio on 15/8/67. It was printed abroad in *Svĕd.*, 32–3 of 1967, p. 591–2.

25. Hamšík, p. 133.

26. The pathologist, Dr Hardmeier, was himself found dead in strange circumstances in Switzerland later in 1967. For a report on his death see *La Suisse*, Dec. 12 and 13th, 1967.

27. *LL*, 5, p. 3.

28. Hamšík, p. 127–9.

29. *Sunday Times*, 10/9/67. (An amusing touch was the remark by Moravia that in any case he wouldn't sign anything approved by Steinbeck. See also *Die Zeit* of 15/9/67, (an open letter from Peter Weiss); *The Times*, 19/9/67; *T.L.S.*, 14/9/67; *Le Monde*, 29/9/67; *N.Y. Herald Tribune*, 3/10/67.

30. Extracts from the speeches made at the CC meeting were printed in *RP* of 30/9/67, and of the 3rd and 4th Oct.; see also *LN*, 40/67 (*Strana a spisovatelé*). For a later summary see *Svĕd.*, 33/67, p. 43–9.

31. According to the extracts released in the Party press the attitude of Party ideologists e.g. P. Hron, K. Hoffman, J. Fojtík, was very hard. But the writers who were present as members of the committee (including I. Skála) seem to have been much more apprehensive about the possible results of reprisals on Union members; and F. Havlíček who, as chief of the Ideological Dept. had to implement policy towards the members, urged a more moderate approach. It was the view of hard-liner Jiří Hájek that the reprisals were the leadership's greatest blunder (see his book *Mýtus a realita*, 1970).

32. See p. 231.

33. *LL*, 4, p. 12 (a letter from Zelenka).

34. The full text of P. Kohout's speech was published in a special supplement to *Svĕd.*, 32–33, 1967, *Dodatky*, p. 106–9.

35. *Svĕd.*, 32–3, 1967, *Dodatky*, p. 89–105.

36. Details of what happened at the CC meeting in October were later given by V. Mencl and F. Ouředník in a series of articles in the newspaper *Život strany* in August-September 1968. Translated excerpts from the articles are available in *Winter in Prague*, ed. R. A. Remington, London, 1969.

37. For the background to the students' demonstration see *LL* 2, p. 7 (*Jak to bylo s tĕmi vysokoškoláky?*).

38. Two years later, in a speech on 18/7/69 V. Bil'ak recalled that it was when he failed to get the Order of Lenin on his birthday that Novotný became convinced that he had lost the confidence of Moscow (A. Ostrý, *Československý problém*, *Index*, Cologne, 1972, p. 16.)

39. In his speech at the CC meeting on 19 December 1967.

40. Brezhnev's comment was reported by Kolder in his speech at the CC meeting.

Chapter X

1. A. Ostrý, *Československý problém* (Index, Cologne, 1972) has documented the political aimlessness of Novotný's conservative opponents: 'We brought down Novotný in January, but we had no idea of any general programme.' (V. Nový): 'We were unprepared either practically or theoretically for further development, (A. Indra). This was also Dubček's view: 'In January we were divided; the Party leadership, which opened the way to this process (of reform) and placed itself at its head, did not, and could not have any concrete plan of campaign.' (A. Dubček, speaking to the Party CC in April, 1968).

2. See e.g. F. Kratochvíl, *Obsah a funkce politické vědy, Nová mysl* 8, 1966.

3. See e.g. the interview with Šik, *Jak zrálo střetnutí* in *KN*, 29/3/68.

4. G. Husák writing in *KŽ*, 12/1/68; J. Smrkovský in *Práce*, 21/1/68. (For translated extracts see Schulz *op. cit.* pps. 263–5).

5. Laštovička's letter was printed abroad in *Svěd.*, 34–6 of 1969, p. 344–5.

6. *LN*, 27/1/68, p. 1.

7. *LN*, 3/2/68, *Nejen dekumulace; Výhrady k parlamentní demokracii.*

8. Z. Mlynář, *RP*, 13/2/68.

9. For his Press conference see *The Times*, 26/8/68. Šejna denied the existence of plans for any coup, but he indicated that there was a powerful group of officers ready to exert influence in favour of Novotný. If we are to believe him, the departments of Defence and of Security contained opposing factions; to Šejna it appeared that the decisive force was the Kolder group, which, with powerful backing from the military establishment, threw in its lot with the reformers to get rid of Novotný. For a contemporary view of Šejna see Procházka, *Politika pro každého*, p. 223, who considered Šejna to be merely the tip of an iceberg of reaction.

10. *Kolik demokracie? KN*, 10/2/68.

11. *Nad jedním pojetím svobody, KN*, 17/2/68. (Answering Hrzal's paper in *Nová mysl*, 25/67).

12. *Občanská společnost hledá své místo, KN*, 24/2/68.

13. *LL*, 1/3/68, p. 12.

14. *KN*, 8/3/68, p. 1.

15. *KN*, 15/3/68, p. 1.

16. *KN*, 8/3/68, *Opět monolog?* (A New Monologue?)

17. *Student*, 10/4/68. A translation of the talk appears in Sviták's *Czechoslovak Experiment*, Columbia U.P., 1971, p. 24–42.

18. The interview appeared in the Slovak journal *Smena*, 28/4/68.

19. A translation of the communiqué is printed in Remington, p. 55–7.

20. *Neues Deutschland*, 27/3/68, Remington, 61–2.

21. *KT*, 4/4/68, p. 23, *Měl profesor Hager mluvit?* (Should Prof. Hager have said it?). In *LL*, 4/4/68 A. J. Liehm amusingly suggested that what was printed in an East German newspaper should not be taken as official German policy.

22. *RP*, 28/3/68.

23. *LL*, 28/3/68, *Procesy, které dělaly dějiny.*

24. *LL*, 21/3/68, published the text of a letter signed by 83 Catholic exprisoners. In the following issue V. Černý introduced an extract from the exiled Czech writer Jan Čep.

25. *LL*, 4/4/68, p. 4. For a detailed account of the aims, life and fate of K-231 see J. Brodský, *Řešení gama*, Toronto, 1971.

26. A case for legalising an official Opposition in Parliament had been put by the writer V. Havel in *LL*, 4/4/68. (*On the Theme of Opposition*).

27. The Action Programme of the Czechoslovak CP, which was accepted at the CC meeting on 5.4.68 was published in *RP*, 10.4.68 (see Remington, p. 88–137). The Programme was, in 1973, placed on the list of publications banned in Czechoslovakia.

28. The Commission of enquiry, under the chairmanship of J. Piller, prepared its report in the summer of 1968, but its publication was deferred by the Presidium, and it never reached the Central Committee, which had called for it. After the August invasion, it was put away in the secret archives of the Party. But it is difficult to keep anything secret in Prague. Many scholars had helped the Commission in researching the material, and although all were sworn to silence, and forbidden to remove or copy anything, inevitably news of the contents spread. Eventually the entire report reached publication in the West, edited by J. Pelikán, *The Czechoslovak Political Trials*, 1950–54, London, 1971.

29. Kruh nezávislých spisovatelů: the author of the announcement was A. Kliment. An account of the Union meeting appeared in *LL*, 4.4.68.

30. The speakers included J. Pistora, P. Kopta, A. C. Nor, and J. Hiršal.

31. The author of this amusing proposal was P. Kopta.

32. e.g. *LL*, 11.4.68, on the horrors of the prison at Bory; *LL*, 25.4.68 on telephone tapping; *LL*, 9.5.68, on the use of drugs by interrogators.

33. *Zpráva dokumentační komise K231*. This, the unofficial report of the K231 commission was printed in Belgium in 1973, and distributed by 68 Publishers, Toronto.

34. *Proces* (The Trial) by E. Loebl; *Zpráva o mém muži* (Report on my husband, by Mme Slánský. Extracts from both books were carried by *LL*, 25.4.68.

35. *Studené slunce* by J. Mucha; an extract appeared in *LL*, 2.5.68.

36. The quotation is from Ivan Sviták, *Student*, 30.4.68 (from a public lecture to K.A.N.).

37. News of the founding of the Society for Human Rights appeared in *KN* 26.4.68; E. Ludvik was chairman of the setting-up committee.

38. For example see the report of CP First Secretary Gustáv Husák to the CC in September 1969, *Czechoslovak Life*, 12/69, p. 2.

39. For some expressions of dissent see Remington, p. 63–86, Oxley, p. 101–45. Any so-called opposition programme is merely a reconstruction of opinions scattered through the media between March and July 1968.

40. Dr Urválek *Jak to bylo s procesy* (The Truth about the Trials) in *RP*, 14.4.68. The interview with Bacílek appeared in *Smena*, 28.4.68. On May 7th The Prague evening newspaper *Večerní Praha* published an interview with the former Security Minister Kopřiva, who confirmed Bacílek's account, and gave details of how Soviet advisors had worked in his department.

41. For a general review of the discussion at the Party Branches, see *LL*, 8.5.68, *Stíny a světla* (Shades and lights). On 12.8.69 *RP* reproduced a summary of the material under the heading *Hlas, který nebyl slyšen* (A voice which was not heeded). There is an interesting analysis of the Proceedings of the Branch meetings and the Secretaries' reports in Ostrý *Československý problém*, p. 62–5.

42. The reference is to Kolder's speech at the Party CC meeting in September 1969. One might have thought that even Security would be sceptical of the idea that the French Intelligence would choose as secret agent a man known for years as a resolute opponent of the regime, whose phone was tapped, and whose correspondence was opened. In August 1970 the popular press published some of the conversations which had taken place in Černý's flat, and had been recorded on the tapes fed by the bugs planted there. Nothing of a treasonable nature was discovered, but the personal and political implications of the conversations were enough to cause serious embarrassment to the participants in the 'normalisation period' after 1969.

43. On 9.5.68, *LL* printed an article by J. Lederer *Polsko těchto týdnů* (Poland these last few weeks) with some sharp criticism of Polish actions. Lederer was arrested in 1971.

44. The remarks were made by Barecki, deputy editor of the journal *Tribuna l'udu*, in a TV interview on 11.5.68.

45. *Neues Deutschland*, 24.5.68.

46. *Literaturnaya gazeta*, 15.5.68.

47. The occasion for this spiteful attack was an interview which Procházka had given in Paris, during the course of which he said that it was impossible not to be moved by the sight of Solzhenitsyn being crucified in his own country. The attack on Procházka was reprinted in *LL*, 16.5.68 on the same page as a summary of Procházka's Paris interview, headed *Solzhenitsyn is our brother*. *LL* also printed in the same issue Procházka's acid reply to the criticism.

48. The article, by V. Stepanov, is included in Remington, p. 158–61.

49. Smrkovský recalled his impression of the meeting in an interview which he gave to David Lajolo, editor of the Italian Communist paper *Giorni - Vie nuove*.

> 'They demanded hard administrative, I should say, police-type action against anybody in Czechoslovakia who spoke his mind in a way that was not absolutely in line with the directives or the policy of the Party'. For the full text see *Listy* 2/1975.

50. The film was a joint production *The Bridge of Remagen*, made in Czechoslovakia, using American uniforms and eight obsolete American tanks brought for the film from Austria by the American producer David Wolper. The al-

legations were first made in the *Berliner Zeitung* on 9.5.68, and angrily refuted in *RP*, 11.5.68; but East German newspapers continued to run the story.

51. The report of Yepishov's incautious remarks was printed in *Le Monde*, 4.5.68. *LL*, 30.5.68 printed a letter from a reader who claimed that similar views were expressed by another Soviet general Zadov to Czech soldiers in an official visit on May 12th.

52. General Yepishov dismissed the report about his alleged remarks as rubbish.

53. P. David, K. Bacílek, V. Široký, B. Köhler, and J. Urválek had all been suspended by June 1968.

54. For a full account of the negotiations between the representatives of the Social Democrats and the Communist leaders, see *Svĕd.* 38, p. 171-188.

55. The bill placed on the shoulders of editors responsibility for safeguarding state secrets etc.; a document for the guidance of editors was drawn up by the Ministries of Defence, Finance, Justice, and the General Prosecutor. Censorship was at the same time removed from the importation of foreign printed matter. During the summer in Prague certain shops carried a fair selection of Western newspapers on sale.

56. *Censura trvá* (Censorship persists) in *LL*, 20.6.68, in which V. Škutina reported that his review of the play *The Trials* was kept off the air by instructions from above because the review involved comments on the Workers Militia. (Škutina was arrested in 1971). In June the social democrats complained that they were unable to defend themselves in the press against attacks, and a petition signed by 30 leading Czech intellectuals asked the National Front to ensure that the Soc. Dem. representatives were not prevented from publishing their side of the case (*Svĕd.* 38, 1970, p. 183).

57. At the September meeting of the Party CC in 1969 V. Biľak claimed that he had suggested to Dubček and brought before the Presidium a plan to occupy radio, TV, and individual newspaper offices (see Ostrý, p. 121). Černík explained his plan for a Broadcasting Control Board at the May CC meeting. The Board was to be representative of media as well as government. (*RP*, 7.6.68).

58. In *LL*, 30.5.68 J. Lederer analysed what he saw as various threats to press freedom, including directives to make taboo discussion of organisations such as K231, and the cause of the social democrats, and threats against *Student*. He commented on news of strike action by Workers Councils, e.g. at Ostrava. In *LL*, 4.7.68, p. 2, a short notice *Na obranu svobody* (In defence of freedom) reported a meeting of Workers Councils to deal with the question of press freedom. A group of historians drawn from several institutes, clubs, and journals, had asked the workers' organisations to put into their programme the defence of freedom of scientific enquiry. A committee for defence of press freedom had been set up at the Central Secretariat of the Socialist Academy; and the Journalists Union had resolved to set up a committee to liaise with Workers Councils. In *LL*, 20.6.68., P. Pithart discussed the whole issue of threats to press freedom:

> Recently, after several months of silence, censorship began again;
> the proscribed information was far from being a state secret, and
> the impulse to stifle its publication certainly did not come from
> the censorship (dept.)... The details (news of the activisation of the
> Soc. Dem. party) are maybe not communicable. The threat is the
> confiscation of an entire edition of a newspaper.

Pithart likewise drew attention to the threat of strike action at Ostrava. A
passage in his article well expresses the mood of hope and anxiety of intellectuals in Prague in June:

> The conditions in which the press, radio, and TV function today in
> Czechoslovakia are unprecedented in contemporary developed
> states. Censorship has faded away, and the market mechanism has in
> practice not begun its harmful effects. Most of the dailies and week-
> lies are more or less independent of the institutions which publish
> them; the dependence of state radio and TV on the state authorities
> is clearly less than e.g. the dependence of the non-communist press
> on the administration of the political parties which publish them.
> It is unbelievable, but the freedom of our press, though not yet
> guaranteed by law, is so far not seriously impaired by either ad-
> ministrative or by material pressure. Not yet anyway...
>
> *Political parties and Press Freedom*
> P. Pithart, *LL*, 20.6.68.

59. The so-called manifesto appeared on June 27 in the Writers' Union
journal *LL*, the youth journal *Mladá fronta*, the Trades Union journal *Práce*,
and the journal orientated to country interests *Zemědělské noviny*.

60. Smrkovský recorded the incident in his newspaper interview (*Listy*, 2/75).

61. Shawcross *Dubček*, p. 161-3.

62. The Presidium statement appeared in *RP*, 29.6.68.

63. Smrkovský himself (see n. 60) is the source of information for his vigorous intervention with the cabinet. The phrase about the manifesto being a
call for counter-revolution was repeated during the Parliamentary debate by
General Kodaj. The phrase was later echoed approvingly in Soviet propaganda
releases, and eventually became quite an important motto in the folk-lore of
the Prague Spring. It is hard to credit that anyone who had bothered to read
the text of the manifesto could have made the claim seriously. General Kodaj
gained a lot of unfavourable publicity by his peppery attitude, and was written
off as an incorrigible Stalinist; he was later to redeem his reputation by a firmly patriotic stance during the early days of the Russian occupation.

64. *LL*, 4.7.68.

65. 'An attack on the socialist foundations of Czechoslovakia', *Pravda*,
11.7.68.

66. The text of the so-called Warsaw letter is included in Remington, p.
225-31; Windsor, App. II.

67. The reply of the Czechoslovak Party Presidium to the Warsaw letter was a confidential document; but it was leaked to journalists, and a copy was printed in the *New York Times* on July 9th. A revised text appears in Remington, p. 234–43.

68. Remington, p. 214–20 prints a report of Prchlík's press conference, the text based on a broadcast from Radio Prague, 15.7.68. At the time General Prchlík was a member of the Party CC, a parliamentary Deputy, and the Officer in Charge of the CC's Security Dept. As such he was involved directly in applying Party policy in the fields of both Security and Defence. Prchlík's statements at the press conference might be taken almost as a pronouncement of official policy, and this is how they were construed in Moscow. On August 22nd, in the aftermath of the invasion, the Russians accused leading personalities in Czech public life of attempts to re-evaluate certain principles in foreign policy touching relations between the two socialist countries, and *Pravda* quoted Prchlík in this connection. After the occupation Prchlík lost all his official functions; was expelled from the Party; reduced to the ranks; and finally court-martialled on March 24th 1971. Private Prchlík was sentenced to three years imprisonment.

69. *Pravda*, 22.7.68. A translation appears in Remington p. 248–52.

70. *LL*, 26.7.68, special edition.

71. Smrkovský, *Listy*, 2/75, p. 13. '(Kohout's) manifesto gave our delegation a mandate of confidence such as few Czechoslovak delegations have even received for international negotiations; but it also put limits upon us. It stressed the need to maintain and defend four points – socialism, alliance, sovereignty, and freedom as the programme of our land and people. In our discussions on the way to Čierná we decided that we had two mandates – to hold on to the programme of revival, expressed in the Party Action Programme, and to avoid a break with the USSR...'

72. Remington, p. 255.

73. For the text of the Bratislava communique see Remington, p. 256–61. A fair example of its rhetoric is the following paragraph:

> Unshakable fidelity to Marxism-Leninism, indoctrination of the masses in the spirit of the ideas of socialism and proletarian internationalism, and an implacable struggle against bourgeois ideology and all anti-socialist forces constitute the guarantee of success in strengthening the position of socialism and repulsing the intrigues of imperialism.

74. Smrkovský, *Listy*, 2/75, p. 14.

75. The communiqué was broadcast over Radio Prague, and printed in the Czech dailies of Wednesday August 21st; among the papers which carried the communique were the Party daily *RP*, and the Trades Union paper *Práce.*

76. One effect of the Presidium communiqué was to stress the difference between the situation in August 1968 and that in March 1939, when the Czech

lands were invaded from Germany after the Czechoslovak President, Hácha, had capitulated in Berlin to pressure and had, in his own name, given an official sanction to the occupation.

77. Bil'ak, Kolder, Rigo, Švestka all cast their votes against the communiqué. President Svoboda was not a member of the Presidium, and so was not asked to vote in the issue.

78. The source is *Sedm pražských dnů*, published by the Institute of History at the Czechoslovak Academy of Sciences, 1968, English translation published by Pall Mall Press 1969 under the title of *The Czech Black Book*. The book is a collection of source material for historians of the events of August 21–27 in Prague.

79. For an eyewitness account of the scene, see *Listy*, 3/1971, p. 32–4.

80. *Czech Black Book*, p. 24–27.

81. *RP* printed an interview with Minister of Information Galuška on 25.8. 68, in which he was asked whether any official organ of Czechoslovakia did in fact request assistance from the USSR. Galuška replied:

> No help, especially no military help, was requested from the USSR or from any of the states whose armies have occupied our country. I repeat: the Government has declared that the occupation of Czechoslovakia is illegal.

82. *Czech Black Book*, p. 203–4. The *Book* includes the published resolutions of official protests against the occupation from a wide range of organisations in industry, education, science, sport, publication, creative art, and politics. *Student*, in a special edition of August 25, published a solemn declaration of support for the arrested leaders and a demand for the withdrawal of the occupation troops, signed by the University Committee of the Communist Party.

83. *Czech Black Book*, p. 235–8.

84. Reports from the Extraordinary XIV Congress of the Czechoslovak CP appear in the *Czech Black Book*. In 1969 Jiří Pelikán, former Director of Television, published in Vienna a complete transcript of the Proceedings, based on a tape recording; an English translation was published by the Penguin Press in 1971 entitled *The Secret Vysočany Congress*, ed. J. Pelikán.

85. The dismissal of Šalgovič and a number of other officers was ordered by the government on August 24th, and all cadre measures taken by them since August 20th were declared invalid (*Czech Black Book*, p. 133–4).

86. This picturesque detail was recalled by Smrkovský shortly before his death (*Listy*, 2/75, p. 22).

Chapter XI

1. For the texts of the letters see *The Czech Black Book*, p. 235-8,(see below, n. 22). Drda's famous letter began: 'The pen is shaking in my hand; my voice falters. For twenty five years I have taught my children to love the Soviet Union, to see Moscow as the surety for our national independence. All that lies now in ruins...'. In 1972 Miss Glazarová made a kind of retraction: Drda died unrepentant.

2. *Czech Black Book*, p. 232-3.

3. *Czech Black Book*, p. 244-56, 261-75 (texts of the Moscow communiqué and the speeches of the four leaders. The text of the communiqué is also printed in Windsor, p. 178-181).

4. *Listy*, 1975/2, p. 23 (interview given by Smrkovský to the correspondent of *Giorni Nuove*).

5. Aspects of Smrkovský's speech which gave especial offence in Moscow were his comparison of the Russian occupation with that by the Nazis; references to the conditions under which the Czechs were brought to Moscow; an admission that acceptance of the Russian conditions might be regarded by the Czech public as a betrayal; admission that the measures to be put into operation (e.g. the restrictions on press freedom and the right of free association) would make more difficult the creation of democratic socialism; and a statement that the Czechs were forced to negotiate in the shadow of tanks and aircraft.

6. The apology was published in *Mladá fronta*, 31.8.68.

7. One member of the Czechoslovak delegation, F. Kriegel, refused to sign.

8. The text of the Moscow Protocol was first published in the exile Paris journal *Svědectví* (IX, 34-6, p. 228-31). A translation is included in Remington p. 379-82.

9. *Pokyny pro tisk, rozhlas a televisi* (Directives for press, radio, and TV) as of 3.9.68, 9.9.68, and 18.10.68. *Svěd.*, 36, p. 347-8).

10. The minutes of the meeting between Kuznetsov and Smrkovský are printed by P. Tigrid as Appendix B to his book *Why Dubček Fell*, MacDonald, London, 1971, p. 215-229. For further discussion of the negotiations during Kuznetsov's visit, see *Le Monde*, 9.9.68 and 13.9.69; *Der Spiegel*, 14.10.68.

11. *RP*, 15.9.68. Remington, p. 388-95.

12. The text of the letter from the preliminary organising committee of K231, asking all branches to liquidate their activities appears in their archives *Zpráva dokumentační komise K231*, printed in Belgium, 1973, p. 166-7.

13. The statement was published by *RP* on 26.9.68.

14. Goldstücker was Visiting Professor in Comparative Literature at the University of Sussex.

15. The text of the proclamation appears in *Czechoslovak Life*, November 1969.

16. 'If a single Czech or Slovak artist, scientist, or journalist, wherever he is, should become the object of persecution or prosecution or his ideas and his work, all the undersigned would consider it as an attack against the entire Czechoslovak cultural community.' (from a resolution passed at a meeting of the Writers Union on October 31st).

17. *Listy*, 1975/2, p. 24.

18. The text of the treaty is printed in Remington, p. 420–4.

19. The speech of one member, Mrs. Sekanina-Čakrtová, who voted against acceptance of the treaty, is printed in *Svĕd*. 34–6, p. 358–60; it appeared originally in *Reporter*, 30.10.68.

20. *Listy*, 7.11.68.

21. An English translation of *The White Book* was printed in Moscow and entitled *On Events in Czechoslovakia* (no publisher or date given). The translation was distributed abroad by Soviet organs and through Soviet Front organisations.

22. *Sedm pražských dnů* (Seven Prague Days), 1968. (*The Czech Black Book*, ed. R. Littell, London, 1969).

23. *Czech Black Book*, p. 284–5.

24. For a vivid picture of Prague on the eve of the CC meeting see L. Pachman, *Jak to bylo* (*What it was like*), 68 Publishers, Toronto, 1974, p. 157–8.

25. The final resolution passed at the November Party CC appeared in *RP*, 19.11.68; an abbreviated text is printed in Remington, p. 430–42.

26. *Pravda*, (Bratislava), 20.11.68; Remington, p. 443–4.

27. A new executive body of seven members, chaired by Dubček, was created at the November meeting; the executive was to act as an inner Presidium.

28. The strike was supported openly by students in Prague, Plzeň, Ostrava, Liberec, Ústí nad Labem, Olomouc, and Brno.

29. In the light of information which has since become known, the attitude of the Czechoslovak Party leadership at the time is more understandable than it appeared then. At the end of September an international Party gathering was held in Budapest, where Lenárt, leader of the Czechoslovak delegation, was approached by two Soviet members who confidentially advised him that the Soviet leadership was split in its attitude to Czechoslovakia and a change of Soviet policy to the advantage of the Czechs was likely. For an account of the secret discussions between Lenárt and Ponomarev see Tigrid *Kvadratura kruhu*, p. 83-4. It is quite unclear what value is to be placed on Ponomarev's story; but Lenárt passed it on to Dubček.

30. For Smrkovský's own account of the December crisis which preceded his fall, see his secret press interview, *Listy*, 2/1975, p. 24–5.

31. *Večerní Praha*, 13.12.68.

32. Remington, p. 449.

33. *Setkání s minotaurem* (Meeting with the Minotaur), by V. Renč; *Čtyři léta* (Four Years), J. Zahradníček; *Sita*, J. Palivec; *Sborník pětadvacíti* (Collection of Twenty four), V. Černý; *Tváře v stínu* (Faces in Shadow), Z. Kalista;

Babel, Má přítelkyně Dora (Babel, My Friend Dora), F. F. Křelina; *Žhář* (The Incendiary), E. Hostovský, *Zeměžluč, Letnice, Děravý plášť* (Gall, Whitsun, The tattered coat), J. Čep; all published in 1968–9.

34. *IV Sjezd Svazu československých spisovatelů*, Prague, 1968.

35. *Spisovatelé a Moc* by D. Hamšík, Prague, 1969. An English translation was published under the title of *Writers against Rulers*, London, 1971.

36. *Čtyři léta*, J. Zahradníček, 1969.

37. *Sborník pětadvacíti*, ed. V. Černý, 1969.

38. *Den Madian*, F. D. Merth, Introd. by Z. Kalista, pub. at Jindřichův Hradec, 1968.

39. *Útěk*, J. Hejda, 1969.

40. *Barva slunce a noci*, L. Reinerová, 1969. Madame Reinerová was the editor of the foreign language weekly *Czechoslovak Life* during the reform period. She was dismissed in 1970.

41. *Presidentův vězeň*, V. Škutina, Severočeské nakladatelství, Liberec, 1969.

42. After being held under arrest for three months, Škutina was released in December 1969, then re-arrested in 1970, and sentenced to four years imprisonment. He was finally released in 1974.

43. *Horečka*, 1967; *Na co umírají muži; Veliký slunovrat*, 1968, by K. Pecka.

44. *Studené slunce*, J. Mucha, 1968. The title is taken from a line of Baudelaire's *Flowers of Evil*. *Studené slunce* was published in English translation under the title of *Living and partly Living*, (tr. E. Osers), London, 1970.

45. *Morytáty a legendy* by B. Hrabal, 1968.

46. *Malé hry* by I. Vyskočil, 1967.

47. J. Opelík in an essay *The Neo-Balzac from Ústí, LL*, 1968.

48. *Veletrh splněných přání*, 1964; *Soukromá vichřice*, 1966; *Katapult*, 1967; *Milenci a vrazi*, 1969, by Vladimír Páral.

49. *Loď jménem naděje* by Ivan Klíma, 1969.

50. *Kladivo na čarodějnice* by V. Kaplický, 1963. The film was directed by O. Vávra and released in 1970.

51. *Oldřich a Božena* by F. Hrubín. The premiere of the play appeared in 1968 in Prague.

52. Indications that an allegory was intended are given by the play's subtitle, by the comments of O. Blanda, who edited the book version, and by remarks of Hrubín himself. ('Each one of us has his own model of history, whose shape is given by facts and data, but whose inner events, based on our inner consciousness, are in constant motion and undergo constant changes and revivals, fading and reviving, thus remaining always contemporary).

53. *Tovarišstvo Ježišovo*, by J. Šotola, 1969.

Select Bibliography

Journals

(All published in Prague except where otherwise stated).

Česká literatura; Československý přehled (New York); *Czechoslovak Life; Dějiny a současnost; Divadlo; East Europe* (New York); *Generace; Host do domu* (Brno); *Impuls; Kritický měsíčník; Kulturní noviny; Kulturní tvorba; Kulturný život* (Bratislava); *Květen; Listy; Listy* (Rome); *Literární listy; Literární noviny; Nová mysl; Nový život; Orientace; Plamen; Proměny* (N.Y.); *Reportér; Rudé právo; Sešity pro mladou literaturu; Student; Svědectví* (Paris); *Survey* (London); *Tvář; Tvorba, Universum.*

Books

Bareš G. *Listy o kultuře.* Praha, 1947.
Básnický almanach. Praha, 1953–60.
Bednář K. *Střepiny o které jsem se sám pořezal.* Praha, 1969.
Blumenfeld Y. *Seesaw.* New York, 1968.
Buriánek F. *Současná česká literatura.* Praha, 1960.
Černý, V. *Sborník pětadvacíti.* Praha, 1969.
Drozda M.—Parolek R. *Umění v kulturní revoluci.* Praha, 1961.
Duben V. *Ledy se hnuly.* New York, 1964.
Dubček A. *K otázkám obrodovacieho procesu v KSČ.* Bratislava, 1968.
Ello P. (ed.) *Czechoslovakia's Blueprint for Freedom.* Washington, 1968.
Gadourek I. *The Political Control of Czechoslovakia.* Leiden, 1953.
Garaudy R. *La Liberté en sursis.* Paris, 1968.
Golan G. *The Czechoslovak Reform Movement.* Cambridge, 1971.
Czechoslovak Reform Rule. Cambridge, 1973.
Grass G.—Kohout P. *Briefe über die Grenze.* Hamburg, 1968.
Hájek J. *Osudy a cíle.* Praha, 1961
Mýtus a realita ledna 1968. Praha, 1970.
Dix ans après. Paris, 1978.
Hamšík D. *Spisovatelé a moc.* Praha, 1969.
Writers against Rulers. London, 1971.
Havel R.—Opelík J (eds.) *Slovník českých spisovatelů. Praha, 1964.*
Havel V. (ed.) *Podoby II.* Praha, 1969.
Jancar B. W. *Czechoslovakia and the absolute monopoly of power.* London, 1971.
Jungmann M. *Obléhání Tróje.* Praha, 1969.
Franz Kafka – Libická konference. Praha, 1963.
Kladiva J. *Kultura a politika.* Praha, 1968.

Kohout P. *From the diary of a counter-revolutionary.* New York, 1972.

Kopecký J. (ed.) *Účtování a výhledy.* Praha, 1948.

Kosík K. *Dialektika konkrétního.* Praha, 1963.

Kozák Y. R. *The Reflection in Czech Literature of Political Changes* (Unpublished dissertation, Ann Arbor) *Kritická ročenka – Pro a proti.* Praha, 1961, 62, 63.

Kusin, V. V. *Intellectual Origins of the Prague Spring.* Cambridge, 1971. *Political Grouping in the Czechoslovak reform Movement.* London, 1972. *The Czechoslovak Reform Movement.* Reading, 1973.

Liehm A. J. *Rozhovor.* Praha, 1965. *The Politics of Culture.* (With an Introduction by Jean-Paul Sartre). New York, 1970. *Le Chemin difficile de la littérature tchèque.* Paris, 1972. *Closely Watched Films.* New York, 1974.

Littel R. (ed.) *The Czech Black Book.* London, 1969.

Loebl. E. *Sentenced and Tried.* London, 1969. *Stalinism in Prague.* New York, 1969.

London A. *The Trial.* London, 1968.

Mlynář Z. *Stát a člověk.* Praha, 1964.

Mňačko L. *Opožděné reportáže.* Praha, 1964. *The Taste of Power.* London, 1967. *The Seventh Night.* London, 1969.

Nezval V. *O některých problémech současné poesie.* (Speech delivered to the 2nd Writers Congress) Praha, 1956.

—(ed. Blahynka M.) *Moderní poesie.* Praha, 1958. *Z mého života.* Praha, 1959.

Novomeský L. *Časová nečasnost.* Praha, 1967.

Novotný A. *Projevy a stati* (vols. I-III). Praha, 1964.

Opelík J. (ed.) *Jak číst poezii.* Praha, 1963. *Nenáviděné řemeslo.* Praha, 1969.

Ostrý A. *Československý problém.* Cologne, 1972.

Pachman L. *Jak to bylo.* Toronto, 1974.

Pelikán J. (ed.) *The Secret Vysočany Congress.* London, 1969. *Potlačená zpráva.* Vienna, 1970. *The Czechoslovak Political Trials.* Stanford, 1971.

Petříček M. *Glosy k současné české poesii.* Praha, 1957.

Petrmichl J. *Patnáct let české literatury.* Praha, 1961.

Procházka J. *Politika pro každého.* Praha, 1968.

Pytlík R. *Příběhy pod mikroskopem.* Praha, 1966.

Rambousek O.—Gruber L. (eds.) *Zpráva dokumentační komise K 231* (Privately printed in Belgium, 1973).

Rechcígl M. (ed.) *Czechoslovak Contribution to World Culture.* The Hague, 1964. *Czechoslovakia Past and Present.* The Hague, 1970.

Reiman P. *O realistickém pojetí umění.* Praha, 1948.

Remington R. A. (ed.) *Winter in Prague.* London, 1969.

Řezáč V. *O pravdě umění a pravdě života.* Praha, 1960.

Richta R. (ed.) *Civilizace na rozcestí.* Praha, 1968.

Civilization at the Crossroads. Praha, 1968.

Ripellino A. M. *Storia della poesia ceca contemporanea.* Rome, 1950.

— *Rok šedesátý osmý v usneseních a dokumentech ÚV KSČ.* Praha, 1969.

— *Sedm pražských dnů.* Praha, 1968.

Schwarz H. *Prague's 200 Days.* London, 1969.

Shawcross W. *Dubček.* London, 1970.

Šik O. *Plan and Market under Socialism.* Praha, 1967.

Alienated Ideology. London, 1972.

Skilling G. *The Interrupted Revolution.* Princeton, 1976.

— *IV Sjezd Svazu československých spisovatelů.* Praha, 1968.

Škvorecký J. *Nachrichten aus der ČSSR.* Frankfurt, 1968.

Škvorecký J. *All the Bright Young Men and Women.* Toronto, 1971.

Sobolev A. I. *Leninská teorie odrazu a umění.* Praha, 1950.

Součková M. *Literature in Crisis.* New York, 1954.

A Literary Satellite. Chicago, 1970.

Štoll L. *Skutečnost tváří v tvář.* Praha, 1949.

Třicet let bojů za českou socialistickou poesii. Praha, 1950.

Literatura a kulturní revoluce. Praha, 1959.

Suda Z. *The Czechoslovak Socialist Republic.* Baltimore, 1969.

Sviták I. *The Czechoslovak Experiment.* New York, 1971.

Dialektika moci. Cologne, 1973.

The Czechoslovak Dream 1968-9. Chico, California, 1977.

Systémové změny. Cologne, 1972.

Szulc T. *Czechoslovakia since World War II.* New York, 1971.

Táborský E. *Communism in Czechoslovakia.* Princeton, 1961.

Taufer J. *Strana, lidé, pokolení.* Praha, 1962.

Tigrid P. *Le Printemps de Prague.* Paris, 1968.

Why Dubček Fell. London, 1969.

Kvadratura kruhu. Brussels, 1970.

Wellek R. *Essays on Czech Literature.* The Hague, 1963.

Windsor P.—Roberts A. *Czechoslovakia 1968.* London, 1969.

Zeman Z. A. B. *Prague Spring.* London, 1969.

Documents

1. A letter sent out to publishing houses in 1948 requiring publishers to place their affairs in the hands of an official appointed by the Ministry of Culture.

2. Statement of the P.E.N. Centre London, and the Executive Committee of International P.E.N., N.Y., 1966.

3. A special edition of the Prague daily *Svobodné noviny* on August 21st 1968 reports the entry of foreign troops into Czechoslovakia, and the official protest of the Central Committee of the Czechoslovak Communist Party.

4. A letter sent out by the Union of Czech Writers to foreign correspondents advising them that the Union had been ordered by the Ministry of Culture to break off all foreign contacts.

(1) MINISTRY OF INFORMATION

Ref. 56665/48-III   Prague 17 November 1948

Subject: Appointment of Official Receivers.
         Publishing House of Youth,
         KLADNO II
         Třebízského 1213

With reference to the prepared law by which the question of publishing policy will be definitely settled; and at the same time reference the need to control Christmas book marketing, I regard it as important to carry out the following interim arrangement, on the basis of Presidential decree No. 130/45 of 26. 10. 45 *On State Responsibility for Education*: I appoint to your publishing (and lending) business a special Receiver of the Ministry of Information and Education Mr.
        Joseph Kos, District Edn. Inspector, Kladno
I delegate to the above Receiver the following authority: you are obliged to hand over to him complete control over your business; to adapt yourself to all his dispositions; and to inform him of all affairs concerning your business.

The responsibility of the Receiver is to last until the new publishing law comes into effect.

Expenses incurred in connection with the actions of the Receiver
are to be covered by your firm.

Minister of Information and Education
Kopecký V.
Received 29/11/48
Acted upon

(2) STATEMENT

by the P.E.N. Centre for Writers in Exile presented to the Executive
Committee of International P.E.N., London, March 30/31, 1966.

The Centre for Writers in Exile considers it its duty to draw the attention of the International executive Committee to recent acts of repression of literary activity in Czechoslovakia and East Germany (GDR).
The Prague literary monthly *Tvář*, characterized by the *Times* of
London (January 14, 1966) as a "lively periodical... whose impact on
the young generation was considerable", had to cease publication on
direct orders of the ideological department of the Czechoslovak
Communist Party. The latter insisted on the recall of the editor-in-chief, several members of the editorial board and, more generally, on
its right to approve editors of all Czechoslovak periodicals.

Earlier, over 270 prominent Czech and Slovak writers – among them
members of the Czechoslovak P.E.N. Centre – have met (on October
15, 1965) at the Architect's Club in Prague and signed a resolution protesting the fact that in the case of *Tvář* "once again administrative
measures were replacing a literary discussion".

Nevertheless, the magazine which had been for years ably edited by a
group of young Czech writers and devoted much of its space to objective information on western arts and letters, had to close down as of
January 1, 1966.

Developments in the German Democratic Republic are even less encouraging.

The Centre for Writers in Exile proposes that the Executive Committee of International P.E.N. should instruct the International Secretary
to convey to the Czechoslovak and German Ost und West Centres the
Executive's concern in this matter and to express its conviction that
the two Centres will continue to uphold the principles of P.E.N.
Charter.

by the P.E.N. Centre for Writers in Exile presented to the Executive
Committee of International P.E.N., New York, June 12, 1966
The Centre for Writers in Exile deems it important to bring the following matter to the consideration of the International Executive.
Three prominent Czechoslovak writers – Václav Havel, Jan Gross-
mann and Hana Bělohradská were invited by the International P.E.N.
to attend the 34th P.E.N. Congress in New York. They accepted the
invitation. According to the London *Times* of June 9th, however,
their passports were withdrawn at the last moment by the Czechoslovak authorities and they were not allowed to leave the country.
The reason for the withdrawal of the passports was given in Prague as
follows: The three writers cannot be permitted to attend a P.E.N.
meeting at which the case of suppression of the Czechoslovak literary
magazine *Tvář*, at the end of last year, might come under discussion.
The Centre for Writers in Exile considers this development a serious
interference with free speech, and an obstruction to the international
dialogue, which P.E.N. fosters. We would like to ask the Secretary
General to explore the matter further. An explanation by the Czechoslovak P.E.N. Centre would be especially desirable. Perhaps, it may
be still possible for at least one of the writers to come over.

RESOLUTION
proposed by P.E.N. American Centre and adopted by the Executive
Committee of International P.E.N., New York, June 12, 1966
That P.E.N. International deplores measures taken by any government which have the effect of preventing P.E.N. members from leaving
their own country or entering a foreign country in response to an
invitation to attend a P.E.N. Congress, a meeting of the International
Executive Committee, or any other meeting called under the auspices
of P.E.N.

(4) Union of Czech Writers

Prague, 18 March 1970.
Dear Colleague,
    By a decision of the Ministry of Culture all external activity by the
Union of Czech Writers has been stopped. Accordingly we are compelled to inform you that in future we are unable to send you either news
of our book publications or journals.
    We are passing your address to the Ministry of Culture with the
request that it should take over our activity as far as possible.

We send you our sincere greetings; we wish you much success; and we thank you for all that you have done for our literature in the past, and will do in the future.

Karel Ptáčník   Dr. Petr Pujman
Vice President of the U.C.W.   Head of the Foreign Section

(3) Prague Thursday 22 August 1968.

FOREIGN TROOPS
ON OUR TERRITORY

Yesterday August 20 at about 11 p.m. the armies of the USSR, the Polish People's Republic, the German Democratic Republic, the Hungarian People's Republic, and the Bulgarian People's Republic crossed the state frontiers of the Czechoslovak Socialist Republic. This took place without the knowledge of the President of the Republic, the Chairman of the National Assembly, the Prime Minister, or the First Secretary of the Communist Party Central Committee and their representatives. At that time the Presidium of the CC was in session, preoccupied with the preparations for the XIV Party Congress. The Presidium of the Party CC calls on all citizens of the Republic to keep the peace and not to resist the advancing armies. For that reason our army, Security forces, and People's Militia have not received orders to defend the country. The Presidium of the Party CC considers this action as contrary to the basic principles of relations between socialist states and also a denial of the fundamental norms of international law. All leading officials of the Party and the National Front remain at the posts to which they were elected, as representatives of the people and members of their organisations, according to Czechoslovak law, and to other norms applicable in the Czechoslovak Republic. The appropriate constitutional bodies have called into session the National Assembly and government, and the Party CC Presidium is calling a full meeting of the Central Committee to consider the situation which has arisen.

THE PRESIDIUM OF THE CENTRAL COMMITTEE
OF THE CZECHOSLOVAK COMMUNIST PARTY.

SPECIAL EDITION

Maintain peace and order! Do not allow yourselves to be provoked to actions for which our enemies are waiting. Do not listen to provocations and rumourmongers. Our strength is in unity, as it has always been in the hours decisive for the life of our nations, in peace, and in calm. In our just resolve for truth and right we are not alone.

V PRAZE VE ČTVRTEK 22. SRPNA 1968

Svobodné slovo

LIST ČESKOSLOVENSKÉ STRANY SOCIALISTICKÉ   NOSITEL ŘÁDU PRÁCE

ZVLÁŠTNÍ VYDÁNÍ

CIZÍ VOJSKA NA NAŠEM ÚZEMÍ

Zachovejte klid a pořádek! Nedejte se vyprovokovat k činům, na které čekají nepřátelé našeho lidu! Nevěřte provokatérům a štváčům! Naše síla je v jednotě, jako byla vždy v rozhodujících hodinách života našich národů, v klidu a v rozvazel V našem spravedlivém zanícení pro pravdu a právo nejsme sami!

KOMUNISTICKÁ STRANA ČESKOSLOVENSKA PŘEDSEDNICTVO ÚSTŘEDNÍHO VÝBORU

Konference o Mnichovu

NOC NA DNEŠEK

PRAVDA ZVÍTĚZÍ!

PRAVDA ZVÍTĚZÍ!

REDAKCE SVOBODNÉHO SLOVA

Létající záhada

Jedna denně

Presidentské sídlo

Úkoly a cíle závodních organizací

Václav KÚRKA, člen předsednictva ÚV Čs. strany socialistické

INDEX